Plantinga's *Warranted Christian Belief*

Plantinga's *Warranted Christian Belief*

Critical Essays with a Reply by Alvin Plantinga

Edited by Dieter Schönecker

DE GRUYTER

ISBN 978-3-11-057758-7
e-ISBN (PDF) 978-3-11-043020-2
e-ISBN (EPUB) 978-3-11-043022-6

Library of Congress Cataloging-in-Publication Data
A CIP catalog record for this book has been applied for at the Library of Congress.

Bibliographic information published by the Deutsche Nationalbibliothek
The Deutsche Nationalbibliothek lists this publication in the Deutsche Nationalbibliografie;
detailed bibliographic data are available on the Internet at http://dnb.dnb.de.

© 2015 Walter de Gruyter GmbH, Berlin/Boston
This volume is text- and page-identical with the hardback published in 2015.
Printing: CPI books GmbH, Leck

♾ Printed on acid-free paper
Printed in Germany

www.degruyter.com

Table of Contents

Preface —— VII

Dieter Schönecker
The Deliverances of *Warranted Christian Belief* —— 1

Christian Tapp
Reference to an Infinite Being —— 41

Winfried Löffler
An Underrated Merit of Plantinga's Philosophy —— 65

Oliver Wiertz
Is Plantinga's A/C Model an Example of Ideologically Tainted Philosophy? —— 83

Thomas Schärtl
Moderating Certainty —— 115

Anita Renusch
Thank God it's the right religion!— Plantinga on religious diversity —— 147

Georg Plasger
Does Calvin teach a sensus divinitatis? Reflections on Alvin Plantinga's Interpretation of Calvin —— 169

Christian Illies
Is Suffering the Rock of Atheism? —— 191

Gregor Nickel
Dwindling Probability. Mathematical and Philosophical Notes in Margin —— 213

Alvin Plantinga
Replies to my commentators —— 237

Index of persons —— 263

Subject Index —— 265

Preface

In the eyes of many philosophers and theologians, Alvin Plantinga is the most important contemporary philosopher of religion. He is widely recognized as an epistemologist and philosopher of great sagacity and originality even by those who do not share his Christian worldview, and his thought has sparked intensive discussions within the philosophical world. All the more striking is that his early works as well as his trilogy on warrant (including *Warranted Christian Belief*, WCB) are still almost unknown to most German philosophers and students, and he is certainly unknown to the German intellectual public at large. There are possibly three reasons for this. First, Germany is a highly secularized nation in which debates on religious questions most often take place under the public proviso that those who hold religious views are peculiarly 'metaphysical' and 'irrational.' In any case, religious perspectives are not taken seriously in public and intellectual life. Unfortunately, this is, secondly, also true for the philosophical and academic field. In contrast to the USA or Great Britain, there is almost no influential philosophy of religion in Germany. Atheistic and agnostic philosophers set the tone, and only very few philosophers are known as religious (let alone Christian) philosophers. Third, there have been no translations of Plantinga's books.

The latter fact sparked the idea to provide a German edition of WCB. Supported by the *John Templeton Foundation*, Joachim Schulte undertook the heavy burden of translating this voluminous and wide-ranging book (the translation is forthcoming from the same publisher, Walter de Gruyter). The present collection of essays provides critical interpretations of many aspects of Plantinga's seminal book: *Dieter Schönecker* (University of Siegen) tries to get a grip on what WCB is really about; at the same time, this paper can be read as an introduction to WCB and Plantinga's religious epistemology. *Christian Tapp* (University of Bochum) deals with Plantinga's critique of negative theology and proposes a more constructive way to read Kaufman's and Hick's reinterpretation of Christian belief; he also provides an assessment of the range of Plantinga's view on divine infinity. *Winfried Löffler* (University of Innsbruck) deals with what he considers an underrated merit of Plantiga's philosophy, to wit, the importance of what Löffler himself calls 'world-view beliefs'. *Oliver Wiertz* (University of St. Georgen) argues that the charge of ideology against Plantinga's Reformed Epistemology is unsubstantiated; however, Wiertz also believes that Plantinga would be in an even better position to defend himself if he took into account the tradition of natural theology. *Thomas Schärtl* (University of Augsburg) critically analyzes Plantinga's concept of certainty that is oriented to the standard of knowledge; alternatively, Schärtl offers a concept of certainty in the tradition of Wittgenstein which he thinks does more justice to the peculiarity of religious belief. With regard to the problem of religious diversity, *Anita Renusch* (University of Frankfurt) argues that believing oneself to be in a better epistemic position is not as easy as Plantinga thinks it is and that he thus disregards part of the trouble the problem causes for religious believers. *Georg Plasger* (University of Siegen) provides reasons why he is not convinced that Plantinga's A/C model is rightly so called with regard to Calvin. *Christian Illies* (University of Bamberg) argues that Reformed Epistemology makes it plausible why the problem of evil does not defeat the strong believer; yet, he says, the problem remains a defeater in the eyes of the strong non-believer. *Gregor Nickel* (University of Siegen) sheds methodological (and mathematical) light as well as doubt on the very idea of using probabilistic reasoning in religious epistemology, with an eye on the debate between Plantinga and Swinburne regarding 'dwindling probabilities'.

We hope that both books, (and most importantly, of course, the translation of WCB), will boost the German reception of Plantinga's idea of what a warranted Christian belief could be. At the same time, the essays, which are all written by native speakers of German (philosophers, theologians, one mathematician), may be or will be of interest to those already familiar with Plantinga's work.

I thank, first of all, Alvin Plantinga, who not only agreed to publish a German translation of WCB, but also was so kind as to take the time and effort to reply to all the essays that critically examine his thought. My thanks also go to all the authors who participated in this project. At a conference in Berlin, sponsored by the *Fritz Thyssen Stiftung*, we had the opportunity for intensive discussions; thanks to the *Katholische Akademie Berlin* for hosting us. Last but not least, I'm grateful to Jonas Höhler, Christian Prust, and Elke E. Schmidt for their support in editing this volume.

Dieter Schönecker
University of Siegen
September 2015

Dieter Schönecker
The Deliverances of *Warranted Christian Belief*

> Die Philosophen unterschätzen die Schwierigkeit
> wirklich zu verstehen, was einer gesagt hat.
> *Friedrich Nietzsche*
>
> We're gonna need a bigger boat.
> *Martin Brody*

After more than 2500 years of philosophy, it is very hard to leave a new and lasting trace in this perennial human enterprise. A pretty sure sign of such a trace is that people begin to wonder what exactly it is that the philosopher claims. To ask such a question is to do historiography of philosophy; its task is not to figure out whether what is being claimed is true and whether how it is argued for is valid. Rather, the task is to decipher *what* is being claimed; after all, how are we to say whether a given proposition is true or an argument sound, if we don't know what the proposition says or the argument is in the first place?[1]

But which proposition? What argument in which book? It is one thing, for instance, to interpret Kant's *Grundlegung*, and another to interpret his *Tugendlehre*. Both are written by Kant, both are even written by the so-called 'critical' Kant, and yet there are enormous differences (or so I'd claim). People speak of Kant's *transcendental philosophy*, but they do not (yet) speak of such a thing as *Plantingianism*.[2] To speak of such a thing as *Plantingianism* would suggest that Plantinga's philosophy is more or less a unified whole; it would suggest that there is one basic idea, or thesis, or an argument, a red line of thought in his oeuvre. (People, and Plantinga himself, do speak of such a thing as *Reformed Epistemology*,[3] but the differences within this camp—Alston, Mavrodes, Plantin-

---

[1] Cf. WCRL, 154, for the distinction between asking what a text means and whether what it claims is true.—I shall use the following abbreviations: GOM = *God and Other Minds*; RBG = *Reason and Belief in God*; SP = *Self Profile*; WCB = *Warranted Christian Belief*; WCD = *Warrant: The Current Debate*; WCRL = *Where the Conflict Really Lies. Science, Religion, and Naturalism*; WPF = *Warrant and Proper Function*.
[2] Though Geivitt and Jesson (2001, 338) once speak of a "loyal Plantingian". And there is, to be sure, an activity called 'to alvinize' and 'to planting' (and people who do this are 'plantingers'); cf. *The Philosophical Lexicon* by Daniel Dennett and Asbjørn Steglich-Petersen (on the web).
[3] Fales (2003, 353) speaks of Plantinga's "trilogy on Reformed Epistemology".—It certainly does not seem clear at all whether the Calvinist ring to this tag is helpful. As we will see, on the A/C model it is important that the human being is created in God's image. As Plasger shows in his

ga, Woltersdorff, among others—are huge; they are probably not as enormous as the differences within, say, *German Idealism*—philosophers such as Hegel, Fichte, Schelling, Herder et al. have next to nothing in common with one another, it seems to me—, but they are significant enough to render such a term almost useless.) What I am interested in here is not (primarily) whether there is such a thing as *Plantingianism*. Rather, my interest is in *Warranted Christian Belief* (WCB). What is the basic idea, or thesis, or argument, or red line of *this* work? My starting point was the impression that readers of WCB take different stances on what this book is really about.[4] Is its basic idea the same idea that Plantinga already presented in his earlier books and texts, to wit, that one can be rational (or something in this epistemic 'neighborhood', to use one of Plantinga's favorite terms) in one's theistic beliefs without having arguments for them? Or is WCB substantially different? In the preface of WCB, Plantinga says his book is a "sequel" (WCB, xi, fn.3 and p. 68) to *God and Other Minds* and to *Reason and Belief in God*; to be more precise, Plantinga says WCB is a sequel "*in a slightly different direction*" (WCB, xi, fn.3, m.e.). This suggests that there is a red line running through those early texts and WCB; there is some 'slightly different direction', all right, but more or less WCB is a sequel nonetheless. What exactly makes a book a 'sequel', Plantinga does not explain; one may assume, however, that a philosophical book that is such a sequel further develops (or goes into the details of) a basic idea, or a thesis, or an argument already presented in earlier books by the same author.

This is not a paper about the plausibility or soundness of Plantinga's arguments. To be sure, I have a number of specific observations to make regarding WCB, and I shall draw attention to certain difficulties directly related to the topic of this paper, i.e. to the question of what the central aim of WCB really is; our discussion and critical remarks in this context will help us to see what that 'red line' is. However, I shall not (really) get into problems that have already been discussed for quite some while and will occupy both sympathetic and hostile readers for quite a while in the future, questions such as: How do we know that a belief is properly basic? Would not too many beliefs be properly basic? How much interpretation is involved in religious experience? Does Plantinga wind up in voodoo epistemology? Do or may we properly and basically believe in the Great Pumpkin or his grand-son? Are there new Gettier woes? If belief

---

paper, however, it is doubtful whether on Calvin's account there is anything left in us after the fall that resembles God, anything like a sensus divinitatis (Plasger 2015, this volume).

[4] As a matter of fact, my very starting point was my reading of a draft of Christian Tapp's paper for this volume. As I saw it, he placed too much emphasis on what I shall call "TW". I am grateful to Prof. Tapp for further discussion of this point.

in the Christian God is as properly basic as the belief in other minds and the past, why don't as many people hold that belief as people hold these beliefs? What exactly is Christian belief in the first place? And so on.[5] So these questions are *not* what concerns me. Rather, the leading question of this essay is this: The main result of WCB seems to be that *if Christian belief is true, then belief in the Christian God is probably warrant-basic*; but can that really be the main result? Is that really what the argument amounts to? One would think not; for even an atheist does not need to deny that if God exists, then in all likelihood he would give us the faculty to know him. That would be so small-bored a result that atheists would have nothing to fear and Christians little to hope from WCB. The principle of charity requires that a given interpretation should not yield the implication that the author of the interpreted text is out of his mind (or something equally implausible) or defends positions that no one denies or would need to deny; and this assumption seems particularly justified in the case of Alvin Plantinga. Thus we have reason to think that such an interpretation of WCB is incorrect. There must be more to it than just that claim. But is there more in WCB? Yes, there is, I submit, and there is a much more. But there is also *less* than in Plantinga's early works.

Obviously, this paper cannot be a comprehensive study of Plantinga's works and their development, and not even a truly close analysis of the aim and structure of WCB. It is at best a very first step in the direction of Plantinga *exegesis*; and there is, of course, some extra appeal to such an attempt given that Plantinga himself will comment upon it. It is quite tempting here to quote Kant's famous dictum that "it is not at all unusual to find that we understand the author even better then he understood himself" (*Critique of Pure Reason*, B 370). Note, however, that Kant continues: "...since he may not have determined his concept sufficiently and hence sometimes spoke, or even thought, contrary to his own intention" (ibid.). As I see it, chances are rather slim that Plantinga 'has not determined his concept sufficiently'; but there might be other reasons that he sometimes speaks or writes, nonetheless, in a way 'contrary to his own intention'. I'm not saying that what matters in interpretation is (only) intention; what matters is the text itself, and so the last authority concerning the interpretation of Plantinga's texts are these texts and its interpreters. Plantinga is just one of these interpreters. So even if he should say something to the effect "This is not what I *meant*" a fair reply would be: "Well, but this is what you wrote".[6]

---

[5] Some of these objections are dealt with in ch. 10 of WCB.
[6] For interpretation as a method of philosophy cf. Damschen/Schönecker (^{2}2013, 205–272).

I shall begin (1) with a sketch of what I think is for the most part a parity argument in the early Plantinga, based mainly on a brief look at GOM as well as RBG. I will then demonstrate that some understand WCB as a 'sequel' to that parity argument, others, however, as a book that shows (even) less than the parity argument since it allegedly only shows that *if* Christian belief is true, then it's probably warranted (2). The next step will be to interpret what Plantinga says himself in WCB about the aim of WCB (3). I'll then make a proposal on how to understand the deliverances of WCB (4). Finally, I'll briefly sum up and also have a look at how Plantinga interprets his own position in texts written after WCB (5).

1 Properly Basic Christian Belief: Plantinga's Parity Argument in the prequels to WCB

God and Other Minds

Let's begin our sketch of the parity argument with *God and Other Minds* (first published in 1967). The book opens, roughly speaking, with what in WCB is called the *de jure* question[7]: Is it rational to believe in God? The basic anti-evidentialist answer is well-known: It is not true that for every proposition in order to be rationally justified in holding it one must have evidence (reasons) for it; if that were true, then we would not be rationally justified in believing in other minds, simply because we have no convincing argument for that belief; however, we are rationally justified in believing in other minds; therefore, that evidentialist claim cannot be true. What is often called the *parity argument* could also be called the 'same epistemological boat' argument. Already in the preface to GOM, Plantinga says that "belief in other minds and belief in God are in the same epistemological boat; hence if either is rational, so is the other. But obviously the former is rational; so, therefore, is the latter" (GOM, viii); and the very last sentence of the book reads as follows: "if my belief in other minds is rational, so is my belief in God. But obviously the former is ration-

---

[7] More on this later; in GOM, Plantinga simply says that he "shall investigate the rational justifiability" (GOM, 3) of God.

al; so, therefore, is the latter" (GOM, 271).[8] This is Plantinga's early answer to what Wolterstorff later in the introduction to his and Plantinga's seminal edition of *Faith and Rationality* called the "evidentialist challenge", namely that "[n]o religion is acceptable unless rational, and no religion is rational unless supported by evidence" (Wolterstorff 1983, 6), where to be supported by evidence means to be supported by propositional evidence. A challenge can be met in two ways: Either you comply and deliver the goods (which in this case is to say you avail yourself of the means of natural theology); or you reject the challenge itself. Plantinga took the latter route.[9]

Reason and Belief in God

The parity argument and with it the basicality claim were developed at some length in *Reason and Belief in God* (1983); therein too we find the 'same boat' allegory.[10] Recall that GOM and RBG are officially declared by Plantinga to be the (main) prequels to WCB, and indeed there can be no doubt that much of WCB is a sequel to RBG.[11] As in GOM, the crucial question is "whether belief in God—belief in the existence of God—is rationally acceptable" (RBG, 19). Since a belief is rationally acceptable, if (but not only if) it is properly basic, the question is this: Is belief in God properly basic? Now properly basic beliefs are beliefs that one

---

[8] This very same formulation is quoted in WCB (70) in quotation marks, but no reference is given.—In his preface to the 1990 Paperback Edition to GOM, Plantinga combines the allegory (or metaphor) of the 'epistemological boat' with the language of 'parity' by saying that belief in other minds and belief in God "are on an epistemological *par*" (Plantinga 1990, xii, m.e.).
[9] This is not quite true. Looking back to GOM in his preface to the 1990 Edition, Plantinga mentions that he "employed a traditional but improperly stringent standard" (Plantinga 1990, ix) in relation to theistic arguments; as he rightly points out, (almost) no philosophical argument is such that it could only be rejected on pain of irrationality (and who sets the standards for the latter?); cf. WCB, 170. Also cf. Plantinga (2001c, 384f.) for a clarification on how Plantinga relates to philosophers such as Swinburne (namely positively); then again, he also says: "I don't know of any such arguments" (2001c, 398), i.e. of arguments that actually show that Christian belief is true; and in (2002, 34), Plantinga says that of all the (two dozen or so; cf. Plantinga, 2007a) arguments for God "none delivers *knowledge*" (his emphasis); also cf. Plantinga 2001a, 217ff.
[10] Cf. RBG, 90: "Belief in the existence of God is in the same boat as belief in other minds, the past, and perceptual objects".—In his famous *Advice to Christian Philosophers* (1984, on the Web), the parity argument is dominant as well.
[11] For instance, Plantinga's very brief discussion in RBG (19–20) of negative theology (Kant, Kaufman, Hick) is much broadened in WCB (3–63) and the same is true for his discussion of the sensus divinitatis, sin, and all that.

does hold, and may hold, without the evidential support of other beliefs; they are beliefs not accepted on the basis of other beliefs (i.e. they are not based on arguments or inferences) and yet they are acceptable. Belief in God, says Plantinga, is such a properly basic belief. The main point behind classical foundationalism, as I understand it, is that some propositions are and must be affirmed (and are thus *properly* believed) without (further) evidence because otherwise there would be an endless chain of propositions.[12] Maybe one can doubt even these propositions and remain skeptical. But it's important to see that Plantinga's task is not to refute skepticism. Rather, he must show that Christian belief is *not* "noetically below par" (RBG, 17). Belief in God, Plantinga aims to show in RBG, is just as rational, i.e. epistemically acceptable as other beliefs (about other minds, the past, perceivable objects) that are acceptable insofar as they are properly basic (if neither kind of belief is considered acceptable by a skeptic, then they are both in *this* boat).[13] From the point of view of classical foundationalism, only beliefs that are self-evident, or perceptual (evident to the senses) or incorrigible beliefs are properly basic; we just *see* them to be true without evidence.[14] Being a non-classical (Reidian) foundationalist, Plantinga adds belief in God to that set of properly basic beliefs. The strategy is twofold:

First, there are two arguments against imperialistic foundationalism (as it were):[15] If only those beliefs are rationally acceptable that are either properly basic or somehow based upon properly basic beliefs, then it would render most (allegedly) non-basic beliefs (about other minds, the past, etc.) that we find rationally acceptable to be unacceptable because it is hard to see how they are based upon basic beliefs; also (second argument), that belief itself (classical foundationalism) is not rationally acceptable because it is neither properly basic nor based on properly basic propositions. So there is no reason to think that *only* beliefs that are self-evident or incorrigible or evident to the senses are properly basic.

---

12 Cf. RBG, 39. "Not even God", says Plantinga in one of his replies (2001c, 390), "can have a proof" that his beliefs are reliable because for such a proof he would already need to rely on the ways he forms these beliefs; the point is that at one point or other one must *trust* in one's cognitive faculties. It is striking, by the way, that Plantinga (as far as I can see) never reflects upon the possibility of something like transcendental *Letztbegründung* (à la Hösle, for instance).
13 There is, says Plantinga, an "analogy between belief in God and belief in the existence of perceptual objects, other persons, and the past" (RBG, 81). On the difference between "God exists" and, for instance, "God is speaking to me" as well as on the difference between "Other persons exist" and "There are other persons" cf. RBG, 80–82.
14 There's quite some (semi-technical) analysis in RGB on 'asymmetry', 'irreflexivity' etc.; I'll ignore all this.
15 "Epistemic Imperialism" is a term used by Alston (1991, 199); but cf. RBG, 28.

However, there is also no reason to think that belief in God is not properly basic and, what is much more: belief in God, *secondly*, has "the *characteristics* a proposition must have to deserve a place in the foundations" (RBG, 59, m.e.). At the end of part II of RBG, Plantinga promises that in part IV[16] he will "look into the proper procedure for discovering and justify such *criteria* for proper basicality" (RBG 62, m.e.). So what are these criteria (characteristics)? To begin with, it is striking that Plantinga in his discussion of the *Great Pumpkin Objection* (which is within part IV) argues that from the fact that reformed epistemologists reject the criteria "of proper basicality purveyed by classical foundationalism" (RBG, 75) one may not infer that they must accept just any belief as properly basic, but that he does *not* explain what exactly a 'criterion' is. The first time Plantinga introduces the term 'criteria', he actually says "*such* criteria" (RGB, 62, m.e.), referring thereby to proposition "(33)" in RBG (p. 60) which formulates the foundationalist claim that a given proposition (belief) A is properly basic "for me only if A is self-evident or incorrigible or evident to the senses for me" (ibid.); this finding is confirmed by the fact that in part IV Plantinga refers to the very same 'criteria' of "modern foundationalism" (RBG, 75). But self-evidence, incorrigibility and perceptual evidence are not criteria of proper basicality; they are *instances*. If they were criteria—which really would be "necessary and sufficient conditions of proper basicality" (RBG, 76)—,[17] then obviously the very idea of showing that belief in God could be a properly basic belief alongside self-evident, incorrigible and perceptual beliefs would be doomed from the outset; by means of criteria one can cognize *which* elements belong to a certain group. If self-evident, incorrigible and perceptual beliefs are properly basic, they must have certain qualities *in common*; once we know what it is that they share and what justifies us in subsuming them under one term (which is 'properly basic'), we can say that other beliefs (Christian belief, for instance) also have these qualities and thus are also properly basic. As far as I can tell, in RBG Plantinga fails to name these qualities.[18]

In any event, Plantinga makes an important point which I'd formulate (in my own words) as follows: Whenever we define terms such as 'knowledge', 'justification', 'rationality', or 'basicality', we need to offer paradigmatic cases of what counts as a relevant instance of the term in question. And for these paradigms, there is no neutral ground, as it were, to start from. This is not to say that there is

---

[16] It actually says "Part III" in RBG (62); in private exchange, Prof. Plantinga has confirmed that this is simply an error.
[17] Cf. WCB, 84: "conditions of proper basicality".
[18] I think that this is a very important point. I'll deal with it in another paper in detail, but will come back to this later.

or could not be a discussion, no revision of what paradigms to use, and no defeaters; properly basic beliefs, and paradigmatic examples of them, are *prima facie* justified, they are not infallible.[19] But it is to say that one cannot simply (imperialistically) claim that belief in God cannot be properly basic because only self-evident or incorrigible propositions or those evident to the senses are properly basic. For how do you know? This is what you say, but I say something else. Plantinga says: "The Christian community is responsible to its set of examples, not to theirs" (RBG, 77).[20] A further important point is this: A belief is basic to me, negatively speaking, if I do not hold it on the basis of other beliefs; still there is a reason why I hold it, some kind of evidence or ground (and this is why Plantinga even endorses a "moderate evidentialism" [Plantinga 2001c, 396].[21] For instance, if I believe that there is a tree in front of me, then I don't hold this belief because I have beliefs about, say, my environment, or my perception; I hold it because I'm having an experience ('being appeared to treely'). This experience is the reason, so to speak, why I have that belief; and this experience is, along with further conditions, all I need in order to be rational, or justified, or within my epistemic rights, to hold that belief.

---

19 Cf. RBG, 77 and WCB, 343f.
20 To give my own example drawn from another context: It would be imperialistic to use only examples from (alleged) knowledge in mathematics and natural sciences in order to define 'knowledge' and then jump to the conclusion that there is no such thing as *moral* knowledge (such an imperialistic move is really what Mackie's famous *argument from queerness* is all about). Moral realists can and should reply that from their point of view moral knowledge is *just as paradigmatic* as mathematical or scientific knowledge; thus moral knowledge is at least one of the foundational (properly basic) beliefs we start from.—Plantinga mentions properly basic *moral* beliefs here and there; cf. RBG, 89; WCB, 148, 174; 208ff., 299, 452f.; and Plantinga (2007a).
21 Therefore, it is a little difficult to see why the version of evidentialism offered by Norman Kretzmann should not be acceptable to Plantinga. According to Kretzmann (the way Plantinga reads him), "what is required is only that the believer have evidence of *some* sort" (WCB, 103). It depends on what 'evidence' means, of course. If one understands evidentialism as the position that the belief in God is acceptable only if there is evidence by means of other propositions, then Plantinga is right. But Kretzmann's position is not a case of evidentialism in this sense. As Plantinga points out, religious experience could be evidence; but if this falls under the rubric of 'evidence', why not the following: Upon reading the Scriptures I find myself convinced that the great things of the gospel are true. Why would the gospel, or reading it with a certain doxastic experience, not count as 'evidence'? You ask me: What evidence do you have for believing in God? I say: the evidence of the Scriptures taken the basic way.

Self-Profile

In his *Self-Profile* (1985), Plantinga says that what he wrote in GOM "still seems to [him] to be substantially true" (SP, 55): "I am obviously rational in believing that there are other minds; so why am I not similarly rational in believing that God exists?" (SP, 156). So "*some* propositions can properly be believed without evidence. Well, why not the proposition that God exists?" (SP, 59). To accept a belief without further propositional evidence is to accept it as basic; Plantinga never tires of arguing for this claim: "my *main aim* was to argue that it is perfectly rational to take belief in God as *basic*—that is to accept theistic belief without accepting it on the basis of argument or evidence from other propositions one believes" (SP, 56, m.e.).[22] So after GOM and before the warrant-books, *the prominent idea in Plantinga's work*—along with an increasing focus on what it means to be *rational, justified,* or something along these lines—is that belief in God is *properly basic* and as such as good as the belief in other minds or the past.

To better understand this, let's briefly compare it with Alston's parity argument.[23] *Very* roughly, Alston's argument goes like this: Perceptual beliefs are prima facie trustworthy (rational, justified, or whatever is epistemically positive); some theistic beliefs are (like) perceptual beliefs; therefore, some theistic beliefs are prima facie trustworthy (rational, justified, whatever).[24] Alston's strategy is to show that theists who claim to have mystical (religious) experiences avail themselves of the same, or at least of essentially the same, cognitive tool (the faculty of perception) as everyone else; therefore, their theistic beliefs based on those experiences are just as trustworthy (until proven guilty) as ordinary perceptual beliefs. Thus the parity in Alston's parity argument is twofold: There is parity regarding the positive epistemic status, *and* there is parity with regard to the source of this status; both ordinary perceptions as well as mystical perceptions have a positive epistemic status, and they do have this status because they are both perceptions (and perceptions are prima facie trustworthy, or so the *principle of credulity* says). The parity argument in Plantinga's work, however, is different. His strategy is not to show that theistic belief is brought about by the same cognitive faculty or the same kind of epistemic input, but by an altogether different faculty of its own; in that sense, theistic belief is unlike other beliefs, and there is no parity in this sense. Still they have something in common with other beliefs;

---

[22] Cf. Plantinga (2007b, 614), where he still speaks of the very same "main aim" (though not with explicit reference to WCB).
[23] Cf. Alston (1991); for a short version, cf. Alston (2005).
[24] Richard Gale's reconstruction of this (or a similar) argument is discussed by Plantinga in WCB, 336f f.; Gale speaks of 'analogy' rather than 'parity'.

they are basic, and they are properly so. That they are basic is easily shown. The propriety of these basic beliefs is a different, much more difficult story. From early on, I submit, Plantinga is successful in showing that classical foundationalism is finished because it is self-referentially inconsistent, and because it is imperialistic in only accepting certain beliefs as foundational. For the same reason, evidentialism with regard to theistic beliefs is criticized (though maybe not finished because it is at least not inconsistent); one need not have an argument for believing in God if belief in God is just as properly basic as other properly basic beliefs. But *is* it a properly basic belief? It would not be so if we had reason to think that belief in God is inconsistent or otherwise somehow false; as we'll see, to show that this is not the case is a major concern of WCB. But how do we know belief in God is proper? What exactly is propriety? '*Well*', says Plantinga in SP, why can the proposition that God exists not properly be believed without evidence? Well, one might reply, why *should* it be believed even if we knew that nothing speaks against it? As Plantinga self-critically points out himself,[25] the "deeper question" (SP, 56) of what rationality and justification are in the first place remains unaddressed in the early works. But note that this is also why the question of the propriety of basic beliefs was not (or at best unsatisfyingly) answered. In RBG (72), a belief is defined as "properly basic" if "it is *rational* to accept it without accepting it on the basis of any other propositions and beliefs at all" (m.e.).[26] So if we don't know what rationality is, we don't know what the propriety of properly basic beliefs is. Do we know better after WCB?

2 The Reception of WCB. Confusion and Friendly Fire

It's too early to say, of course, but if I were to bet on which books of the last 50 years or so will still be read in another 50 years from now, I'd bet that one of them will be Plantinga's WCB. It is extremely difficult to come up with something novel in philosophy, especially in disciplines such as philosophy of religion and epistemology, but I am convinced that Plantinga has managed to give us some truly fresh ideas (and not just some old wine in new analytic bottles).[27] But

---

25 Cf. SP, 56 and WCB, 67–70.
26 Cf. Plantinga's definition in Plantinga (1982, 15) and (2007b, 614, Fn.).
27 To be fair to Plantinga and his predecessors, it should be noted that Plantinga himself always points out that there are predecessors such as Thomas Reid, Herman Bavinck and, of

what exactly are those novel ideas? To be more precise: What is the basic idea of Plantinga's WCB? What is its aim?

To many it seems that WCB boils down to this: "if theistic belief is *true*, then it seems likely that it *does* have warrant" (WCB, 188; let's refer to this claim with "TW", I will be more precise later). But obviously, it is one thing to say that Christian belief *has* warrant, and another to say that it has warrant *provided* Christian belief is true. This is exactly what Plantinga's antipode, Richard Swinburne, finds problematic about WCB.[28] According to his interpretation of WCB, it is Plantinga's claim that "we cannot in any interesting sense ask whether it is rational to believe that Christian belief *has* warrant—he [i.e. Plantinga] says, or seems to say" (Swinburne 2001, 207, m.e.). All that Plantinga succeeds in doing, says Swinburne, is "showing what *would* give warrant to Christian beliefs" (op. cit., 205, m.e.), but Plantinga does not show that Christian beliefs *are* warranted: "a monumental issue which Plantinga does not discuss, and which a lot of people will consider needs discussing. This is whether Christian beliefs *do* have warrant" (Swinburne 2001, 206, m.e.).

Swinburne's worry is pervasive. Take Moreland and Lane Craig (2003, 160 – 169): They are, in principle, certainly friendly readers of Plantinga's project, and yet they also attack his argument in this regard; the "aim of this project" (Moreland/Craig, 167)—that is of what they call the "private" (ibid.) project of providing "from a Christian perspective an epistemological account of warranted Christian belief" (Moreland/Craig, 161)—is just to show TW; and even that, they claim, is not sufficiently argued for. In the same vein, Groothius expresses the worry that "some may be disappointed that Plantinga never tries to make a compelling case that Christianity is true" (Groothius, on the web) which is why these people will seek out resources "to argue that Christianity is not merely warranted, but true"[29]; similarly, Anderson in his review (on the web) notes that Plantinga's abandonment of a proof for the truth of Christianity "may strike some readers

---

course, Calvin (and even Aquinas) who already developed some of the principal ideas involved in what has become Reformed Epistemology.

28 It is, by the way, an interesting question whether there really is such an enormous gap (as is often claimed) between Swinburne's approach and Reformed Epistemology. Certainly, Swinburne has much more confidence in arguments for God; but note that the entire cumulative argument rests upon the argument from religious experience: If the probability of theism on the other evidence is not very low, the testimony of those with religious experience strengthens the cumulative probability. Since the argument from religious experience itself is based upon the principle of credulity (which is a reformed principle, as it were), Swinburne is not a complete evidentialist; cf. Plantinga's brief remark in WCB (91, footnote 43); on Swinburne's approach, cf. (Nickel/Schönecker, 2014).

29 There is confusion here; for if Christianity is warranted, then it is (in all likelihood) true.

as an anticlimax and even as a glaring omission"; Moser (2001, 371) is afraid that Plantinga's achievement "will doubtless disappoint many"; and Helm (2001, 1112) finds Plantinga's strategy "not so ambitious". To Greco, the "central thesis of Reformed Epistemology [...] is that some beliefs about God *can* be properly basic" (2007, 629, m.e.); Plantinga's project, Greco then says, "is to explain how Christian beliefs might be warranted or properly basic, as opposed to *showing* that they are" (op. cit., 636, his emphasis). For Senor (2002, 391), Plantinga's "aim is not to show that belief in God is warranted but only that there is no good reason to think it is not" (Senor 2002, 392). Then he says: "In sum, what we get in WCB is an argument for a conditional claim" (393), namely TW ('if theistic belief is true, then it seems likely that it does have warrant'). Daniel von Wachter (2007, 496) also reduces WCB to this claim: "In *Warranted Christian Belief* [...] Plantinga argues that Christian beliefs probably are knowledge if they are true". Similarly, Forrest in his review of WCB (2002, 109) says: "In this work Plantinga argues for [TW]". All in all, Forrest (2009) finds the lack of argument for the truth of Christian belief or the A/C model to be the "most pressing criticism of Plantinga's recent position".

So what is the impression yielded by a brief survey of the reception of WCB? TW is what really occupies these readers; they tend to take TW as the main result of the entire book, and they also think this is an insufficiently ambitious claim. But is the result of Plantinga's *opus magnum* really so meagre? The book's title, after all, is "*Warranted* Christian Belief", not "*Possibly* Warranted Christian Belief". As it turns out, there are other readings of WCB. It seems likely that entries in *Wikipedia* reflect a rather common interpretation of his project; if so, it is illuminating that according to the *Wikipedia* article on *Reformed Epistemology* Plantinga, having begun with a parity argument in GOM, has gone on in WCB to "argue that theistic belief *has* 'warrant'" (Wikipedia 2012, m.e.). Similarly, in his contribution to *Religious Epistemology* in the *Internet Encyclopedia of Philosophy*, Kelly Clark briefly explains the parity argument and then continues: "For the sake of parity, we should trust the deliverances of the faculty that produces in us belief in the divine (what Plantinga [2000], following John Calvin, calls the *sensus divinitatis*, the sense of the divine)". Here Clarke—as well as Trigg (2002) and Hibbs (2001)—obviously understands Plantinga's warrant-argument in terms of the parity-argument: The early Plantinga is well-known for his parity-argument and the concept of proper basicality; thus the expectation is that Plantinga now avails himself of the same strategy, based on the new and seminal epistemological concept of warrant. And this is not just the impression we receive from encyclopedia articles. Take Linda Zagzebski, for instance: In her introduction to a collection of "Catholic Responses to Reformed Epistemology" (1993) she speaks of Plantinga's "new account of warrant" (Zagzebski 1993, 2), referring to the publication of *Warrant and Proper Function* (WCB was not yet written). Zagzebski understands the (then new) warrant-project—obviously against the background of GOM and RBG—as providing the "resources to defend the positive position that religious beliefs *have* warrant and, when true, constitute knowledge" (ibid., m.e.); and she finds Plantinga's new warrant-approach "obviously much stronger than the earlier claim that no one has shown it to be irrational to hold theistic belief in the basic way" (1993, 2).[30] Then WCB was published, and other readers also made the same assumption as Zagzebski. Thus Phillips (2004, 251) says: "Basic beliefs in religions *are* as warranted as they are in perception and memory" (m.e.). On Wykstra's interpretation, TW along with the claim that the idea of a *sensus divinitatis* is possible "entail that for all we know, Christian theism *has* warrant" (2002, 94, m.e.). Paul Copan (2001, 940) begins his brief review by describing Plantinga's aim as follows: "Theistic belief *has* good warrant, Plantinga wants to show" (m.e.); a little later, however, Copan writes: "Plantinga states that if Christian belief is true, it is also warranted" (ibid). Yet again, Winfried Löffler (2006)—one of the few German-speaking philosophers that are familiar with Plantinga's philosophy—has quite another view: With reference to RBG, he says that Plantinga's claim is only that one "*könne*" (*could*, Löffler 2006, 92) entertain basic theistic beliefs whereas with reference to WCB, Löffler believes that Plantiga's position became *stronger* because he (Plantinga) now argues, according to Löffler, that most theists are "*tatsächlich erkenntnistheoretisch vernünftig*" (*really* are epistemologically rational, ibid., 94)—as we will see, it is just the other way round.

After GOM and RBG, Plantinga developed his theory of warrant and published *Warrant: The Current Debate* (WCD) and *Warrant and Proper Function* (WPF; both 1993); as a matter of fact, Plantinga considers WCB to be a "sequel" (WCB, 68) to these two books as well. So both the pre-warrant-texts GOM and RBG as well as WCD and WPF are prequels to WCB; and this, I claim, has caused confusion in the book's reception. Some people read WCB as if its main result were TW; others still see the good old pre-warrant-parity-argument at work and even believe that it is shown that Christian belief is warranted; yet others seem more or less confused. What is the proper reception?

---

30 In her review of WCB, however, Zagzebski (2002, 117) criticizes Plantinga for showing too little: "*if* Christian belief is true, belief in it has the kinds of epistemic value that philosophers routinely discuss: it is justified, internally and externally rational, and warranted" (her emphasis).

3 The Aim of WCB: The Official Position

Authors typically describe their aim in a preface, and so does Plantinga. So let's turn to WCB itself, and let us first look at its *Preface* to see what Plantinga himself declares to be the aim of WCB. Central to the entire project is Plantinga's distinction between *de facto* objections and *de jure* objections. De facto objections—such as the argument from evil—are about the truth of Christian belief; if such an objection is viable, Christian belief is false (or very unlikely). WCB is not primarily concerned with these objections, says Plantinga; according to him, de facto objections are not as "prevalent" (WCB, ix) as de jure objections. Roughly speaking, de jure objections concern "the intellectual or rational acceptability of Christian belief" (WCB, vii). To be more precise, there are three main candidates for de jure objections, to wit, "that Christian belief is *unjustified*, that it is *irrational*, and that it is *unwarranted*" (WCB, x). From scratch, Plantinga puts great emphasis on the claim that de jure objections are supposed to work *regardless of the truth of Christian belief*; these objections hold that Christian belief, "whether or not true, is at any rate" (WCB, ix) unjustified or irrational or unwarranted (or all of it). There is, says Plantinga, "the common suggestion that Christian belief, whether true or not, is intellectually unacceptable" (WCB, xiii); what is wrong with Christian belief, according to de jure objections, is "something other than falsehood" (WCB, ix). Thus, Plantinga formulates "the main question of the book" (WCB, x) as follows: "is there a *de jure* objection to Christian belief? One that is independent of *de facto* objections and does not presuppose that Christian belief is false?" (WCB, x).

There are numerous general formulations of the de jure question (JQ). As it turns out later, these general formulations are only preliminary (or sometimes merely summary in character). For there is a "metaquestion" (WCB, 67). This is the question JQ is really asking about; what, exactly, *is* the de jure question? Given those three candidates for de jure objections, the de jure question can be broken up into three questions:

(JQ1) Is Christian belief justified?

(JQ2) Is Christian belief rational?

(JQ3) Is Christian belief warranted?

But this is not the crucial step for answering the 'metaquestion'. The crucial step is to pose and answer the following question: What do 'justified', 'rational', and 'warranted' *mean*? (Or: What *is* it for a belief to be justified, rational, or warranted?) It is this question that Plantinga himself says he did not raise when he wrote

GOM (and did not fully appreciate when writing RBG).³¹ When it comes to justification, Plantinga took evidentialism in GOM for granted, and he didn't ask what exactly 'justification' and 'evidence' mean. In WCB, a huge part (the entire second part) is dedicated to the 'metaquestion': What do 'justified', 'rational', and 'warranted' mean, both in general and with regard to Christian beliefs? Once this is accounted for, the 'metaquestion' can be answered, i.e. JQ1, JQ2, and JQ3 can be reformulated and, if possible, be answered. To put a highly interesting and useful debate in a nutshell, here are the answers to that 'metaquestion', i.e. here are the reconstructed variants of JQ:

> (JQ1)* Is Christian belief justified, i.e. do those who hold Christian beliefs flout any epistemic obligations?
>
> (JQ2)* Is Christian belief rational, i.e. are those who hold Christian beliefs internally and externally rational?³²
>
> (JQ3)* Is Christian belief warranted, i.e. are these beliefs produced by cognitive faculties functioning properly in a cognitive environment, according to a design plan successfully aimed at truth?

In the *Preface* Plantinga himself says that the de jure objection both with regard to justification (justification-objection) and to internal rationality (internal-rationality-objection), unlike the external-rationality-objection and the warrant-objection, do *not* presuppose the falsity of theism;³³ so the claim is not that there aren't *any* de jure objections that do not depend on de facto objections, but there aren't any "*decent*" (WCB xiii, m.e.) such objections.

It is Plantinga's contention that such a dependence between the falsity and the de jure objection holds when it comes to warrant as that which "makes the difference between knowledge and true belief" (WCB, xi) and thus to the warrant-objection. The argument for this claim is very simple: "As is turns out, this *de jure* objection [the objection, say by Marx or Freud, that Christian belief lacks warrant] is really dependent on a de facto objection. That is because (as I argue) if Christian belief is true, then it is also warranted; the claim that theistic

---

31 Cf. Plantinga (1990).—In RBG, Plantinga uses terms such as 'to be rational', 'justified', or 'within one's epistemic rights' more or less interchangeably; here too, WCB is a sequel, but a sequel that is *much* more detailed and explicit then its prequel.
32 As we shall see later, the proper question is this: (JQ2)** Is Christian belief rational, i.e. are those who hold Christian beliefs internally rational?
33 Cf. WCB, xiii. The reason is obvious: Neither flouting my duties nor properly sticking to my experience guarantees truth. It is therefore misleading of Plantinga (2001b, 327 f.) to say that in WCB he argues that "*all*" (m.e.) de jure objections "presuppose the falsehood" of Christian belief.

(and hence Christian) belief is unwarranted really presupposes that Christian belief is false" (WCB, xii). As Plantinga already notes in the *Preface*, in order for a belief to have warrant, it must be produced by a cognitive faculty that is "successfully aimed at the production of true belief" (WCB, xi). So if a belief is warranted, then it is produced by a faculty that is successfully aimed at the production of true belief, and hence it is probably true; and if a belief is unwarranted, then for the same reason it probably is not true. And then a major point Plantinga believes he makes against Freud&Marx&Others is that they, when claiming that Christian belief is unwarranted, already presuppose that it is false: "their objection presupposes its falsehood" (WCB, xii). Again, a de jure objection is dependent on a de facto objection; '*that is*', says Plantinga, because of TW.[34]

Judging from our brief glance at the reception of WCB, one might easily get the impression that at the end of the day (and much sharp-witted reasoning) Plantinga's position really amounts to no more (or not much more) than TW. So it's about time we looked more closely at TW. In the section that those critics have in mind, Plantinga raises the following question: "Is Belief in God Warrant-Basic?" (WCB, 186). Then there are two brief answers: "If false, probably not" (WCB, 186); and: "If true, probably so" (WCB, 188). These are the headings of the subsections. A little further on, Plantinga provides the following answers to that question: "if theistic belief is false, but taken in the basic way [and not taken on testimony], then it probably has no warrant" (WCB, 186); and: "if theistic belief is *true*, then it seems likely that it *does* have warrant" (WCB, 188). How are we to understand this? To begin with, we should note that those statements (in WCB, 186 ff.) are statements about '*theistic* belief' in general because Plantinga has not moved on to the extended A/C model. Once he has done that, he writes: "If *Christian* belief is true, then very likely it does have warrant" (WCB, 285, m.e.). But the difference between theistic and Christian belief is not the problem; rather, the problem is that in the official formulation of his argument there is a probability condition built into TW: If theistic (or Christian) belief is true, then *probably* theistic (Christian) belief has warrant; and if theistic (or Christian) belief is false, then *probably* theistic (Christian) belief has no warrant. I take it that this is not a very serious doubt or possibility; as a matter of fact, in the *Preface* Plantinga himself does *not* say: 'if Christian belief is true, then it is also *probably* warranted'; rather, he formulates TW *without* the probability caveat: "if Christian belief is true, then it is also warranted" (WCB, xii). So maybe we could put this caveat aside. If we do that and follow the formulation of the *Pref-*

---

34 Cf. Plantinga (2001c, 387): "My reason for refraining from arguing that Christian belief is warranted is my belief that the latter is warranted if and only if it is true".

ace, we read Plantinga as claiming 'if true, then warranted' as well as claiming 'if false, then not warranted'. Since the latter is equivalent to 'if warranted, then true', we get: If Christian belief is true, then it is warranted, and if Christian belief is warranted, then Christian belief is true. On this reading, therefore, Plantinga's alleged main position (or proposition, for that matter) would be a bi-conditional:

> **(TW)** Christian belief is warranted if and only if Christian belief is true.[35]

But the official (more rigid) formulations in WCB are different:

> (i) If Christian belief is false, then Christian belief probably has no warrant.
>
> (ii) If Christian belief is true, then Christian belief probably has warrant.

On the assumption that (i) is equivalent to

> (i)* If Christian belief probably has warrant, then Christian belief is true.

we get: If Christian belief probably has warrant, then Christian belief is true, and if Christian belief is true, then Christian belief probably has warrant. Thus, in this version, there is also a bi-conditional:

> **(TWP)** Christian belief is probably warranted if and only if Christian belief is true.

But is that assumption (i.e. (i) and (i)* are equivalent) sensible? It depends on how exactly we understand the negation of the consequent of (i) ('Christian belief probably has no warrant'). Generally speaking, the negation expresses that it is not the case that Christian belief probably has no warrant. But what exactly is being negated? On the first reading it is the claim that Christian belief probably has *no* warrant; the claim is that it probably has no warrant, and this claim is negated by saying that it probably *does have* warrant. Thus we get:

> **(NC1)** Christian belief probably has warrant.

---

[35] This is how Plantinga put it in an interview with Robert Lawrence Kuhn for PBS; cf. the video on the web. Note, however, that in this interview too Plantinga sometimes mentions the probability caveat, sometimes not.

(This is the reading used in (i)*).³⁶ On the second reading the negation refers to the probability condition: the claim is that Christian belief *probably* has no warrant, and this claim is negated by saying that it *not* probably has no warrant. Thus we get:

> **(NC2)** Christian belief improbably has no warrant.

Or more naturally speaking: It is improbable (unlikely) that Christian belief has no warrant. And then the question is this: Is there a difference between saying that Christian belief probably has warrant and saying that it is improbable that it has no warrant?

Possibly yet another meaning comes into focus by a formulation Plantinga uses in a text written after WCB: "I argue that (probably) Christian belief has warrant if and only if it is true" (Plantinga 2001a, 216). Thus we have:

> **(TWP)*** Probably, Christian belief is warranted if and only if Christian belief is true.

Here the probability condition is put in front of the entire bi-conditional itself, and I'm not sure that TWP and TWP* are equivalent.

So on the face of it, there is reason indeed to believe that Plantinga has only claimed something fairly meager and even something that is quite obvious: If God, as Christians typically understand him, exists, then our belief that He does exist is what He wants us to think about Him and so our belief that God exists is true, or as Swinburne in his review of WCB puts it: "It is natural to suppose that God created us in such a way that we would come to hold the true belief that He exists" (Swinburne 2001, 205). I'm not sure what Swinburne means by saying that this is '*natural*'; as it happens, Plantinga himself also finds it "natural" (WCB, 188). I think what they both mean is that it is obvious or very plausible to think so; if God is a loving God, and if he creates us in his image, then why should He do so in a way that we would have *no* knowledge of Him? Why would he (entirely) hide himself?³⁷ And yet, God's possible *hiddenness* is a seri-

---

36 In email-exchanges, Christian Tapp provided the following counter-example to argue that (i) is not equivalent to (i)*: If my car begins to stutter and then stops running, then probably it has no gas; however, if probably it does have gas, then this still does not imply that it does not begin to stutter and stops running.—I am grateful to comments made regarding this issue by Christian Tapp and Gregor Nickel.

37 Geivett and Jesson (2001, 333) think that this point brings TW "close to the edge of tautology"; maybe that is rather strong, but Moreland and Lane Craig (2003, 167) are certainly right in saying that Plantinga's argument for TW "is surprisingly thin".

ous and much discussed topic; so I think it is surprising that Plantinga says little (in WCB) about the possibility of God hiding himself.[38] Given that TW obviously is a very important result of WCB (to some even the main or only result), this is quite disappointing. (Note that the subsections in which these answers are given are hardly four pages long.) This objection is all the more relevant given that TW is introduced with regard to theism in general, not with regard to Christian belief; so even if the God of Christianity cannot be understood as a (completely) hidden God, another God (a God from a Non-Christian perspective) could possibly have reasons not to reveal himself so TW wouldn't be 'natural'.[39]

In the *Preface*, Plantinga goes on to describe what happens in part III the title of which is "Warranted Christian Belief". This title is, *nota bene*, identical with the title of the book itself. So one would expect it to be the central part of the book; as a matter of fact, Plantinga says that part III (except for chapter 10 that deals with objections) is the "central part of the story line" (WCB, xiv). In this part, Plantinga lays out his extended Aquinas/Calvin model which is a theory of a Christian *sensus divinitatis* as a cognitive faculty[40] that, supported by the Holy Spirit, produces Christian beliefs; the extended A/C model is thus a theory of what warrant is when it comes not only to theistic belief, and theistic belief before the Fall (then the model is unextended), but to Christian belief proper.[41] And then Plantinga says: "I propose the extended A/C model; according to this model, Christian belief *is* warranted" (WCB, xii, m.e.). That certainly sounds as if, at least according to this model, Christian belief '*is*' warranted;

---

38 There is only a brief discussion of a similar objection by Keith Lehrer (WCB, 282–284).
39 However, the God relevant in these subsections is already described as a "person who has created us in his image [...] who loves us" (WCB, 188), etc.
40 The sensus divinitatis itself (not just the instigation of the Holy Spirit) is sometimes described as a "*process*" (cf. WCB, 256, 331) rather than a faculty; I'll ignore this difference.
41 For my purposes, I will not (usually) differentiate between the A/C model and the extended model and often just speak of the 'model'.—Sometimes it sounds as if the model is a model of how a broad theistic belief in (some kind of) personal God is brought about and can have positive epistemic status (cf. the "essence" of the unextended model as described in WCB, 204) and the extended model of how "*specifically* Christian belief" (WCB, 200, 241, m.e.) is triggered; sometimes, however, it sounds as if the extended model is the model that describes our cognition and volition *after* the "fall into sin" (WCB, 205) whereas the unextended model is the model that accounts for the sensus divinitatis *before* the 'Fall'. But knowledge of God based on the sensus divinitatis *before the Fall* must still be knowledge of the Christian God, and thus, among other things, knowledge of the (typically Christian) Holy Trinity.—By the way, Plantinga has a good deal to say about the cognitive and affective effects of sin, but in WCB he is almost silent on how we are to understand the 'Fall' as described in *Genesis* (he says that "the model need not take a stand" on this issue, WCB, 207 and 213; cf. 211f., however, and 212 for a brief case of "speculation" regarding how the very first act of sinning sin was possible).

since the model is one 'proposed' by Plantinga, one would think that he claims Christian belief is warranted. But then he continues: "What I officially claim for the extended A/C model is not that it is *true* but, rather, that it is *epistemically possible* (i.e., nothing we know commits us to its falsehood); I add that if Christian belief is true, then very likely this model or something like it is also true" (WCB, xii). Christian belief is warranted, but only '*according to*' the model.

Several things are noteworthy here: *First*, TW is presented here as something *added* ('I add…'); it's not the only claim, and it seems it isn't even the main claim. Rather, *secondly*, the main claim seems to be this:

(EP) The extended A/C model is epistemically possible.

(I'll get back to this.) *Thirdly*, we should note that EP is what Plantinga '*officially*' claims. So officially he doesn't claim that the extended A/C model is true (but only possible). This is to say, obviously, that *un*officially (personally) he very well believes it to be true[42] (though, certainly, he doesn't *know* he *is* warranted for then he would need to know that his beliefs are true which he doesn't).

Plantinga himself puts his two claims—TW and EP—in a certain perspective. WCB, he says, "can be thought of in at least two quite different ways" (WCB, xiii): as an "exercise in apologetics and philosophy of religion" (ibid.) and as an "exercise in Christian philosophy" (ibid.). In this context, Plantinga repeats that what he claims for the extended A/C model "is twofold: first, it shows that and how Christian belief can perfectly well have warrant, thus refuting a range of *de jure* objections to Christian belief. But I also claim that the model provides a good way for Christians to think about the epistemology of Christian belief, in particular whether and how Christian belief has warrant" (WCB, xiii). Here Plantinga seems to promise an answer to the question of '*whether*'[43] Christian belief has warrant; and a little later in the *Preface* Plantinga says the A/C model "is a defense of the idea that Christian belief *has* warrant" (WCB, xiv)— on pain of contradiction, however, it can only be a defense inasmuch the 'idea' itself is epistemically possible and thus *could* have warrant.[44]

The "public" project, says Plantinga, "does not appeal to specifically Christian premises or presuppositions" (WCB, xiii), whereas the "Christian" (ibid.) project is "starting from an assumption of the truth of Christian belief" (ibid.).

---

42 Cf. WCB, 347 and 499, where Plantinga clearly says that he holds Christian beliefs to be true (and thus probably warranted).

43 On page xiv of the *Preface*, Plantinga repeats this point: "… asking *whether and how* such [Christian] belief has warrant" (my emphasis).

44 Maybe this observation made Copan write what he did write (see above, p. 13).

It is very important *not* to interpret this from a logical point of view (so to speak). The point is not that the A/C model can convince only those who already believe in Christianity. It is certainly particularly helpful to Christians to be offered an epistemology that fits their basic beliefs; but since officially the truth of this epistemology (the A/C model) is not claimed, in principle everyone could have come up with it. Dennett could have done so:[45] Assume, for the sake of the argument, that Christian belief is true; how could we then account for knowledge of God? How is knowledge of God possible? How is it brought about? So to argue "from a Christian perspective" (ibid.) is not to claim that what speaks for the A/C model is that God exists; what speaks for the appropriateness of the model is that if God exists, then it is probably true.

So much for the *Preface*. Later in the book Plantinga says that he claims "*four* things for these two models" (WCB, 168, m.e.), i.e. for the A/C model and the extended A/C-model. Plantinga begins, *first*, with epistemic possibility; "related to" this claim, he says, is, *second*, the claim "that there aren't any cogent objections to the model" (WCB, 169). It seems rather difficult to see what the difference is to the first claim; I'll get back to this once we understand what exactly epistemic possibility is. The *third* claim really is not a claim at all, but rather a proposition Plantinga says he does *not* claim: "I don't claim to *show* that they [the models] are true" (WCB, 169); this is an important piece of information when it comes to our understanding of the aim and scope of WCB, and I'll get back to this as well. The *fourth* claim is a variant of TW inasmuch the idea is that there might be other models than the (extended) A/C model and that, in any case, for these other models as well it is also true that "if classical Christian belief *is* indeed true, then one of these models is very likely also true" (WCB, 170).

Still later in the book, Plantinga says that what he claims for the model is *threefold*, namely that "it is (1) possible, (2) subject to no philosophical objections that do not assume that Christian belief is false, and (3) such that if Christian belief is true, the model is at least close to the truth" (WCB, 351). Here, (1) is EP, and (3) is TW (or very close to it). (2) is a variant of the second claim; what is missing is the idea that no claim to truth is made regarding the model, which, again, is no direct or positive claim that something is the case.

Last but not least, it should not go unnoticed that Plantinga offers, I think, a brilliant critique of negative theology or, put another way, a defense of theolog-

---

[45] Cf. Plantinga (2001c, 400), where he says that "non-Christians may find it [the model] of interest in the same way that Christians may be interested in seeing whether and how naturalists can give an account of, say, intentionality".

ical realism: Human beings, argues Plantinga, can meaningfully think and speak about God. I only mention this in passing, but it should be mentioned nonetheless.[46]

So according to the *Preface* and some other strategic passages, the aim of WCB is to argue for the following propositions:

> **(TR)** Human beings can meaningfully think and speak about God.
>
> **(EP)** The (extended) A/C model is epistemically possible.
>
> **(TW)** Christian belief probably has warrant if, and only if, it is true.

Based on this analysis, we can already see that TW is far from being the only claim in WCB, and that it isn't even the main claim; after all, TW is presented in the *Preface* as something '*added*'. To understand TW as the main target of Plantinga's theory is thus a misunderstanding; and even TR, EP and TW are not all that is argued for. This will become clearer once we look a bit deeper into the deliverances of WCB.

4 The deliverances of WCB: Epistemic Possibility, the Parity Argument, Proper Basicality, and TW

Plantinga presents JQ as 'the main question of the book'. He does so despite the fact that he himself admits that the de facto question (is Christian belief true?) is "the *more important* question" (WCB, 63, m.e.). Since Plantinga presents JQ as 'the main question of the book', he seems mainly interested in arguing for the A/C model and TW. And yet at the very end of WCB, Plantinga writes: "But *is* it [the extended A/C model] true? This is the really important question" (WCB, 499), a question, however, which he acknowledges he is unable to answer within "the competence of philosophy" (ibid.). If the model is true, i.e. if we do have a sensus divinitatis that works according to a design plan successfully aimed at truth, then, in all likelihood, we are warranted. But are we? If Plantinga really did not argue for more than the A/C model and TW, then atheists could feel safe. But there *is* more.

---

46 For a discussion cf. Tapp (this volume, p. 41 ff.).

4.1 Epistemic Possibility

The (extended) A/C model, says Plantinga, is epistemically possible. The claim, he says, is not simply that the model is logically possible; the idea is not only that the model is in itself consistent. It certainly is, but many theories are possible in that sense. Rather, the claim is "much stronger" (WCB, 168). The claim really is that the model is "consistent with what we know, where 'what we know' is what all (or most) of the participants in the discussion agree on" (WCB, 169); thus, to say that the model is epistemically possible is to say that "nothing we know commits us to its falsehood" (WCB, xii). We would be committed to its falsehood if either there is a successful objection—such as the notorious *Great Pumpkin Objection*—to the model as a model (these objections are dealt with in chapter 10); or if there were successful defeaters, i. e. good reasons to believe that Christian belief itself is false,[47] such as historical Biblical criticism, postmodernism, pluralism, or the problem of evil (these are all dealt with in part IV of WCB). Other possible defeaters could arise from the sciences, such as classical mechanics, quantum mechanics, evolutionary theory, evolutionary psychology, but they are dealt with only in Plantinga's latest book *Where the Conflict Really Lies. Science, Religion, and Naturalism* (WCRL, 2011).[48]

I already mentioned that Plantinga's first claim regarding the two models is EP; the second is the claim that there are no 'cogent objections' to the model. But what is the difference? To show that the model is epistemically possible is to show that it is consistent and that there is no contradiction with something else most of us claim to know. Accordingly, one way to show that there is a cogent objection to the model is to show that it is somehow internally inconsistent, in which case it would be epistemically impossible; another is to show that it is not consistent with something else we know, in which case it would also be epistemically impossible. A third way to cogently object to the model, I take it, would be to demonstrate that one of its (entailed) propositions is just false; not because

---

[47] For the difference between objections to the model and defaters for Christain belief, cf. WCB, 285.
[48] With regard to the sciences, the idea is, roughly speaking, that there is no *conflict*: Evolutionary theory, for instance, can be true and Christian belief can be true belief as well. This is possible because evolutionary theory gives room for evolution to be guided. Nothing we know about evolution (if we know anything here: that there is an evolution at all, and if so, that the earth is very old, that men and other living beings have common ancestors, that evolutionary descent is governed by the mechanism of natural selection based upon random genetic mutation, and so on) commits us to believe that Christian theism is false.

it entails a contradiction or is inconsistent with what we know but simply because what is claimed to be the case really is not.

EP is a very important part of WCB, and as such it has not received the credit it deserves; there is more involved than just TW, and Plantinga, in his reply to Swinburne, is entirely right in pointing this out.[49] If one understands Plantinga's WCRL as an addition to part IV of WCB, one can easily see how important this defense is for the entire project. To have a good defense is no warrant that you will win; however, it *almost* is. For if warrant is what makes a true belief knowledge, and if there are only two possible worldviews that have an account for how such warrant (and hence knowledge about the world) is possible, to wit, theism and naturalism, and if naturalism is self-defeating, then theism remains; and then we not only have an account of how on such a view knowledge of God (and other things) is possible, but also of how it is possible in a 'strong' sense (by means of countering alleged defeaters); I shall get back to this in a moment.

4.2 The Parity-Argument in WCB: Answering the de jure justification-objection and the rationality-objection

The answer to JQ1*

Recall the first version of JQ:

> **(JQ1)*** Is Christian belief justified, i.e. do those who hold Christian beliefs flout any epistemic obligations?

If one understands justification deontologically, i.e. in terms of epistemic duties (such as a duty to search for and stick to the truth, to reflect objections, to be honest and serious in one's intellectual activities, and the like), then the answer to (JQ1)* is quite easy, and Plantinga says so; if this is what it means to be justified, then a Christian at least can be justified and often "*obviously*" (WCB, 101)

---

49 Cf. Plantinga 2001a, 217.—Another example of how deeply Plantinga can be misunderstood is Rentsch's interpretation. According to Rentsch (2005, 191), Plantinga argues that theistic belief is warranted if it can be reconstructed as possible. Rentsch even charges Plantinga for uncritically adopting scientific criteria of sense (or meaning); this is not only against the spirit of everything Plantinga says, but the latter explicitly argues that we should *not* understand "belief in God as or as like a sort of scientific *hypothesis*, a *theory* designed to explain some body of evidence" (WCB, 330).

is; no epistemic obligation is flouted in holding Christian beliefs. In this sense, responsible Christians and Non-Christians are in the same boat.

As we shall see later, however, there is a problem here; for the claim could be stronger and actually *was* much stronger in RBG. Still it is regrettable that Plantinga himself downplays the importance of (JQ1)*. He considers it (and the de jure objection) hardly "worthy of serious disagreement and discussion" (WCB, 102); and he says twice that JQ cannot be (JQ1)*.[50] Now it might be true that the answer to (JQ1)* is obvious. But it's only obvious once you have the insights provided by Plantinga's analysis. 'Justification' is a concept that still plays an important role in epistemology and certainly in ordinary language and discourse. Plantinga's treatment of (JQ1)* is therefore very important and of great help for the theist; to show that on any sensible interpretation of justification, Christian belief *is* justified is of tremendous value and should be recognized. There's more to the argument than just TW.

The answer to JQ2*

Let's now turn to the second version of JQ, the de jure question with regard to rationality. Plantinga distinguishes at least *six* different conceptions of rationality, and so there are (or would be) six different ways to further specify JQ2 or JQ2* respectively.[51] I have no space to discuss this. The really important conceptions are *internal* and *external* rationality.[52] A belief, says Plantinga, is "externally rational if it is produced by cognitive faculties that are functioning properly and successfully aimed at truth" (WCB 204; cf. 112). Obviously, the concept of external rationality is very close to the concept of warrant, so close that it's *prima facie* hard to see what the difference really is. In any event, Plantinga himself says that because external rationality "is *included in warrant*, the real question, here, is whether Christian belief does or can have warrant" (WCB, 204, m.e.).[53]

---

50 Cf. WCB, 102 and WCB, 108.
51 Cf. WCB, 109. Note that there is some overlapping here; e.g. justification broadly construed is very close to what Aristotelian rationality is.
52 Plantinga discusses Alston-rationality at length (WCB, 117–134); but whenever he returns to the JQ-issue (203f., 255–258, 365), he only discusses internal and external rationality.
53 Cf. Plantinga (2001c, 394): "the notion of warrant, as I understand it, includes rationality".— In WCB, 257, Plantinga identifies external rationality with "the *first* condition of warrant" (m.e.), namely with the proper function of the cognitive faculties; however, in that passage in WCB (204), 'successfully being aimed at truth' (the fourth condition of warrant) is part of the definition of 'external rationality'.

For this reason I suggest that we can further reconstruct JQ with regard to rationality as follows:

> **(JQ2)***** Is Christian belief rational, i.e. are those who hold Christian beliefs internally rational?

My cognitive faculties work properly (in the sense of *internal* rationality), if I only form beliefs that are "*coherent*" (WCB, 112)[54] and "appropriate" (WCB, 111) with regard to my experience, that is, with regard to my "phenomenal imagery and doxastic experience" (WCB, 111). The basic idea of internal rationality, I take it, is that one is not insane *on one's own standards*. This is important because one can be a madman without being internally irrational; external rationality, on the other hand, excludes this. When it comes to internal rationality, there is (as with the justification-objection) no serious de jure objection.

As he did with JQ1, Plantinga repeatedly claims with regard to the different concepts of rationality, that *none* of the different variants of JQ *can be* ('can't' he says several times) equivalent to the de jure question. But what does that mean? One certainly *can* ask (both logically, physically as well as psychologically speaking) whether, for instance, Christian belief is internally rational.[55] The answer is easily given in this particular case, that's right. But still those questions *can* be raised, they certainly *have been* raised and still are *being* raised by one philosopher or other, and, what is more, the answers are not always straightforward. Plantinga writes: "What we have seen so far is what the *de jure* question and criticism are *not:* it is not the complaint that the believer is not within her intellectual rights in believing as she does" (WCB, 135)—and this holds for any of the other versions of the de jure questions and objections: "None of these criticism has much of a leg to stand on. So the *de jure* criticism has proven elusive" (ibid.). Again, this is misleading. *All* these objections can be raised, and they have been raised; they might be easily fended off, but that does not make them elusive; they can clearly be stated and discussed. When it comes to the objections against his model, Plantinga calls those critics "excessively naive" (WCB, 325) who simply assume that the meaning of terms such as 'justified', 'rational', and so on, is clear; these critics, he says, "seldom make a serious attempt to explain what they

---

54 There's some tension here between saying that coherence is part of internal rationality and presuming (as Plantinga does in WCB, 115) that those who raise the rationality-objection do not (or could not) mean to claim it is inconsistent; the objection could indeed be this: It is irrational of you to hold firm to Christian belief given that this belief is full of inconsistencies.

55 As Plantinga points out himself (WCB, 112, Fn.4) philosophers such as Rorty and Dennett tend to think Christians are somewhat insane.

mean by these terms" (ibid.). But once it is clear what 'justification' is, "the question of justification is too easily answered to be interesting" (WCB, 327). Yes, once you see things right, it might be easy to answer this question; and yet, since such an attempt at clarification is seldom made, it is worthwhile to pursue and successfully complete one.[56]

The answer to JQ3*

By asking whether this or that variant of JQ really *is the* de jure objection (both 'is' and 'the' emphasized) and claiming in each case that it is not, Plantinga tends to downplay the effort he puts into discussing those 'questions' and 'objections'. But these are important discussions even if, as Plantinga says, the *"proper de jure* question" (WCB, 137, m.e.) is this:

> **(JQ3)*** Is Christian belief warranted, i.e. are Christian beliefs produced by cognitive faculties functioning properly in a cognitive environment, according to a design plan successfully aimed at truth?

The warrant-objection (the 'F&M objection') claims that Christian belief (or rather holding on to it) is *"irrational"* (WCB, 151); what this means, however, is that such belief is either produced by cognitive faculties (reason, perception, memory, introspection, etc.) that *malfunction* (Marx) or by faculties and processes that are *not aimed* at the production of true beliefs to begin with (Freud). The de jure objection behind JQ, Plantinga says, "is best construed as the claim that Christian belief, whether true or false, is at any rate without warrant" (WCB, 153).

Before we look at the answer to (JQ3)*, let us consider whether the issue behind JQ is really 'best construed as the claim that Christian belief, *whether true or false*, is at any rate without warrant'. I already argued that the other versions (or constructions) of JQ are just as good.[57] But there is another problem. Already in the *Preface*, Plantinga puts much emphasis on his claim that JQ actually can*not* be answered without answering the de facto question. There is a certain "attitude" (WCB, xii), he claims, described as an "agnostic attitude" (WCB, 499),

---

[56] Note that crucial parts of Plantinga's critique of Anthony O'Hear (WCB, 326–328) and John Mackie (WCB, 328–331) rest upon the conceptual analysis of 'justification', 'rationality' and 'warrant'. The importance of Plantinga's achievements here is particularly evident in his reply to Michael Martin's version of the (Son of) Great Pumpkin Objection (WCB, 343–349).

[57] Plantinga says JQ3* is "viable" (WCB, 152). As it turns out, it's not 'viable' at all; so why is it, as a question, in any better position than JQ1* and JQ2**?

which is the main target of his critique. The attitude is this: "'Well, I don't know whether Christian belief is *true* (after all, who could know a thing like that?), but I do know that it is irrational (or intellectually unjustified or unreasonable or intellectually questionable)" (WCB, xii); at the end of his discussion of the M&F complaint, Plantinga describes the position again as follows: "Christian belief may be true, and it may be false; but at any rate, it is irrational to accept it" (WCB, 152).[58] It is striking, however, that Plantinga claims he addresses an important question (JQ), but really does not provide any evidence regarding who *actually has* such a pseudo-agnostic attitude. There are plenty of examples for foundationalism, evidentialism, and so forth; but is there an example of someone who has that de jure attitude? Plantinga refers to "Freud, Marx and Nietzsche" (WCB, xi).[59] But do they share that attitude? Take Freud, for instance. He "seems to assume", says Plantinga, "that such [theistic] belief is false, and then infers in rather quick and casual fashion that it is produced by wish-fulfillment and hence doesn't have warrant" (WCB, 186); Freud "simply presupposes that theistic and hence Christian belief is false" (WCB, 498). But if this is a correct interpretation of Freud, then he is *not* the alleged opponent who has that 'agnostic attitude'; it's at best a *pseudo*-agnostic attitude. For it is one thing to argue that people *have* that attitude, or claim to have it, and quite another to argue, as Plantinga does, that they cannot or could not sensibly hold it (i.e. cannot or could not argue that they do not know whether Christian belief is true but still claim to know it is intellectually questionable). If Freud *assumes* or *presupposes* that Christian belief is false (and knows that he assumes it), as Plantinga claims he does, then he does not even entertain that attitude; for if he did, he would not make any claims, or assumptions, as for the truth of Christianity ('well, I don't know whether Christian belief is true'); after all, Freud calls it an *illusion*. To be sure, Plantinga claims that according to Freud an illusion is "not necessarily false; and he goes on to add that it isn't possible to prove that theistic belief is mistaken" (WCB, 139). This is what Freud "says" (ibid.), according to Plantinga; but he provides no textual evidence for his claim, and it contradicts what he (Plantinga) says later in WCB (186, 498) about Freud 'assuming' and 'presupposing' that Christian belief is false. It even contradicts what Plantinga says just one page later where he says that according to Freud psychoanalysis "provides arguments against the truth of religious belief" (WCB, 140); according to Plantinga's Freud, the function of illusion and wish-fulfillment

---

[58] Very similar formulations of this attitude can be found in WCB, 169, 191, 242, in Plantinga (2001a, 215), and in Plantinga (2001c, 380); in the latter text, Plantinga calls it the position of a "skeptic" (a.a.O).

[59] Nietzsche, however, is later dismissed; cf. WCB, 136.

"is not to produce *true* belief" (WCB, 142).⁶⁰ So Freud does *not*, as a matter of brute fact, raise his de jure objection '*whether true or not*'; neither does Marx, and so neither of them actually evinces the 'agnostic attitude'.⁶¹ Nor do they *presuppose* that there is some malfunction or wishful thinking in order to then come to the conclusion that, *therefore*, Christian belief is false (this is what Plantinga claims in WCB, 162). Rather, they assume, for whatever reasons (materialism,⁶² psychoanalysis, evidentalism) that Christian belief is false and *then* they seek a naturalistic *explanation*⁶³ of how people come to hold that belief (just as Plantinga assumes that Christian belief is true and then seeks an Christian explanation of how people come to hold that belief). This is even what Plantinga at the very end of his discussion of the F&M complaint says himself: Freud "takes it for granted that there is no God and that theistic belief is false; he *then* casts about for some kind of explanation of this widespread phenomenon of mistaken belief" (WCB, 198, m.e.).⁶⁴—In his reply to Swinburne, Plantinga claims that "many or most objections to Christian belief" (2001, 215) are of that pseudo-agnostic ilk ('Well, I don't know...'). But not only is there a big difference between 'many' or 'most'; there is no evidence that even many, let alone most or "an enormous amount of recent and contemporary" (WCB, 191) people argue this way;

---

60 Plantinga says that, according to Freud, "the proper intellectual attitude toward these beliefs isn't merely agnosticism; it is that the beliefs in question are unwarranted and furthermore are very probably false" (WCB, 162). Elsewhere, Plantinga describes it somewhat differently: "Freud thinks, once we see that theistic and religious belief has its origin in wishful thinking, we will also see that it is very probably false" (WCB, 162). In WCRL, Plantinga says: "in fact Freud thinks theism is false" (2011, 148).
61 Plantinga quotes Marx: "The basis of irreligious criticism is *man makes religion*" (WCB, 140); that is hardly compatible with the de jure attitude. Nor do the other philosophers who are mentioned by Plantinga and argue along Marxian and Freudian lines actually have that attitude either. Plantinga quotes Hume's observation, for instance, that the Christian religion "cannot be believed by any reasonable person without [a miracle]" (WCB, 143); and so too with the others (Carroll, Cupit, Daniels, Ellis, Frye, Rousseau, Wilson). Wykstra (2002, 94) coins the de jure attitude "Demure De Jure Objection"; but note that he too provides no evidence about who actually made or makes such an objection.
62 As a matter of fact, this is what Plantinga says *himself* when it comes to Marx: He (Marx) draws the conclusion that Christian belief is false from materialism: people "will see that materialism is very probable true, *in which case* Christian and theistic belief is very likely false" (WCB, 162, m.e.).
63 Cf. WCB, 145, where it says Freud and Marx give "naturalistic explanations of religious belief".
64 Cf. WCB, 315, where Plantinga speaks of Freud's "presupposition" that God doesn't exist with regard to a possible Freudian explanation that some human beings have a desire for union with God.

Freud and Marx appear not to. So I think Plantinga is right in claiming that one *cannot* "adopt" (WCB, 191) the de jure attitude because it is not independent of the de facto question; but he should not argue with such emphasis that Freud&Marx&Nietzsche&others "can't *any longer* adopt" (WCB, 191, m.e.) that de jure attitude because they never really had adopted it in the first place.

Now what is Plantinga's answer to (JQ3)*? The answer is not, as some commentators think it is, that Christian belief *is* warranted; the answer is just TW. The gist of the whole story is this: By definition, one necessary condition (among others) for a belief to have warrant for a person is that it is produced by a cognitive faculty according to a design plan successfully aimed at truth; that it is 'successfully aimed at truth' is to say that there is a (very) high objective probability that the belief is true.[65] Since we cannot say whether Christian belief *is* true, we cannot say that Christian belief is warranted, and that the A/C model is true. But we can say that the model is epistemically possible, that there are no (other) cogent objections to it, and we can say that Christian belief is true if, and only if, it has warrant.

4.3 Proper Basicality

Basicality

Just as in RBG, Plantinga understands a belief as basic if one does not hold it on the evidential basis of other propositions or some inference; rather, such beliefs are *occasioned* in us by certain circumstances—we *find* ourselves having them. The perception of a tree brings about the belief that there is a tree; and so it goes with God: "we find ourselves with [beliefs about God], just as we find ourselves with perceptual and memory beliefs" (WCB, 172f.). Circumstances in which belief in God is triggered are, for instance, seeing a wonderful night sky or feeling guilty about having done something bad. With regard to basicality, says Plantinga, the *sensus divinitatis* "resembles perception, memory, and *a priori* belief" (WCB, 175, partly m.e.); in this respect, Christian beliefs "*are like* memory beliefs, perceptual beliefs, some *a priori* beliefs, and so on" (WCB, 343, partly m.e.).

---

[65] For a final word Plantinga's on warrant cf. WCB, 153–156; for the idea of a successful aim with regard to truth cf. *Warrant and Proper Function*, in particular 49, 55, 75, 194.

Propriety as justification

What about *proper* basicality? That depends on what propriety consists in. As we saw, there are three fundamental epistemological concepts for interpreting JQ: justification, rationality, and warrant. So is theistic belief properly basic if we understand the propriety of such a belief to consist in being justified, and justification in turn as a deontological concept? Yes.

But there are two problems here. Proper basicality is discussed in a brief section as one of the "six further features of the model" (WCB, 175). The first 'feature' is the very idea of there being a *sensus divinitatis* that, under certain circumstances, triggers belief in God as something that we 'find' in ourselves. The second feature is that this sensus is a "capacity" (WCB, 173) or "disposition" (ibid.) for belief in God rather than innate knowledge in a strict sense. Then basicality is introduced as the first of those 'six *further* features of the model'. "*According to* the A/C model" (WCB, 175, m.e.), says Plantinga in the first section on these 'features', theistic belief is basic; and he begins the next section on proper basicality with respect to justification Plantinga by saying: "*On* the A/C model, then, theistic belief as produced by the *sensus divinitatis* is basic" (WCB, 177, partly m.e.). That sounds as if Plantinga is saying that only '*according to*' or '*on*' the model is belief in God (properly) basic, i.e., only if the model is true.[66] Then, however (since it cannot be argued that the model *is* true), we cannot argue that belief in God is properly basic; as a matter of fact, Plantinga points out that the A/C model is a *model* inasmuch it shall show "*how it could be*" (WCB, 168, Plantinga's emphasis) that belief in God is true. Yet when he discusses *proper* basicality as the fourth 'feature' of the model, Plantinga says that "it is really pretty obvious that a believer in God *is* or can be deontologically justified" (WCB, 178, m.e.). And then the claim, it seems, really is that belief in God can be and often even '*is*' justified and hence properly basic: "the believer in God *is* within her epistemic rights in accepting theistic belief in the basic way" (WCB, 179). The problem, I think, is that the A/C model is a model "of theistic belief's [sic] having *warrant*" (WCB, 168, m.e.), and if the concept of warrant is part of the model itself, it cannot be shown that belief in God is basic and justified (properly basic in that sense). However, if we understand the A/C model just as the claim that human beings have the 'capacity' to form 'basic' beliefs about God, then, given a correct understanding of what justification really is, the claim is this:

---

[66] Later too Plantinga speaks as if Christian belief is justified and internally rational "If" (WCB, 252) the model is right or "On" the model (WCB, 255); maybe passages like these have led Zagzebski (2002, 117) to her interpretation (s.a., p. 12f.).

(BJ) Belief in God is basic and justified.

And so, later in chapter 8, when he discusses the extended A/C model, Plantinga says that "even *apart* from the model" (WCB, 255, m.e.), Christian belief often *is* justified.

The second problem is much harder; as a matter of fact, I think it is crucial both to the interpretation of Plantinga's philosophy as well as to his philosophy proper. For lack of space, however, once again I can only be brief here: As Plantinga points out (WCB, 85–8), there is a deontological and theological ring to the terms 'justification' and 'justified'; in the epistemological context, to be justified means to abide by one's epistemic duties. But *what* duties? According to what Plantinga calls the "classical package: evidentialism, deontologism, and classical foundationalism" (WCB, 88), one is obliged to believe only in propositions that are properly basic, i.e. in propositions that are self-evident, incorrigible or evident to the senses, or in propositions that are, in one way or other, supported by these properly basic propositions; if one does so, one is justified. As we saw, the strategy in RBG was to find a bigger boat: Belief in God is *just as* properly basic as self-evident propositions, memory beliefs et al. But we also saw that Plantinga had difficulties in RBG to find a way to identify necessary conditions such that they are jointly sufficient to define what makes a belief *properly* basic. Now in the context of his discussion of the A/C model and its 'six features', Plantinga claims that belief in God *is* basic and justified (BJ). The section in which he does so is very short, just half a page; Plantinga obviously thinks that he can be brief because he can refer back both to RBG and chapter 3 of WCB. But this self-interpretation is misleading: Whereas in RBG he has a strong concept of justification such that the propriety of theistic basic beliefs consists in their being in one bigger boat alongside self-evident propositions (et al.), the concept of justification in WCB—the one that is used to claim BJ[67]—is weak, much weaker indeed: one is weakly justified if one thinks carefully, pays attention to possible problems, reacts to counterarguments, is open to discussions, maybe reads a lot, and the like; it is only the weakness of this concept of justification that makes Plantinga believe that it is 'obvious' that Christians at least often are justified.[68] As I have argued, in RBG Plantinga failed to provide 'criteria' by which we can define 'properly basic' such that we can subsume theistic belief under properly basic beliefs; but he did at least *claim* that theistic belief *is* justified

---

[67] This concept is expounded in sec. V of chapter 3 (WCB, 99–102).
[68] This concept of justification is so weak that even someone believing in "rotational reproduction" could be justified; cf. WCB, 101 f.

in this strong sense, just like other paradigmatic examples of properly basic beliefs. (I shall return to this.)

Propriety as internal rationality

On rationality there is only a footnote in this context,[69] but later Plantinga clearly states that "just as for theistic belief, I'll argue that many or most Christians *can* be but also *are* both justified and in internally rational in holding their characteristic beliefs" (WCB, 200).[70] So a further result is:

> **(BIR)** Belief in God is basic and internally rational.

Propriety as warrant

When it comes to warrant (and external external rationality as part of warrant) things are "harder" (WCB, 200). Plantinga explicitly does talk about proper basicality with respect to warrant. Here the claim is much weaker; it's only claimed that according to the model belief in God "*can*" (WCB, 178; 186; m.e.) have warrant. Then the question is raised whether belief in God "*is*" (WCB, 186, Plantinga's emphasis) warranted. The answer is a conditional; the answer is TW.[71]

---

[69] Cf. WCB, 179, Fn.15.
[70] Cf. WCB, 203f. and 324 for other clear statements of this kind. In early replies to critics of WCB, Plantinga repeats that he argues that Christian belief *is* justified and internally rational; cf. Plantinga (2001c, 387) and Plantinga (2002, 132). Thus, Zagzebski (2002, 117), for instance, underrates the deliverances of WCB when she says that in this book "Plantinga wants to show that such [Christian] beliefs *can* be properly basic, rational and warranted" (m.e.).
[71] Cf. WCB 245f. for a brief summary of the epistemic status of specifically Christian belief. Note, however, that Plantinga in this summary speaks as if Christian belief is justified, internally and externally rational as well as warranted only "given" or "on the model"; but that caveat is only necessary for warrant.

5 Ecce WCB! Interpretation and Self-Interpretation

We noted in the beginning that there is some confusion in the reception of WCB. So let's, by way of summary, see what the deliverances of this work really are; let's also have a brief look at how Plantinga himself interprets WCB—*ecce WCB!*

What are the deliverances of WCB?

We now have the deliverances of WCB at hand (well, at least as far as I interpret WCB). To begin with, there is a solid foundation:

> **(TR)** Human beings can meaningfully think and speak about God.

Then, we have a clear understanding of how to apprehend the vexing problem of the intellectual acceptability of theism and Christian belief:

> **(JQ1)*** Is Christian belief justified, i.e. do those who hold Christian beliefs flout any epistemic obligations?
>
> **(JQ2)**** Is Christian belief rational, i.e. are those who hold Christian beliefs internally rational?
>
> **(JQ3)*** Is Christian belief warranted, i.e. are Christian beliefs produced by cognitive faculties functioning properly in a cognitive environment, according to a design plan successfully aimed at truth?

Not only is there a detailed analysis of what these questions mean; there are even answers to (or related to) these questions:

> **(EP)** The (extended) A/C model is epistemically possible.
>
> **(BJ)** Belief in God is basic and justified.
>
> **(BIR)** Belief in God is basic and internally rational.
>
> **(TW)** Christian belief has warrant if, and only if, it is true.

And there is one more thing I haven't mentioned yet; there is an evolutionary argument against naturalism that, if correct, yields the following conclusion (I'll get back to this in a moment):

> **(NSR)** Naturalism is self-refuting.

On Plantinga's interpretation, WCB is a 'sequel' to GOM and RBG, though in a 'slightly different direction'. Since the decisive move in GOM and RBG was to provide a parity argument, for WCB to be a 'sequel' it also needs to contain a parity argument. So what happens to the good old parity argument? Is it no use any more? Well, not quite. Theists (or Christians) cannot claim that their belief is warranted without answering the de facto question; and if one assumes that the de facto question cannot be answered ('after all, who could know a thing like that?'), then the question of whether Christian belief is warranted cannot be answered by the theist either. However, it *cannot* be answered by the atheist either; and so the theist and the anti-theist are back in 'same boat' again. But we should note that the boat they are both in is a different boat from the one they used to be in on the basis of the old parity argument. By introducing the concept (and theory) of warrant, Plantinga makes it impossible to use the old parity argument any longer. A crucial aspect of the old parity argument, as I understand it, is that it works even if the belief that is shown to be justified or rational inasmuch it is properly and basically believed is not true. On the old parity argument, one can be justified and (internally) rational in one's beliefs (and justified and rational in believing that one has true beliefs) without actually (but not knowingly, of course) having true beliefs. The theist can reply to the atheist: I'm just as justified as you, even if what I believe should be false; I'm just as (internally) rational as you, even if what I believe should be false. He cannot, however, reply: I'm just as P-warranted[72] as you, even if what I believe should be false, and he cannot do so for two reasons. First, P-warrant for a theist is obviously very different than P-warrant for an atheist (not with regard to the formal conditions but with regard to what they mean; a naturalistic account of design and proper function is different—"by God or evolution" (WCB, 155)—from a theistic account). Secondly, and again, for a belief to be P-warranted it must in all likelihood be true. But who could know a thing like that?

So does WCB make stronger or weaker claims than GOM and RBG? I think both yes and no. If I were to put Plantinga's early philosophy in one sentence, then, I think, it would be this: *Christian belief is properly basic.* In WCB, this claim is considerably weakened: TW is a conditional; the claim is only that Christian belief *can* be warranted, and if true, probably is (and in that sense can be properly basic). Certainly, WCB's claim that Christian belief is justified and internally rationally (and in *that* sense properly basic) is helpful; but since justifica-

---

[72] Note that "warrant" is first introduced in WCB (xi, cf. 153) in very general terms as that third element that distinguishes knowledge from mere true belief; so what is called 'warrant' here is what others call 'justification', for instance. What Plantinga then specifies as warrant (proper function and all that) is what I mean here by P(lantinga)-warrant.

tion and internal rationality are understood in a much weaker way than in RBG, the claim is weaker here too. Put another way: The claim in RBG that Christian belief *is* properly basic—that is, is in the same boat as self-evidential beliefs et al.—is reduced to the claim that it is properly basic in a somewhat unchallenging way, and only *can* be properly basic in a substantial way (by way of warrant), and this only if true.

What are the deliverances of WCB? Self-Interpretation

A major problem, I think, in the literature on Plantinga is the, sometimes exclusive, focus on TW; Swinburne, for instance, made this point *cum organo pleno*. As we have seen, however, there is much more than just TW involved; as a matter of fact, TW is one of several findings, and in one place it is even characterized as something 'added'. As was shown in passing already, Plantinga in his early replies (2001a, 2001b, 2002c, 2002) does (almost) his best to clarify things; all in all, I think he does a good job in interpreting himself and WCB in these early replies. (His interpretation of GOM and RBG is not as convincing.) He is also right in defending himself against the charge that, on account of TW, he does too little to support theists who have their doubts or even agnosticists or atheists to overcome their lack of faith. He says as much in his reply to Swinburne, and he says it even more clearly in another reply: "I don't provide argument for Christian belief in *WCB* […]; it doesn't follow, however, that there is nothing in my program that might help the nonbeliever reconsider his or her doubts" (Plantinga 2001c, 385). In his reply to Zagzebski, Plantinga (2002, 132) indirectly (and modestly) refers to EP and the deliverances in part IV of WCB: "And finally, is it really all that difficult to defend the truth of Christian belief? As far as I can see, none of the objections to its truth have much to be said for them; all are easily refuted". Not so easily, really; so it is good to have that little help from our *spiritus rector*.

On the negative side, there are three problems: First, Plantinga (and his future readers) should not join or even conduct the choir of those who understand the claim that there is no sensible de jure objection to Christian belief that does not presuppose the falsehood of the latter as the main thesis in WCB.[73] It is only an implication of TW (or rather of the concept of warrant); it is based on a strawman-attitude; and there is more, and more important, material to consider here.

---

[73] Cf. Greco (2001, 461) who thinks that to refute the pseudo-agnostic attitude "is the main target of the book"; according to Geivett/Jesson (2001, 329f.), the "major thesis [of WCB] is that there are no *de jure* objections to Christian belief that do not presuppose some *de facto* objection".

Second (and again), Plantinga (and his readers) should resist the temptation to focus on TW. I see such a tendency in Plantinga's most recent work. In his debate on "Science and Religion" with Daniel Dennett (Dennett/Plantinga, 2011), Plantinga argues, among other things, that contemporary evolutionary theory with its doctrine of random mutation is compatible (unlike naturalism) with theistic belief, and that, even if it weren't, "it wouldn't follow that theistic belief is irrational or unwarranted" (Dennett/Plantinga, 2011, 3). The reason Plantinga provides for his claim is this: "As I argue in *Warranted Christian Belief*, if theistic belief is true, then very likely it has both rationality and warrant in the basic way, that is, not on the basis of propositional evidence" (Dennett/Plantinga 2011, 9). Putting aside that Plantinga here parallels rationality and warrant (as we saw, external rationality is part of warrant), the basic argument ('as I *argue* in WCB...') or claim of WCB seems to be TW; there's no mention of EP at all, and also no word on justification and internal rationality. (Something similar can be said for WCRL.)

What happens then in the further debate with Dennett is all the more remarkable, and not so much because Dennett in his opening essay does *not* deny the compatibility of evolutionary theory and theism; rather, it is striking that Plantinga in his reply to Dennett's essay does *not* rely on TW. Dennett's main point is that the compatibility of theism and evolutionary theory doesn't prove anything; many quite absurd theories (Flying Spaghetti Monsterism et al.) are compatible with evolutionary theory, and still Plantinga believes in the Christian God (and not in Buddha, Allah, Krishna, monsters, or whatever). So the "burden of proof", says Dennett, "falls on Plantinga to show why his theist story deserves any more respect or credence than" (Dennett/Plantinga 2011, 28) Dennett's Supermanism (which is a version of the Flying Spaghetti Monsterism). It is tempting to think that the reason why Plantinga in his reply does not get back to TW is that he can at best show that theism is not as silly as Flying Spaghetti Monsterism; but why believe in it in the first place? Given the basic idea of WCB and Plantinga's critique of evidentialism, this question might seem to miss the point; for the very point is that theists do not need a reason to be warranted. All they need to be warranted is that theism is true, i.e. that God exists: "if theistic belief is true, it probably doesn't require propositional evidence for its rational acceptance" (Dennett/Plantinga 2011, 9), says Plantinga. Fair enough; but *is* it true? That we cannot know, as Plantinga must say (and does say).

This brings me to my last and final point. Would it be fair to reconstruct Plantinga's most important argument (or strategy) as follows: The best way to understand what knowledge is to say that it is warranted true belief. But there are only two models to understand the elements of design and proper function in such a theory of knowledge as warranted true belief: theism and naturalism.

Whereas naturalism is epistemically impossible (and hence false), theism is epistemically possible. Now skepticism cannot be refuted; we never know anything in a very strict sense, because we never can be sure whether what we believe is true. And since warrant and truth are closely related to each other, we can also never say that our beliefs are warranted. Still we cannot help but have certain beliefs such as beliefs about the past, other persons, external things, or God; we also feel that these beliefs constitute knowledge. But if they do, they must be warranted; but they only can be warranted if theism is true; hence theism is true, if anything is true. Or in one sentence: If anything is warranted, then Christian belief is warranted.

Literature

Alston, William (1991): Perceiving God. The Epistemology of Religious Experience, Ithaca/London.

Alston, William (2005): "Mysticism and Perceptual Awareness of God", in: William E. Mann (Ed.): The Blackwell Guide to the Philosophy of Religion, Blackwell 2005, 198–219.

Anderson, James N. (2002): "Faith Without Reason? A Review of Warranted Christian Belief by Alvin Plantinga" (online).

Clark, Kelly James (2004): "Religious Epistemology", in: Internet Encyclopedia of Philosophy (online, October 2, 2004).

Copan, Paul (2001): "Review of Warranted Christian Belief", in: The Review of Metaphysics, Vol. LIV, No. 4, June 2001, 939–941.

Damschen, Gregor/Schönecker, Dieter (^{2}2013): Selbst philosophieren. Ein Methodenbuch, Berlin/Boston.

Dennett, Daniel C./Plantinga, Alvin (2011): Science and Religion: Are they Compatible? New York/Oxford.

Fales, Evan (2003): "Alvin Plantinga, Warranted Christian Belief", in: Noûs 37:2, 353–370.

Forrest, Peter (2002): "Review of Alvin Plantinga, Warranted Christian Belief", in: Australasian Journal of Philosophy, 80 (1), 109–111.

Forrest, Peter (2009): "The Epistemology of Religion", in: Stanford Encyclopedia of Philosophy (online, March 11, 2009)

Geivett, R. Douglas/Jesson, Greg (2001): "Plantinga's Externalism and The Terminus of Warrant-Based Epistemology", in: Philosophia Christi, Ser. 2, Vol. 3, No. 2, 329–340.

Greco, John (2001): Review of "Warranted Christian Belief, in: American Philosophical Quarterly 75 (3), 461–466.

Greco, John (2007): "Reformed Epistemology", in: Chad Meister/Paul Copan (ed.): The Routledge Companion to Philosophy of Religion, London and New York, 629–639.

Groothius, Douglas: "Review of Alvin Plantinga, Warranted Christian Belief" (on the web).

Helm, Paul (2001): "Review of Warranted Christian Belief", in: Mind, Vol. 110. No. 440, Oct. 2001, 1110–1115.

Hibbs, Thomas S. (2001): "Review of WCB", in: The Weekly Standard, Dec. 24, 2001.

Löffler, Winfried (2006): Einführung in die Religionsphilosophie, Darmstadt.

Moreland, James P./Craig, William Lane: Philosophical Foundations for a Christian Worldview, InterVarsity Press, Downers Grove, Illinois, 2003.
Moser, Paul K. (2001): "Man to Man with Warranted Christian Belief and Alvin Plantinga", in: Philosophia Christi, Series 2, Vol. 3, No. 2, 367–377.
Nickel, Gregor/Schönecker, Dieter (2014): "Richard Swinburne's Concept of Religious Experience. An Analysis and Critique", in: European Journal for Philosophy of Religion, 6, 1, (2014), 177–198.
Philipps, D.Z. (2004): Review of "Warranted Christian Belief, in: International Studies in Philosophy, 36 (1), 251–252.
Plantinga, Alvin (1982): "On Reformed Epistemology", in: Reformed Journal, January 1982, 13–17.
Plantinga, Alvin (1983): "Reason and Belief in God", in: Alvin Plantinga and Nicholas Woltersdorff (ed.): Faith and Rationality: Reason and Belief in God, Notre Dame, 16–93.
Plantinga, Alvin (1984): Advice to Christian Philosophers
Plantinga, Alvin (1985): "Self-Profile", in: James E. Tomberlin/Peter van Inwagen (eds.): Alvin Plantinga, Dordrecht/Boston/Lancaster, 1985, 3–97.
Plantinga, Alvin (1990): "Preface to the 1990 Paperback Edition" [of God and Other Minds], ix-xiii.
Plantinga, Alvin (1993a): Warrant: The Current Debate, New York.
Plantinga, Alvin (1993b): Warrant and Proper Function, New York.
Plantinga, Alvin (2000): Warranted Christian Belief, New York.
Plantinga, Alvin (2001a): "Rationality and Public Evidence: A Reply to Richard Swinburne", in: Religious Studies, Vol. 37, No. 2, 2001, 215–222.
Plantinga, Alvin (2001b): "Warranted Christian Belief. A Précis by the Author", in: Philosophia Christi, Series 2, Vol. 3, No. 2, 327–328.
Plantinga, Alvin (2001c): "Internalism, Externalism, Defeaters and Arguments for Christian Belief", in: Philosophia Christi, Series 2, Vol. 3, No. 2, 379–400.
Plantinga, Alvin (2002): "Reply" [to Sudduth, Wykstra, Zagzebski], in: Philosophical Books 43, 117–135.
Plantinga, Alvin (2007a): "Two Dozen (or so) Theistic Arguments", in: Deane-Peter Baker (ed.): Alvin Plantinga (Contemporary Philosophy in Focus), Cambridge, 203–226.
Plantinga, Alvin (2007b): "On 'Proper Bascality'", in: Philosophy and Phenomenological Research Vol. LXXV No. 3, 612–621.
Plantinga, Alvin (2011): Where the Conflict Really Lies. Science, Religion, and Naturalism, Oxford.
Plasger, Georg (2015): "Does Calvin teach a sensus divinitatis? Reflections on Alvin Plantinga's Interpretation of Calvin", this volume, 169–189.
Rentsch, Thomas (2005): Gott, Berlin.
Senor, Thomas D. (2002): "A Critical Review of Alvin Plantinga's Warranted Christian Belief", in: International Philosophical Quarterly, 42,3, Issue 167, 389–396.
Swinburne, Richard: "Plantinga on Warrant", in: Religious Studies, Vol. 37, No. 2, 2001, 203–214.
Tapp, Christian (2015): "Reference to an Infinite Being", this volume, 41–64
Trigg, Roger (2002): Review of "Warranted Christian Belief", in: Faith and Philosophy, 19 (1), 123–126.

Wachter, Daniel von: "Philosophy of Religion in Protestant Theology", in: The Routledge Companion to Philosophy of Religion, Hg. P. Copan & C. Meister, London: Routledge, 2007, 487–497.
Wiertz, Oliver (2015): "Is Plantinga's A/C Model an Example of Ideologically Tainted Philosophy?", this volume, 83–113.
Woltersdorff, Nicholas: "Introduction", in: Alvin Plantinga / Nicholas Woltersdorff (ed.): Faith and Rationality: Reason and Belief in God, Notre Dame, 1–15.
Wykstra, Stephen J.: (2002): "'Not done in a Corner': How to be a sensible evidentialist about Jesus", in: Philosophical Books 43, 92–116.
Zagzebski, Linda (1993): "Introduction", in: Linda Zagzebski (ed.): Rational Faith. Catholic Responses to Reformed Epistemology, Notre Dame, 1–13.
Zagzebski, Linda (2002): "Plantinga's Warranted Christian Belief and the Aquinas/Calvin Model" in: Philosophical Books 43, 117–123.

Christian Tapp
Reference to an Infinite Being

Languages are complex systems. Even if we hold that most of our linguistic expressions obtain their meanings in observable, empirically determined circumstances and that only some expressions obtain their meanings by virtue of their positions within the language system alone, it is crucial that the ranges of meaningful discourse and of what can be expressed by a language are not confined to these roots. We can form meaningful statements not merely about (hitherto) empirically determined circumstances and about language itself. For example, we could discuss, in early 2011, the upcoming first speech of the pope in the German parliament and say that we like or dislike such an event for this or that reason. Although nobody has ever witnessed such an event previously, we can successfully form assertions that refer to it, predicate properties of it and, *post festum*, may turn out to be true or false.[1] We can successfully talk about events that have not yet occurred, types of events that have never been exemplified before, or even events that will never occur. (Perhaps in the last case, we would not say that we have successfully *referred* to them). What is true about events is *mutatis mutandis* also true for things. We can meaningfully discuss the first human being to run 100 meters in less than 9 seconds or the first 1000 dollar note I will ever have in my hands. However, some people doubt that by the linguistic devices we have acquired in the lowlands of mundane reality, we can refer to a being as lofty as God.

In the first part of *Warranted Christian Belief* (WCB), Alvin Plantinga addresses some prominent representatives of such doubts. My task in this paper is to present and discuss Plantinga's arguments and positions in that part. First of all, I must state that I am quite sympathetic to most of what Plantinga writes in that section of his splendid book. Hence, I cannot attempt to write a profound and incisive critique. Instead, I will offer something like a shift in perspective that might be of interest to people who do not completely embrace Plantinga's contagious enthusiasm for Christian apologetics.

Therefore, in what follows, I will perform my compulsory program of summarizing and discussing Plantinga's line of argument in the first part of WCB, and I will enrich the discussion with some considerations on the possibility of

---

[1] This statement does not mean that no problems of reference could possibly occur; for example, if the pope falls ill and the speech is cancelled. However, such problems do not preclude describing such utterances as cases of successful reference in the event that everything occurs as expected.

referring to God and on the role the divine predicate of infinity plays in Plantinga's first section. The reason for focusing on infinity is that this particular divine predicate is central for both some strands of negative theology, that locate divine infinity in the proximity of divine ineffability,[2] and some strands of the philosophy of religion (such as the Plantingean strand) that consider infinity primarily a positive notion that is a useful kind of shorthand for some of the classical divine attributes suggested by a perfect-being conception of God.

1 Plantinga's argument in the first part of WCB

As Plantinga notes in the very first sentence of WCB, his book is "about the intellectual or rational acceptability of Christian belief" (WCB, vii). The main question of the book is: "Is there a viable *de jure* objection to Christian belief?" (WCB, x). Plantinga's overall project in WCB is to show that a negative *de jure* attitude toward Christian belief (i.e., taking it to be unreasonable to believe what Christians believe) is either incoherent or implies a negative *de facto* attitude toward it (i.e., taking what is believed to be false or senseless). Hence, according to Plantinga's argument, continuously upholding an agnostic attitude toward the truth of Christian belief is incompatible with the denial of its rationality. Plantinga realizes this project by working out what he calls the extended Aquinas/Calvin model, an epistemological model that he takes to have strong support in Christian belief. The model postulates something like a sixth sense, the *sensus divinitatis*, a faculty by which we can know divine things. As the *sensus divinitatis* is deranged by sin, it functions properly only because of divine grace and salvation (this constitutes the *extended* version of the A/C model).

Defeaters of Christian belief notwithstanding, this argument amounts to the following sequence of conditionals: If Christian belief is true, then the extended version of the A/C model is likely to be a correct model of our faculty to form true beliefs about God. If there is such a faculty, then (given some additional conditions, such as we exercise this faculty in appropriate circumstances) those beliefs have warrant, i.e., constitute knowledge. Additionally, if Christian beliefs are warranted (i.e., are produced by a cognitive faculty whose design plan is "successfully aimed at truth", WCB, 156), then it is not irrational, unreasonable or in any other way epistemologically defective to hold them. Therefore, by a chain inference, we have the following "large conditional": IF Christian belief is true,

---

[2] For instance, John Hick holds this view (cf. below and WCB, 43); this view is also common in continental theology; cf. the discussions in Striet (2003).

THEN it is not irrational to hold it. Hence, by contraposition, if it were irrational to accept Christian belief (negative *de jure* attitude), then one would also have to doubt its veracity (negative *de facto* attitude).[3] One might have wished that Plantinga had also presented arguments for the antecedent of the conditional, i.e., for the truth of Christian belief. But, he holds that this would be "beyond the competence of philosophy" (WCB, 499).[4]

However, before Plantinga can begin working on his overall project, he needs to address a fundamental obstacle to it: Is the presupposed realistic interpretation of Christian belief possible at all? Is it possible and adequate to take the assertions of believers at face value? When believers say, "God made the heavens and earth", do they say that God made the heavens and earth? Do they refer to a being, God, of whom they predicate a certain property, having created the heavens and earth?

Plantinga brackets this category of questions together into one question of whether there is "any such thing as Christian belief, conceived as Christians conceive it?" (WCB, x). This question does not mean he doubts that there are Christians, i.e., people who hold Christian beliefs. It rather means whether the beliefs the Christians have can be properly called "Christian" in the sense in which Plantinga understands that term. The point is that Christians think they have beliefs about God conceived of as an ITUB (an infinite, transcendent and ultimate being

---

[3] One may challenge Plantinga's project by suspecting it to be trivial: If Christian belief is true, then it is epistemically acceptable to hold it—simply because it is epistemically acceptable to hold a truth. However, this critique falls short of Plantinga's point. His point is that if Christian belief is true, then by virtue of the A/C model, it has warrant. Warrant is what distinguishes knowledge from mere true belief. Hence, according to Plantinga, in the case of Christian belief, truth entails warrant. Such entailment is by far not trivial, because a belief to be warranted in Plantinga's sense includes that the belief is "produced by cognitive processes or faculties that are functioning properly, in a cognitive environment that is propitious for that exercise of cognitive powers, according to a design plan that is successfully aimed at the production of true belief" (WCB, xi).
A critique of Plantinga's overall account has much better prospects if it challenges either Plantinga's externalist warrant conception of knowledge or his claim that Christian faith does imply the A/C model (or the likelihood of its correctness). I am not sure that a *"sensus divinitatis"* supplemented by grace has strong support from most varieties of Christian belief.

[4] Cf. Swinburne (2001): "There is, however, a monumental issue which Plantinga does not discuss, and which a lot of people will consider needs discussing. This is whether Christian beliefs do have warrant (in Plantinga's sense). He has shown that they do, if they are true; so we might hope for discussion of whether they are true" (206). Plantinga replied that he takes his extended A/C model to show how Christian belief "could have warrant, justification and rationality when taken in the *basic* way" (220), and this is warrant for me, with respect to my private evidence, and not with respect to public evidence (Plantinga, 2002).

—my abbreviation). However, following Kant, some people claim that it is impossible to have beliefs about ITUBs because our concepts cannot apply to them: "Our concepts can apply only to finite beings, beings who are not transcendent in the way Christians take God to be" (WCB, x). Therefore, Christians are sometimes understood to believe something actually quite different from what they say and what they think they believe.[5] Adopting a technical term from epistemology, one might follow Plantinga in calling such a position an example of (theological) anti-realism.

As an advocate of (theological) realism, Plantinga's task in the first part of WCB is to rebut the claims of anti-realists and to disprove their arguments (insofar as they exist). In doing so, he is, as it were, *clearing the deck* for the large-scale questions of whether there is "a viable *de jure* objection to Christian belief" (x), and if there is, whether this objection implies the falsehood of Christian belief.

In anglophone and continental theology, theological realism is often rejected as naive. One reason is a certain Kantian attitude that Plantinga calls "conceptual agnosticism" (WCB, 31) according to which we cannot refer to or know anything about God, at least nothing substantial. In the first two chapters of WCB, Plantinga discusses and disproves three lines of argument to that effect: the arguments of Kant (or a Kantian), Kaufman and Hick.

1.1 On Kant

Plantinga traces conceptual agnosticism (CA) back to Immanuel Kant, "a virtual titan of philosophy" whose work, however, is marked by "grave hermeneutical difficulties" (WCB, 9) because there is no settled interpretation of his work. In

---

[5] There are at least two different ways to understand "believing that p". They differ according to a difference in using descriptions p of a belief of a person S in sentences of the form "S believes that p". According to the one way one should, in forming p, stick to the words/concepts S uses in describing her belief. According to this way it is necessary to conclude from S uttering "I believe in the existence of God" that S believes that God exists. According to the other way, what matters is how an observer would describe what S believes on the basis on his observations of S's behavior. According to this second way it is well possible that S utters "I believe in the existence of God" while S does not believe that God (in our sense of the term) exists but, say, that there are certain cosmic forces. In the first way, it is almost impossible to say that S believes something different from what he believes to believe. In the second way, it seems well possible. In any case, Plantinga uses "believe that" in the second way when he describes his adversaries as rational beings who hold that Christians "*think* they have beliefs about an infinite and transcendent being, but in fact they are mistaken" (in thinking to have beliefs *of this kind*; WCB, x).

particular, Kant often writes as if we can think about and refer to God but cannot obtain metaphysical knowledge of him. However, other passages of his works are much more supportive for a skeptical thesis such as CA. One particular argument, which Plantinga cites, begins from the denial of intellectual intuition as part of our faculty of knowledge. From this denial, he infers that "categories can never extend further than to the objects of experience" (WCB, 10), which is a fundamental thesis of the *Critique of Pure Reason*. If the categories are only applicable to the phenomenal realm (the realm of experience), then they are, in particular, not applicable to God, who is "a noumenon *in excelsis*" (WCB, 10).

This argument hinges on at least two elements: the relation of the phenomenal to the noumenal realm and the assumption that predication is exhausted by categorical predication. I will treat the second point further below regarding the question of the scope of logical negation, and I will focus on the first point in what follows.

Plantinga distinguishes two interpretations of Kant, the two worlds and the one world interpretation, which constitute different ways of understanding the duality of A and B in epistemically basic sentences such as "A appears to p as B". Both interpretations enable the thesis that our concepts do not apply to God.

According to the two worlds interpretation as Plantinga takes it, there exist the two worlds of "noumena" and "phenomena" (these terms are used here only approximatively). Only the world of phenomena is epistemically accessible to us. Hence, as we have no access to the world of noumena, our concepts apply only to the world of phenomena, which is somewhat of a construction of ours. Therefore, according to the two worlds interpretation, our concepts apply not to God but to our mental construction, in which case, it is almost absurd to maintain the literal claim that a God in this sense was the creator of the heavens and earth because his existence would depend on ours as he is part of our mental construction (the phenomenal world). According to Plantinga's diagnosis, the problem with this account is that the same would hold for any of our concepts, which makes both the case of God non-special and the whole interpretation ridiculous. The one world interpretation, in contrast, regards the phenomena not as a separate world besides the noumenal world but more similar to the aspect we see or the image we obtain from the real, the noumenal world.

With respect to Kant there is much disagreement among historians of philosophy. Since some important aspects of Plantinga's critique will show up in discussing the positions of Kaufman and Hick, I will not go into detail here. Suffice it to say that Plantinga's conclusion after his discussion of Kant is quite negative:

> There is really nothing in Kant to suggest that in fact we can't think or talk about God. More generally, it is exceedingly hard to see how to construct an argument—an argument for the conclusion that we cannot refer to and think about God—from materials to be found in the work of Kant (WCB, 31).

As I confessed above, I embrace the major part of Plantinga's Kant interpretation. Nevertheless, I would like to focus on one point that seems not conclusive to me. If, in the sentence "God is the creator (of heavens and earth)", someone takes "God" to refer to a mental construction (call this interpretation "anti-realist" for short), then it truly seems absurd to predicate "is the creator" of this mental construction. But my impression is that this absurdity is somehow forced onto the anti-realist interpretation. Doesn't it seem absurd mainly for the reason that the meaning of "God" is located at the anti-realist reinterpretation level while the meaning of "the creator" is taken in the realist sense? A real property such as 'being creator' is predicated of a mental construct—that is indeed absurd. Wouldn't it be a much more charitable interpretation of a Kantian standpoint to locate the predicated property (being creator) also at the anti-realist reinterpretation level, i.e. to take it too as some sort of mental construction (a mental construction that applies to certain other mental construction as their property in a very special sense)? If one does so, the absurdity is by far not that obvious. If one refuses to do so, one might call for a justification for that discrimination between two concepts so closely related as the concepts of God and creator, of whom the one is interpreted at the anti-realist reinterpretation level while the other is taken literally.

1.2 On Kaufman

In section 2.I, Plantinga discusses the position of the late Harvard theologian Gordon D. Kaufman (1925–2011), who is an adherent of CA (i.e., the thesis that we cannot think or talk about God because our concepts do not apply to him). Plantinga analyzes Kaufman's position as follows: Because God is infinite, he is not identical with any finite reality; hence, he is not within the realm of our experience; therefore, the reference of the term "God" is highly problematic. We can neither know nor experience what Kaufman calls "the real referent" of the term "God". What is available to our worship, prayer and all other practical purposes is only an imaginative construct called "the available God" or "the available referent of the term 'God'".

Plantinga criticizes Kaufman's position along two lines. The first line of critique is that he doubts both steps of the argument from God's infinity to the problematic reference of the term "God". Let me reserve the discussion of the first step of the argument, which proceeds from infinity to not being within the realm of our experience, for the section below on infinity (Section 3). With respect to the second step, from unexperienceability to the problem of reference, Plantinga's critique focuses on entities or events postulated in the natural sciences: Despite the fact that many such entities or events, such as the Big Bang, cannot be experienced by us, no one would ever doubt that "Big Bang" is a meaningful term which can be used to form true sentences. Hence, according to Plantinga, there is no reason to support the general inference from unexperienceability to the problem of reference.

One might conjecture that this conclusion is a little too quick for, in fact, there *are* problems of reference with terms like "Big Bang". Anti-Realists in the philosophy of science, for example, claim that such terms do not refer, at least not to events in empirical reality. Structuralists, for example, will say that scientific terms refer to places in theoretical structures. According to this conjecture, then, Plantinga would need an additional argument in support of realism here.[6] It is, however, not clear that Platinga does really need it. The point of his counter-example to Kaufman's thesis is not that there are no problems of reference concerning terms like "Big Bang". The point is that unexperiencability alone is not a sufficient reason for raising doubts about the reference of a term. The "Big Bang" is indeed a counterexample to Kaufman's first conditional from unexperiencability to problems of reference.

Plantinga's second line of critique consists in revealing several points of incoherence in Kaufman's view. For example, it is incoherent to interpret a Christian believer as thinking to predicate properties of the "real" God while managing only to predicate them of a mental construction of his own. Since nobody will consciously acknowledge that it was his own mental construct that created the heavens and earth, there remain only two possibilities: Either one must suppose that the Christian is utterly wrong when he thinks that he predicates the divine properties of God, whereas he unconsciously predicates them of his mental construct; or one must suppose that not only the reference of the proper name 'God' but also the meaning of the divine predicates differ from what they are ordinarily taken to be. However, this interpretation would be so alien to the belief system interpreted that "a strong argument would be required to make this even reasonably plausible" (WCB, 37)—and there is no such argument.

---

6 Cf., for example, Plantinga (1982). In that famous address Plantinga argues chiefly against anti-realism. He embraces only part of the anti-realist intuition that truth is not independent of mind—insofar as it is necessarily coextensive with God's mind.

Plantinga identifies further incoherence in the idea that "our concepts do not apply to the real referent, if indeed there is such a thing" (WCB, 38). This argument is incoherent, Plantinga states, because if a concept P does not apply to x, then x does not have the property expressed by P (the property P, abbreviated); thus, x has the property non-P, and thus we *can* attribute a property to God, after all. Furthermore, the argument is self-refuting in the case of formal properties such as being self-identical. If the predicate 'is self-identical' does not apply to the real referent, then 'is not self-identical' does. Additionally, the same is true for any property of which we have a concept, implying in consequence that "there could be a being that had no properties, didn't exist, wasn't self-identical, wasn't either a material object or an immaterial object, and didn't have any properties" (WCB, 38). Such a position is clearly incoherent, Plantinga concludes.

In his later works, Kaufman changed his position somewhat. He abandoned the real referent and focused more strongly on opposing the reification of God—an opposition that is very common among continental theologians today. "It is a mistake", Plantinga quotes Kaufman,

> to regard qualities attributed to God [...] as though they were features or activities of such a particular being. [...] These terms and concepts do not refer directly to 'objects' or 'realities' or their qualities and relations, but function rather as the building blocks or reference points which articulate the theistic world-picture or vision of life (WCB, 39).

This argument explains why Kaufman presents an elaborate reinterpretation of central theistic and Christian doctrines. Religious language and practice are still important insofar as they are "used to promote human flourishing, 'human fulfillment and meaning'", as Plantinga quotes Kaufman (WCB, 40).

Plantinga's critique of Kaufman's new position is biting: Kaufman needs the reinterpretation of God as a symbol because he thinks that there is no such being (a God in the sense of ordinary Christian belief). Hence, he is an atheist-theologian—a type of person whom Plantinga analogizes to a mountaineer skeptical about the existence of mountains. Insofar as Kaufman advises us to continue to use the term 'God' and other traditional phrases, even though there is no being such as the traditional God who has the properties traditionally predicated of him, he wants to assign those terms quite a different meaning: "We are to say such things as 'God is real', meaning that in fact there are forces in the world that contribute to human flourishing" (WCB, 42). In Plantinga's view, this is misleading double-talk:

> It is not even a matter of throwing out the baby with the bathwater; it is, instead, throwing out the baby and keeping the tepid bathwater, at best a bland, unappetizing potion that is neither hot nor cold and at worst a nauseating brew, fit for neither man nor beast (WCB, 42).

I can understand the emotions guiding such polemic assessment. Taken as it stands, Kaufman's position (which can be taken *pars pro toto* for ways of thinking that are prevalent in contemporary theology) is highly inadequate to the self-understanding of Christian belief. To a full-fledged traditional Christian believer, taking "God is real" to express *nothing but* that "there are forces in the world that contribute to human flourishing" must seem to be a blunt misrepresentation of some of the most central elements of her belief. However, I have the impression that Plantinga's warranted aversion against Kaufman's "devotion to the bath water" has caused Plantinga, the passionate advocate of the baby, to overlook that even the moldy Kaufmanian bath water may be of some worth if used appropriately. Let me disclose the meaning of these metaphorical terms.

What I would like to propose is a more constructive way of understanding Kaufman's claims. To be sure, in the interest of Christian faith, some of Kaufman's statements cannot be upheld, for instance, the idea that we cannot refer to God or that God (in the sense of classical theism) does not exist (if Plantinga's reconstruction of Kaufman's position is correct with respect to this point). However, other claims might be preserved. To specify these, I need to say somewhat more exactly what a reinterpretation of Christian faith is. A reinterpretation of a body of beliefs is a mapping from the set of traditional beliefs (or their verbalizations) onto a set of beliefs that the traditional verbalizations are now taken to express. For instance, "God is real", which is a verbalization of a traditional Christian belief, is mapped onto the belief that there are forces in the world that contribute to human flourishing. Suggesting theologically such a reinterpretation has two elements: first, endorsing the images of the traditional beliefs under the mapping (endorsing the belief that, for instance, there are forces in the world that...) and, second, endorsing the meta-thesis that the mapping constitutes a meaning function, i.e., a function that assigns a meaning to the beliefs in the set it operates on, viz. a meaning that is adequate to Christian belief. If one abandons this meta-thesis including all suggestions to *identify* Christian belief with its weak image under the reinterpretation function, the result will be a collection of weak images of Christian beliefs, that are well compatible with Christian belief traditionally understood. This collection can be taken as a type of secular interpretation of Christian belief. It is an "under-interpretation" as it surely falls short of what it intends to interpret. However, is it therefore worthless? The point is that according to a traditional understanding of Christian faith, "God is real", for instance, does (in connection with several other doctrines of Christian faith) well *imply* that there are "cosmic forces working toward the fully humane existence for which we long" (Kaufman's words as quoted by Plantinga), but not the converse. Another example is the fact that the worshipping practice of a Christian community does indeed "orient selves and communities so as to facilitate development toward loving and caring selfhood, and toward communities of openness, love, and freedom" (Kaufman according to Plantinga, WCB, 41; at least this accords to the ethical ideals of true Christian faith). A just critique of Kaufman should not assert that those claims are false. In fact, most of them are implied by Christian faith even though falling short of it. Kaufman's error does not consist in indicating and endorsing those implications (and Plantinga accordingly does not say it does). Kaufman's cardinal error is to identify implications of Christian belief with that belief itself. This is what in my eyes ultimately warrants Plantinga's rejection of Kaufman's *Ansatz*.

Thus, my proposal results in interpreting most of what Kaufman writes as a secularized extraction from Christian belief even if it falls short of an adequate interpretation of such belief. As it stands, such an extraction may be helpful for mystagogical and apologetic purposes and represents something akin to a preliminary stage of Christian faith for modern, rational and open-minded people. By Kaufman's work we may learn that an interpretation of Christian faith exists that, when considered in itself (i.e. without adequacy issues), makes sense, is morally appealing and in accordance with reason, touches on some deep streams of religious feelings or desires in people, and strikes some necessary chords to enable a secular-minded person to discover his "religious musicality" (Max Weber).[7]

Again, to believe that God exists is to believe *much more* than that there are "cosmic forces working toward the fully humane existence". However, belief in God implies belief in such forces, or rather, in one such force. Such belief may well serve as a preliminary stage, a first-order approximation or an educational simplification of a full theistic and Christian belief. I cannot see that this way of reading Kaufman would in any way contradict Christian faith or intellectual integrity as long as one does not attempt to identify what is not identical.

1.3 On Hick

Plantinga then discusses the work of John Hick. According to the version of CA that Hick holds, our concepts—or at least our 'substantial' concepts, see below—

---

[7] "I absolutely lack religious musicality and I have neither the desire not the ability to erect any mental 'constructions' of religious character within myself..., though after careful consideration, I have to say that am neither anti-religious nor irreligious". My translation; the German original reads: *"Ich bin zwar religiös absolut unmusikalisch und habe weder Bedürfnis noch Fähigkeit, irgendwelche seelischen 'Bauwerke' religiösen Charakters in mir zu errichten..., aber ich bin nach genauer Prüfung weder antireligiös noch irreligiös"* (Weber 1994, 65).

do not apply to God or 'The Real' as it is in itself. As our language has developed in contact with experienceable reality, it does not apply to the noumenal reality of "The Real *an sich*".

Plantinga indicates two ambiguities in Hick's position, the first one concerning the one world vs. two worlds interpretation of Kant and the question of whether the noumenal Real is experienceable and the second one concerning the strength of the CA thesis that Hick embraces. Regarding the first point, Plantinga can dismiss the ambiguity quite easily by proposing the view that

> perhaps it doesn't matter whether we say that we actually experience it [= the Real, C.T.] or say, instead, only that it contributes to our experience (WCB, 45).

Resolving the second point requires further elaboration. Although Hick admits that it makes no sense to assert that none of our concepts apply to the Real, the question is which ones do and which ones do not.

To that end, Hick draws on an elaborate distinction of types of properties or concepts.[8] He distinguishes formal from nonformal properties, negative from positive properties and properties of which we have a grasp from those of which we do not have a grasp. These distinctions are displayed in the following table.

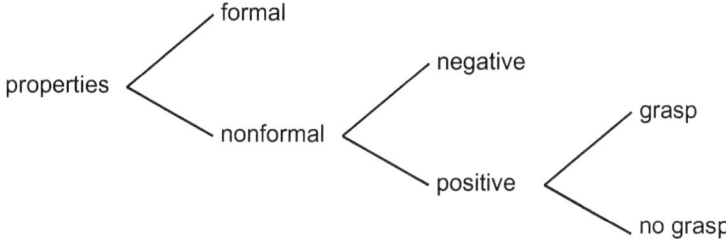

Plantinga develops the theoretical division of concepts even further. He distinguishes two groups of formal concepts: the concepts of one group are essential for a thing to have and are necessarily had by everything (such as *being self-identical* and *being such that 7+5=12*), whereas the concepts of the other group

---

[8] In the multi-layered relation of our language to the world, there are two different levels that are closely connected with and broadly analogous to each other: the level of concepts and the level of properties. Concepts express properties, and properties of which we have a grasp can be expressed by concepts. Hence, there is always a sort of redoubling between a theory of concepts and a theory of properties. In the following text, I will cheerfully toggle between both levels.

are of a different, more contingent, relational character (such as *being referred to by human beings* and *being thought of by John*).

According to that scheme of properties, Hick's theory can be formulated as follows: The Real has formal properties (such as having some properties, being self-identical, etc.), has all formal properties that everything has and it has some of the other formal properties. In addition, if P is a positive nonformal property of which we have a grasp, the Real does not have P (Hick's version of negative theology); therefore, the Real has the complementary negative property P^c (such as not being a horse, not being good), which exists because P was such that we have a grasp (a conception) of it (note that $P \vee P^c$ is universally valid for properties P of which we have a grasp). Furthermore, the Real can and perhaps must have some positive nonformal properties, but only such properties of which we have no grasp.

Thus, Hick's idea with respect to the Real is that only formal properties and negative properties apply to it. If we call the remaining properties 'substantial' according to Hick, we can summarize his position in his own words as

"that our substantial concepts do not apply to the Ultimate" (WCB, 46).

According to Plantinga, Hick's theory of religious belief attributes a striking error to the practitioners of great religions: Although believers think that their beliefs refer to a being with certain positive properties of which they have a grasp, in fact they refer to the Real, a being with no positive nonformal properties of which we have a grasp. More precisely, such practitioners aim at talking about the Real *an sich* but manage to refer to the Real *für mich*, the phenomenal "version" that is available to us in contrast to the noumenal reality "*an sich*".

However, how *could* we refer to a being such as the Real that has no nonformal positive properties of which we have a grasp? Plantinga considers several possibilities. Obviously, definite descriptions using classical divine properties will not do because those are positive properties of which we have a concept (see Section 2 below for a more detailed account of this way of referring to something). Furthermore, the description "the being that has no nonformal positive properties" does not work because there might be several such beings differing from each other only in positive properties of which we have no grasp. Nonetheless, there must be some type of connection between the person referring to the Real and the Real referred to. The only remaining possibility is that there is "some kind of experiential contact" with that being (WCB, 51). However, that possibility comes at a high price for Hick's position because "then the Real enjoys at least one positive nonformal property of which we have a conception: the property *being experienced by us*" (WCB, 51). Although this property might be considered a formal property in Hick's sense, Plantinga shows that it entails nonformal properties depending on one's theory of experience: According to the standard causal theory, *being experienced by us* entails the positive nonformal property of being causally connected with us (WCB, 52). Hence, Hick's position is incoherent as it presupposes that a being that is defined as having no nonformal property of which we have a grasp does indeed have the nonformal property of being experienced by us.

The significant error that Hick imputes to religious practitioners is a different matter. Although such imputation reduces the plausibility of his position, it does not necessarily threaten coherence because even in quite ordinary circumstances, it is possible to successfully refer to a being even though one has mostly false beliefs about that being.

Overall, Plantinga judges the coherence of Hick's position much more favorably than Kaufman's. Although we have no positive evidence that a being such as Hick's Real does exist, we cannot assert that it does not exist. To successfully refer to the Real, one must make an exception for the rule that it does not have positive properties because there must be some type of experiential contact with it. The distinction of positive and negative properties is not incoherent, although it is not completely overt. Plantinga in fact proves its coherence by constructing a basic theory of positive and negative properties and mapping it onto basic propositional logic.[9]

---

9 Although there surely are positive and negative predicates, i.e., linguistic expressions of properties that either do or do not contain linguistic negation particles (such as the word "not" or the particle "un-" or the like), it is not clear that the distinction makes equally good sense with respect to properties. If one considers abstractness and concreteness, for example, it seems arbitrary which one of these properties to take as the positive, more basic property and which one as the negation of the other (either "concrete" means "not abstract" or "abstract" means "not concrete").

Plantinga's basic theory of positive and negative properties has the following axioms:
(1) Every property is either positive or negative.
(2) Every property has a complement.
(3) The complement of a property P has the opposite sense from P.
(4) A property equivalent to a given property has the same sense as that property.
(5) No negative property of which we have a conception entails a positive property of which we have a conception (otherwise the Real would have that entailed property).
(6) The Real has no positive properties of which we have a conception (perhaps there are exceptions to the generality of this axiom).

Given an appropriate definition of conjunctive and disjunctive properties, this theory of positive and negative properties can be formalized and mapped onto propositional logic so that one can understand that it is consistent, decidable, complete etc; cf. WCB, 53.

There is another problem with Hick's position, which concerns the concept of infinity; hence, this problem will be discussed in the section on infinity (Section 3 below). To anticipate a result, Hick's position leads to the conception of the Real as a being that is limited with respect to all properties of which we have a grasp simply because it does not exemplify them. The Real can be called 'unlimited' only in the sense of possessing, to the maximal degree possible, "some properties of which we have no grasp" (WCB, 55).

Hence, Hick's conception fairly passes Plantinga's tests for coherence. However, in the course of the conjunct procedure of being tested and modified, the concept of the Real becomes sharpened in a way that makes it vulnerable in the sense of religious relevance. The basic problem is, Plantinga states,

> that if the Real has no positive properties of which we have a conception, then we have no reason at all to think that it is *in religion* that human beings get in experiential contact with this being, rather than in any other human activity: war or oppression, for example. This being has none of the properties ascribed by the practitioners of most of the great religions to the beings they worship: it is not good, or loving, or concerned with human beings, or wise, or powerful; it has not created the universe, does not uphold it, and does not pay attention to the universe or the creatures it contains. It is an unknown and unknowable X (WCB, 56).

If the Real had the properties of the theistic or even the Christian God, there would be strong reasons for thinking that we "live in relation to the Real" and that "some ways of behavior are appropriate to the Real and others are not" (WCB, 57), as Christian belief considers when it holds that "self-centered behavior is less appropriate with respect to [the Real] than living a life of love" (WCB, 58). However, if it is true that the Real is emptied of all positive properties of which we have a conception and is conceived of as a mere unknowable X, the reasons for this conclusion vanish. Moreover, one cannot find any criterion for deciding which ideas in religions are *authentic* manifestations of the Real (Hick's "*personae*" and "*impersonae*", WCB, 58). Whereas Plantinga presents this last point as a question about religious relevance, one might consider emphasizing it further and taking it as another question about the coherence of an account that is indebted to the possibility of judging the authenticity of manifestations of a being that is conceptually emptied of almost all grounds for judging.

2 Elements of a theory of reference (to God)

According to the self-image of Christian belief, God (who is an ITUB) exists. He is the only ITUB and it is the case "that we are able to address him in prayer, refer to him, think and talk about him, and predicate properties of him" (WCB, 3). As far as classical theology is concerned, the last point is not unopposed. There is a strong tradition of so-called "negative" theology. Claims of different strength are offered under that label, ranging from certain epistemic restraints such as that God is not completely cognizable or that his essence is not knowable (what he is)—via restrictions of property ascription (such as that God is more unlike than like what our predicates express) to full-blown apophatic claims that come close to incoherence (such as that we can neither say nor know anything about him at all). Plantinga reconstructs all the positions we have discussed thus far as strands of negative theology, although they differ in the strength of the CA thesis they embrace.

Once the pros and cons of Kant's, Kaufmann's and Hick's positions have been discussed, the systematic questions remain: Can we refer to such a being as Christian believers think they do in prayer, praise and preaching? How could that work?

Generally, it is a fact that the (successful) use of the linguistic devices that we have acquired in empirical situations is not confined to such situations. We can refer to objects or events in empirical situations of quite a different type from the situations in which we have acquired their names (just consider the example of the papal speech given in the introduction to this paper); moreover, we can successfully discuss non-empirical objects such as numbers. Leaving aside the question of the exact ontological nature of mathematical objects, we might suppose that numbers are not part of physical reality and that we can successfully refer to the number three with the word "three". We acquire mathematical language in empirical situations, such as when we face three apples, three green cars or three family members, but then we proceed to use such language successfully in talking and thinking about abstract objects, such as numbers.

Alternatively, consider scientific theories that propose certain types of theoretical entities. Most people are usually inclined to believe a scientific theory that has explanatory and prognostic success to be true and to treat it as if it were wholly unproblematic to refer to the entities it presupposes and to predicate properties of them.[10]

---

[10] However, Anti-Realists in the theory of science, such as Bas van Fraassen and others, challenge this "usual inclination".

Those examples provide the foundation for God's case. If our linguistic faculties are such that we manage to refer to such diverse types of non-experienced or non-experienceable things or events, then there is also a certain initial plausibility that such faculties will also serve for the case of God. However, God's case is somewhat special. Plantinga adduces the divine predicates of infinity, transcendence and ultimacy to illustrate this specialty. I will discuss this further in the following section on infinity (Section 3). Additionally, in most of the cases above, we use some of our ordinary terms in their ordinary meaning and combine them in definite descriptions for something non-ordinary. As, for example, when we use the terms "pope", "parliament", "speech" and a date expression, terms with whose meanings we are well acquainted, in order to refer to an event with which we are not acquainted yet.[11] This use is quite different from God's case. Most nonformal predicates used to distinguish him, such as "the all-knowing, all-powerful, and wholly good creator of the heavens and earth", are not ordinary predicates in their ordinary meaning, but their meanings are already modified. God does not perform morally good actions in the way that we do; he does not come to know things in the ways that we do; and his creating things is an "activity" of a nature that is quite different from the nature of our activities of "creating", such as building, constructing, breeding or designing.

Nevertheless, reference to God must be possible if one pursues a realistic account of religious belief that should be open to the possibility of such belief to be (literally) true. Plantinga presents a rudimentary theory of reference to God in the context of his discussion of Kaufman's *Ansatz*. Before presenting this theory, I would like to clarify another point concerning predication.

Plantinga frequently argues that it is plainly incoherent (or even self-refuting) to claim that no predication of God is possible at all. His argument is that if for a property P, God does *ex hypothesi* not have P, then he must have the complementary property P^c, which is simply the property not to have P. Although this argument is in some sense unobjectionable, a Kantian may take it to miss the point in question. To understand this, it is helpful to distinguish logical from contentual or "real" (to use a Kantian term) predication. Plantinga's argument

---

[11] The situation in case of the number word "three" is not that easy. We might say that by "three" we mean the number that these three apples and those three pears have in common, but this presupposes a meaningful concept of "number" that seems to be too abstract so as to be introduced by more ordinary concepts. One might think about reducing this case to forms of definition by pointing out exemplary cases, but even then there remains at least one term for quite an abstract operation, namely the instruction to form the general term that those examples are examples of. But let's not move into details of the ontology of numbers at this point.

is cogent for logical predication: If one holds that predication is impossible in the sense that for each predicate P, P does not hold for any ITUB, then predication *is* possible insofar as the opposite predicate non-P necessarily holds for the ITUB (because if P does not hold for x, x belongs to the complement of the extension of P, and that is the extension of non-P.) Thus, the impossibility of predication in the logical sense is self-refuting; therefore, predication is clearly possible.[12] Another issue is "real" or "contentual" or "categorical" predication, by which I mean the ascription of (logical) predicates of certain types, namely predicates that fall under certain distinguished categories of predicates or are composed of such predicates. Call such predicates "categorical predicates". There might thus be two reasons that a categorical predicate P does not hold for some x (i.e., there are two negations of "Px"), namely that the converse categorical predicate "non-P" holds or that the categorical predicates generally do not apply to x; therefore, neither P nor non-P holds. According to this view, non-P is not the logical contradictory to P; hence, the *tertium non datur* "for all x Px or non-Px" does not hold. (Or it holds only for x such that x is a categorizable object. This object is what is usually called a "finite object"—one for which the categories can be applied.)

Kantian philosophy is by no means the only branch of philosophy that has a problem not with broadly logical but with such a special, categorical predication. According to Aquinas, for instance, predication is the intellect's action of dividing and composing, such that it cannot work in the case of a simple being that has no parts (Aquinas STh I,13). Furthermore, according to the Aristotelian theory of predication, which Aquinas largely embraces, conceptual determination is by sorting and shelving according to a *genus proximum* and a *differentia specifica*. Hence, this type of determination does not work in the case of a being that is from the outset taken as not falling into any genus whatsoever.

In chapter 2.I of WCB, Plantinga presents some elements of a theory of reference in the context of his discussion of Kaufman's arguments for the CA thesis. He considers two ways of referring to God: via definite descriptions and via social communication. Definite descriptions such as 'the creator of heavens and

---

12 Another argument for the self-refuting nature of strict apophatic theses can focus on the meta-assertion that something, s, has no properties. This argument is performatively self-refuting because it predicates the property *having no properties* of s. One may defend the claim by taking refuge in the distinction of object- and meta-level properties, restricting the negative claim to object-level properties and taking the objection to concern a meta-level property. However, this distinction would seem to considerably reduce the strength of the thesis. The distinction is perhaps even incoherent because having meta-level properties may imply having object-level properties.

the earth', 'the omnipotent and omniscient creator of the world' or 'the divine person who spoke to Abraham' pick out a referent by a property that the referent and only the referent possesses. More precisely, a definite description in natural language has the form 'the x such that ... x ...' where '... x ...' is replaced by a predicate or a formula (i.e., a logical combination of predicates) $\phi(x)$. Since Frege and Russell first studied definite descriptions in a systematic manner, it has become clear that the successful use of them in the context of true statements requires two conditions be satisfied, an existence condition ($\exists x\, \phi(x)$) and a uniqueness condition ($\forall x,y\, (\phi(x) \wedge \phi(y) \to x=y)$). If one or both conditions are not satisfied, philosophers of language have different opinions on how to address sentences containing such "defective" definite descriptions (they consider the sentences false, senseless, devoid of meaning, forbidden or respectively ill-formed). In case the conditions are satisfied, one may introduce a new name into the language ("new" in the sense that it will obtain its meaning now) by defining it as the object selected by the description. As one may use different description formulas for that purpose, the meaning of the expression "God" for different people is fixed differently depending on what description they have chosen as basic (this is a significant problem in texts on natural theology as there are so many different "definitions" of the concept of God). Elsewhere—in "The Boethian Compromise"[13]—Plantinga has argued that different descriptions may in fact "express logically equivalent (even if epistemically inequivalent) essences of God" (WCB, 35).

Although the definite description method of fixing the reference of the term "God" is the more important one in scholarly contexts such as the philosophy of religion or theology, the more common way of fixing the reference is much simpler. This method consists in obtaining the name from others, who already use it, either during one's childhood or whenever one first encounters other people talking about God. This method amounts to a causal theory of meaning quite consistent with that of Saul Kripke: the linguistic items I use commonly obtain their meanings through my picking them up from the discourse of or with others and through my intention to use them with the same meaning as others do. This way of acquiring meaningful vocabulary is much more common, but it is also more risky. Imagine that someone has just invented a new word that in fact refers to nothing, but he begins to use it in some ways that others do not completely understand but find interesting enough to continue telling others, and so forth. Ultimately, all language use that is only obtained from others and not actively connected to one's own experiences or at least actively struc-

---

[13] Plantinga (1978).

tured by ordering concepts is on credit from one's linguistic predecessors. If these predecessors have just invented a meaningless word, then the whole path through generations of language users on which this theory of meaning is based may lead to a dead end. Although this aspect may be judged a slight disadvantage of the causal theory of meaning, it fits well with Plantinga's views because he indicated already in his *Warrant and Proper Function* that "the success of my noethic ventures depends on the success of similar ventures on the parts of those around me" (see ibid., 77–78; WCB, 35).

3 Infinity and the role of divine attributes

Plantinga is not known to support philosophical theology. Nevertheless, he does support the use of divine predicates as he takes Christian belief to have two subsets: classical theism (including beliefs such as the existence of an ITUB) and its subset of specifically Christian beliefs (including beliefs about trinity and salvation).

In what follows, I would like to focus on Plantinga's conception of the divine predicate 'infinity'. This predicate is of particular interest because on the one hand, it appears in all of his discussions in the first part of WCB and in the definition of an ITUB (an infinite, transcendent, ultimate being); on the other hand, it does not appear in his standard formulations of theistic belief, including the following two formulations:

> there is an all-powerful, all-knowing, wholly good person (a person without a body) who has created us (WCB, 3)

and

> God is a person: that is, a being with intellect and will. A person has (or can have) knowledge and belief, but also affections, loves, and hates; a person, furthermore, also has or can have intentions, and can act so as to fulfill them. God has all of these qualities and has some (knowledge, power, and love, for example) to the maximal degree. God is thus all-knowing and all-powerful; he is also perfectly good and wholly loving. Still further, he has created the universe and constantly upholds and providentially guides it (WCB, vii).

However, in the second quotation, there is a point of contact with Plantinga's understanding of infinity, as will become clear.

In WCB, infinity is explicitly mentioned first in a paragraph of the preface dedicated to summarizing the argument of the first part (WCB, x). In that description, Plantinga does not use any elaborate theory of that predicate's meaning. Instead, as is currently very common in philosophy and theology, he appeals to its contrary, finitude, and to the commonplace that we are finite beings living in a finite world of finite things. This strategy is sufficient to gain what he wishes: to furnish the claim that our concepts do not apply to ITUBs with some degree of initial plausibility. We are finite beings forming our concepts immanently and in contact with a world of finitude. Hence, it is immediately plausible that our concepts will not, at least not without further ado, apply to a transcendent and infinite reality such as that of an ITUB. This argument is the opponent's thesis that Plantinga sets out to criticize in the first part of his book.

Subsequently, in considering the argument that concepts cannot apply to ITUBs, Plantinga is more explicit on his notion of infinity. The most relevant explanation is quoted in full:

> An infinite being, we might say, is an unlimited being—unlimited, that is, with respect to certain properties. Among these properties might be power, knowledge, goodness, love, and the like. (A being is unlimited with respect to power and (propositional) knowledge, for example, if there is a maximal degree of power and knowledge, and the being in question enjoys that maximal degree of those properties. It might be hard to say precisely what the maximal degree of these properties is; with respect to knowledge, we might begin by saying that a being displays that maximal degree if it knows all true propositions and believes no false proposition.) (WCB, 6)

According to this explanation, infinity is quite a complex concept, which seems to amount to a two-place relation with (a term for) a being x as the first argument and (a term for) a set of properties $P = \{P_1,...,P_n\}$ as the second argument. The relation holds in the case where the being has the properties in P to the maximal possible degree. Thus, P_i must come in degrees, and there must exist a maximal degree. Let us suppose the degrees can be represented as real numbers from the interval [0,1] with the maximal degree reached with the value of 1. Then, each P_i is itself a two-place relation $P_i(x,d)$ with the intended meaning that x enjoys P_i to the degree d. Hence, we obtain the following definition of infinity:

> A being x is called infinite with respect to a set of (great-making) properties $P = \{P_1,...,P_n\}$—Inf(x,P)—if and only if for all $P_i \in P$: $P_i(x,1)$.

This understanding of infinity is not unusual in philosophical and religious theology. However, one may discuss several points: Is it plain to identify infinity, unlimitedness and (here comes the point in question) maximality? At least if these concepts are intended to keep in touch with their precise counterparts in mathematics, it seems odd to identify them. Maximality and infinity are different because there are maximal values that are not infinite and infinite values that are not maximal. For example, the function $f(x)=-x^2$ has its maximum at $x=0$ / $f(x)=0$ which is, for sure, not infinite. And the identity function $f(x)=x$ on, say, the first uncountable transfinite ordinal number ω_1 has infinite values (ω_0, for instance) but no maximum. Additionally, unlimitedness and infinity are distinct, for there are unlimitedly growing functions that do not reach infinite values and functions with infinite values that are limited. For example, $f(x)=x$ as a function on the natural numbers is growing without limit but does not take on infinite values. And the constant function $f(x)=\omega_0$ is limited (by ω_0 and every larger ordinal number) although it has only an infinite value. Furthermore, limitedness seems to be a property of functions (roughly, the function f is limited by a if for all x the value f(x) is equal to or less than a), whereas maximality seems to be a property of single values of a function (roughly, a value f(x) is a (local) maximum of f if there is a small environment of x such that in that environment, the values of f are equal to or less than f(x)). Surely there are connections between both concepts (if f(x) is a local maximum, then in an environment of x, f is limited by f(x); if f is limited by a, and f reaches a somewhere (for example, x is a point such that f(x)=a), then f has a local maximum there), but such connections between the concept do not permit to identify them.[14]

Whereas this point concerns the precise structure of the conceptual network Plantinga employs, another point is more relevant from the perspective of the philosophy of religion: does he truly presuppose that maximal degrees of each of the properties in P are then combined in the definition of an infinite being with regard to P? This issue is a special case of a general problem connected with the extension of properties: does the predicate "infinite" signify the combination of maxima or the result of maximizing them as far as their combination is still possible? Problems of that type are familiar in the philosophy of religion. For example, maximal power (all-powerfulness) as considered in itself will probably include the ability to produce a state of affairs no one can ever know about. However, if a being is not only all-powerful but also omniscient, it is hard to understand how such an unknowable state of affairs could be brought about without the all-powerful and omniscient being ceasing to exist or at least ceasing to have these properties (which are ordinarily thought to be essential properties of a being divine). Hence, combining after maximizing can make the conjunctive property incoherent. Instead, one should demand that a perfect being have all great-making properties to an extent to which it is logically possible for them to be combined. The Bohemian philosopher, mathematician and theologian Bernard Bolzano has, accordingly, incorporated that into his definition of a perfect being when he defines a being as perfect if it has all powers that are possible to

---

[14] For a more detailed discussion of the relation of mathematical and theological infinity-talk, cf. Tapp (2011).

have simultaneously and has these powers to the highest degree possible given the existence and degrees of the others.[15] A similar point has been made recently in an award-winning paper by Yujin Nagasawa, who claims that Anselmian perfect being theology implies the "MaximalGod Thesis" (which comes close to what I have presented as Bolzano's view), whereas most Anti-Anselmians base their attacks on the wrongly supposed "OmniGod Thesis" (which comes close to what I take to be the position Plantinga seems to unintentionally embrace).[16]

The notion of infinity becomes systematically most central in Plantinga's discussion of the position of the theologian Kaufman, who holds a version of the CA thesis. Plantinga analyzes Kaufman's argument for that thesis roughly as follows: God is infinite, hence not within the realm of our experience, and hence unreferrable. Plantinga doubts the first transition, from infinity to unexperienceability. He takes infinity to mean that God is "unlimited along several dimensions" (WCB, 34), especially with respect to power. However, how does that support the non-experienceability thesis? Plantinga asks a rhetorical question: "If God is omnipotent, infinitely powerful, won't he be able to manifest himself in our experience, bring it about that we experience him?" (WCB, 34). Plantinga has supported the claim implied by this question in advance by presenting examples from religious traditions claiming that God spoke to human beings and by recourse to William Alston's important work on not mere experience but perception of God. The infinite power of God warrants the assumption that he can produce every state of affairs he likes except those that are logically impossible. However, as there is no reason to interpret a state of affairs in which we experience God as logically impossible, there is good reason to suppose that an infinite God can produce such a state. Therefore, in light of Plantinga's analysis, it is "initially implausible to declare that God, if he is infinite and omnipotent, could not bring it about that we experience him" (WCB, 34). Hence, contrary to Kaufman's argument, God's infinity is more of a *pro* than a *con* with respect to the possibility of our experiencing him.

In Plantinga's discussion of Hick's position, infinity plays a crucial role in the context of the strongest argument against the coherence of Hick's position. The problem is that, according to Hick, infinity is a negative property: it signifies the absence of limits. Although that statement seems fairly standard, infinity entails, if it is not equivalent to, positive properties. In the spatial analogue Plan-

---

15 Cf. Bolzano (1834, I, §74). Bolzano calls all great-making properties "powers" as they all enable a being to acquire something: knowledge by the power to think (*denken*), perception by the power to perceive (*empfinden*), actions by the power to will (*wollen*), creation of beings by the power to create (*schaffen*), and influence of beings by the power to change (*verändern*).
16 Cf. Nagasawa (2008).

tinga mentions infinity means *having no borders,* which implies *occupying all of space.*[17] In the case of infinity as a divine predicate, there is a similar implication. To understand this notion, we need to follow Plantinga's further analysis of the concept of divine infinity.

According to Plantinga, the doctrine of divine infinity has two components: divine infinity involves the *absence of limits in a certain respect* and *not to suffer limitations by anything else.* He takes his definition of divine infinity, which we have discussed (having all properties of a certain set of properties to the maximal possible degree), to cover both components. With respect to the second component, it is simply the maximal degree to which the Real has its properties that ensures that it cannot suffer limitations from other beings. For example, being omniscient, the Real has knowledge to such a degree that no other being can ever limit his knowledge, i.e., can ever bring it about that he does not know something that can be known. The same idea holds for omnipotence, which means having power to a degree such that "nothing can prevent him from doing what he wills" (WCB, 55).

With respect to the first component, Plantinga specifies his earlier considerations with an argument to the effect that God is not unlimited in every respect. Were God unlimited in every respect, he would have to have "every property to the maximal degree, which is impossible" (WCB, 55) because in that case, God as a spirit would also have to be a material object: "Rather, the traditional idea has been that God has every *great-making* property to the maximal degree" (WCB, 55). Thus, Plantinga specifies the set of properties included in the definition of infinity discussed above as being the set of *great-making properties.* However, infinity with respect to great-making properties entails positive properties of which we have a grasp. Being unlimited with respect to power, omnipotence, entails having power, which is not only a great-making but also a positive property of which we have a grasp, and this is a problem for Hick's negative theology approach that explicitly excludes all positive properties from God. The only resolution for Hick seems to be to take infinity as unlimitedness with respect to properties of which we have no grasp. This interpretation leads to the following bizarre construction of an image of God/the Real according to Hick: "It has the complement of every property we have a grasp of; it has other properties we have no grasp of; and the way in which it is infinite is that it has to the maximal degree some properties of which we have no grasp" (WCB, 55).

---

[17] In understanding spatial infinity as implying *occupying all of space*, Plantinga overtly departs from the mathematical standard use of "infinite". According to that standard use, the space between two parallel lines in the euclidean plane is infinite; according to Plantinga's use, it is not. What he has in mind while talking about "infinity" seems to be more like what mathematicians commonly call "unlimitedness", as will become clear in the next paragraph.

4 Conclusion

In the first part of WCB, Alvin Plantinga suggests a realist interpretation of Christian belief and defends the possibility to think about and linguistically refer to an infinite being such as God. I embrace most of what Plantinga argues on that topic in the first two chapters of WCB, in particular his critique of the Kantian, Kaufmanian and Hickian ways of endorsing versions of the thesis of conceptual agnosticism, i.e., the thesis that our concepts (at least the substantial ones) do not apply to the being to which religious speech acts and acts of worship are directed.

Besides pointing to the slightly artificial flavor of the alleged absurdity of predicating "being the creator of heavens and earth" of a mental construct, I have proposed in this paper, relative to Plantinga's view, a more constructive way to read Kaufman's (short-coming) reinterpretation of Christian belief, a stronger reading of Hick's conceptual emptification of the Real as a problem of coherence, an assessment of the range of logical arguments against a being with no properties, and a reconstruction of Plantinga's interesting ways of discussing divine infinity.

Literature

Bolzano, Bernard (1834): Lehrbuch der Religionswissenschaft, Sulzbach.
Nagasawa, Yujin (2008): "A New Defence of Anselmian Theism", in: Philosophical Quarterly 58, 577–596.
Plantinga, Alvin (1978): "The Boethian Compromise", in: American Philosophical Quarterly 15,2, 129–138.
Plantinga, Alvin (1982): "How to Be an Anti-Realist", in: Proceedings and Addresses of the American Philosophical Association 56,1, 47–70.
Plantinga, Alvin (2000): Warranted Christian Belief, New York.
Plantinga, Alvin (2002): "Rationality and Public Evidence: a Reply to Richard Swinburne", in: Religious Studies 37, 215–222.
Striet, Magnus (2003): Offenbares Geheimnis. Zur Kritik der negativen Theologie (=ratio fidei, vol. 14), Regensburg.
Swinburne, Richard (2001): "Plantinga on Warrant", in: Religious Studies 37, 203–214.
Tapp, Christian (2011): "Infinity in Mathematics and Theology", in: Theology and Science 9/1, 91–100.
Weber, Max (1994): Max Weber—Gesamtausgabe, Abt. 2: Briefe, Bd.6, hg.v. M.R. Lepsius/ W. Mommsen, Tübingen.

Winfried Löffler
An Underrated Merit of Plantinga's Philosophy

1 Introduction

Compliments from philosophical colleagues are at times slightly ambivalent: below the surface they often contain a well-wrapped "yes, but" as well. The present paper intends something like that: I want to stress a valuable, yet still underrated point that I see in the background of Plantinga's philosophy. But I suspect that perhaps Plantinga himself underrates this merit as well; my proposal, hence, is to make more of that achievement. This might lead into a certain tension with some other of Plantinga's current tenets (as in *Warranted Christian Belief*); on the other hand, it could help to block some recurrent objections to his religious epistemology.

I see this underrated merit of Plantinga's philosophy (beginning with *God and Other Minds*) in his rehabilitation of the reputation of a special group of beliefs, which I would for brevity like to call *world-view beliefs* (I will address the terminological problem connected with them in a minute). A first key text in Plantinga's works where world-view beliefs get the strongest attention is surely *God and Other Minds:* Plantinga argues there that belief in the existence of God is, in terms of justification, not worse off than our belief in the existence of other minds. I bracket the question whether these 1967 arguments were convincing, but I want to highlight and recommend the very idea of inquiring into the rationality of a belief like 'there are other minds beyond my own'. It is a paradigmatic example of a world-view belief; others would be Plantinga's examples of Moore-style beliefs like 'there are material objects', 'the world has existed for more than five minutes', but of course also 'there is such a person as God' etc.[1] These were the examples used by Plantinga later on in RBG and WCB, but we can add other items to that list, and I hope Plantinga would agree to that: 'the world consists of relatively stable objects with attributes of a certain plasticity', 'the objects of the world neither emerge out of nothing nor disappear', 'changes in states of affairs have a cause (or a network of causes)', etc. My point is that

---

[1] RBG, 81f.; GOM.—I shall use the following abbreviations: GOM = *God and Other Minds*; RBG = *Reason and Belief in God*; WCB = *Warranted Christian Belief*; WCD = *Warrant: The Current Debate*; WPF = *Warrant and Proper Function.*

these world-view beliefs, although they play a crucial role in our cognitive organisation, still have an ambivalent position in Plantinga's thought: on the one hand, he did much to bring them back to the philosophical agenda, but on the other hand they still don't enjoy his deserved attention (with the belief 'God exists', of course, as a notable exception).

2 A note on terminology: "world-views", thin and thick

The beliefs in question are burdened with a terminological problem, and I should briefly address it early in order to avoid misgivings. Many speakers (in the German, but I think likewise in the Anglo-Saxon realm) tend to confine matters of "world-view"/*Weltanschauung* to issues in practical contexts like "what do you think about abortion/artificial fertilization/direct democracy/constraints of civil liberties to the benefit of the environment and/or future generations and/or public security/adoption for singles, female or male couples/assisted suicide/etc.?". "World-view" is here understood as a bundle of axiological, evaluative stances with high political and often religious relevance. The belief or disbelief in a God-like being, other religiously significant objects like the Virgin Mary, angels, or Satan, one's personal attitude towards the interplay between science and religion, or religious commandments and human rights may also count as instances of "world-view" beliefs in the "thin" sense. Likewise, "world-view" is sometimes understood as something you are likely to find in political manifestos, party programs, ideological guideline books, religious confession texts etc.[2]

I want to clearly point out that I am intending something different (or at least "thicker") here. The conception of world-view I am after is much more general and more theoretical in character. The world-view of persons provides the most general structure of orientation in our thinking, it provides an interpretation of all the manifold phenomena that we come across in our lives, and it guides our decisions and actions. Hence, it does not only contain the aforementioned "big" evaluative beliefs in political, ethical and religious matters, it comprises the trivialities of common sense as well. Much of it made up the object of traditional metaphysics, even if the average speaker would most probably not talk about it in terms of "substance", "accident", "efficient cause" etc. The aver-

---

[2] Naugle's (2002) otherwise valuable book focuses somewhat too much on these axiological/evaluative sides of world-view.

age, philosophically uncontaminated speaker is not even aware that such world-view beliefs are implicitly at work in his practice: they come to his mind, if at all, perhaps in non-standard situations where the usual, well-greased course of our thought and practice is being disturbed, like in situations of error, deception, and frustrated expectations. This circumscription might make clear why I would subsume the Moore-style beliefs mentioned before under the scope of world-view beliefs.[3]

"World-view" is not the only terminological candidate in town to single out the beliefs I intend. Widely used terms with a partly overlapping semantic scope are "world-picture", "descriptive metaphysics" (in the sense of P.F. Strawson),[4] "implicit metaphysics" (in the sense of Stephan Körner),[5] "conceptual frameworks", "hinge propositions" (in the sense of the very late Wittgenstein), and recently perhaps also "implicit theology". Nevertheless, I have a preference for the term "world-view / *Weltanschauung*" for two reasons. Firstly, it is crucial that a person has exactly *one* world-view, even if there might be tensions (like inconsistencies and incoherencies) and underdeveloped regions in it. This uniqueness is important since it is one and the same person that expects guidance and orientation from his or her world-view. "Hinge propositions" and "conceptual frameworks", to the contrary, clearly admit of plurality, and even "world picture" does so: It does not sound awkward that a person has more than one world-picture, e.g. the one of the sciences and the one of some religion. Secondly, I would like to retain a *certain* allusion to the practical, evaluative function of the beliefs in question, even if I sharply rejected the *purely* evaluative/axiological/politico-religious reading of "world-view" some lines above. It depends on your world-view how you act in certain circumstances. World-*view* preserves this practical, evaluative aspect better than "descriptive metaphysics" and "world-picture", which both sound like purely descriptive-theoretical stances (whereas you can have "views" on descriptive as well as on evaluative issues). "Implicit religion / implicit theology", to mention a further terminological candidate,[6] is perhaps misguiding in content: granted that every person (who is able to (more or less) understand his or her world and act in it) has a world-view, and that many utterly a-

---

[3] I tried to expose this conception of world-view and its relevance in ch.5 of my introduction to the philosophy of religion: Löffler (2006). My position there draws substantially from ideas that Otto Muck has developed since the 1960's; see his collection of articles in Muck (1999). For a recent English publication, see Muck's article "J.M. Bochenski on the Rational Aspect of *Weltanschauung*" (Muck 2012).
[4] Strawson (1959).
[5] Körner (1984).
[6] See, e.g., http://www.implicitreligion.org/journal.htm.

religious world-views will share points with religious ones, this does not mean that every world-view must do so. Moreover, "implicit theology" brings back the danger of reducing world-views to the "big" politico-religious questions.

World-views, to summarize loosely, are bundles of fundamental life-carrying convictions of a partly theoretical and partly practical character, which guide our orientation in the world and our evaluations, and which hence guide our thinking and acting. We shall come back to the structure of world-views in section 4.

3 World-view beliefs in RBG and WCB— and their ambivalent status

In WCB, there is a passage that at first glance seems to come closest to describing the role of world-view beliefs:

> What you properly take to be rational, at least in the sense of warranted, depends on what sort of metaphysical and religious stance you adopt. It depends on what kind of beings you think human beings are, what sorts of beliefs you think their noetic faculties will produce when they are functioning properly, and which of their faculties or cognitive mechanisms are aimed at the truth. Your view as to what sort of creature a human being is will determine or at any rate heavily influence your views as to whether theistic belief is warranted or not warranted, rational or irrational for human beings. And so the dispute as to whether theistic belief is rational (warranted) [...] is at bottom not merely an epistemological dispute, but an ontological or theological dispute. (WCB, 190)

However, at closer inspection this passage about "metaphysical stances" has more to do with "thin" world-view beliefs than with "thick" ones. It revolves around the ontological copestone of some world-views, namely the belief in a personal God and its consequences for our account of the human being and its cognition of God. These are of course high-rank world-view beliefs, but beliefs of a rather optional kind: some people share them, some do not, and removing or replacing these beliefs would leave wide regions of our world-view untouched. What this WCB passage is not talking about are the more common and (in a way) trivial world-view beliefs like "there are other minds". In this section, I intend to track the role of this sort of belief in Plantinga's work. Where do we find references to "thick" world-view beliefs across Plantinga's work?

Plantinga's early parity argument between our belief in the existence of other minds and belief in God was mentioned before.[7] This is the first prominent appearance of world-view beliefs in his œuvre.[8] A next crucial passage is in *Reason and Belief in God*, a key text in the development of Reformed Epistemology. (As far as I can see, Plantinga later on never retracted the positions uttered in RBG, and WCB may be seen as an impressive elaboration and epistemological refinement of the views delineated in RBG.) In RBG, Plantinga extends his attention to other world-view beliefs: not only the existence of other persons[9] is considered here, but also the existence of perceptual objects and of the past:

> Suppose we return to the *analogy between belief in God and belief in the existence of perceptual objects, other persons, and the past*. Here too it is relatively specific and concrete propositions rather than their more general and abstract colleagues that are properly basic. Perhaps such items as
>   (13) There are trees,
>   (14) There are other persons,
> and
>   (15) The world has existed for more than five minutes
> are not in fact properly basic [...]. (RBG, 81, my italics)

Notice that Plantinga's statement is somewhat open about the epistemological status of such beliefs: we are told that they are not properly basic,[10,11] but Plantinga also would presumably not call them inferential. And this is for good reason: it would be somewhat awkward to say that my belief in the existence of

---

[7] GOM. On this parity argument, its later career, and the relation between RBG and WCB see also Dieter Schönecker's article in this volume.
[8] Important sources of Plantinga's attention to world-view beliefs seem to be Reid and Hopkins; see Marsden in RBG 226, 235.
[9] I take "other persons" as the RBG sequel of "other minds" here. Whether there is a difference here, is not important for present tasks.
[10] Plantinga's central notion of the "proper basicality" of some beliefs, which comes in here, means, briefly summarized, that these beliefs are not relying on other beliefs for their justification and need not rely on any others. Sloppily expressed, these beliefs may just emerge in us in certain situations and it is OK to have them. This epistemological, justificatory sense of proper basicality is sometimes conflated with a psychological, descriptive sense: beliefs are psychologically properly basic if they just appear in us in certain situations and there is no indication for psychological malfunction. We shall come back to the question whether this basic/non-basic distinction is fruitful or not.
[11] It should be mentioned that on p.82 in RBG, Plantinga considers that it might perhaps be harmless to call them properly basic, but he adds a disclaimer: "even though so to speak is to speak a bit loosely". I take it that "loose proper basicality" is not proper basicality, since proper basicality is a Y/N-attribute which does not admit of degrees.

other persons would be inferred from beliefs like 'Emma is angry', or my belief in the existence of the past from my belief 'I had breakfast this morning'. The information content of the conclusion would clearly transgress that of the premise. (The prima facie promising way to propose that 'there are other persons' could be inferred from a *longer list* of beliefs like 'Emma is angry', 'Charlie is in pain' etc. would look equally artificial.) Typically, inferential beliefs are at roughly the same level of generality and abstraction as their inference-bases, e. g. 'Joseph is in his office' might duly be inferred from 'I see his car on the parking ground'. But the content of a highly general belief in the heart of our belief system cannot be inferred from a very particular one or even a long list of very particular ones.[12]

That our beliefs in the existence of other persons, perceptual objects, the past etc. can't simply be inferential may also be seen from the following consideration. Usually, the degree of certainty of inferential beliefs is smaller than or equal to their corresponding basic beliefs. This however does not seem to hold for our three belief examples in question: most people would assign higher certainty to 'there are other persons' than to 'Emma is angry' and the like.

Here is another consideration that goes in a similar direction: A local belief like "I had breakfast at 7" would not simply and by itself allow an inference to a world-view belief like "The world has existed for more than 5 minutes", but only provided that a whole lot of other world-view beliefs function as tacit premises: that there is world, that it is diachronically identical with the world at 7, that I am diachronically identical with me at 7, and much more.

Hence, we may note as an intermediate result that in RBG world-view beliefs appear more clearly as an object of epistemological consideration, but that beliefs like (13)-(15) are neither properly basic nor good candidates for inferential beliefs. Hence they seem to fall into another camp of beliefs.

In *Warranted Christian Belief*, we find a confirmation that these world-view beliefs are neither properly basic nor inferential. Plantinga first widens the list of examples again, by citing—as I take it, with approval—a passage from ch. 6 § 1 of John Henry Newman's *A Grammar of Assent* (1870):

> Nor is the assent which we give to facts limited to the range of self-consciousness. We are sure beyond all hazard of a mistake, that our own self is not the only being existing; that there is an external world; that it is a system with parts and a whole, a universe carried on by laws; and that the future is affected by the past. We accept and hold with an unqualified

---

[12] Uninteresting counterexamples to this claim are simple logical inferences like existential generalisation: from "97 is prime and between 90 and 99" we might infer that "there is at least one prime between 90 and 99".

assent, that the earth, considered as a phenomenon, is a globe; that all its regions see the sun by turns; that there are vast tracts on it of land and water; that there are really existing cities on definite sites, which go by the names of London, Paris, Florence, and Madrid. (WCB, 97–98)[13]

Plantinga immediately adds an epistemological reflection on the status of such beliefs. It confirms that such beliefs are not inferential:

> But how much of this can be seen to be probable with respect to what is certain for us? How much meets the classical conditions for being properly basic? Not much, if any. I believe that I had cornflakes for breakfast, that my wife was amused at some little stupidity of mine, that there are really such 'external objects' as trees and squirrels, and books, apparent memories, crumbling mountains, and deeply carved canyons. These things, according to classical foundationalism, are not properly basic; they must be believed on the evidential basis of propositions that are self-evident or evident to the senses (in Locke's restricted sense) or incorrigible for me. Furthermore, they must be probable and seen to be probable with respect to propositions of that sort: there must be good arguments, deductive, inductive, or abductive, to these conclusions from those kinds of propositions.
>
> If there is any lesson at all to be learned from the history of modern philosophy from Descartes through Hume (and Reid), it is that such beliefs *cannot* be seen to be supported by, to be probable with respect to beliefs that meet the classical conditions for being properly basic. (WCB, 98)

This passage needs some hermeneutic care, since it is primarily intended as a *reductio ad absurdum* of the "classical picture" (i.e., narrow-minded foundationalism in the style of Descartes, Locke, etc.). Nevertheless, it is obviously also Plantinga's own position that not only on "classical" criteria, but on *any* reasonable criteria these beliefs do not appear as inferential. But are they, hence, basic? On "classical" criteria they are surely not, but neither do they seem to be clearly basic according to Plantinga's criteria: Interestingly, Plantinga's list of examples for basic beliefs contains local beliefs as well as world-view beliefs. The examples 'I had cornflakes for breakfast' and 'my wife was amused at some little stupidity of mine' do not neatly fit with the world-view-like beliefs such as "the world was not created ten minutes ago".[14] This move back to more local examples for basic beliefs makes it appear as if Plantinga hesitated to call the exam-

---

[13] Newman's original text is available online: http://www.newmanreader.org/works/grammar/chapter6–1.html.
[14] Of course, 'I had cornflakes for breakfast' and 'my wife was amused at some little stupidity of mine' *imply* world-view beliefs about the existence of other minds and the past (with the caveat concerning such inferences mentioned above), but they are not world-view beliefs themselves.

ples of world-view beliefs basic. Likewise, in his subsequent examples for basic beliefs he again just mentions local beliefs: "I believe in the basic way that there is a lot of snow in the backyard just now and that I met my class yesterday; I don't believe either of these things on the basis of propositions that meet the classical conditions for proper basicality [...]" (WCB, 98). As far as I can see, Plantinga nowhere says unambiguously that the world-view beliefs are basic according to his criteria.

We may summarize that WCB leaves a somewhat ambivalent impression in regard to world-view beliefs. On the one hand, WCB is well in line with RBG, and we get some further examples of world-view beliefs as well as a confirmation: world-view beliefs are indeed neither properly basic nor inferential. On the other hand, the importance of world-view beliefs remains rather underexplored and their positive epistemological characterization remains open: if they are neither basic nor inferential, what are they? Or, to open a more general question, is the basic/inferential distinction perhaps misleading, after all?

4 Noetic structures and a collateral damage of classical foundationalism

Seen in itself, Plantinga's critique of classical foundationalism (or "the classical picture", in what follows "CP") is one of the most convincing parts of RBG and WCB.[15] As is well known, Plantinga develops arguments in order to show that the classical picture (a) is self-undermining since it can itself not be justified according to its own epistemological standards (since the basic tenets of CP are themselves neither properly basic nor properly based according to CP conditions) and (b) would leave a huge bulk of our most robust and unproblematic everyday beliefs in a highly dubious epistemological status. These arguments are doubtlessly a strength of the RBG/WCB position.

I want to show, however, that Plantinga's RBG/WCB position still involves a sort of residual bewitching by CP. Even if Plantinga is—duly!—an opponent of CP, he still seems to apply a tacit presupposition of it, namely the presupposition that the distinction between "basic" and "inferential" beliefs (or, more recently,

---

[15] It is another question whether anybody in the history of philosophy really ever fully shared this classical picture, and another story again whether classical philosophical theology really presupposes this classical picture, as Plantinga suggests. Especially in the latter point I would raise serious doubts; but a serious treatment of this problem would go beyond the scope of this paper.

and more exactly: "properly basic" and "properly based" beliefs) is sufficient and useful. It may be seen as a sort of collateral damage of CP (false as it is anyway!) that some basic assumptions of it even return in the thought of its most prominent opponent.

My point, however, is that this distinction between basic and inferential beliefs, even if it is regarded as mutually exclusive and exhaustive by many contemporary analytic epistemologists, is rather misguiding, since it seduces to analyze our belief systems in an unduly simplified (or "undercomplex", if a Germanism is tolerable and helpful here) fashion. A first hint that something could be wrong with the basic/inferential (or properly basic/properly based) distinction was the insight that world-view beliefs seem neither clearly basic nor clearly inferential, which was developed in the foregoing paragraph.

Another hint that the basic/non-basic distinction could be insufficient is the defectiveness of one of its derivative notions, namely Plantinga's rendering of "noetic structures". Let us hence have a look at Plantinga's analysis of "noetic structures" or belief-systems in the *Warrant* trilogy.[16] Interestingly, this whole notion of noetic structures remains rather pale and underexplored in WCB, and something similar holds for *Warrant and Proper Function* (where one would expect an elaboration of it, since it exposes Plantinga's own systematic views in epistemology).[17] The only explicit remarks on noetic structures or belief systems can be found in *Warrant: The Current Debate:*[18]

> Say that *S's noetic structure* is the set of propositions he believes, together with certain epistemic relations that hold among him and them. An account of S's noetic structure will specify, for example, which of his beliefs are basic and which nonbasic. It will also include something like an index of degree of belief, specifying, for each proposition he believes, how firmly he believes it. (We could add, if we like, that it specifies for each proposition to which he affords some degree of confidence, the degree of confidence he affords it.) Further, it will include, for any belief *B* that is a member of it, an account of which beliefs (and

---

16 One should add that a comparatively long passage on noetic structures had been contained in RBG (48–55), and that it even sketches a center/periphery distinction which I will endorse later on (RBG, 50). The examples mentioned there for beliefs in the center of a noetic structure are world-view beliefs. However, as far as I can see these achievements have not found much echo in the *Warrant* trilogy.

17 In WPF, the topic of belief systems primarily appears indirectly in ch.10 on coherentism.

18 They appear in ch.4 on coherentism, but they are a sort of general characterisation of belief systems preparing the stage for Plantinga's distinctions between coherentism and foundationalism. Hence I take it that the following quotation represents Plantinga's views and not just his rendering of coherentist positions; even if the second last period might sound like a coherentist addendum. A non-coherentist could easily subscribe to that period as well; he would just not take coherence as a (or: the) criterion for justification.

which sets of beliefs) *support B*, and the degree and kind of support they provide for it. It will also include an *epistemic history* of each belief, specifying the conditions under which the belief was formed and has been sustained, and a *deontological history*, which specifies for each belief whether it was formed and has been sustained in accord with epistemic duty. Finally, it will include a coherence index of the structure, which measures both the coherence of the structure as a whole and, for each of its members, its coherence with the rest of the structure. Still other properties of a noetic structure are relevant and important in some contexts, but I shall ignore them for now. (WCD, 72)

Of course, this description is intended as a reconstructive model and not a phenomenologically adequate description: the average, epistemologically uncontaminated speaker/thinker/reasoner can do (and successfully does) his cognitive business without ever caring about or even thinking of such structures. The guiding metaphor along which belief systems are reconstructed here is something like a list (or perhaps the file sheet of some databank software like Access): belief systems are basically long lists of beliefs with additional columns for their further attributes: "basic/non-basic", "degree of belief", "supported by what?", "gained how?" etc. But even taken as a model, this description has at least two blind spots.

Firstly, the model suggests an overall atomistic conception and does not sufficiently emphasize the network character of our beliefs. For instance, my strong (non-basic) belief that the temperature in Vienna at the present moment, July 26, 11.50 a.m., will not be below 10 Celsius, is supported by a vast, hard-to-survey mass of beliefs of manifold content: my memory belief about the weather forecast and my own perceptions when going out this morning; my geographical beliefs about the distance to Vienna and its altitude above sea-level, the shape of the globe and the landscape of central Europe; my climatological beliefs about the seasons in Austria and the course and usual speed of temperature changes during a day; these in turn are related to my beliefs about the chemical composition of the atmosphere, the behaviour of water vapour in the air, the declination of the axis of the earth, the effect of sun-radiation to surfaces, and so on and so forth. All in all, a network would be a more appropriate guiding metaphor for belief systems than a list. Of course, this network character *can* in principle be represented in the list model (provided the file sheets may get sufficiently huge), but the overall flavour of the model is rather atomistic: beliefs are isolated items coined by our cognitive machinery, based on other isolated beliefs (in the case of nonbasic beliefs) or isolated episodes of experience, memory etc. (in the case of basic beliefs).

Secondly, world-view beliefs seem hard to integrate into that model, since the only sort of "stratification" of beliefs which appears in the model is that between basic and non-basic beliefs. World-view beliefs, however, neither seem clear candidates for basic nor for inferential beliefs, as we saw in the previous section. The file sheet lines for world-view beliefs would contain lots of empty fields; e.g., what beliefs could reasonably support my beliefs that objects usually don't disappear or emerge, that time does not reverse its direction etc.? And when did I form these beliefs? Any answers to such questions would seem odd, nevertheless such beliefs enjoy a high degree of belief and confidence, and I don't seem to violate any duties by holding them.

5 Noetic structures: a refined model

What could a more sophisticated and more realistic model of noetic structures or belief systems look like, and where could world-view beliefs find their place in it?[19] Noetic structures display more stratifications than just the basic/non-basic distinction; even in a preliminary analysis one could distinguish at least seven groups of beliefs (the ordering principle are rough considerations of locality/generality; however, the question for the exactly right principle is not important here). To begin with, we have

(1) a lot of "local" beliefs concerning particular circumstances in our world. These beliefs may be basic ("I saw Emma just 5 minutes ago") or non-basic ("Emma is not in Spain"), and they may be more singular ("this cucumber is yellowish") or more generalizing in character ("my apple tree brought a rich crop over the last 15 years").

(2) Certain fields of these beliefs are governed by yet more generalizing theories, from everyday theories ("cucumber grows best in warm and sunny places", "garlic gets an unpleasant smell and bitter taste when roasted to strongly") up to scientific theories in the various disciplines. However, these theories alone will not do to solve our problems: we need and indeed have

(3) beliefs about the appropriate fields of application of our theories (which theory fits to what sort of phenomenon?), and we have

(4)—usually somewhat vague and unstable—beliefs about "collision/preference rules" for cases when different theories recommend different actions. E.g., when a commercial enterprise slides into a crisis, economic theories might recommend to set free one third of the workforce, whereas our everyday moral theories might consider this inacceptable. Any action carried out in this situation will display a respective (implicit) preference rule. Related with that, we have

---

[19] For the background of these ideas, see footnote 3 above.

(5) beliefs about the domains of objects in the various fields, and the relations and priorities between them. These beliefs are also usually vague and implicit. Most people believe, for example, in the existence of protons, molecules, cells and the like on the one hand, and in the existence of sugar cubes, pencils and persons on the other hand. If asked what "really" exists, the cells or the persons, the molecules or the sugar cubes, most people would provide some answer, be it vague, inconsistent or incoherent.[20] That there must be some beliefs in that direction operative can be seen in certain patterns of behaviour: e.g., someone who takes a medication for pain or depression obviously believes (at least in a vague way) that certain molecules exert an influence on the mental states of persons; this is a specimen of a belief about the relation between objects of different domains.

(6) There are beliefs (usually implicit, yet deep-rooted) about general traits of our world like its composition of relatively stable objects with somewhat variant attributes, causal principles, variants of the Leibniz principle, the principle of the regular course of natural processes, and perhaps some more. Finally, there are

(7) beliefs concerning a core or unifying factor in the world-view; this might be a theistically conceived God or something else, e.g. an venerable global process of nature, a hierarchy in the cosmos etc.[21] This core of the world-view assigns a place to all other beings assumed in that world-view, and it typically has some practical consequences (e.g., other persons might be seen as co-creatures and hence worthy of empathy and solidarity in a theistic world view).

I regard this as a more realistic model of belief systems or noetic structures since beliefs from various groups collaborate in manifold ways in the forming of newly gained beliefs. Especially beliefs from the "higher" groups (in my numerical ordering) are tacitly involved in the forming of beliefs in lower groups. E.g., my memory belief about my breakfast this morning involves beliefs about material objects, the course of time etc.; my belief that my children have eaten up all the eggs in the fridge involves my beliefs about objects like persons and their

---

20 They may vary from a kind of "folk reductionism" (a person is nothing else than a conglomerate of cells, which are in turn just a conglomerate of atoms or subatomic particles") to a kind of "folk antirealism" ("what really interests me are persons, pencils and sugar cubes, the rest are fictions of the scientists").
21 Such core beliefs of world-views may sometimes draw some of their content from beliefs at lower layers as their models; e.g., the experience of intact, benevolent human relations to caring parents etc. may provide a model experience for a theistic world-view, the fascination of research in natural processes may foster an a-religious, naturalistic core of the world-view, and the like. There is, however, no psychological automatism or determination in any direction. For a recent treatment of related issues, cf. Koltko-Rivera (2004). See also Körner (1984).

needs and habits, the regular course of nature, etc., or—to take a Plantingian example—a particular religious belief like "God made this flower" involves at least my belief about the existence of material objects and the existence of God. Spelled out in another terminology, we may say that a world-view has a guiding function and provides the necessary context and background in light of which we understand our world.

We may bracket the (difficult, yet minorly important) questions about the exact assignation of single, particular beliefs to one of these groups (1) to (7). But three other points are more relevant for our concerns: Firstly, it may seem clear now that at least beliefs from groups (4) to (7), perhaps also from group (3) may appropriately be called "world-view beliefs"; Plantinga's aforementioned example ('there are other minds') is obviously a member of group (5), and the belief in the existence of God is best assigned to group (7). Secondly, it is now easier to see why the basic/non-basic distinction was of limited utility: especially in the higher groups there are lots of beliefs which are neither clearly basic nor clearly non-basic (e.g., do we basically believe that changes have causes, or do we infer that from our experiences of change? Neither nor.) Thirdly and consequently, we now see why especially world-view beliefs seemed to elude the basic/non-basic distinction.

6 A side-remark: how to justify world-view beliefs

It may at first glance seem worrisome that world-view beliefs are neither clearly basic nor clearly non-basic. Does this imply that they are unjustified and hence irrational? Not at all. Instead of getting trapped by evidentialist ideas again, we should endorse Plantinga's (and Alston's) proposal that justification is not the only way to give beliefs a positive epistemic status. For world-view beliefs, as more or less fundamental beliefs, we may expect very special ways to bestow them their warrant. A more detailed treatment of this issue would go beyond the scope of this paper, so I just want to adumbrate one possible line of thought. Maybe it is fruitful to revive the old Aristotelian and Scholastic idea that certain fundamental beliefs cannot be proven true (in the strict sense of proving by inferring from external, indubitable premises), but just "defended" (however, in a quite convincing way): some world-view beliefs are so fundamental that even the attempt of their denial presupposes their truth. Aristotle famously showed this for the principle of non-contradiction (PNC): the opponent of the PNC utters his position (call it P) and by this he presupposes that $\neg P$ is false. Hence, he presupposes that P and $\neg P$ cannot be true at the same time. He has hence made use of the PNC in his very act of utterance. In a similar, yet somewhat less rigid fashion, the belief that our world consists of persisting objects with variant attributes could be defended: Someone who tried to convince me of the negation of this claim tacitly presupposes this claim: he talks to me and tries to change my opinions, i.e. he obviously distinguishes between me as a persisting object (whose opinions are in need of change) and my modifiable opinions as my attributes.[22] In a more loose way, one could show for most of the world-view beliefs in groups (3) to (6) that their warrant comes from their efficacy in structuring our experience and guiding our manifold cognitive activities, even if strict, presupposition-free proofs for them might be hard to find.

World-views have some rather intersubjective and some rather personal segments; especially the core of world-views has personal character and reflects, among other things, influences of biography and socialisation. This does not mean that world-views are immutable and beyond rational discussion. To the contrary: it is to be expected that world-views change and that they mature in the course of one's life. Usual occasions for such change and refinement are the confrontation with other world-views and experiences that are hard to integrate in the previous world-view. And there is a long tradition of at least defending the rationality of certain world views: classical philosophical theology, Plantinga's arguments in GOM, but also arguments in favour of naturalism and atheism are examples of it.

7 Warranted Christian belief in the refined model

What could all this imply for theistic belief in God or for Christian belief in particular? Theistic or Christian belief is clearly a central part of certain people's world-view, and it belongs to belief group (6). Where and how could it get its warrant? And in what light would my proposal put Plantinga's tenet that religious belief can be properly basic?

Let us start by a comparison with other basic beliefs, like simple experiential or memory beliefs. Even beliefs of that kind tacitly rely on world-view beliefs, which provide their context of interpretation and plausibility. Someone who forms his memory beliefs about his breakfast or his belief that Emma is angry also believes, e.g., in the existence of the past, of external objects, of persons and their minds in special, in regularities in the world, in patterns of behaviour

---

22 "Retortion" arguments in that style were widely studied around the mid 20th century, e.g. by Isaye (1954). For an English overview see Moleski (1977). They are still scarcely studied, but it would be well-worth investigating into logically and epistemologically up-to-date versions of this pattern of arguments.

etc.²³ Without this whole net of framework beliefs an isolated experiential or memory belief could not be formed and would have no information value at all. The apparent basicality of beliefs like "Emma is angry" or "I had cornflakes for breakfast" comes from the fact that this integration of experiential situations into our world-view framework normally runs tacitly and reliably. We need not draw any conscious inferences to successfully interpret situations like these. This tacitness and automaticity, however, does not mean that our world-view background beliefs would not be operative.

In principle the same holds for experiential situations of religious significance. If religious beliefs emerge in a person in certain situations (be it overwhelming impressions of nature, the attentive reading of the Scripture, participation in services, moral challenges, pleasing interpersonal encounters, or others), they do this before the background of the person's world-view beliefs: a religious interpretation of such situations must have a certain "default plausibility" in order to trigger such religious beliefs, and as a minimum condition, the semantics of religious talk must be sufficiently clear for that person.²⁴

In order to avoid misunderstandings, two remarks should be added: Firstly, I do not want to suggest that every religious belief is *nothing else but* a psychological product of personal interpretations, of a certain "religious way to look at things". My analysis does not preclude the possibility that some religious experiences are veridical, that they "really come from God". My analysis leaves open the whole spectrum of possibilities, from authentic religious experience to pathological cases. But the interpretation function by the personal world-view is operative in all these cases. Secondly, I do not suggest that having religious experiences presupposes previous religious belief. This would be implausible: There is, e.g., a credible stock of conversion stories from St.Paul to the present which suggests the contrary: religious experiences can be made by former non-believers and sometimes change their mind. But it is necessary that they roughly understood religious language before and basically knew how religious explanations work. This provides the necessary world-view background; religious experience does not fall on a *tabula rasa* in such cases.

What could be a benefit of this refined position? I think that a stronger attention to the world-view background of religious belief could help to neutralize

---

23 "Believing", of course, is taken here in the tacit, dispositional sense: you need not actually think of these contents, but on being asked about them, you would assent to them. I think that any plausible analysis of belief systems relies on this sense of believing.
24 I take Antony Flew's well-known suggestion to take a presumption of "A-Theism" as default hypothesis as a thought-experiment to create a world-view without any such semantic knowledge.

three recurrent patterns of opposition to Plantinga. The first two are the accusation of circularity (since theistic or Christian premises about the *Sensus Divinitatis* and the assistance of the Holy Spirit are crucial for Plantinga's epistemology) and the accusation of a certain arbitrariness: since Plantinga regards religious and Christian belief as properly basic, this seems to open the doors too wide for weird religious claims (this is often labelled "The Great Pumpkin objection"). Religious beliefs, so says a third line of criticism, seem too closely assimilated to simple, everyday experiental and memory beliefs. God however, so it is suggested, is very unlike the usual objects of experience, and it would reduce him to an intra-world object if he appeared as the object of single, experience-like beliefs.

There is perhaps some grain of truth in these objections. In light of my refined position, I think that Plantinga could answer them as follows.

Concerning the circularity accusation, Plantinga could frankly admit that the *Sensus Divinitatis* and the influence of the Holy Spirit are premises stemming from a theological anthropology. But the inclusion of such premises into an epistemology loses a lot of its extravagance when the role of world-view beliefs is taken into account: these theological premises belong to the world-view background of certain epistemic subjects, but every epistemic subject has *some* world-view beliefs in the background. (The defence of the rationality of such theological premises is of course another issue; Plantinga—in his "Defeaters" chapter of WCB—has a lot to say about it.)

Addressing the second accusation (that of arbitrariness of content), the world-view approach proves especially helpful: As Plantinga rightly claims, it is simply not true that any (and arbitrarily strange) religious claims can be equally warranted. It is, e.g., just rubbish to claim that the Great Pumpkin or Jupiter appear from time to time. In my analysis, this has to do with the necessary integration of religious beliefs into the whole of a world-view: The weirder religious claims are, the more they tend to violate commonly accepted beliefs on various levels of functioning world-views, e.g. well-entrenched scientific and common sense theories or well-entrenched ontological claims.

The third accusation of downsizing God to a sort of unusual object of experience would also lose some of its bite, for two reasons: Firstly, God is not only a special object of experience, he is also (and in the first place) an object in the core of a theistic world-view, and the belief in his existence is backed by various other segments of the world-view. Secondly, where religious experiences occur, they happen—like any other experiences—not completely isolated from other beliefs, but embedded into the interpretative horizon of a world-view, as we saw. These background assumptions function as a critical filter to judge the credibility of religious experiences (there is, e.g., a long spiritual tradition of "Discerning the Spirits" which reflects exactly this critical filtering of religious experiences before the background of other, reliable beliefs.)

To sum up: I have tried to shed some more light on an important achievement of Plantinga's early philosophy which seems to have lost attention in his later work: his rehabilitation of world-view beliefs. My suspicion is that in Plantinga's later epistemological turn his analysis of belief systems / noetic structures on the basis of the insufficient distinction between basic and nonbasic beliefs did not leave much room for world-view beliefs—they are neither clearly basic nor clearly non-basic and hence do not fit into that picture. An alternative analysis of belief systems, however, could assign them a plausible place. This might even help to answer some common objections to Plantinga's religious epistemology. There is, however, a (modest) price to be paid for that: religious belief, even experiential religious belief, might appear as psychologically basic, but in terms of justification it is not as basic as Plantinga thinks—it is always embedded into a network of world-view beliefs.[25]

Literature

Isaye, Gaston (1954): "La Justification Critique par Rétorsion", in: Revue Philosophique de Louvain 52, 205–33.
Koltko-Rivera, Mark (2004): "The Psychology of Worldview", in: Review of General Psychology 8, 3–58.
Körner, Stephan (1984): Metaphysics: Its Structure and Function, Cambridge.
Löffler, Winfried (2006): Einführung in die Religionsphilosophie, Darmstadt.
Moleski, Martin (1977): "Retortion: The Method and Metaphysics of Gaston Isaye", in: International Philosophical Quarterly 17, 59–93.
Muck, Otto (1999): Rationalität und Weltanschauung (Rationality and World-View), Innsbruck, Vienna.
Muck, Otto (2012): "J.M. Bochenski on the Rational Aspect of Weltanschauung", in: International Philosophical Quarterly 52, 63–78.
Naugle, David K. (2002): Worldview: The History of a Concept, Cambridge.
Plantinga, Alvin (1983): "Reason and Belief in God", in: Alvin Plantinga and Nicholas Wolterstorff (ed.): Faith and Rationality: Reason and Belief in God, Notre Dame, 16–93.
Plantinga, Alvin (1990): God and Other Minds: A Study of the Rational Justification of Belief in God, Ithaca, New York.
Plantinga, Alvin (1993): Warrant: The Current Debate, New York.
Plantinga, Alvin (1993b): Warrant and Proper Function, New York.
Plantinga, Alvin (2000): Warranted Christian Belief, New York.
Strawson, Peter (1959): Individuals. An Essay in Descriptive Metaphysics, London.

---

[25] I would like to thank Dieter Schönecker, Patrick Todd and Terry Walsh for numerous helpful comments on an earlier version of this paper.

Oliver Wiertz
Is Plantinga's A/C Model an Example of Ideologically Tainted Philosophy?

Ever since I began giving lectures in the philosophy of religion, I've treated Alvin Plantinga's version of Reformed epistemology, especially as found in his magnum opus *Warranted Christian Belief*. And every year, I'm challenged by students who express a distinct aversion to Plantinga's treatment of the epistemic status of theistic beliefs. This aversion sometimes takes very emotional forms. Quite often, accusations of "fundamentalism" or "ideology" are bandied about. Apparently, Plantinga's epistemology of religious belief strikes some students as an ideological justification of religious beliefs in the guise of philosophy, a position which is not only philosophically mistaken, but is also a provocation because Plantinga seems to be playing with the philosophical cards stacked in his favor. As a result, we usually don't make much headway during class discussions.

In the following paper, I want to investigate whether my students' negative reactions have any basis in fact i.e. whether Plantinga's epistemology of theistic belief is based on an ideologically tainted philosophy.

A principal difficulty in posing this question is the ambiguity and vagueness of the term "ideology" and its derivatives. Definitions and uses of the term "ideology" vary to such an extent that one gets the impression that "the same word serves to describe a variety of phenomena—not just a single one..." (Boudon 1988, 25). Correspondingly, theoretical reflection on the concept and the phenomenon of ideology is many-sided and confusing. "If one looks at the literature that exists on the concept of ideology and explanations of the phenomenon of ideology, then one is overcome by the irresistible feeling that above all there is a great deal of confusion." (Boudon 1988, 25)

Fundamentally, one can distinguish between a pejorative and a purely descriptive (non-evaluative) use of the term. Since evaluative elements are part of the meaning of the one expression, these two uses of "ideology" cannot involve the same concept, but rather the terms "ideology" or "ideological" must involve two or more different concepts.[1] Since my students were using the expression "ideology" in the pejorative sense to express their disapproval of Plantinga's position, I will focus in this present context only on the pejorative mean-

---

[1] The question of whether "ideology" is used equivocally or analogically is a question which can remain open in the present context.

ing of the term. But even then there is no uniform picture. Even Marx' and Engel's famous "The German Ideology" presents neither a coherent concept nor a developed theory of ideology.[2]

For my purposes I define the basic idea of the pejorative use of "ideology" as a divergence between the real underlying purpose of something and an ideology's intellectual justification for it. Characteristically, ideologies in this sense are not concerned with weighing the reasons for and against the truth of a belief i.e. not concerned with the search for truth, but rather about providing legitimacy for already fixed beliefs by providing them with an "intellectual alibi" (Thielicke 1958, 44). As a result, ideologies are not open to critical inquiry but try to avoid it at all costs.[3] Ideology thus bars our access to reality. Correspondingly, Hans Kelsen has defined "ideology" (in the pejorative sense) as "… a representation of the object which is non-objective, influenced by subjective value judgments, concealing, transfiguring or disfiguring the object of knowledge …" (Kelsen 2000^2, 111).

Ideologies have a practical function of achieving specific goals rather than giving priority to the epistemic goal of achieving knowledge.[4] A philosophy is ideological when it is not concerned with the search for truth by way of reasoned argument, but rather with a retrospective legitimation of beliefs which one is unwilling under any circumstances to subject to serious discussion. Philosophy is ideological when it takes the form of a rationalization of what in fact are irrational attitudes and beliefs by producing theories and arguments which are created solely for the purpose of justifying such irrational phenomena.[5] In contrast to deception or fraud, however, the ideologue is personally convinced of the truth of his ideology.[6]

On this view, a critique of ideology consists in exposing or unmasking the real motives behind an assertion or line of argument by reference to these underlying but hidden motives.[7] My students probably have the impression that Plantinga's theories and arguments are not primarily concerned with providing neu-

---

[2] Marx/Engels (1962^3) The "German ideology" characteristically describes the divorce between philosophical ideas and social reality; ideology is the illusion that ideas rather than material social conditions are the driving force behind historical change that serves to maintain the dominant social order and to which even the ruling class is subject; cf. Bohlender (2010, 41f.).
[3] Cf. Thielicke (1958, 46).
[4] Cf. Althusser (1968, 181f.).
[5] Cf. Vilfredo Sun Paretto's theory of "derivations", see Paretto (1970).
"Derivation" is Paretto's term for ideologies.
[6] Lübbe (1963, 15).
[7] However, such a critique has no implications for the truth of an assertion or the validity or soundness of an argument.

tral, rational philosophical analysis and argument, but are rather an attempt to provide legitimation to certain religious beliefs and defend them philosophically at all cost.

In Plantinga's epistemology of theistic Christian belief,[8] especially as developed in *Warranted Christian Belief* (WCB)[9], there are primarily three main areas which might be interpreted as corroborating the suspicion of ideology in the sense described above: the charge that Plantinga's argument is circular, the so-called "Great Pumpkin Objection", and the role of defeaters and internal defeater-defeaters (in the following abbreviated as defeaters[2]) in Plantinga's epistemology.[10] After providing a brief overview of the most important issues in WCB for the question under consideration, I will consider each of these three issues in turn.

1 A Brief Overview of Plantinga's Epistemology of Theistic Belief in WCB

In WCB Alvin Plantinga pursues two main goals: First, he wishes to contribute to Christian apologetics by showing that if the Christian faith is true, it is most likely in good epistemic order. Second, he wants to provide an epistemology of theistic belief from a Christian perspective, and in so doing make a contribution to Christian philosophy.

His starting point is the distinction between *de facto* objections to Christian theistic belief which challenge its claim to truth and *de jure* objections which challenge its positive epistemic status. In particular, Plantinga has in mind a version of the *de jure* objection which argues that theistic belief is epistemically defective and therefore unacceptable, independently of the question of its truth. Plantinga's argument is that this form of the *de jure* objection fails, because the success of any viable *de jure* objection assumes the success of the *de facto* objection.

---

[8] In the following, "theism" is used as a generic term. Unless expressly stated otherwise (especially in the context of Plantinga's so-called *extended A/C model*) no sharp distinction is made between theism and Christianity.

[9] I shall use the following abbreviations: FT = *The Foundations of Theism: A Reply*; RBG = *Reason and Belief in God*; WCB = *Warranted Christian Belief*; WPF = *Warrant and Proper Function*.

[10] In addition to these three issues, one could also explore Plantinga's remarks on the relationship between Christian presuppositions and autonomous science as a starting point for an ideological critique of his position.

Plantinga focuses on a form of the *de jure* objection which challenges whether Christian belief has warrant. According to Plantinga, warrant is that epistemic property which when combined with true belief produces knowledge. Central to Plantinga's notion of warrant is the concept of proper function. If a belief is produced by a cognitive mechanism that is functioning properly in accordance with a design plan directed at generating true beliefs, then this belief has warrant, if it is produced in the appropriate cognitive environment and unless it faces any undefeated defeaters.[11] How a belief is produced is crucial for whether that belief has warrant, but this does not mean that the epistemic subject who has the belief must know how it was produced or be able to show that the respective cognitive module that produced the belief is reliable. If all warrant conditions are fulfilled, then the degree of warrant for a belief depends upon the strength of that belief.

In a second step, Plantinga develops his so-called *A* (quinas) / *C* (alvin) model for the warrant of the theistic core of Christian faith. This model claims to be logically consistent and epistemically possible i.e. it is consistent with our current state of knowledge and is free from outstanding non-defeated defeaters. Plantinga holds this model to be true, but he does not claim to have proven this; nevertheless he believes that if the Christian faith is true then this model or some model very similar to it is very likely to be true. The A/C model says that God has created in human beings a *sensus divinitatis*, a cognitive module which reacts to various stimuli to produce (basic) theistic beliefs.[12] Since, by hypothesis, the *sensus divinitatis* is a work of God, it is reliably aimed at truth and therefore beliefs generated by means of it have warrant. If the Christian God exists, it is very likely that there is a *sensus divinitatis* or some similar capacity which is reliably directed toward truth and functions properly. In other words, if the Christian God exists, then it is very likely that as a product of the *sensus divinitatis*, theistic-Christian beliefs have warrant.

However, according to Plantinga's extended A/C model, the *sensus divinitatis* has been badly damaged (though not completely destroyed) by original sin. Therefore, because of the noetic effects of original sin, our *natural* knowledge of God is both limited in scope and damaged, distorted or completely destroyed.[13] But God does not abandon humanity to this ruinous condition; rather He offers them a way to salvation. In the life, death and resurrection of Jesus

---

11 In the following, the formulation "properly functioning cognitive faculties," includes the fulfillment of all warrant conditions.
12 Basic beliefs are not the result of argument. Properly functioning basic beliefs are beliefs that have positive epistemic status immediately (independently of evidence or argument).
13 WCB, 184, 186.

Christ, human beings are offered salvation. This salvation includes the restoration of the *sensus divinitatis* by the Holy Spirit, whose work in the believing Christian brings forth faith, in order that the Christian teachings proclaimed in the Bible can be understood and their truth recognized.

2 The Alleged Circularity of Plantinga's Position in WCB

Ideologies in the pejorative sense are closed systems in that the arguments they produce always presuppose what they are required to prove and thus are circular.

The charge of circularity has been sometimes raised against Plantinga's position in WCB.[14] To assess the strength of this charge, one must first clarify what exactly is meant by "circularity" because this is not always clear. At any rate circularity is a possible property of arguments and it counts as a fallacy. The most obvious case of a circular argument is an argument which is meant to prove p to someone not accepting p, using p as one of its premisses (i.e. "begging the question") or an argument in which one proposition is justified by reference to a second, and the second is justified by reference to the first.[15] Such arguments are not necessarily formally flawed (i.e. invalid solely because of their circularity).[16] But they are dialectically impotent, because they afford their conclusions no support. We expect from arguments for a certain proposition p offering the unconvinced reasons to accept p. But if the offered reasons contain or presuppose p, they won't convince S who exactly does not believe p. They won't possess any dialectical force. "If an argument is to be successful, the truth of the premisses must be admitted by both sides. When a disputant asserts a premiss, he is, therefore, asking his opponent to grant it to him (cf. "claim"). When he asserts the conclusion as one of his premisses, he is asking his opponent to grant him the truth of the statement whose truth has been questioned..."[17] Via circular arguments one can produce arguments for any odd claim.[18]

---

[14] E.g. Löffler (2003, 143).
[15] Cf. Mackie (1967, 177).
[16] The nature of the charge of circularity is not logical but dialectical or epistemic. "If the charge of circularity were logical and not epistemic ... all deductive arguments would be viciously circular." Psillos (2012, 42).
[17] Sparkes (1966, 462f., 462).
[18] Moser (1993, 4f).

An argument is a covertly circular argument for p, if its logical validity or the truth or epistemic justification of one of the premises of the argument assumes the truth of p without expressly stating it.

Evident and covert logical or propositional circularity are to be distinguished from epistemic-performative circularity.[19] Epistemic circularity is involved when the reliability of a belief forming mechanism or doxastic practice is argued for in a way that presupposes the reliability of that very mechanism or practice, because it assumes or relies on beliefs whose positive epistemic status[20] (in the sense of their probable production of true beliefs) depends upon the epistemic reliability of that practice or belief forming mechanism. Epistemic circularity consists in the "… commitment to the conclusion as a presupposition of our supposing ourselves to be *justified* in holding the premises …" (Alston 1996, 15). In this epistemic sense, the inductive argument for the general reliability of memory beliefs based on the fact that my memorial beliefs have been reliable in the past is circular because it assumes that I can *correctly* remember that my previous memory beliefs were reliable.

Is Plantinga's A/C model circular in one of the above senses and would such circularity justify the charge that the theory is ideological?[21] To answer this question I will consider the objections of two German philosophers of religion. Saskia Wendel holds that Plantinga's argument in WCB is circular because he attempts to justify one religious belief ("God has forgiven my sins") by the appeal to another religious belief (the existence of a *sensus divinitatis*).[22] Even if we leave aside the terminological vagueness of her objection (the A/C model is mainly not concerned with epistemic justification but rather with (possible) warrant), she overlooks that Plantinga's aim in WCB is not to prove that theistic beliefs such as "God has forgiven my sins" are *de facto* warranted. Plantinga does not argue from the (actual) truth of theism to its (actual) being warranted, but rather he argues that if theism is true, then theistic beliefs very likely have warrant. *Pace* Wendel, Plantinga does not need to presuppose the truth of theism or the existence of a properly functioning *senus divinitatis* to provide reasons for his positive assessment of the epistemic status of theism, since his positive assessment of its actual status does not play any role in his philosophical argument (although he is convinced that theistic beliefs do in fact have warrant).[23]

---

[19] On epistemic circularity, cf. Alston (1996, 15–17), cf. also: Alston (1996b, 271).
[20] In the following "positive epistemic status" serves as a generic term that includes positive epistemic concepts such as "epistemically justified", "rational", "warranted" etc.
[21] For Plantinga's answer to the circularity objection cf. WCB, 351f.
[22] Cf. Wendel (2010, 88).
[23] Plantinga considers it impossible to show that theism has warrant; cf. WCB, 169f.

The circularity objection raised by Friedo Ricken is more complicated. He describes Plantinga's approach as circular in the following way:

> ... It's hard to see how he [Plantinga; OJW] can avoid the charge of circularity. We can summarize his [Plantinga's; OJW] argument as follows: theism's epistemology is correct, therefore if theistic belief is true, it is possible to know God. But this evidently leads to the following circular argument: if theistic belief is true, then it is possible to know it is true. But the possibility of knowing it is true already presupposes that it is true (Ricken 2003, 26, my translation).

Ricken doesn't show that Plantinga's argument is self-evidently circular. Ricken seems to understand Plantinga as presupposing the truth of his theistic-based theory of knowledge (i.e. Plantinga's A/C model, with its hypothesis of a properly functioning *sensus divinitatis*) and it therefore follows that if theism is true, one can be epistemically warranted in knowing that God exists. However, in order to make the alleged circularity of Plantinga's argument evident, Ricken seems to assume that a theistic-based theory of knowledge presupposes the truth of theism; since Plantinga's A/C model involves theistic assumptions the positive epistemic status of theism does not non-circularly follow (only assuming the truth of Plantinga's theistic theory of knowledge) from theism's being true.

Using the following abbreviations: *TTE* (truth of theistic epistemology), *TT* (truth of theism) and *WT* (warrant of theistic beliefs) we can present Ricken's reconstruction of Plantinga's argument as follows:

```
1) TTE
2) TTE → TT          A/C model
∴ 3) TT              from 1) and 2)

4) (TTE & TT) → WT
∴ 5) WT              from 1), 3) and 4)
```

This argument is not obviously circular.

However, according to Ricken, 1) already presupposes TT. If one understands "presuppose" in its ordinary sense, this means that TT is a necessary condition of TTE. In this case you get the following reconstruction of Plantinga's argument:

```
1) TTE → TT          A/C model
2) TTE               from 1) (and 4))
∴ 3) TT              from 1) and 2)/
4) (TTE & TT) → WT
∴ 5) WT              from 2), 3) and 4)
```

This reconstruction is identical with the previous version and therefore not obviously circular.

If you understand "presuppose" in the sense that TT is a sufficient condition of TTE, you get the following reconstruction:

1) TT → TTE	A / C model
2) TTE	from 1) (and 4))
3) TTE → TT	
∴ 4) TT	from 2) and 3)
∴ 5) TTE	from 1) and 4)
6) (TTE & TT) → WT	
∴ 7) WT	from 4), 5) and 6)

This reconstructed version of Plantinga's A/C model is in fact obviously circular. However, it misunderstands Plantinga, and confuses two distinct epistemological projects in WCB with each other.

Plantinga's A/C model does not claim that an epistemically justified belief in TT (i.e., WT) presupposes any belief in TTE. I don't have to have *even heard* of a *sensus divinitatis*, much less Plantinga's A/C model, for my theistic beliefs to have warrant. It is only required that my theistic beliefs are (at least in part) the product of a properly functioning *sensus divinitatis*. Nothing more is required for WT according to Plantinga's epistemically externalist warrant theory and correspondingly, nothing more is required by his A/C model either. Therefore, the theist does not need arguments for the warrant of (at least of some of) his theistic beliefs.

On the one hand, WCB is an exercise in apologetics in the sense that Plantinga defends the possibility of properly basic warrant for theistic belief; on the other hand, Plantinga pursues the project (internal to Christian faith) of providing an epistemology of theistic-Christian belief.[24]

Plantinga's apologetic project in WCB is to defend the possibility of the A/C model and to seek to prove that in the case that theism is true, then it highly likely has warrant. For this project, he must neither presuppose TT or WT. By contrast, the project of providing an internal epistemology of theistic belief presupposes the truth of theism. This project is *theological* insofar a theistic-Christian theory of knowledge is a project internal to Christianity, and as a result, Plantinga can assume the truth of Christian theism.

However, Ricken's objection to Plantinga's argument can also be understood as follows: According to Plantinga, one can recognize the truth of theism in a le-

---

24 For other aims in WCB cf. Dieter Schönecker's article in this volume.

gitimate way only if theism is true. The truth of theism is therefore a necessary condition for legitimately believing that it is true.

"Legitimate" in this context can be understood in two ways:

a) in the sense of "alethically legitimate" viz. appropriate to something's being true; or

b) in the sense of "epistemically legitimate" viz. that a cognition is legitimate or justified if the resulting belief has positive epistemic status.

Interpreting Plantinga as saying a) would be trivial since it applies to every proposition and every type of knowledge. I can only appropriately recognize the truth of a proposition if that proposition is in fact true. "Legitimate" in the sense of b) is more interesting and relevant to the issue of circularity. Plantinga does in fact assume that one can legitimately come to know the truth of theism only if the A/C model (or something like it) is true, since he considers the arguments for the truth of theism too weak to justify an epistemically legitimate knowledge of its truth.[25] No obvious circularity is apparent here.

The suspicion of a *covert* circularity in Plantinga's argument might focus on Plantinga's hypothesis that his theistic theory of knowledge is correct only if theism is true. From this one might conclude that my belief in theism can only have a positive epistemic status, if the theistic theory of knowledge is correct and I know that it is correct. This would mean that if I am to be reasonably convinced of the truth of theism, I have to be convinced of the correctness of the theistic theory of knowledge, which implies in turn that I know the truth of theism. This would amount to a circle in that if I am to be reasonably convinced of the truth of theism, I must already assume theism is true.

However, the circularity of this reconstructed argument does not reflect Plantinga's position. Plantinga's A/C model does not claim that I have to assume the theistic theory of knowledge is correct in order to be epistemically reasonable in accepting the truth of theism. Indeed Plantinga does not require any meta-beliefs *at all* about the conditions for the positive epistemic status of my theistic beliefs in order for them to enjoy positive epistemic status. The only requirement is that these beliefs are (at least in part) the product of a properly functioning *sensus divinitatis*. Nothing more is required on Plantinga's epistemically externalist warrant theory and correspondingly, neither is his A/C model. Therefore, Plantinga's A/C model is not covertly circular.

However, this version of Ricken's objection suggests two other senses in which Plantinga's A/C model might be epistemically circular. I see two possible starting points for making that case:

---

[25] WCB, 170 can be understood in this way.

1. The epistemic justification of Plantinga's argumentation for a belief being warranted is that it is a product of a properly functioning *sensus divinitatis*, that is, a reliable cognitive capacity for knowledge of theism's truth. But this presupposes that there is such a capacity and that it functions reliably. However, in WCB Plantinga does not argue that there is in fact a properly functioning *sensus divinitatis* and therefore doesn't present any argument that could be epistemically circular.

2. The warrant for the belief that there is a reliable and proper functioning *sensus divinitatis* and therefore that belief in the truth of theism might be epistemically justified, presupposes that theistic beliefs are warranted and therefore the existence and proper functioning of the *sensus divinitatis*. In fact, according to the A/C model, theistic beliefs only have warrant if they are the result of a properly functioning *sensus divinitatis*. However, in WCB Plantinga does not assert that there is such a *sensus divinitatis*. And according to Plantinga's theory, the theist *need not* be convinced that a properly functioning *sensus divinitatis* for his theistic beliefs exists, in order for those beliefs to have warrant. Therefore, there is no basis in fact for the suspicion that Plantinga's position is epistemically circular in this sense either.[26]

But even if Plantinga's epistemology of theistic belief *were* circular, this would not imply it was ideological. The problem of epistemic circularity has plagued (non-skeptical and non-relativist) theories of knowledge since their inception.[27] So unless one wants to brand every (non-skeptical and non-relativistic) philosophical theory of knowledge as ideological from the outset, the presence of epistemic circularity will not be sufficient to support the allegation of ideology.

Yet these reflections on epistemic circularity point to another potential starting point for suspecting Plantinga's approach is ideological. An important aspect of defending Plantinga's A/C model and his theory of warrant against the charge

---

26 In a way Plantinga's entire Christian philosophy is epistemically circular in the sense that he presupposes that the possibility that our beliefs have warrant and the possibility of knowing that naturalism is false requires him to presuppose some form of supernaturalism since according to Plantinga, the conjunction of evolutionary theory (which he accepts) and philosophical naturalism (which he doesn't) is irrational. As a result, the probability that our cognitive faculties function properly and are aimed at truth under the assumption that evolutionary theory and philosophical naturalism are true, is extraordinarily low. See: WPF, Chapter 12. This kind of epistemic circularity, however, is not relevant to a possible ideological criticism of Plantinga, since if Plantinga's evolutionary anti-naturalist argument is valid, any claim to rationality and truth presupposes the truth of theism (on the assumption that evolutiontheory is true).

27 "Epistemic circularity has dogged epistemology from the time of the Greek skeptics, Descartes through Hegel's circle and serpent biting its tail ..." (Sosa, 1996, 303).

of circularity is the insight that theism's being warranted does not depend upon arguments for its truth / for its warrant. This could suggest however, that Plantinga's theory is ideological insofar as it frees theism from any requirement to provide rational grounds or answer to criticism.

3 The Great Pumpkin Objection

Another interpretation of the ideological objection to Plantinga is that his epistemology of theistic beliefs is overly lax by allowing (in theory) even fantastic and abstruse systems of belief to claim epistemic warrant but (in practice) limiting this epistemic liberality to theistic beliefs, unjustifiably excluding the beliefs of other religious or quasi-religious world views.

Michael Martin has objected that Plantinga's thesis that theistic beliefs are possibly properly basic is radically relativistic because any belief can be immunized from criticism by declaring it to be basic.[28] To be sure, Plantinga does not say that all beliefs which are taken to be basic *are* in fact *properly* basic. And from the fact that Plantinga holds theistic beliefs to be (possibly) properly basic, it obviously does not follow that any belief whatsoever is properly basic or that the epistemic subject's belief that his beliefs are properly basic necessarily means they have positive epistemic status.[29]

Warrant-basicality does not provide a belief with epistemic immunity either. Even beliefs that are properly basic or held to be so are subject to defeaters. According to Plantinga's warrant theory, a belief B for an epistemic subject S has sufficient degree of warrant, only if S is unaware of any defeaters for B or if S can defeat all known defeaters for B, and hence possesses a defeater-defeater (defeater^2) for B. Plantinga already addressed the concern voiced by Martin in his seminal essay "Reason and Belief in God"[30] under the section "The Great Pumpkin Objection" (hereinafter: GP).[31] The term is lifted from Charles Schultz's

---

[28] Cf. Martin (1990, 272ff.). For lack of space, I will abstract from the different senses in which epistemic subjects or their beliefs can be defective (or epistemically legitimate). I will not always be explicit about the kind of epistemic merit under consideration: whether the merit in question is warrant, a deontological understanding of justification, rationality, entitlement or whatever. I appeal to the goodwill of the reader to choose the most benign interpretation of the strongest reading in each case.
[29] Martin (1990, 272): "Plantinga's proposal would generate many different communities that could legitimately claim that their basic beliefs are rational ... Among the communities might be devil worshipers generated, flat earthers ..."
[30] RBG, 74–78.
[31] GP surfaces first in: Plantinga (1980, 49–63).

cartoon *Peanuts*. In the cartoon, Linus van Pelt, Charlie Brown's best friend, expects the arrival of the Great Pumpkin in the pumpkin patch every year on Halloween. The objection is that if theistic beliefs are properly basic, then on Plantinga's A/C model, Linus' belief in the appearance of the Great Pumpkin could also be considered properly basic.[32] Plantinga correctly responds to this objection by noting that even if theistic beliefs are properly basic under particular circumstances, it does not follow that they are basic under all circumstances or that other beliefs are basic under all, the same or different circumstances, respectively.[33] However, there is a question about the relevant difference between theistic beliefs and Great Pumpkin beliefs which allows Plantinga to distinguish between their epistemic statuses. What epistemically relevant *difference* is there between theistic belief and Linus' Great Pumpkin faith?

The assumption that theistic beliefs and Great Pumpkin beliefs have unequal epistemic statuses points at an ambiguity in Plantinga's formulation of GP (at least in RBG). Plantinga formulates GP primarily as if it's a question of whether (under certain circumstances) the possibility of properly basic theistic beliefs implies the (possible) proper basicality of all possible beliefs.[34] In some places, however, GP runs as follows: the possibility that even apparently absurd beliefs can justifiably be held as properly basic is inferred from the fact that theists hold some of their beliefs as properly basic.[35] The difference between the two formulations of the objection is not without significance. The second version of the GP is not concerned with the connection between the *fact (possibility)* that some belief B is properly basic and the *fact (possibility)* that theistic beliefs are properly basic, but rather about the warrant for the *meta-belief* M, that if theists hold theism for properly basic, then one can be equally justified in holding completely absurd beliefs for properly basic. This second issue is explicitly addressed by Plantinga in WCB under the heading "The Son of Great Pumpkin Objection" (SGP).

---

[32] In WCB, this objection is found in the following modal version: "if belief in God can be properly basic then so can any other belief, no matter how bizarre ..." (WCB, 344).
[33] Cf. Plantinga (1983, 74).
[34] In WCB Plantinga does not argue that theistic beliefs are actually properly basic, but that they are possibly properly basic and *in the case* of the truth of theism, are actually properly basic.
[35] "If we say that belief in God is properly basic, will we not be committed to holding that just anything, or nearly anything can properly be taken as basic, thus throwing wide the gates of irrationalism and superstition?"; RBG, 74 (underlining OJW). Cf. to the first formulation of the objection: "If belief in God is properly basic, why can not *just any* belief be properly basic?"; RBG, 74 (italics by AP; underlining OJW).

SGP in WCB is stated as follows:[36]

1) If it is epistemically legitimate to hold theistic beliefs as basic, then epistemologists of any community are epistemically permitted to hold the central beliefs of their community as properly (rationally) basic, no matter how absurd these beliefs are.

2) But it is not epistemically legitimate to hold any belief whatsoever as properly basic, regardless of how absurd it is.

3) Therefore, one cannot legitimately hold theistic beliefs for properly (rationally) basic.[37]

Some distinctions and clarifications show that even apart from the fact that Plantinga only claims that basic theistic beliefs *can* have warrant, this variant of the SGP is not a good objection to Plantinga's A/C model. It does not follow necessarily from the warrant of the claim that theistic beliefs can have warrant that the meta-belief of the Great Pumpkinites, viz. that their Great Pumpkin beliefs are properly warrant basic, actually has warrant. If the A/C model is correct, theistic beliefs have warrant *qua* products of the *sensus divinitatis* in a basic manner, but it does not follow that Great Pumpkin beliefs which are *not* products of a properly functioning *sensus divinitatis* are properly (rational) or warrant-basic.

At this point, however, perhaps the one decisive weakness of the A/C model and Plantinga's apologetic strategy centering on this model[38] becomes clear: Plantinga has no good (dialectical) reason[39] to accept the truth of central theistic beliefs. Correspondingly, Plantinga's remarks on the *sensus divinitatis* and the proper basicality of central theistic beliefs in his A/C model take the form of a conditional: *if* theistic beliefs are true, *then* they are most likely the products of a properly functioning *sensus divinitatis* and therefore have warrant. But the A/C model leaves open the following issues: the question of the truth of theism,

---

36 Cf. WCB, 345.
37 Cf. WCB, 345. As a *reductio ad absurdum* (and not a *modus tollens)* argument SGP can be formulated as follows: a warrant theory or a doxastic practice which allows you to hold obviously bizarre beliefs as properly basic leads to a *reductio ad absurdum*. With respect to his response to GP or SGP there is an interesting development to be found in Plantinga's thinking. If in RBG he attacks the first premise on the grounds that Great Pumpkinism is epistemically defective but basic, then in WCB he admits that at least in some respects, Great Pumpkinism is epistemically in order, and his criticism is directed primarily to the second premise of the objection.
38 I understand Plantinga's apologetic strategy as having two parts: one part consists in the rejection of the evidentialist objection by pointing to the possibility of having proper warrant-basicality for at least some theistic beliefs; whereas the second part is concerned to argue that the success of the *de jure* objection to theism depends upon the success of the *de facto* objection.
39 A dialectical reason for *p* is a reason which in a discussion is accepted by all parties as a relevant reason for *p*.

the reasons for the truth of theistic belief, and the reasons for believing in the existence of a properly functioning *sensus divinitatis*. As a result, it remains open which reasons speak in favor of the claim that theistic beliefs actually have warrant or are properly warrant-basic.

But if the question of the truth remains an open question in the A/C model, then it is unclear whether there is indeed *any* relevant epistemic difference between Great Pumpkinites and theists, because according to Plantinga, the crucial epistemic difference between Great Pumpkinism and theism is that there is a *sensus divinitatis* such that the beliefs produced by it are warrant-basic, whereas there is no corresponding cognitive module for the Great Pumpkin believer, a *sensus cucurbitatis* as it were. Thus within the framework of his Reformed Epistemology[40] (within the A/C model), Plantinga's apologetic project can not assume that there is any relevant epistemic difference between theism and Great Pumpkinism.

If one understands the main thrust of SGP as a good objection to Plantinga's apologetics of theistic faith to show that he cannot point to any epistemically relevant difference between theism and bizarre belief systems, and views the ability to cite a relevant difference as a *necessary precondition* for the rationality of the denial of the (possible) warrant basicality of bizarre beliefs, then it seems that Plantinga has no good answer to SGP.

Plantinga might argue that it is unclear why the theistic apologist should have any *interest* in citing any epistemically relevant difference between theism and Great Pumpkinism. In order to examine this as a possible response, I will introduce three hypothetical characters: the theist, Christian; the Great Pumpkinite, Linus; and the neutral observer between these two worldviews, Philo.[41] Linus and Christian hold key elements of their respective creeds[42] to be true and hold these beliefs in an epistemically basic way; furthermore, they are not aware of any other evidence for these beliefs, so that any warrant for these beliefs must be based (directly or indirectly) on their having been produced by a *sensus divini-*

---

40 This is true at least in terms of the apologetic aspect of Plantinga's Reformed epistemology.
41 Insofar as Philo's position is neutral between theism and Great Pumpkism (and other philosophical, religious and quasi-religious belief systems, such as naturalism), it represents the perspective from which Plantinga's apologetic project must be judged. Plantinga understands his apologetic project as a "contribution to an ongoing public discussion of the epistemology of Christian belief; it does not appeal to specifically Christian premises or presuppositions. I shall argue that, from this public point of view, there isn't the faintest reason to think that Christian belief lacks justification, rationality, or warrant ...", WCB, XIII.
42 The term "creed" will be understood as a collection of the central tenets of a religious or general philosophical community, the acceptance of which is required for membership in that community; for a similar treatment; cf. Swinburne (2005, 198).

tatis or *sensus cucurbitatis*, respectively. Furthermore, let's assume that both Christian and Linus are convinced that the warrant for their religious beliefs or worldviews fundamentally depends upon their having been produced through a properly functioning, truth-oriented, etc. cognitive module and that their beliefs have warrant, if they are true on the A/C model or, alternatively, the *L(inus) / S(chultz)* model of the Pumpkinite apologist, and that both view their (respective) models as epistemically possible. Finally, let's assume that the truth of theism and Great Pumpkinism are mutually exclusive and that Christian, Linus and Philo know this.[43]

What reasons does Philo have for granting theistic beliefs a higher epistemic status than Linus' Great Pumpkinite beliefs? Under the assumptions of our example (and Plantinga's Reformed Epistemology), it seems that he has *no* good reasons to do so. Since Linus' creed is incompatible with the Christian faith, on pain of inconsistency Philo cannot hold both creeds to be true, and since he does not have any good (epistemic) reason to hold one of the two creeds as more likely to be true than the other or one of the two creeds as more epistemically reliable than the other, then, unless he has additional relevant evidence, Philo should suspend judgment about the truth of the two creeds. Plantinga's claim in RBG that there is an epistemically relevant difference between theistic belief and Great Pumpkin belief because there is no Great Pumpkin and therefore no cognitive faculty which functions properly to produce Great Pumpkin beliefs etc.[44] is irrelevant for Philo since God's existence and the existence of a *sensus divinitatis* is precisely what is contested. From this perspective, there is no independent evidence either for theism or Great Pumpkinism i.e. evidence independent of the belief in their respective truths. Any attempt to privilege theism over alternative belief systems which are equally (internally) consistent, in keeping with our current knowledge etc. will seem irrational because it treats seemingly similar things differently.

If, however (at least) one of the two creeds must be false, and there is no neutral ground (i.e. in terms of the probability of the truth of one of the two faiths) to give one priority over the other, then it is not epistemically possible to exclude the truth of the pumpkinite creed which would imply the falsity of

---

[43] Great Pumpkinism can be considered a religion (or quasi-religion) similar to theism although there are differences between the God of theism and the Great Pumpkin, e.g. that Great Pumpkin is creator of the universe and possesses all compossible great making properties but does possess them neither essentially nor in an unsurpassable extent. In addition to all theistic attributes he possesses a predilection for pumpkins (because of the high intrinsic worth of pumpkins) and has the habit to appear to some of his devotees on halloween.
[44] Cf. RBG, 78.

the theistic creed. If the theistic creed should be false, however, the theistic hypothesis of the existence of a (universal and properly functioning) *sensus divinitatis* (and thus the A/C model) is questionable on two counts:

1. If the theistic creed is false, then there is no God and hence no *sensus divinitatis* created by God, whose deliverances can be trusted as reliable by virtue of its having been created by God. In this case, theistic beliefs are not only false, but have no warrant.

2. If theistic faith is false but nevertheless the product of a cognitive module that is at least functionally equivalent to the *sensus divinitatis*, then this module must function for the most part falsely, or its design plan cannot be directed toward truth or alternatively, it is not working in an environment for which it was designed etc. In this case also theistic beliefs are not only false but have no warrant.

Philo therefore has no reason to give preference to theism over Great Pumpkinism with regard to either truth or warrant. Viewed from his neutral perspective, there is no perceptible difference between the epistemic status of the L/S model and the A/C model, or between Christian's use of Plantinga's apologetic strategy such that if theism is true it has warrant such that a *de jure* objection against theism assumes the success of the *de facto* objection (or the stronger claim, which Plantinga does not argue for, that properly basic theistic beliefs possess warrant), and Linus' analogous application of this defensive strategy, or the stronger claim that Great Pumpkinism has properly basic warrant.

For Philo there is every indication that there is no discernable difference to the neutral observer that would make it (epistemically) impossible for Linus to adopt the theists' defensive strategy. That means that from the perspective of Plantinga's *apologetic* project, there is no difference between the application of his strategy by Great Pumpkinites and by theists. In this case, SGP (at least on my interpretation) has achieved its aim.

On my interpretation, SGP—perhaps it would be better to call my objection the G(rand) S(on of the) G(reat) P(umpkin) GSGP—is less concerned with the unacceptable epistemic permissiveness of the A/C-model or its epistemic principle; rather it shows that Plantinga's A/C model and the apologetic strategy associated with his theory of warrant could be taken captive by representatives of some obviously bizarre belief system, since one is unable to point to any epistemically relevant difference (from an apologetic perspective) in the way the strategy should be applied.

If the same apologetic strategy can be applied with equal apologetic force to the beliefs of Great Pumpkinism and theism, then this raises question what theism gains by this strategy. Plantinga could argue that his apologetic project is primarily concerned with clarifying the relationship between *de jure* and *de facto* objections and this goal is not called into question by SGP or GSGP. However, Great Pumpkinism, whose truth and warrant is incompatible with the truth and warrant of theism, also benefits from clarifying this relationship such that now two mutually exclusive religious (or quasi-religious) systems can both point out that, firstly, their potential positive epistemic status is independent of positive evidence, and secondly, the question of their epistemic status can not be answered independently of the question of their truth.

The fact that some[45] bizarre belief systems, such as Great Pumpkinism, can appropriate Plantinga's apologetic strategy to advance their cause, sheds a bad light on the strategies' epistemic value or utility. An epistemological and apologetic strategy that protects some (not all) absurd or bizarre belief systems from some (not all) types of objections (such as certain evidentialist objections), gives the impression of following a mere immunization strategy, from which even absurd systems can profit and use to their ideological advantage.[46]

A neutral observer (but probably also some theists) would probably recommend that Christian find a strategy which (regardless of the condition of the truth of theism and the falsity of Great Pumpkinism) can point to a relevant epistemic difference between Pumpkinism and theism, and so show that Pumpkinites can not use Plantinga's strategy with the same epistemic legitimation as the theist, so that his strategy is at least in principle immune to ideological abuse or misuse. However, in the context of Plantinga's Reformed Epistemology, this seems impossible or at least very difficult, which must leave theists as well as all Philo sympathizers unsatisfied.

Plantinga would perhaps respond that the theist/christian *qua* theist/christian knows that the Great Pumpkinite cannot apply Plantinga's apologetics or theory of knowledge simply because there *is* no Great Pumpkin and therefore no *sensus cucurbitatis*. But at least the neutral observer of his apologetic project should reserve judgment about the A/C model (and all other competing models) because there is a possible strong objection to its truth: the (possible) truth of Great Pumpkinism and the L/S model. And the question of the truth of the two competing models cannot be settled without recourse to arguments like those of traditional natural theology.

---

[45] I do not claim that *any* belief or system of beliefs whatsoever can adopt this strategy (cf. WCB, 350), but only that in addition to theism, *some* evidently absurd systems like Great Pumpkinism can.

[46] The possible counter-argument, that the abuse of a principle does not refute the principle itself, overlooks the fact that from the perspective of Plantinga's own apologetic strategy, it is not possible in *principle* to distinguish evidentially between the two.

Finally, from GSGP it follows that doubts concerning the truth of the A/C model and the warrant of theistic belief do not necessarily presuppose the belief that theism is false. Rather GSGP shows that a neutral observer need not deny the truth of theism in order to be justified in withholding assent about the truth of the A/C model as well as Plantinga's theory of the (possible) proper warrant-basicality of theistic beliefs, but that it is enough to suspend judgment about the truth of the theistic creed (or Great Pumpkin creed), which implies withholding judgment about whether theism has warrant and about the epistemic possibility of the A/C model. There does seem to be at least a "faintest reason" (WCB, XIII) for this suspension of judgment.

Our examination of GP, SGP or GSGP has not proven that Plantinga's apologetic strategy is evidently ideological. However, there is some reason to believe that it can be understood ideologically or abused for that purpose-especially if one plays down the importance of defeaters for the warrant or the lack of warrant of religious beliefs. I will conclude by considering this point.

4 Defeaters and Internal Defeater-Defeaters

Up to this point GP, SGP and GSGP have been considered from a perspective external to theism. But this is not the only possible perspective. SGP, GSGP and the underlying concerns that motivate them can also be formulated from a perspective internal to theism.

As we've described the situation, from Christian's perspective there are reasons for thinking that Linus is right, or at least that he is in an equally good or bad epistemic position as Christian himself. Suppose that Linus' other beliefs (i.e., the beliefs in his noetic system which do not belong to his Pumpkin creed) prove to be as reliable as the average person's, that there are no obvious internal inconsistencies in his Great Pumpkin creed, that it does not conflict greatly with the background knowledge he shares with non-Pumpkinites, and that there is no (ideologically neutral, i.e. dialectical) reason[47] to doubt the sincerity and seriousness of Linus' faith; in this case, are his Great Pumpkin creed and his epistemological model of the production of core Pumpkin beliefs (which are warrant-basic because they are produced by a properly functioning *sensus cucurbitatis*, the L/S model) as epistemically legitimate (e.g. justified or warrant

---

[47] In this context, an ideologically neutral standpoint is one which is independent of the truth or warrant of theism or Great Pumpkinism, i.e. beliefs whose propositional content, truth or falsity or epistemic status can be agreed upon in principle by all participants in the discussion; cf. WCB, 169.

rational) as Christian's beliefs on the A/C model and which (apologetically neutral) reasons does Christian have to postulate an epistemic difference between himself and Linus and to doubt the epistemic legitimacy only of Linus' Pumpkin creed and L/S model but not of his own creed and model?

Linus' Great Pumpkin belief would gain plausibility for Christian (via the principles of credulity and testimony)[48] if Linus was to sincerely claim that he had a religious encounter with the Great Pumpkin or if his experience could be understood under such an interpretation. However, since the truth of Linus' creed is incompatible with the truth of Christian theism, it is (according to Christian's A/C model) incompatible with theistic belief having warrant, because if the Great Pumpkin creed is true, then there is no properly functioning *sensus divinitatis* producing true theistic beliefs according to a design plan aimed at truth etc.

In this situation, Christian might ask himself what impact his knowledge of Linus' Great Pumpkin faith and Philos' assessment of the epistemic parity between Great Pumpkinism and theism should have on his own epistemic position. Under these circumstances, can Christian simply assume a decisive epistemic difference between Great Pumpkin faith and theism such that Great Pumpkinism is false and therefore without warrant? Formulated in contemporary epistemological terms: Does Christian's knowledge of Linus' Great Pumpkin faith and Philo's assessment of the epistemic parity between the two creeds constitute a defeater for his theistic faith?

A defeater provides a reason to give up a belief that one already has.[49] The belief D is a defeater (simpliciter) for the belief B of an epistemic subject S, if the proper functioning of S's relevant cognitive capacity requires that S give up B, if S's noetic structure contains D and the defeater function of D is not neutralized by any other belief in S's noetic system.[50] Whoever has a defeater (which is undefeated) for a belief can not rationally continue to hold that belief.[51] Defeaters do not need to be products of a properly functioning cognitive capacity nor do they need to have their origins in our rational capacities.[52] Even a belief that

---

[48] To these two principles and their religious and philosophical relevance, cf. Swinburne (2004², 322).
[49] WCB, XIIf.
[50] For Plantinga's notion of epistemic defeaters cf. WCB, 363.
[51] Cf. WCB, 357. Nearly every belief is subject to possible defeat. Plantinga, however, makes certain exceptions: for example, one's own mental states e.g. pain sensations, beliefs about one's own existence, perfectly self-evident beliefs and those which are held to be true with a maximum degree of certainty (WPF, 41).
[52] WCB, 363–366.

is not acquired by rational means can function as a defeater for a rationally acquired belief.

As a result of his encounters with Linus and Philo, Christian can ask himself whether it was he rather than Linus who was wrong about the epistemic status of his creed and its truth, i.e. whether his own creed isn't false or at least epistemically deficient.[53] Such reflections constitute a (potential) defeater for his belief in the truth and warrant of his theistic beliefs.

The (in Plantinga's view) apologetically justifiable belief in the mere *possibility* that his theistic beliefs are properly basic does not help Christian, since from the latter's perspective, nothing except for theistic convictions speaks against the epistemic possibility of the L/S model and the possible truth of Great Pumpkinism, and in this situation, Christian is no longer certain of the truth and warrant of his theistic beliefs.

But why shouldn't Christian simply assume the truth and properly basic warrant of theism and thus infer that Great Pumpkinism and the L/S model are false?[54] In this case, Christian would not weigh the reasons for Great Pumpkinism and theism against each other like a neutral observer, but take sides, although he has no neutral epistemic grounds (i.e. reasons that are independent of his theistic position) for preferring theism. The use of theistic grounds does not arise for him in this context, since he has called the truth of theism, and hence whether it is warranted, into question. That is to say, in this ambivalent situation he has no good epistemic reason to favor theism over the alternative, if he doesn't know of any independent reason to believe its truth. As a result, Christian cannot defend his choice by arguing that his theistic beliefs spring from an epistemic source which Linus lacks, viz. a properly functioning *sensus divinitatis*. Perhaps Christians' theistic beliefs are in fact the product of a properly functioning *sensus divinitatis* and his theistic faith implies that this is the case, but in his situation he cannot rely on this assurance because the truth and origins of his theistic creed is what he questions. This does not mean that

---

[53] Indeed two reasons speak in favour of such pessimistic thoughts. The first reason is theological in nature. It is the Christian belief that the sensus divinitatis suffers heavily from the cognitive consequences of original sin and perhaps even in a Christian is still in a very poor condition. The second reason is more epistemological in nature and is based on the fact, that every reflection on the reliability of some of one's beliefs and of one's epistemological capacities presupposes a basic trust in the principal reliability of one's cognitive capacities. But which reason allows me to withhold such epistemic trust from other people? If this is so the detection of disagreement with others lowers one's own epistemic trust at least prima facie; cf. Foley (2001).

[54] Christian's reaction would correspond to Plantinga's response to the original GP viz. that the difference between theism and Great Pumpkinism is that there is no Great Pumpkin and hence no sensus cucurbitatis; cf. RBG, 78.

Christian must deny that his theistic convictions have a special epistemic source which gives them warrant,[55] but only that in the situation he is in, he must withhold judgment about whether there is an epistemically relevant difference between the reliability of the source of his theistic creed and the source of Linus' Great Pumpkin faith.

But can't Christian call upon what Plantinga describes as the phenomenology of a "doxastic experience" (WCB, 111) or "impulsional evidence" (WPF, 192) to ground his theistic beliefs? A doxastic experience is a kind of experience that always accompanies the formation of a belief. It consists in the feeling that the belief is true and an experience which seems to compel acceptance of the truth of the belief. The assumption is that beliefs I have and hold to be true are accompanied by feelings different from the beliefs I hold to be false. Why can't Christian appeal to this experience as a sign of the truth of his theistic beliefs, arguing that he has no doxastic experience of Great Pumpkin beliefs, and that this constitutes an epistemically relevant difference between his and Linus' situation, which in turn is evidence of the falsity of Linus' Great Pumpkin beliefs?

The problem with this line of argument is that doxastic experiences are not an appropriate criterion for distinguishing true and false beliefs because they are too subjective. They do not consist in the fact that true beliefs "feel" different from false beliefs, but only that the beliefs which I *hold* to be true, "feel" different to me from the beliefs I *hold* to be false.[56] For any epistemic subject, doxastic experience is linked with propositions that are believed to be true.[57]

---

55 For example, Plantinga in WCB, 453.
56 Strictly speaking, one must say: *propositions* which I hold for true feel differently than those I hold for false. If doxastic experience is recognized as a criterion for truth, then *ceterus paribus*, all my present beliefs must be true, since all my beliefs are accompanied by doxastic experiences. But since not all my present, past or future beliefs are true, doxastic experience is no reliable indicator of the truth of my beliefs. This is evident by considering the following thought experiment: Assume that at time t I believe p but at time t_1 I believe non-p. P and non-p cannot both be true, but both p and non-p are accompanied by doxastic experiences at the respective times t and t_1. The proposition p (in contrast to non-p) does not result in a doxastic experience at t_1, but this is not an argument against the truth of p and for the truth of non-p, since the reverse is true at time t and perhaps at some time t_2. Or put differently, my doxastic experience is no reason for me to hold a proposition as true, but the doxastic experience associated with p is a consequence of my holding p as true (or my growing conviction of the truth of p).
57 One could argue that every form of arguing and reason depends on doxastic experiences in that I have no other reasons than my doxastic experiences for believing a certain proposition or viewing an argument as valid. Maybe, but especially in such controversial areas as in matters of religion one should search for reasons which do not convince alone me but also other people (who I value as rational beings) because this minimizes the danger of being mistaken and maximizes mutual understanding and confirmation or correcture between human beings. Perhaps

Therefore, Linus could equally well cite his own doxastic experiences associated with his Great Pumpkin beliefs, which challenge Christian's theistic beliefs (and Christian is aware of such a possible response by Linus). Therefore, there is no epistemic significance in the fact that Christian's doxastic experience is associated with his theistic beliefs rather than with Great Pumpkin beliefs, since this difference is trivial; it only suggests that Christian is (was) convinced of the truth of theism and the falsity of Great Pumpkinism—but it doesn't say anything about the truth aptness or epistemic status of these beliefs.[58]

Could Christian perhaps point to the strength of his basic theistic convictions and claim that the certainty of these convictions speaks for their truth and thus against the truth of Linus' Great Pumpkin beliefs? "Certainty" here can be understood in at least two different ways. First, "certainty" can mean the epistemic certainty of a belief i.e. the degree to which the belief is based on evidence.[59] However, according to the A/C model, the warrant for Christian's theistic beliefs is not primarily based on (propositional or non-propositional) evidence, but on the proper production of those beliefs by the *sensus divinitatis*. Therefore, only the second, subjective and psychological sense of certainty is at issue: In this sense, "certainty" is the degree to which I hold a belief to be true, or the strength of my convictions.[60] On Plantinga's model for meeting the conditions for warrant, the degree of warrant of a belief corresponds to its degree of psychological

---

even our ordinary arguments rest on doxastic experiences but these doxastic experiences are intersubjective—contrary to most of the doxastic experiences in religious matters.

58 Finally, it is questionable whether in the situation as I've described it, Christian's beliefs regarding the truth and positive epistemic status of theism are accompanied by the corresponding doxastic experience or whether, by contrast, his theistic faith now appears doubtful to him and leaves him "cold". Moreover, according to the extended A/C model, Christian, as a pure theist, does not have a *sensus divinitatis* that functions perfectly, but its proper function is damaged by the effects of original sin. If we assume that Christian is a Christian believer and that the Holy Spirit has restored his *sensus divinitatis*, then, according to Plantinga, the "restoration" of the damaged *sensus divinitatis* by the Holy Spirit does not happen in an instant, but occurs over a period of time, and thus one cannot assume that on Plantinga's extended A/C model Christian presently finds himself in the best possible epistemic position (since the work of the Holy Spirit is not complete) so that other evidence i.e. the differences in the religious convictions between him and Linus, Linus' sincerity in believing etc. might not foreclose the possibility that his faith is still relatively weak, perhaps even so weak that it no longer has positive epistemic status for him.
59 Whether "evidence" is understood as propositional or non-propositional can remain open here.
60 In this sense, I'm more sure that I'm sitting in my office writing this paper than I am that Shakespeare is the author of Hamlet.

certainty.⁶¹ Therefore, Christian might argue that the high degree of psychological certainty of his basic theistic beliefs constitutes a reason for assuming they have a high degree of warrant. If theistic beliefs possess a strong warrant, they are probably true and if they are probably true, it follows that Great Pumpkinism is probably false and lacks warrant. In this case, the high degree of psychological certainty of his theistic belief speaks for an epistemically relevant difference between theism and Great Pumpkinism. However, this argument assumes that Christian's theistic beliefs in fact have warrant, i.e. that they are the product of a properly functioning *sensus divinitatis*. The plausibility of this assumption, however, is precisely what Christian's knowledge of Linus' Great Pumpkin beliefs calls into question. In addition, it cannot be ruled out that even Linus' Great Pumpkin beliefs possess a high degree of psychological certainty for him and therefore Linus could argue in the same fashion as Christian—with the only difference being that for Linus this line of argument is used to defend his Great Pumpkin faith against theism and not vice-a-versa. Put somewhat differently: in this situation it is neither evident nor can Christian simply assume that his (probable) strong psychological certainty of the truth of theism is truth-tracking.⁶²

It seems that once Christian is aware of Linus' Great Pumpkin faith, he possesses a defeater for his theism that he can not easily refute. In some respects this conclusion is not surprising if we call to mind Plantinga's apologetic goal in WCB. He wants to show above all that the anti-theistic *de jure* objection is dependent upon the anti-theistic *de facto* objection. But it remains an open question what grounds the theist has for the truth of his beliefs and therefore for the epistemic distinction between theistic and Great Pumpkin beliefs. But if the theist cannot answer this question, he can not remove the suspicion of epistemic favoritism, viz. that theism and Great Pumpkinism are not being treated equally, even though he has no reasons or at least gives no reasons for this unequal treatment.

The theist is thereby subject to the suspicion of having violated the fundamental principle of rationality, viz. treating similar cases similarly, which also means (prima facie) treating what appears to be the same in the same way.⁶³ This

---

61 Cf. WPF, 47, at least if "degree of belief" is understood as "psychological certainty of belief".
62 This consideration speaks against Vogelstein's argumentation, especially his "Principle of Testimonial Evidence" in: Vogelstein (2004).
63 The rational principle of treating similar cases similarly and dissimilar cases differently requires criteria for determining what is "similar" and "different". However, in most cases, we understand the relevant sense of equal (unequal) treatment. If I'm considering the appropriate gift for a wine lover who is blind and has a penchant for Chardonnay wines, the sort of grape and

not only represents a possible violation of a rationality requirement, but it also moves dangerously in the vicinity of ideological thinking, since it unintentionally gives the appearance that there is a relevant epistemic difference between theism and Great Pumpkinism; but this relevant difference is only presented from a perspective internal to theism and can only be recognized from within it. As a result, Plantinga's presentation of the epistemic status of Great Pumpkinism seems to be "influenced by non-objective, subjective value judgments", which is Kelsen's definition of ideology.[64]

However, Plantinga could respond, that the considerations presented thus far ignore the distinction between intrinsic and extrinsic defeaters^2 or at least misunderstand the role of intrinsic defeaters^2.[65] Intrinsic defeaters^2 are beliefs that can be challenged by potential defeaters but defeat these because their warrant is greater than the warrant of the potential defeater in question.[66] Plantinga supports the theory of intrinsic defeaters^2 with his example of the missing letter.[67] Peter is a philosophy professor who writes a letter to a colleague in which he tries to bribe him into writing a glowing letter of recommendation on Peter's behalf for his latest research project. The colleague, however, indignantly refuses and sends the letter to the faculty dean. Soon the letter disappears from the dean's office under mysterious circumstances. Peter had the means, motive and opportunity to steal the letter and was known to have done such shiftless things in the past. In addition, an extremely reliable faculty member reported he had seen Peter near the dean's office during the time when the letter must have been stolen. The evidence against Peter is very strong and all his colleagues are convinced he was the perpetrator. However, Peter is in fact innocent. At the time of the crime, he distinctly remembers going for a walk in the woods and therefore believes in a basic way that he did not steal the letter. The evidence against Peter is very strong and all of his colleagues are convinced of his guilt. This evidence is also available to Peter and it constitutes a potential defeater for his memory belief. The only reason Peter has for holding this defeater for false is his memory belief which therefore acts as an intrinsic defeater^2. He has no addi-

---

color (texture, flavor etc.) of the wine is important, but not the color or design of the label. Whoever doesn't understand this, does not understand what it means to be blind and have a strong preference for Chardonnay wines (or what it means to choose an appropriate gift); or she suffers from a cognitive disorder which makes it unable to come to this conclusion.

64 Cf. Kelsen (1960^2, 111).
65 On the role of intrinsic defeaters^2 cf. FT, 310 f.
66 Cf. FT, 311: "When a basic belief **p** has more by way of warrant than a potential defeater **q** of **p**, then **p** is an intrinsic defeater of **q**—an intrinsic defeater-defeater, we might say."
67 Cf. FT, 310; WCB, 371.

tional defeater² independent of this belief. For Plantinga the case is clear: Peter is perfectly rational in continuing to hold his memory belief because the warrant conferred by this belief is greater than the warrant (conferred by the available independent evidence) of the potential defeater. Peter's first-person epistemic perspective is thus decisive for determining whether or not he has a defeater.

Analogously, basic theistic beliefs can act as intrinsic defeaters² because of their high degree of non-propositional evidence.[68] For theists, whose *sensus divinitatis* is working perfectly, even the problem of evil is not a valid defeater, but is "only" an occasion for perplexity and for questioning what reasons God could have for permitting terrible evil.[69] An important assumption behind Plantinga's story of the missing letter is the high degree of basic warrant and psychological certainty that Peter's memory beliefs have for him (or at least which he associates with them). This can be made clear by the following sequel to the story. Let's assume the case is never resolved and in time is forgotten. Meanwhile, Peter develops a scientific ethos, such that his past attempt at bribery appears to him as irresponsible, indeed reprehensible. To find why he let himself succumb to bribery, he undergoes psychoanalysis. Over the course of his therapy, he comes to realize that his desire for academic recognition was so strong that he not only attempted to bribe his colleague, but he also tried to cover up any traces of evidence that he had done so and suppressed any unpleasant memories of the fact or alternatively, interpreted them in a self-serving manner. Under these circumstances, Peter should rationally begin to doubt the reliability of his memory belief (and his innocence) regarding the missing letter. He should ask himself whether his recollection of taking a walk in the woods at the time of the crime is not simply an instance of his general tendency to suppress or falsify unpleasant memories. It would seem plausible to assume that by this time, the testimony of Peter's colleague—who saw him near the dean's office at the scene of the crime—represents an effective defeater for his memory belief that he was

---

68 WCB, 485, 489f.
69 WCB, 490. Another area in which Plantinga appeals to intrinsic defeaters² is the apparent conflict between religious belief and natural scientific hypotheses. He writes, "even if, contrary to fact, there were scientific evidence for unguided evolution and hence for atheism, that would by no means settle the issue. Suppose there is scientific evidence against theism: it does not follow that theism is false, or that theists have a defeater for their beliefs, or that theistic belief is irrational, or in some other way problematic. Perhaps there is also evidence, scientific or otherwise, for theism. But second ... if theism is true, it is likely that it has its own intrinsic and basic source of warrant... If so, the warrant for theistic belief doesn't depend on the state of current science" (Plantinga, 2011, 1–23, 15f.).

walking in the woods at the time (and hence for the belief he is innocent), and therefore his memory belief can no longer function as an intrinsic defeater².⁷⁰

To return to our three characters, whether Christian's theistic beliefs can function as an intrinsic defeater² depends essentially on its degree of basic warrant and psychological certainty. The question of the degree of certainty and warrant for Christian's beliefs cannot be answered with certainty, however, because the warrant for these beliefs depends on the extent to which Christian's *sensus divinitatis* is affected by the noetic effects of original sin or, by contrast, whether it has been healed by the work of the Holy Spirit, and this eludes human judgment. Instead, one can ask what degree of warrant it is rational for him to ascribe to his Christian beliefs.

If "rational" is conceived in terms of Plantinga's warrant approach, the rationality of Christian's assessment of the warrant for his beliefs cannot be determined with certainty because we do not know if Christian's assessment of the warrant for his belief comes about through a process that is epistemically reliable (and neither does Christian). By contrast, if "rational" is understood in the sense of internal rationality,⁷¹ then Christian's assessment of the warrant for his Christian beliefs depends not only on his own experiences (including his doxastic experiences) but also upon his other beliefs and the conclusions he draws from them.⁷² If Christian already has beliefs that from his perspective speak against the truth or the warrant of his theistic beliefs and if his relevant doxastic experience is relatively weak, then he doesn't have a high degree of internal rationality for his claim to have strong warrant for his Christian beliefs. For the sake of his internal rationality, he should not judge the warrant for his theistic beliefs as being very strong. In this case, Plantinga's analogy with the example of the missing letter breaks down. It seems to me that among intellectual christians in some modern Western societies, cases such as this are not that rare.⁷³

The situation of many contemporary christian intellectuals in Western society with regard to the degree of certainty of their beliefs seems rather like Peter's situation *after* his psychoanalysis. They are uncertain whether the potential defeater they have encountered doesn't point to the dubious epistemic status of

---

70 For a similar argument cf. Sennett (1993, 189–207, 195 ff.).
71 For Plantinga's understanding of internal rationality cf. WCB, 110–113.
72 Cf. WCB, 111 f.
73 Psychological certainty distinguishes theistic beliefs from more pragmatic types of beliefs that Plantinga sometimes mentions as paradigm cases of basic beliefs, such as memory beliefs, whose fundamental reliability we presuppose and whose justification or epistemic status we question more for academic reasons rather than from a genuine concern about their reliability. Cf. also Alston (1999, 238 ff.).

their theistic beliefs, or even to their falsity.[74] Many present-day Christian intellectuals are plagued by doubts and intellectual difficulties with their faith, not only of a superficial or momentary kind, but of a more profound nature.[75]

In our pluralistic Western societies "... all see their option as one among many .... We all learn to navigate between two standpoints: an 'engaged' one... and a 'disengaged' one ..." (Taylor 2009, 31, original; 12), and under the conditions of secularization not all, but many Christians, "... cannot help looking over their shoulder from time to time, looking sideways, living our faith also in a condition of doubt and uncertainty...." (Taylor 2009, 28, original; 11). The cognitive situation of Christians in the present seems to be more differentiated and difficult than Plantinga's remarks on Christian intrinsic defeaters[2] assume. In this situation of pluralism, Plantinga's apologetic approach seems more easily interpreted as ideological than in a situation of greater religious uniformity and certainty.

However, Plantinga argues that even if theism were improbable with respect to the rest of what the theist believes, and even if the theist's other beliefs offer only evidence *against* theism, nothing epistemically decisive follows from this.[76] He argues that there are many true beliefs which are improbable with respect to the rest of what we believe. Plantinga illustrates this point by the following example: When I play poker, it must be improbable to me, based on the rest of my beliefs (for example, that the deck has exactly 52 cards), that I have drawn an inside straight. But it doesn't follow in the least that it is irrational to believe that I've drawn an inside straight, because my warrant for the belief is not based on its being highly probable with respect to the rest of my beliefs, but it is rather based on sense perception.

But Plantinga's poker example cannot be easily applied to the case of theistic beliefs.

In a poker game, every player is dealt some combination of 5 cards (otherwise it wouldn't be a poker game). Hence the probability of the event type in

---

[74] In addition, it is unclear how many theists have had religious experiences that confer such a strong degree of certainty that defeaters simply bounce off them. Very few theists find themselves in a similar epistemic position to Moses standing before the burning bush (Ex 3,1 to 15), whose belief that God has spoken to him, according to Plantinga, could not be invalidated by any precursor to Feuerbach or Freud; cf. FT, 312.

[75] Even exemplary Christian believers like Therese of Lisieux and Mother Teresa of Calcutta suffered years of doubt and spiritual darkness (Plantinga cites in WCB, 491 from a letter in which Therese describes her "dark night of faith"). Their faith in these periods does not seem to be characterized by the steadfastness and liveliness which Plantinga characterizes as an internal defeater[2].

[76] Cf. WCB, 464.

which every player is dealt a combination of five cards is 1.0. Since every combination of cards is equally likely, it's possible to have any combination of cards (i.e. any particular token of the type that a player has a certain combination of 5 cards), since this combination is no less likely than any other combination of cards (the antecedent probabilities of the various combinations of cards being the same) and since a player must have *some* combination of 5 cards. Since the relevant event type (I have a combination of 5 cards) is highly probable, and the individual event tokens are equally likely, the sensory perception of the event tokens has, *ceteris paribus*, sufficient justification.

However, if the relevant event type is itself unlikely, or the individual event tokens differ greatly in their likelihood, my perceptual experience does not (automatically) provide me sufficient justification for the belief that a particular event token is present, or alternatively, the experience is more vulnerable to defeaters. If Hans claims that he has seen a UFO, we have good reason, based on our well-justified belief that the antecedent probability of the event type "encounter with a UFO" is low, not to believe Hans, although we otherwise trust his perceptual beliefs as generally reliable.

If Plantinga's poker example is to contribute to the question how theistic beliefs can respond to defeaters based on counterevidence, we have to determine the initial probability of events of the type "I met God," "I know God", etc. Assessing the probability of these event types in turn depends largely on how one accesses the probability, based on the available evidence, that God exists. The arguments of natural theology (and natural atheology) seem to me to play an important role in answering this question.[77] But if this is the case, then natural theology plays a more important role in the success of Plantinga's apologetic project than he thinks.

5 Conclusion

I conclude that Plantinga's epistemology of theistic belief does not represent a clear case of ideologically tainted philosophy. This result should not surprise those who have followed Plantinga's efforts to provide a plausible theory of warrant and warranted Christian belief, with all its modifications, responses, defens-

---

[77] Reasons for affirming God's existence should not be based directly on perceiving God since it is a matter of debate what sort of force such perceptions have in the face of (undermining or undercutting) defeaters. However, they might play an indirect role of providing cumulative or mutually inferential support for other arguments e.g. cosmological arguments from natural theology.

es etc. over the last several decades. For some, Plantinga's acumen together with his acerbic wit and hyperbole in dealing with objections to his theory or objections to the truth of Christian theism may occasionally give the impression that he is unwilling to take these objections seriously. However, this impression is mistaken. Less mistaken, it seems to me, is the impression that Plantinga at times appears to underestimate the concrete epistemic situation of many intellectual theists in contemporary, pluralist, liberal Western societies and consequently the epistemic starting point for an apologetic for theism. This also probably contributes to the suspicion that Plantinga's epistemology of theistic beliefs is ideologically tainted.

This limitation, and thus the potential starting point for an ideological critique of his position, is one which Plantinga can relatively easily overcome, since he is convinced that there are enough good, if not cogent arguments for the existence of the theistic God.[78] The fact that natural theology doesn't have to commit itself to a concept of proof as demanding as that proposed by Aristotle in the *Posterior Analytics*, viz. of deductive proof from self-evident premises, but that it can appeal to cumulative probabilistic arguments, has been shown by authors as diverse as John Henry Newman, Basil Mitchell and Richard Swinburne, each in their own way. By giving greater consideration to such forms of natural theology, Plantinga not only could more easily sidestep the charge of circularity, he also would have a plausible response to the Great Pumpkin objection and its assorted descendants, while leaving himself less exposed to possible suspicions and charges of ideology.[79]

Literature

Alston, William P. (1996): The Reliability of Sense Perception, Ithaca, London.
Alston, William P. (1996b): "A 'Doxastic Practice' Approach to Epistemology", in: Paul Moser (ed.): Empirical Knowledge: Readings in Contemporary Epistemology, Lanham 1996.
Alston, William P. (1999): "The Distinctiveness of the Epistemology of Religious Belief", in: Godehard Brüntrup/Ronald K. Tacelli (eds.): The Rationality of Theism, Dordrecht 1999, 237–254.

---

[78] Cf. Plantinga (2007).
[79] This publication was made possible through the support of the grant 15571 ("Analytic Theology") from the John Templeton Foundation. The opinions expressed in this publication are those of the author and do not necessarily reflect the views of the John Templeton Foundation. I am also grateful to Dr. Michael Parker for translating an earlier draft of this paper and to the members of the Berlin-conference for many helpful suggestions, especially Professors Löffler, Schönecker and Tapp.

Althusser, Louis (1968): Für Marx, Frankfurt/Main.
Bohlender, Matthias (2010): "Die Herrschaft der Gedanken. Über Funktionsweise, Effekt und die Produktionsbedingungen von Ideologie", in: Harald Bluhm (ed.): Karl Marx/Friedrich Engels: Die deutsche Ideologie (Klassiker Auslegen Bd. 36), Berlin 2010, 41–57.
Boudon, Raymond (1988): Ideologie. Geschichte und Kritik eines Begriffs, Reinbek b. Hamburg.
Foley, Richard (2001): Intellectual Trust in Oneself and Others, Cambridge.
Kelsen, Hans (2000²): Reine Rechtslehre, Wien.
Löffler, Winfried (2003): "Externalistische Erkenntnistheorie oder Theologische Anthropologie? Anmerkungen zur Reformed Epistemology", in: Ludwig Nagl (ed.): Religion nach der Religionskritik, Wien 2003, 123–147.
Lübbe, Hermann (1963): Politische Philosophie in Deutschland, Basel, Stuttgart.
Mackie, John Leslie (1967): "Art. 'Fallacies'", in: Edwards (ed.): The Encyclopedia of Philosophy III, New York, London 1967, 169–179.
Martin, Michael (1990): Atheism: A Philosophical Justification, Philadelphia.
Marx, Karl/Engels, Friedrich (1962³): "Die deutsche Ideologie. Kritik der neuesten deutschen Philosophie in ihren Repräsentanten Feuerbach, B. Bauer und Stirner, und des deutschen Sozialismus in seinen verschiedenen Propheten", in: Marx Engels Werke 3, Berlin.
Moser, Paul (1993): Philosophy after Objectivity. Making Sense in Perspective, New York, Oxford.
Paretto, Vilfredo (1970): "Die Derivationen", in: Kurt Lenk (ed.): Ideologie. Ideologiekritik und Wissenssoziologie, Neuwied, Berlin 1970, 217–225.
Plantinga, Alvin (1980): "The Reformed Objection to Natural Theology", in: Proceedings of the American Catholic Philosophical Association 15, 49–63.
Plantinga, Alvin (1983): "Reason and Belief in God", in: Alvin Plantinga/Nicholas Woltersdorff (eds.): Faith and Rationality: Reason and Belief in God, Notre Dame, 16–93.
Plantinga, Alvin (1986): "The Foundations of Theism: A Reply". In: *Faith and Philosophy 3* (1986), 298–313.
Plantinga, Alvin (1993): Warrant and Proper Function, New York.
Plantinga, Alvin (2000): Warranted Christian Belief, New York.
Plantinga, Alvin (2007): "Two Dozen (or so) Theistic Arguments", in: Deane-Peter Baker (ed.): Alvin Plantinga, Cambridge, New York 2007, 203–227.
Plantinga, Alvin (2011): "Science and Religion: Where the Conflict Really Lies", in: Daniel C. Dennett/Alvin Plantinga (eds.): Science and Religion: Are They Compatible? Oxford, New York 2011, 1–23.
Psillos, Stathis (2012): "Reason and Science", in: Christina Amoretti/Nicla Vassallo (ed.): Reason and Rationality, Heusenstamm 2012, 33–51.
Ricken, Friedo (2003): Religionsphilosophie, Stuttgart.
Sennett, James F. (1993): "Reformed Epistemology and Epistemic Duty", in: Elisabeth Radcliffe/Carol J. White (eds.): Faith in Theory and Practice: Essays of Justifying Religious Belief, Peru/Ill. 1993, 189–207.
Sosa, Ernest (1996): "Philosophical Scepticism and Epistemic Circularity", in: Paul Moser (ed.): Empirical Knowledge. Readings in Contemporary Epistemology, Lanham 1996, 303–329.
Sparkes, A.W. (1966): "Begging the Question", in: Journal of the History of Ideas 27.

Swinburne, Richard (2004²): The Existence of God, Oxford.
Swinburne, Richard (2005²): Faith and Reason, Oxford.
Taylor, Charles (2009): Ein säkulares Zeitalter, Frankfurt/Main.
Thielicke, Helmut (1958): Theologische Ethik II/2, Tübingen.
Vogelstein, Eric (2004): "Religious Pluralism and Justified Christian Belief: A Reply to Silver", in: International Journal for Philosophy of Religion 55, 187–192.
Wendel, Saskia (2010): Religionsphilosophie, Stuttgart.

Thomas Schärtl
Moderating Certainty

In *Warranted Christian Belief* (WCB)[1] Alvin Plantinga offers an interesting picture of human capacities concerning the knowledge of God. A brief sketch will get us the following layout: Human nature is equipped with a sense of the divine (*sensus divinitatis*), which allows the 'production' of basic propositions referring to God. And under the conditions of sin it is the Holy Spirit himself (IIHS) who readjusts the SD and guarantees warrant. In both cases, the religiously relevant propositions aren't derived from any non-theistic premises. Nor are they subject to any further questioning regarding their probability. This is good news insofar as even the cornerstone doctrines of faith can be 'known' and layers of mutually weakening probabilities don't water down their certainty. Given that an externalist account of epistemological challenges is sound, we are entitled to say that, under certain circumstances, human beings can actually have 'knowledge of God' since knowledge can be defined as 'warranted true belief' with 'warrant' replacing the unsatisfactory notion of 'justified'. Here is the good news for the Christian believer:

> Christian belief is properly basic, where the propriety in question embraces all three of the epistemic virtues we are considering. On the model, the believer is justified in accepting these beliefs in the basic way and is rational (both internally and externally) in doing so; still further, the beliefs can have warrant, and warrant sufficient for knowledge [...].
> (WCB, 259)

But *isn't* this picture of human capacities too good to be true?[2] And isn't the whole idea of a human nature equipped with a cognitive capacity that secures the 'production' of reliably basic beliefs a rather *theological* answer to a *philo-*

---

[1] I shall use the following abbreviations: WCB = *Warranted Christian Belief*; WCD = *Warrant: The Current Debate*; WCRL = *Where the Conflict Really Lies. Science, Religion, and Naturalism*; WPF = *Warrant and Proper Function*.
[2] If this were the essence of Plantinga's way to approach religious epistemology, it would be subject to Michael Levine's very harsh accusations stating that contemporary analytic philosophy of religion produces oversimplifying solutions to complex problems and furthermore doesn't even care about philosophical neutrality any longer but eagerly embraces certain denominational convictions; cf. Levine (2000, 89–119). Levine predominantly treats John Haldane's approach to the Bible, Peter Van Inwagen's remarks on the problem of theodicy, and Nicholas Wolterstorff's Divine Discourse. Still, his attack could be extended to Plantinga's religious epistemology insofar as it seems to blur the lines between theology and philosophy while burning the classic bridges between theology and philosophy: namely natural theology.

sophical problem?³ It is not just that the number of people who might be able to claim knowledge of God is fairly limited, even if it is permitted, from an externalist's point of view, to have knowledge without actually claiming it. Moreover it is hard to believe that in an area of great disagreement among individuals and cultures there might be even the slightest chance to gain knowledge. Well, the theistic externalist is in a position to explain the diversity of knowledge of God in two ways: 1) The complexity of the object (especially divine transcendence, infinity and God's character as a free agent) does not allow us to apply a simplified concept of gaining knowledge or even to have too high an expectation of the resulting amount of knowledge. 2) Even if we take the complexity into account, there might be a number of disturbing factors left, showing that we aren't always in favorable and suiting circumstances when it comes to knowing God. 3) There is no good argument from diversity, which could seriously threaten the externalist's approach. While 1) may be associated with William P. Alston's way of addressing the problem of how the experience of God is not universally instantiated or accessible in terms of a law-like regularity,⁴ 2) and 3) are along the lines of Alvin Plantinga's answer to the problem.

But I would like to show that 1) addresses a deeper problem of religious epistemology. It is a problem, which will force us to rethink the nature of faith in addition to the nature of certainty, while critically examining whether it should be our goal to gain knowledge of God in the first place. And as a result, it could also follow that strategies 2) and 3) cannot satisfy either. To get there, it might be helpful to refer to Immanuel Kant again and to his cornerstone argument, which basically says that the concept of God is beyond our pay-grade of 'serious' and conceptually unchallenged knowledge. While Alvin Plantinga focused on Kant's admittedly highly problematic notion of the *Ding an sich* and the story of *noumena*,⁵ I will point out that there are additional problems Kant hinted at, which are still worth discussing, even after one has admitted that Kant's combination of epistemological antirealism with some sort of empiricism isn't convincing.

Before I turn to the problem of certainty and concept-formation, I need to address some aspects of Plantinga's theoretical layout. For there is yet another, even more pressing problem attached to the above-mentioned picture of human nature: that human beings are capable of getting 'in touch' (let's leave the specific meaning of this phrase undetermined for the moment) is a conviction,

---

3 Cf. Löffler (2003); cf. also Mascord (2006).
4 Cf. Alston (1991).
5 Cf. WCB, 9–30.

which by itself is an integral part of a religious worldview. Nevertheless, it might be hard—if not impossible—to claim that this conviction is true, unless the overall (Christian) worldview is true. In other words: Does the proposition, which says that human beings are meant to have a *sensus divinitatis*, have to be a product of this very same *sensus divinitatis* in order to be reliable? This is precisely the moment when the circularity objection enters the picture.

1 Meta-Rationality

Although it is impossible to actually accuse Plantinga's Aquinas/Calvin model of being trapped in a vicious circle, there is something odd in the layout of his account, which at least somehow looks like a circle. Consider the problem Richard Swinburne has frequently pointed at:[6] Plantinga offers an argument *ex hypothesi:* if belief in God is true, it has warrant [T → W]. But what can we do with this? And how should any endeavor in religious epistemology proceed? Plantinga, as it seems, plays the modus tollens card, because from (T → W) and (¬W) we can derive (¬T); but what one can do—and what Plantinga actually does—is to show that there is no reason to give possible defeaters too much credit. In other words: There isn't a strong enough reason to accept (¬W) in a variety of cases: Neither postmodernism nor the plurality of religious belief-systems nor the problem of evil can create a convincing argument against the assumption that Christian belief has warrant. Such arguments may in one way or the other minimize the degree of warrant for a certain individual, but the opponent would not (necessarily not?) be in a position to show that these problems could ever destroy warrant generally, i.e. universally undermine the rationality of Christian belief. So any individual who believes (despite these defeaters) is, according to Plantinga, rational in doing so.[7] I am inclined to call this strategy a "Despiteology Apologetics" which rests simultaneously on a *Tu-Quoque*- and *Why-Bother*-Strategy. In short: whenever a possible defeater comes in sight, Plantinga seems to advise the Christian believer to stick to her guns, because she doesn't really have to bother, since the proponent of a defeater isn't in the superior position to deliver a good enough argument:

> The central question here […] is whether the Christian's beliefs are or are not on an epistemic par with the beliefs of those who don't agree with her. This is the crucial issue. If something like the extended Aquinas/Calvin (A/C) model […] is in fact correct, then there is a

---

6 Cf. Swinburne (2001).
7 Cf. WCB, 422–499.

> significant difference between the epistemic situation of those who accept Christian belief and those who do not; the objector is therefore assuming, unjustifiably and without argument, that neither that model nor any other according to which there is a source of warranted Christian belief is in fact correct and that there is no such source for Christian belief. This assumption has nothing to be said for it [...]. (WCB, 455).

Well, even at the risk of being blunt: Something has to be said here, because atheists usually do not just produce a mere assumption or a guess. They usually point to an argument which is, at least inductively, meant to raise suspicion. Some atheists would underline that there are sufficient hints which show that any religious believer has some pretty hard work to do in order to justify the rationality of her point of view: belief in God is rational *if and only if* there is some evidence for its rationality (R ↔ E) and in the face of lacking evidence no believer has the right to claim rationality (¬E → ¬R). In other words, a believer would have to produce some *positive evidence*. This problem is analogous to what Richard Swinburne said[8] when he pointed to the *modus ponens aspect* of Plantinga's working hypothesis (T → W): somebody has to start arguing *in favor* of T in order to derive W. Anything less would be like discussing the possibility of a fancy car to be the fastest automobile ever built without anybody starting the engine and pushing the pedal to the metal.

It might be that addressing these problems and being in favor of (R ↔ E) is like falling off the wagon of non-evidentialist sobriety. And indeed, Plantinga's despiteology apologetics could not in the least be as successful as it is if he did not make use of another tactic rather frequently. I'm inclined to call this his trump card of non-inferentiality, which has to back up the idea that theistic propositions are properly basic. As he wonders whether theistic propositions could be produced by natural mechanisms rather than by a *sensus divinitatis* and whether religious belief can be explained in purely naturalistic terms, Plantinga writes:

> The crucial point, here, is that on the model (and in actuality as well) theistic belief is not ordinarily accepted as an explanation. It is not that the theist sizes up what the world appears to be like (including the existence of theistic belief itself) and then proposes the existence of God as the best explanation of these phenomena. If that were how she was thinking, then the fact that theistic belief is explanatorily idle (if it is) with respect to some range of data might be relevant. But it isn't. On the model, the believer in God ordinarily believes in the basic way, not on the evidential basis of other propositions, and not by way of pro-

---

[8] Cf. Swinburne (2001, 206): "There is, however, a monumental issue which Plantinga does not discuss and which a lot of people will think needs discussing. This is whether Christian beliefs do have warrant (in Plantinga's sense)".

posing belief in God as an explanation of something or other. Hence the fact that there are better explanations of some range of phenomena (if there are) does not so far cast any doubt on belief in God. (WCB, 371)

The first part of the above-quoted paragraph sounds like a relief insofar as faith would not have to compete explanatorily with scientific theories.[9] Nevertheless, the second half of the paragraph sounds wrong or, to say the least, completely underestimates the complex situation of having faith in a postmodern and global setting. Actually, believers *do* want to know whether their faith is able to stand up to especially those theories that offer a naturalist's explanation of how the concept of God was furnished by evolution. Even if they do not want to enter the evidentialist's game of deducing theistic propositions from non-theistic premises, they still want to know whether what they believe makes sense. Their beliefsystem has to fulfill at least certain standards, which means that it ought not run against basic intuitions, which tell us how the world is, it should not be at odds with basic convictions in science or society (when those have proven to be close to the truth), it should not demand intellectual sacrifices etc.

To allude to a Davidsonian and to a Wittgensteinian term, we can presume: Not just a few believers want to know whether their faith is *rooted in experience*. Although being rooted doesn't endorse evidentialist inferentialism, it still says that these roots, under certain circumstances, have to be made explicit as propositions, which reveal the most fundamental intuitions people have with regard to the world.[10] As Ludwig Wittgenstein concisely put it: a believer does not seek explanation when she refers to God, but still she expresses an attitude towards any sort of explanation.[11] Within the Catholic tradition of natural theology, Bernard Lonergan emphasizes that the human relation to transcendence is an offspring of the more general *desire to know and to understand*.[12] While this version of knowledge and understanding is different from scientific understanding, it is still somewhat related to it insofar as it consists of knowing the faculty and process of knowing, and understanding the desire to understand. Consequently—for Lonergan—the concept of God is predominantly rooted in the human ability to (I am using my own words here) 'contemplate' existence in the light of the mystery of being. Is it really true that we will not find many religious believers who will

---

[9] For the layout of the theism-explanation-dilemma cf. Dawes (2009).
[10] Cf. Schärtl (2008).
[11] Cf. Wittgenstein (1990, 570): "Wenn der an Gott Glaubende um sich sieht und fragt 'Woher ist alles, was ich sehe?', 'Woher das alles?', verlangt er *keine* (kausale) Erklärung; und der Witz seiner Frage ist, daß sie der Ausdruck dieses Verlangens ist. Er drückt also eine Einstellung zu allen Erklärungen aus.—Aber wie zeigt sich die im Leben?"
[12] Cf. Lonergan (RP 2005²).

not evaluate their religious faith in at least some rudimentary form of the contemplation of being? Is the proper basis of theistic propositions indeed as basic as Plantinga wants us to believe? Aren't there at least some of those propositions rooted in the contemplation of the mystery of being?

As a matter of fact, reductionist 'explanations' of religion or religious experiences (take for instance Newberg's neuro-theology)[13] can be at odds with basic intuitions, which are an outcome of the contemplation of being. It is not just that these explanations may serve as possible defeaters; their true role is to possibly undermine the theistic propositions' status as basic propositions. But, as Plantinga does, to play the trump card of non-inferentiality in this context sounds to me like missing the entire point of any philosophical, let alone theological quarrel with reductionist ways of explaining the origins of religion.

Saying that there is nothing to explain here is 'cheesy', unless you can show —as, for example, the late Dewi Z. Phillips did—that there is the tendency and risk of misunderstanding religion once you start to *explain* religion. But you have to *justify* a non-reductionist view of religion, even if this is not done by an evidentialist course of arguments but rather by 'contemplating the phenomenon'.[14] The more classic approach, however, would be to show that a theistic explanation of religion is superior to a reductionist one; but this would have to be done using the tools of natural theology, or at least its surrogates (if one likes to include, for example, Kant's argument from morality in favor of religion).[15] To simply claim that those religious propositions are basic and therefore not subject to the business of explanation sounds like a trick which, at the end of the day, rather avoids the confrontation with any serious critique of religion. No atheist is going to buy the postulate that referring to the possibility-wise unrefutable claim that there might exist a *sensus divinitatis* (strengthened by IIHS) will be enough to establish the religious believer's entitlement to be considered rational; to the atheist the whole strategy might look like a sophisticated way applied by religious people to duck and to henceforth ignore the 'gunfire' of an enlightenment and post-enlightenment critique of religion.

Fortunately, Plantinga does not duck at all. Quite the opposite, his approach is an admirably sophisticated way to demonstrate that presupposing an externalist concept of religious knowledge is far from being irrational. Part of this eagerness can be detected where Plantinga spends quite some time to demonstrate that our cognitive capacities are not produced by evolution's blind procedures

---

[13] Cf. Newberg/Waldman (2006, 167–245).
[14] Cf. Phillips (2001, 4–8).
[15] Cf. for an initial discussion of the problem Zagzebski (1993).

and cannot completely be explained in naturalistic terms.[16] This argument, in my opinion, is much more important than Plantinga might admit, because it serves as nothing less than a renewed version of the so-called *alethological* proof of God's existence combined with an indirect version of an *argument from design* dressed up in the clothes of *an argument from consciousness*. As a matter of fact, Plantinga takes naturalism seriously and realizes that a reductionist's account of cognitive capacities indeed poses a threat to religious epistemology. Therefore, we need to have good reasons to trust our cognitive capacities so that we can suppose with some confidence that they are really aimed at truth and that they are, in one way or the other, capable of dealing with a transcendent God. Indeed, it is a requirement of rationality to evaluate whether or not naturalistic approaches are truly threatening. And Plantinga's anti-naturalistic argument is one impressive masterpiece of natural theology (and nothing less).[17]

I wonder, however, what kind of rationality this might reveal. Since Plantinga tries to furnish a sound argument, prepared by the two preceding volumes of his 'Warrant' trilogy, which are eager to prove that our cognitive capacities are aimed at truth and that externalism is superior to any other kind of epistemological model, his own rationality, as it appears on the pages of WCB, cannot be simply equated with warrant. There is nothing non-inferential about the different steps Plantinga has to take (and has in fact taken) in order to show that an externalist concept of knowing God is adequate and, even in the face of its presumably worst enemies (namely Freud and Marx), still unrefuted. So we will find in WCB a working idea of rationality, which is not equivalent with warrant. This idea mainly consists of the good old practice of giving good reasons for certain assumptions, although Plantinga drifts towards the impression that these reasons are good enough as long as there are no counterarguments, which can outweigh them. We could refer to this working idea of rationality, which couches several strategies to defend the idea of religious knowledge in terms of warrant, as *meta-rationality*. Meta-rationality of this sort is paramount for philosophy as a scientific endeavor. But, isn't meta-rationality precisely the version of rationality we should go for? It may be a relief for the religious believer to know that she is entitled to be treated as a rational person if her knowledge of God has a sufficient degree of warrant, but this very same person is, as our friends from the postmodern camp constantly remind us, an inhabitant of very different worlds

---

[16] Cf. WPF, 216–237. Cf. also WCB, 227–240; furthermore WCRL, 307–350.
[17] For further discussions of the complicated relationship between Reformed Epistemology and natural theology cf. Rehnman (2012).

(in a Goodmanian sense of the word).[18] For me as a religious believer it is not enough to rest assured that even the most intriguing defeaters will not harm me; actually I would like to have good reasons to think that my faith has a lot going for itself, especially in the light of a plurality of (Goodman-) worlds, which offer differing belief-systems. It is this very same version of rationality that we are seeking in religious epistemology and in fundamental theology: We want to have good reasons, at least we want to be offered good reasons to rely on, since the plurality of Goodman-worlds makes basicality a status that has to be 'earned' (even if this process of earning is not a process of inferring) and which cannot be presupposed or taken for granted.

2 Warrant Tracing Truth?

My appeal to *meta-rationality* becomes less disturbing once we look again at the layout of Plantinga's overall idea of defending his A/C-model—an idea which has for all propositions p related to the model in question: $T(p) \to W(p)$ with "T" signifying "true" and "W" denoting "warrant".[19] But since $T(p) \to W(p)$ is equivalent to $\neg T(p) \vee W(p)$, we are left with the troubling possibility that our (model-relat-

---

[18] A Goodman-world is, to my understanding, a holistic (but after all not completely closed) system with its internal semantic relations and its specific concepts. These relations and concepts result in different belief-systems rather than presupposing them; cf. Goodman (1978).

[19] This idea of a connection between truth and warrant seems to be alluded to in WCB, 188: "So if there is no such person as God, it is probably not the case that the process that produces theistic belief produces a true belief in most of the nearby possible worlds. Therefore, it is unlikely that belief in God is produced by a process that is functioning properly in a congenial epistemic environment according to a design plan successfully aimed at the production of true belief." In this case the formula must be read like this: $\neg T(p) \to \diamond \neg W(p)$; this is sound on the basis of the *ex falso quodlibet*. But then the opposite conclusion would be valid as well: $\neg T(p) \to \diamond W(p)$. The modus ponens version of the connection between truth and warrant can be found in WCB 188: "On the other hand, if theistic belief is true, then it seems likely that it does have warrant. If it is true, then there is, indeed, such a person as God, a person who has created us in his image […], who loves us, who desires that we know and love him. And if this is so, the natural thing to think is that he created us in such a way that we would come to hold such true beliefs as that there is such a person as God, that he is our creator, that we owe him obedience and worship, that he is worthy of worship, that he loves us, and so on." The formula we might extract from this might look like that: $\diamond T(p) \to \diamond W(p)$. As a matter of fact, given the implicitly significant modalities, this is a very careful claim. My main interpretation of Plantinga's approach sounds comparably optimistic.

ed) beliefs could have warrant even if belief in God is false.[20] The problem is not only that this sounds counter-intuitive; the mere obvious separation of truth from warrant remains puzzling.[21] For only within an extremely pure conception of truth, usually associated with metaphysical and epistemological realism, it might be possible that truth and warrant go separate ways.[22] But any other theory pointing at truth as a *result* of warrant *under ideal circumstances* would have to say that it simply cannot be the case that $\neg T(p) \wedge W(p)$, since "warrant" is too strong a notion. With $\neg(\neg T(p) \wedge W(p))$ being equivalent to $\neg T(p) \rightarrow \neg W(p))$ we arrive at the bi-conditional $\forall p\ (T(p) \leftrightarrow W(p))$.[23] Of course, this formula does not conflate truth with warrant; it just denies that they could go entirely separate ways. But what might this do for meta-rationality? Referring back to the bi-conditional, the answer is simple: Plantinga's overall strategy of rebutting possible defeaters to the ascription of warrant is only one part of the theistic job that needs to be done. The other part is to refute those atheistic or a-theological accounts that are eager to claim: $\neg T(p)$ or at least $\diamond\neg T(p)$. But then natural theology is back in the saddle, because in order to show that a-theology is untrue one must somehow show that it is true that a loving God exists, who might have equipped us with a *sensus divinitatis* or with IIHS.[24]

---

[20] Intuitively, I would go for the alternative: $T(p_1) \vee \neg W(p_1)$ which is equivalent to $W(p_1) \rightarrow T(p_1)$ so that $\neg T(p_1) \rightarrow \neg W(p_1)$ may be generalized as $\forall p\ (W(p) \rightarrow T(p))$ or $\forall p\ (\neg T(p) \rightarrow \neg W(p))$ respectively. This converse version of symbolizing the connection between truth and warrant would do justice to the idea that the *proper function* of our cognitive capacities, which is a necessary prerequisite of warrant, is aimed at truth. But, of course, from this angle even Freud and Marx, let alone Feuerbach and Nietzsche or, nowadays, Dennett and Dawkins could put a real threat to theistic beliefs.

[21] For a detailed analysis of the problem cf. Merricks (1995).

[22] It is this separation that would allow that our best explanations or our best theories, which deserve this attribute based on their degree of warrant, be completely wrong. But this is way too counter-intuitive. If we don't want to ridicule our cognitive capacities altogether, we cannot help but assuming that truth and warrant go hand in hand.

[23] Of course, one has to emphasize that there is a reasonable distinction between "being true" and "being justified". For I may be justified in believing that my neighbor is mocking me, while this is not true etc. However, as Plantinga has underlined in WCD and WPF, "warrant" wants to be more and better than justification. Warrant wants to replace "justification" and surpass it. Furthermore, "warrant" is meant to be applicable where justification fails or is out of place, i.e. in cases of non-inferential knowledge. So what is ok for *justification*—$(\neg J \wedge T) \vee (\neg T \wedge J)$, which is equivalent to $\neg(\neg J \rightarrow \neg T) \vee \neg(\neg T \rightarrow \neg J)$—might not be correct for warrant. For further discussions of warrant or—with regard to the standard definition of knowledge—any other crucial ingredient tracing truth, cf. Roberts/Wood (2007, 9–20).

[24] We could shoot for a disjunctive syllogism: $T \vee \neg T$, aiming at T through $\neg\neg T$. But is $\neg\neg T$ *adequately* served in just rebutting atheistic arguments? There needs to be more. However, Plantin-

This topic becomes even more crucial as soon as we approach how Plantinga deals with prominent critiques of religion, namely Freud and Marx.[25] Plantinga discusses Marx and Freud in the light of the question whether or not their approaches undermine warrant.[26] Plantinga is right in stating that Marx and Freud (among others) think religious faith is suspicious because it lacks warrant right from the start. But how would the Aquinas/Calvin model be able to make the Freud and Marx complaint 'futile'? How would that model help Christian believers to realize that their faith isn't a result of illusion, projection or cognitive facilities that aren't aimed at truth but maybe (to point to Nietzsche) at resilience or self-sustaining or to the simple amusement of our brain? Again we find two strategies: Plantinga *demands* good reasons why anyone should think that $\forall p \; \neg W(p)$. Since Freud and Marx are in no position to present evidence 'beyond reasonable doubt', their attack boils down to $\forall p \; \diamond \neg W(p)$.[27] Therefore, we don't have to take them seriously at the end of the day. The strategies performed here are, once again, a combination of *Tu-quoque* and *Why-bother*-tactics. Especially the latter is used to let Freud's so-called legacy fade away completely:

> Freud offers no arguments or reasons here at all. As far as I can see, he simply takes it for granted that there is no God and that theistic belief is false; he then casts about for some kind of explanation of this widespread phenomenon of mistaken belief. He hits on wish fulfillment and apparently assumes it is obvious that this mechanism is not 'reality-oriented' [...]. As we have seen, this is a safe assumption if in fact theism is false. But then Freud's *de jure* criticism really depends on his atheism: it isn't an independent criticism at all, and it won't (or shouldn't) have any force for anyone who doesn't share that atheism. (WCB, 198)

Well, Plantinga seems to play the 'Ex-falso-quodlibet'-card in addition to the above-mentioned strategies. But seriously, why would he demand solid evidence from Freud without delivering it himself? At the end of the day, all Plantinga seems to show is that there might be a *sensus divinitatis*, which might come from a benevolent God. But this theory needs to have something going for it before we can buy it and before Freud can be blamed for his atheistic attitude and prejudice. As long as theists just stick to a mere implication which says $\forall p \; (T(p) \to W(p))$, they do not really present anything else but an attitude them-

---

ga's theory of warrant wouldn't even have to care about the need to refute ¬T. Nevertheless, Plantinga cares—which is a clear sign of endorsing meta-rationality.

25 As Swinburne had pointed out, Freud and Marx aren't really the strongest and best paradigms of critique religion. It would have been way more interesting to deal with Nietzsche or Feuerbach; cf. Swinburne (2001, 212).
26 Cf. WCB, 152–153.
27 Cf. WCB, 192–198.

selves. And one must ask whether this sort of prejudice is rational? Is it rational to believe in the *sensus divinitatis* and its unique features?

Especially Nietzsche would have pointed out that our cognitive aims are a mixed bag; and nowadays neurosciences may give us even more evidence for that: it is not always truth we are seeking; sometimes it is *peace of mind* or consolation even at the costs of being delusional. Who can actually guarantee that the *sensus divinitatis* is really aimed at truth and not predominantly aimed at peace of mind or consolation,[28] delivering true propositions merely as byproducts of statements, which are meant to ease our existential tragedy or to cut off the edges of boredom that might appear to be the horizon of our restless mind?[29] But even if Plantinga still wants to hold that these considerations do not put any serious threat to our faith in the *sensus divinitatis*, we are not off the hook if what I have said earlier is right with respect to the connection of warrant and truth. Once we agree that this connection looks like this: $T(p) \leftrightarrow W(p)$, even Freudian atheism will threaten the assumption that religious faith enjoys warrant, because $\neg T(p_1) \to \neg W(p_1)$, which is validly based on the bi-conditional.[30] Therefore, the answer must be that religious faith *has something going for it*—something which is stronger than the weight of atheist attacks.[31] Again, this would be a plead in favor of natural theology, which will allow us to catch two birds with one stone: we might be able to give good reasons for the

---

28 The situation gets even more complicated, if we grant that cognitive capacities can be used in ways which may not count as malfunction but won't be reliable in terms of producing propositions that are aimed at truth. Cf. Steup (1995).
29 For reductionist approaches that need to be addressed compare Alper (2006); Broom (2003); Wilson (2002).
30 It is interesting to note that contemporary atheism feels entitled to this strategy and even provoked by Reformed Epistemology to use it; cf. Parsons (2007, 111): "In other words the atheist can turn Plantinga's argument upside down and argue that the fact that theistic belief is not warrant basically shows that there probably is no God! Further, when it comes to arguments questioning the rationality of theism, Marx and Freud are now the least of theists' worries. A number of recent works offer challenging naturalistic accounts of religious belief in terms of neuroscience, anthropology, and evolutionary theory [...]. If the arguments of these authors are cogent—and Plantinga gives no reason why they cannot be (unless we *presuppose* theism true)—then there is excellent reason to doubt that theistic belief is warrant basic, for such belief will have natural, non-rational causes—and not be caused by the proper functioning of a cognitive faculty designed to produce beliefs. If the rationality question is contingent on the reality question (and vice versa), as Plantinga claims, these arguments will be doubly dangerous. Arguments against the rationality of theistic belief now become arguments also against the truth of theism. Reformed epistemology does indeed have an ironic conclusion: Its net effect is to multiply the arguments against the existence of God."
31 Cf. Parsons (1990).

existence of a benevolent God and, along the way, find a number of good reasons why to trust the *sensus divinitatis* is reasonable, although we are aware of the mixed-bag situation of our cognitive aims. And this is precisely the business of meta-rationality discussions.

3 Barthianism in Disguise?

Plantinga's God is the God of post-reformation traditions: it is a God of mercy and justice, grace and punishment, love and decision. It is this God the *sensus divinitatis* is meant to refer to. But let us use our imagination for a moment: Let us enter a time-machine which brings us back to the year 360 B.C. around the time when famous Greek philosopher Plato might have finished the final touch-ups of his dialogue *Timaios*. Invited to the academy, we might learn more about Plato's interesting concept of God, a God who made all things, but who clearly did not create them from nothingness, because his making is bound to coping with primary matter, a God, furthermore, who lacks omnipotence, since he is subordinate to the realm of ideas and their eternal beauty, which he seeks to imitate in his making procedures. From the outside, this realm of ideas looks even more divine than a God who serves as a maker of all earthly things.[32] As you can see, Plato's God is crucially different from the God of Christianity. Plato's God is interested in harmony, truth, and justice; but he doesn't demand worship and doesn't really care about our love. Clearly, for ourselves as Christian time-travelers, we would ascribe warrant to our concept of God. But it would be awkward to ascribe the same degree of warrant to Plato's concept of God, although we might grant Plato's concept a considerable amount of rationality.

But how could Plantinga's concept deal with such a concession? If we look at the situation as a result of religious pluralism, the Christian's degree of warrant could be increased or diminished, either way.[33] Apparently, the impact the

---

[32] Cf. Bordt (2006, 177–180).
[33] Cf. WCB, 456f. My guess would be that Plantinga did intend to have objective standards of warrant. But if the act of belief (which may or may not be affected by defeaters) plays into the degree of warrant, there will be an unavoidably subjective side to warrant. This will have two painful consequences: 1) The subjective aspect can and, to my estimation, will undermine the externalist notion of warrant which claims to untie knowledge from predominantly subjective (especially inner-subjective) aspects of knowing. 2) A stubborn believer (who might be wrong all the way down but who is stubborn enough not to be affected by it) may have more warrant and therefore be entitled to be more rational than, in comparison, a doubting believer.

mere existence of an alternative worldview has on us is, according to Plantinga, an impact on our degree of warrant. But is there a chance to grant Plato warrant? From the viewpoint of pure metaphysics, nobody can seriously deny that Plato in fact has developed a sophisticated concept of God, who is meant to mediate between eternal truths on the one side and contingent existence on the other side. Furthermore this concept gives us a very powerful understanding of why there is a gap between universals and their instantiations. But from a post-reformation Christian point of view Plato's concept looks deficient. Did Plato lack the *sensus dvinitatis* or IIHS? And if so, why did he? Didn't he meet certain (moral?) requirements to be infused with IIHS? Or was this '*remedium ignorantiae*' not available before incarnation? From the viewpoint of 'pure reason' Plato is rational in sticking to his concept of God, because it is developed from accessible metaphysical principles. And especially this concept of God may count as a result of what we earlier have called the contemplation of being. As a matter of fact, for quite a few medieval theologians (take Peter Abaelard for instance)[34] Plato's concept of God was one framework to start from. Medieval scholars were convinced that the Christian God must meet certain metaphysical standards even in surpassing the Platonic concept of a mediator-God at a certain point. Hence, for some medieval theologians Plato's concept did have a very high degree of warrant. And to justify this, it was enough to refer to the rather general capacities of human reasoning without feeling an urge to postulate the existence of a *sensus divinitatis*. But how could that be? In Plantinga's picture, appealing to pure reason is as problematic as dangerous; it can never guarantee the proper basicality of theistic propositions and, therefore, cannot safely lead to knowledge of God. Without being assured of the *sensus divinitatis* at work, Plato's concept of God might just remain guesswork. But would that not be a rather chauvinistic Christian position? Against possibly charging the time-travelling Christian of being egoistic and self-centered, Plantinga might say the following:

> She may agree that she and those who dissent are equally convinced of the truth of their belief, and even that they are internally on par, that the internally available markers are similar, or relevantly similar. Still, she must think that there is an important epistemic difference: she thinks that somehow the other person has made a mistake, or has a blind spot, or hasn't been wholly attentive, or hasn't received some grace she has, or is blinded by ambition or pride [...] or something else; she must think that she has access to a source of war-

---

But this would spit in the face even of an everyday concept of rationality. If what Plantinga says about the impact of the strength of personal belief in warrant is true, then warrant cannot be meant to replace either being justified or being rational. For comparable discussions cf. Zagzebski (1998², 326–329). For further aspects of this problem cf. Zeis (1998).
34 Cf. Abaelard (1997, 5–6).

ranted belief the other lacks. If the believer concedes that she *doesn't* have any special source of knowledge or true belief with respect to Christian belief—no *sensus divinitatis*, no internal instigation of the Holy Spirit, no teaching by a church inspired and protected from error by the Holy Spirit, nothing not available to those who disagree with her—then, perhaps, she can properly be charged with an arbitrary egoism, and then, perhaps, she will have a defeater for her Christian belief. But why should she concede these things? She will ordinarily think (or at least *should* ordinarily think) that there are indeed sources of warranted belief that issue in these beliefs. (WCB, 453).

In this paragraph Alvin Plantinga very clearly reveals that his concept of a *sensus divinitatis* is plain Barthianism in disguise. Let's name it: what in fact makes the Christian believer superior to a non-Christian believer is *revelation*. As long as she can count on revelation as an additional source to gain knowledge, she has the right not to be ashamed of feeling superior. I have to admit that this is an attractive position *theologically*; nevertheless, *philosophically* it is disastrous, because the appeal to revelation does no good in the philosophers' rule-books. It is simply leaving the soccer game of rational discourse in suddenly applying the bully rules of American football by introducing God and the Holy Spirit himself as quarterback. A stubborn philosopher might still remain unconvinced and raise the question whether the Holy Bible or the teaching of the church—sources of warrant Plantinga was referring to—are trustworthy. Well, if there is a God, they may be trustworthy; if there is no God, they are liars all the way down. Again, we are left with the cornerstone question whether we have good reason to believe that there is a God. And we would have to try to fulfill the even harder task to demonstrate that the God who is responsible for the *sensus divinitatis* has more going for himself than Plato's God (for anyone interested in how this might be carried out and where one will get trapped I recommend St. Augustine).

But let's go back to our thought-experiment; let us even take a step further while imagining that the Christian theist is eager to corner Plato and to make him admit that he doesn't have comparably reliable sources of warrant. Let's just, for the time being, think that Plato was smart enough to make use of the Christian strategy while appealing to the Socratic 'Daimonion' as a heavenly source of gaining cognitive access to the divine. Plato could produce an argument for the existence of such a special, spiritual, and conscience-related cognitive capacity, the *daimonion*, as people could have seen it at work in Socrates' way of life. To be literally driven towards truth even at the risk of one's own death, to seek higher knowledge and understanding, to fulfill the innermost wishes of God—all of this, as Plato might respond, has to be regarded as the working of the Daimonion in us, with Socrates being the role-model. In this scenario, Plato could confront us with the following formula: $T(d) \rightarrow W(d)$ with "T"

signifying "true" and "*W*" denoting "warrant" for the set of all *daimonion*-model-related propositions *d*. Now, we have exactly the case when belief-systems are on par; and any externalist-style appeal to higher sources or higher powers won't help. But what would be the advice for a philosophical referee to acquiesce this situation? I would guess she will appeal to 'pure reason' hoping that one or the other concept of God might uncover itself as being more in alignment with natural theology.[35]

But the whole time-travelling story might also reveal that any appeal to higher powers (like revelation dressed up as *sensus divinitatis* or IIHS) becomes an idling wheel once any other religious belief-system starts claiming comparable sources as their own. This situation would result in a dead-end, if we had to come to the conclusion that any party has the right to claim access to special cognitive mechanisms and to treat religious sentences as basic propositions. How would we ever be in a position to say that any religious belief that spits in the face of reason is suspicious?[36]

4 Limitations for Knowing God?

The overall problem was generated, however, by a very ambitioned idea—namely by the idea that faith can be or should be regarded as knowledge (under certain circumstances). But why would we have to treat faith as some sort of knowledge? Are we not aiming to high? My guess would be that the certainty of knowledge is seen as the only form of certainty that suits the certainty of religious belief; the basic connection seems to look like this for all instances *b* of belief, "*C*" denoting

---

[35] For further discussion of having the right concept of God but risking misidentification cf. Geach (1969, esp. 113): "I have spoken [...] of natural theology as a means of exposing errors about God. But it has on the contrary been argued that a God whose existence and attributes were established by natural theology would not really be the same God as the true and living God of religious belief, that natural theology of its very nature lays hold of the wrong God, an abstract sort of God. This argument appears to me confused. Suppose Sherlock Holmes established from his data both the existence of a murderer—i.e. that the case actually is one of murder—and some of the murderer's characteristics; suppose the police later on arrested a man with those characteristics and found confirmatory proofs of his guilt: it would occur to nobody, I imagine, to distinguish between the abstract murderer of Sherlock Holmes's deductions and the real live murderer raging in his cell; surely nobody would wish to deny this plain statement of the case, that Holmes had abstract knowledge relating to a concrete individual."
[36] And isn't the appeal to reason the justification for condemning certain religious practices (think of cannibalism) or for calling certain beliefs primitive or below reason (think of astrology, polytheism or animalist images of deities)?

"certainty", "*K*" signifying "knowledge", and ***O*** being some sort of "ought-to-be" operator: $\forall b\ \boldsymbol{O}(C(b) \rightarrow K(b))$. But I doubt whether there is a close-to-necessary connection between certainty and knowledge. Sometimes certainty comes with knowledge, sometimes it doesn't.[37] Moreover, the certainty of faith, which is the noblest aspect of a believer's perseverance, needn't be the certainty of knowledge. And this is the moment when I have to refer to Immanuel Kant again, as I did briefly in my introductory remarks.

I agree with Alvin Plantinga that Kant's remarks on 'theology' and the concept of God are complicated. It is, nevertheless, interesting that we can isolate Kant's theological concerns somewhat from his anti-realism. Basically, Kant says that the concept of God is beyond our pay-grade of gaining knowledge. This thesis is built on a number of different arguments, they vary widely especially within Kant's treatise of the classic arguments for God's existence. But I will pick just two of them, which seem to me sufficient enough to make the point.

A first argument says that nothing can be known which is seriously underdetermined. So, let "*A*", "*B*", "*C*" be the properties that are crucial for determining, let's say, the kind-membership or the identity-criteria of an entity *x*. And let "*K**" be the property of "being known", then, according to Kant: $\forall x\ (A(x) \wedge \diamond(B(x) \wedge \neg B(x)) \wedge \diamond(C(x) \wedge \neg C(x)) \rightarrow \neg K^*(x))$.[38] We could call this Kant's *dogma of serious or relevant knowledge*. If we don't have serious knowledge, it usually is the business of sense experience to help us out. On the contrary—and this is a very important aspect of Kant's dogma—once we have serious knowledge we will know how for example $A(a)$ entails $B(a)$ and $C(a)$ etc. Thus, knowledge of entailments can serve as Kant's litmus test for serious knowledge. Now, is Kant's concept of

---

[37] I think this is even true from the part of knowledge—at least if we start from an internalist's picture of knowledge. Imagine that I am really capable of fixing extremely delicious Bavarian roast pork. Intuitively I perform the right steps: I 'know' *how* to spice it, *when* to turn it in the oven, when to turn up the heat slightly, when to add some broth or the right mixture of sautéed vegetables etc., but I might not be able to write every single step down appropriately or to explain it to somebody in propositional form. The result of my cooking will proof that I know how to fix a wonderful dinner menu, although once I am forced to explain each step of the procedure I might lose all certainty and start stuttering and rethinking. This situation, I guess, would be a situation which could account for knowledge without certainty.

[38] Cf. Kant (*Kritik der reinen Vernunft*, A 571–572): "Ein jedes *Ding* aber, seiner Möglichkeit nach, steht noch unter dem Grundsatze der *durchgängigen* Bestimmung, nach welchem ihm von *allen möglichen* Prädikaten der *Dinge*, sofern sie mit ihren Gegenteilen verglichen werden, eines zukommen muß. Dieses beruht nicht bloß auf dem Satze des Wiederspruchs; denn es betrachtet, außer dem Verhältnis zweier einander widerstreitenden Prädikate, jedes Ding noch im Verhältnis auf die *gesamte Möglichkeit*, als den Inbegriff aller Prädikate überhaupt, und, indem es solche als Bedingungen a priori voraussetzt, so stellt es ein jedes Ding so vor, wie es vor dem Anteil, den es an jener gesamten Möglichkeit hat, seine eigene Möglichkeit ableite."

serious knowledge far-fetched? Honestly, I don't think so. Just imagine that I am going to tell you a story about my elementary school, for which I have to rely on my memory. In case I shouldn't remember crucial information about my former school (like the sizes of the classes, the layout of the building, the number of faculty members etc.), you would agree that I don't have serious knowledge of my former school (any longer). To help me out I would have to make a journey hoping to get enough information based on sense perception in order to fill the gaps of my memory.

Now Kant's dogma, $\forall x\ (A(x) \wedge \diamond(B(x) \wedge \neg B(x)) \wedge \diamond(C(x) \wedge \neg C(x)) \rightarrow \neg K^*(x))$, puts the concept of God in some sort of *double luck situation*. The idea of serious knowledge presupposes the ideal of complete determination, which according to Kant unfolds into the idea of a Supreme Being that is (in the long run) ultimately responsible for entity x's being A, $\neg B$, and $\neg C$ or A, B, and $\neg C$ or A, $\neg B$ or C.[39] For the *idea of a Supreme Being* is meant to ensure epistemically[40] that my endeavor to achieve serious knowledge isn't shallow and futile right from the start. Furthermore, it backs up some very basic ontological commitments I want to stick to with respect to the world around me: for instance the commitment to a, in principle, successful encounter with the things in the world in order to arrive at knowledge. That's good luck for the notion of a Supreme Being, because it conceptually serves as the backbone of this epistemological endeavor and its ontological underpinnings. But the dogma itself is bad luck for any attempt to gain serious knowledge of the Supreme Being.[41] If I had to admit that there are gaps

---

39 Cf. Kant (*Kritik der reinen Vernunft*, A 573–578).
40 Cf. Kant (*Kritik der reinen Vernunft*, A 577–578): "Es versteht sich von selbst, daß die Vernunft zu dieser ihrer Absicht, nämlich sich lediglich die notwendige durchgängige Bestimmung der Dinge vorzustellen, nicht die Existenz eines solchen Wesens, das dem Ideale gemäß ist, sondern nur die Idee desselben voraussetze, um von einer unbedingten Totalität der durchgängigen Bestimmung die bedingte, d.i. die des eingeschränkten abzuleiten. Das Ideal ist ihr also das Urbild (Prototypon) aller Dinge, welche insgesamt, als mangelhafte Kopien (ectypa), den Stoff zu ihrer Möglichkeit daher nehmen, und, indem sie demselben mehr oder weniger nahe kommen, dennoch jederzeit unendlich weit daran fehlen, es zu erreichen."
41 Cf. Kant (*Kritik der reinen Vernunft*, A 580): "Wenn wir nun dieser unserer Idee, indem wir sie hypostasieren, so ferner nachgehen, so werden wir das Urwesen durch den bloßen Begriff der höchsten Realität als ein einiges, einfaches, allgenugsames, ewiges etc. mit einem Worte, es in seiner unbedingten Vollständigkeit durch alle Prädikamente bestimmen können. Der Begriff eines solchen Wesens ist der von *Gott*, in transzendentalem Verstande gedacht, und so ist das Ideal der reinen Vernunft der Gegenstand einer transzendentalen *Theologie* [...]. Indessen würde dieser Gebrauch der transzendentalen Idee doch schon die Grenzen ihrer Bestimmung und Zulässigkeit überschreiten. Denn die Vernunft legte sie nur, als den *Begriff* von aller Realität, der durchgängigen Bestimmung der Dinge überhaupt zum Grunde, ohne zu verlangen, daß alle diese Realität objektiv gegeben sei und selbst ein Ding ausmache. Dieses letztere ist eine

in the ways in which (essential, kind-related or identity-preserving) properties are ascribed to the Supreme Being, I could not gain serious knowledge of the Supreme Being.[42] According to Kant, I would have to turn to sensory input to fill the gaps. But with regard to the Supreme Being, this is a dead-end street by definition. Anyhow, whatever we might want to say about God, in Kant's view, it won't pass the litmus test of knowing entailments.[43]

Theoretically, we have three options to deal with Kant's dogma: 1) we could refuse to be convinced. But I think the dogma has something going for it. For if I cannot decide, based on solid evidence, whether an archaeopteryx is a (sophisticated) saurian or a (weird) bird, I clearly don't have serious knowledge of an archaeopteryx. 2) We could underline the necessity of experience while denying that only sense perception will do the trick. In an Alstonian way we could emphasize the role of mystical experience. Or, in a more Hegelian way, we could point out that the contemplation of the inner logic of the universe of properties—that has the existence of a supreme being as their necessary presupposition—will ultimately serve as a determining factor, even if this process is not really comparable to sense experience. Both ways—and I guess there are even more subcategories to this possibility—are promising but require quite an amount of conceptual grunt work for the theist, facing the risk of rebuttal at every turn. 3) For knowing God we don't need serious knowledge; even the most rudimentary form of getting acquainted will do. Of course, this is a viable way. Nevertheless, for the realm of knowledge it is a very pricy one, since we would be left with mere scratches of what God might be like. Maybe our knowledge of God would be less than we need in order to have a discussion with an atheist beyond the enterprise of testing conceptual possibilities.

---

bloße Erdichtung, durch welche wir das mannigfaltige unserer Idee in einem Ideale, als einem besonderen Wesen, zusammenfassen und realisieren, wozu wir keine Befugnis haben, so gar nicht einmal die Möglichkeit einer solchen Hypothese geradezu anzunehmen, wie denn auch alle Folgerungen, die aus einem solchen Ideale abfließen, die durchgängige Bestimmung der Dinge überhaupt, als zu deren Behuf die Idee allein nötig war, nicht angehen, und darauf nicht den mindesten Einfluß haben."

42 Especially in his critique of cosmological arguments, Kant makes us aware of a series of serious conceptual gaps. Cf. Kant (*Kritik der reinen Vernunft*, B 640–642). Essentially, Kant says that we do not understand the connections between God as the supreme cause of everything and as God instantiating maximal greatness, which is meant to lead us to an understanding of God's necessary existence. In his critique of the cosmological argument do not Kant points to the fact that we do not know how these concepts entail each other, although to know these entailments would be necessary to arrive at the conclusion that a supreme cause necessarily exists.

43 Cf. Kant (*Kritik der reinen Vernunft*, A 581–582).

So, what would be Plantinga's stand on this? I guess he would recommend a combination of 2) and 3)—in his sophisticated way as usual. He might want to convince us that the sensus divinitatis does not need very much to get 'triggered' in order to 'produce' serious knowledge of God. As a matter of fact, the *sensus divinitatis* is able to replace sense-experience at low costs. There is no need to have any sort of direct encounter with God to get the *sensus divinitatis* going. Looking at the night sky or standing on a mountain-top might be just the situation you need to trigger the *sensus divinitatis*. Isn't that wonderful news? And wouldn't this be a very comfortable detour around Kant's problem? Well, it could be that there is a *sensus divinitatis* and that it indeed works that way. But, to say the least, there is something very odd and very unique about it: given the low costs of input it seems to produce a formidable, even splendid result (namely serious knowledge of God). Unlike all the other mental capacities we are blessed with, the *sensus divinitatis* doesn't need sensory input that is *equivalent* to the output. No, this *sensus divinitatis* makes gold from straw, because the sensory input of the night sky will (given the required circumstances and the absence of disturbing factors) lead to the statement: "There is a creator of this universe." But none of our cognitive capacities work that way: whenever memory leaves us, we need a sensory input, which is (in the broadest sense of the word) equivalent to our loss; when our imagination fails, we need sensory input to replace fading parts equivalently. If I offer an inductively based conclusion, I must not claim it unrestrictedly, since the bill of sensory input is going to strap me severely. There is no free lunch in our mental and epistemic life. But, all of a sudden, this very special cognitive apparatus—called *sensus divinitatis*—offers an almost free ride? Given the inner analogies of our cognitive faculties, this is truly unbelievable.

But there is a second argument that can be extracted from Kant's *Critique of Pure Reason*. We can call it the *straight knowledge dogma*.[44] Again, let "A", "B", "C" be the properties that are crucial for determining the kind-membership or the identity-criteria of an entity x. And let "K*" be the property of "being known", then, according to Kant, we need to be aware of: $\forall x \ ((A(x) \to (B(x) \land$

---

44 As a matter of fact this idea is more prominent in Kant's remarks on the so-called 'paralogisms' concerning the self and the antinomies concerning the idea of world; cf. Kant (*Kritik der reinen Vernunft*, A 348–405; B 432–599). Nevertheless, it can be found in footprints when Kant discusses inconsistencies in our notion of God—especially when he talks about the argument from design and the status of the concept of God in general. Cf. Kant (*Kritik der reinen Vernunft*, A/B 620–630, 631–642).

$\neg B(x)) \vee (C(x) \wedge \neg C(x))) \rightarrow \neg K^\star(x))$.[45] With regard to our concept of God, straight knowledge would remind us of the impossibility of arriving at knowledge of God, because inevitably we will get trapped in inconsistencies. Kant himself discusses the problem that—given the notion of God as a supreme wisdom (based on an argument from design) is cogent—we can conclude that God works like an engineer forming primary matter into ordered existence or that he brings about being itself. It could go either way, since there is nothing in the concept of a supreme wisdom that necessarily requires a creation ex nihilo.[46] The same goes, following Kant, for the theistic concept of God versus the deistic conception of God. From the notion of God as a supreme cause we could derive both mutually exclusive concepts. And, this is my guess, Kant would be amused and put in good humor by contemporary discussions within analytic philosophy of religion, because the ongoing debates between eternalists and temporalists, theistic libertarians and compatibilists, free-will-defense-theorists and fatalists would be enough evidence to show that there is no chance to finally overcome the ambiguities within the concept of God insofar as certain cornerstone properties ascribed to God (omnipotence, goodness, foreknowledge, wisdom) may lead us entirely different, yet mutually exclusive ways, whereas such a paradoxical situation might be avoided only if we seriously modify the content of the properties we started out with. Aren't these debates enough evidence of the fact that we do not have straight knowledge of God and that we do lack certainty?

Classically, apart from negative theology, two alternatives offered some solution: 1) The first alternative, let us call it the Thomistic viewpoint, while bowing our head before the medieval tradition, will unswervingly remind us of the fact that with respect to God there are no unequivocal concepts available. Through the looking glass of analogy we may come to a concept formation that avoids inconsistencies by entering a certain level of abstraction and by opening gaps of conceptual determination or conceptual entailment respectively. Although this position is attractive and very useful, it could fall prey to what I have called Kant's *serious knowledge objection*. Anyhow, if this solution should eventually be able to provide us with knowledge, it clearly will not have the merit of being properly basic. 2) The second alternative became prominent in German Idealism (but was also foreshadowed in Nicolaus Cusanus). According to this solution, the concepts in question are meant to expose an inner dialectics,

---

[45] To me it seems that at least part of this dogma is the motive for Gordon Kaufman's *God the Problem*, which, therefore, deserves more attention than Plantinga offered in WCB, 32–38. Kaufman's problems of referring to God are a subcategory of Kant's problem of serious knowledge, because successfully referring to x presupposes serious knowledge of x (according to Kant).
[46] Cf. Kant (*Kritik der reinen Vernunft*, A 620–630, 631–642).

which includes that the content and meaning of the divine properties in question literally start embracing the content and meaning of the opposite predicate/property—once we add *divine infinity* to the picture. This would be the reason why in God freedom and necessity, for instance, are 'the same' or why being substance and becoming are mutually inclusive etc. I admit that this solution is really hard to swallow, if you apply the law of non-contradiction without making excuses for Hegelian dialectics. But even if this pill somehow gets down the throat, the question still remains whether what we conceptually gain at the end of the day is knowledge. For Hegel this is undoubtedly so, although nevertheless it will not be properly basic, but must be the result of getting a grip of knowledge as knowledge in a, well, very long run.[47]

At this point I don't see how referring to the *sensus divinitatis* could help us out, unless this truly miraculous equipment would not only be responsible for the production of basic propositions, but also for concepts and conceptual entailment. I don't believe that we are equipped with such stupendous and unique facilities. A sober look at the Bible might simply show that this is a document of how human beings have tried to conceptualize God, while conceptually great inconsistencies still remain. So, if the Bible should be treated as divine revelation, God apparently was not too concerned of getting across a consistent (i.e. consistent entailment-wise) concept of divine nature, of eliminating human shortcomings right from the start or of providing us with the certainty of infallible knowledge.[48] Maybe God's purpose has been that faith remains faith and is, as a genuine intellectual as well as moral virtue, *different* from knowledge. Instead of chasing the shadows of knowledge, I would like to advise the benign reader to look for a different conception of certainty, which can be detected in Kant and even more (but I guess this can mean a great deal of annoyance to Alvin Plantinga)[49] in Wittgenstein and in the writings of first generation Wittgensteinans like Rush Rhees.

---

47 Cf. Wenz (2012).
48 Again, Plantinga could point to the IIHS that eliminates the ambiguities, since the Bible itself is just a stimulus meant to trigger the higher cognitive capacities (infused by grace). But, once again, this sounds like a theological answer to a philosophical problem. Similarly, the Swiss theologian Ingolf Dalferth has recommended that a sound theological hermeneutics of Scripture has to be based on the Holy Spirit's engagement in our reading the Bible; cf. Dalferth (1998). Philosophically, such an answer implies that neither the rationality of faith nor the trustworthiness of faith's sources can be justified relying on the capacities of human reason only. This result sounds like a combination of Barthianism from the inside with fideism from the outside. For further discussion cf. Askew (1988); Penelhum (1983); Evans (1998, 45–47).
49 It is obvious that Plantinga isn't very fond of Kant, although he tried to approach him with due respect. For Wittgenstein's case the whole situation is different; given that Plantinga has

5 Certainty without Knowledge

In combining Kant and Wittgenstein we can spell out another kind of certainty—practical certainty that is the practical implication of what we might call 'living by' a concept. *Living by a concept* is an everyday phenomenon; there is nothing esoteric about it. For instance, most of us—if not all of us—live by the concept of ontological stability and endurance. Usually, nobody would favor a position that casts doubt on the idea that things vanish and come back to existence invisibly. Although I do not exactly know that things are stable and endure periods of time, because my sensory equipment and my cognitive capacities might just be too slow or too sloppy to pick up the instances of vanishing and popping back into existence, I am committed to this concept because it makes sense of the ways in which I lead my life and perform my everyday actions or answer to my everyday responsibilities. Living by a concept may still be possible if I cannot spell out logical connections between the concepts I live by or if I seem to face certain gaps between the concepts I live by, because these concepts aren't internally connected by logical implications (or anything of that sort) but by their impact on my life.

Living by a concept is a matter of decision in one way, but seen from a different angle it is not: Thus, I can try to switch concepts I am meant to live by inasmuch as I can try to influence my health or my body weight, i.e. I can do something for it or come up with a decision, although many aspects of the switching process are simply beyond immediate control. Wittgenstein once said that faith is a passionate decision for a system of reference or, in my words, a concept to live by.[50] The decision Wittgenstein is talking about is not so much what we mean by 'deciding', but rather an act of affirmation. Therefore, faith includes the affirmation of the concept I live by. For it is this concept that determines much of how I see the world and estimate what is going on as well as what is valuable and trustworthy. The certainty of faith, in the Wittgensteinian picture, is the certainty of acting out my affirmation. For example, to be certain that the things surrounding

---

dedicated only one single footnote to the topic, one will get the impression that a Wittgensteinian epistemology of religion isn't even worth talking about. Cf. Plantinga, WCB 8, fn. 22. Assuming that 'Wittgensteinian fideism' is, however, an entirely misleading label, invented and coined by the atheist philosopher Kai Nielsen, we should be encouraged to think that Ludwig Wittgenstein's philosophy of religion is quite different from Nielsen's cliché. Cf. Nielsen/Phillips (2005).
50 Cf. Wittgenstein (1990, 540–541): "Es kommt mir vor, als könne ein religiöser Glaube nur etwas wie das leidenschaftliche Sich-entscheiden für ein Bezugssystem sein. Also obgleich es Glaube ist, doch eine Art des Lebens, oder eine Art das Leben zu beurteilen. Ein leidenschaftliches Ergreifen *dieser* Auffassung. […]."

me are (ontologically) stable requires that I am acting on it without hesitation and second thoughts: putting my car into the garage and taking my keys with me is an everyday example for living by the concept of ontological stability. Usually I do not have to think about whether or not my car will be there in the morning. I may worry about thieves, but I surely do not worry about remote ontological possibilities. In other words: The concepts I live by determine my alleys of doubt as well as the instance for which I can effectively collect evidence. Religious faith is, according to Wittgensteinians, just like that: It consists of a variety of concepts we live by:

> ('The divinity of Scriptures' is not an 'objective fact' [...]) Once again, what do I recognize, and in what sense is it *recognition*, when I recognize the divinity of the Scriptures?
> It is not to *find out something about them*, comparable to discovering the date when they were written down.
> It is to live by them. (Rhees 1997, 53)

Concepts we live by have meaning and make sense as long as we are in a position to act on them. Of course, as in everyday life we can lose certainty and become insecure. This happens predominantly when the concept we live by starts to deracinate, i.e. to lose its roots in our experience. Once we get to this point we need to use all our cognitive capacities in order to either re-root the concept or to switch to another concept. Re-rooting the concept presupposes, in parts, collecting evidence but, moreover, it demands the will to live by it while evaluating whether or not living by it does any good—at least in the sense of staying in touch with the broader aspects of life experience. Just to give an example: Any sort of 'through the roof' supernaturalism (like believing in ghosts that haunt people, believing in demons that inhabit rivers or trees, believing in godlike entities that resent us) has become a deracinated concept humans used to live by. The technological aspects of our everyday life have taught us to embrace some sort of naturalism with no chance to this 'through the roof' supernaturalism to become a concept to live by again (at least in Western cultures). From this point of view, we cannot help but treating the deracinated concept like superstition, and as something irrational even if the implications of this very concept, seen in themselves, might still enjoy some sort of functional or procedural rationality. What qualifies as rational is, therefore, determined by its power and ability to be 'lived by' with perseverance as well as with all the curiosity and desire to understand human intellect is blessed with. But, again, there is no chance to sell the certainty of the concept we live by as knowledge or as the outcome of assessing probabilities.

It is important to notice that our primary business concerning concepts we live by isn't justification or, seen from the opposite angle, error: In a sense, we cannot be mistaken with regard to the concepts we live by, although we can be horribly 'far off' once we consider the impact of the concept in question to our life:

> You might make a mistake about physical objects, as you would if you said that there are no black swans. But you would not make a mistake—not that kind any-way—if you said there are no physical objects. (Rhees 1997, 53)[51]

People who said that there are no physical objects would seem really far off to us; to us they would not be able to find their way out of a paper bag. But there is no use in calling them mistaken because of the strangeness of their viewpoint. This strangeness remains, unless we could find a common concept to live by that can serve as a common denominator for assessing the impact the differing concepts have on our lives. For Wittgenstein and Rhees, the concept of God is, predominantly, a concept to live by;[52] this is the very reason why it is not subject to a specifically evidentialist way of justification:

> The worship of God is not regulating one's life in accordance with a highly probable hypothesis.
> 'Holding to a belief which we have every reason to think is true.' (And what is meant by 'true' would be shown by the sorts of reasons that are given for it.)
> This is the idea of a possible *justification* of religious beliefs, or the suggestion that a religious belief is something that can be borne out. Otherwise, what is it that we 'have every reason to think'? (Rhees 1997, 56–57)

It is tempting to think that for Wittgensteinians religious belief is self-sustaining. But this would be misconceived. Rather, they would emphasize that there exists no unequivocal notion of 'giving reasons' or 'being rational'. Especially for con-

---

51 Cf. also p. 55: "Would you say that someone who denied the existence of physical objects was mistaken? Certainly not like the mistake of one who denies the existence of black swans."
52 Cf. Rhees (1997, 54): "But what is it to have an idea of God? That 'having an idea' is different from having an idea of an iceberg or of a quality. For one thing, you don't get the idea the same way. I might form my idea of an iceberg from having seen one or having seen a picture. Neither does the idea of God play the same sort of role. It does not help me to identify or anticipate anything. I should hardly say that my idea of God was my idea of God's properties (or of 'the sort of being that God is'). And it would not be natural to ask, 'Does God really have the properties that I suppose he has?' [...] When I speak of God I am not speaking about my idea. And if we say that God has an independent reality this means partly that it is impossible to be mistaken in what one says of God, and for people to disagree. Only, then it is important to see what kind of disagreement this is and what they are disagreeing about. How do we know that we are talking about the same thing?"

cepts we live by, giving reason cannot be performed without contemplating the ways in which these concepts are rooted in our experiences and our lives.⁵³ Of course, these ways are meant to differ individually and culturally. Moreover, there exists no special cognitive capacity responsible for the concepts we life by. Instead, all the cognitive faculties we have are affected by the concepts we live by—insofar as they form and prescribe the development of cognitive virtues, direct our curiosity, pre-determine the shape of our inevitable consequences and empower the passions we reveal in sticking to our commitments. The concepts we live by are basic seen from the angle of evidentialist justification. Since their strength is determined by their impact on our lives, we do not arrive at the cornerstone concepts we live by through inference and discursive conclusions.⁵⁴ But on the other side the concepts we live by are crucially dependent on their impact on our lives; apart from that they are lifeless. Seen from this angle, the concepts we live by cannot be basic. They are nourished by our life-experience; and, therefore, they are meant to be judged by their fruitfulness. However, for the concepts we live by there is neither a direct nor an immediate way of understanding their meaning, referring to their addressee or knowing them. But this doesn't imply that the concepts we live by denote merely abstract objects. Instead, understanding, referring, and (to a certain extent knowing) with respect to concepts we live by is crucially bound to the ways in which we lead our lives.⁵⁵ That is the reason why Rush Rhees equates referring to God with worshipping God.⁵⁶ Likewise referring to the stability of physical objects must be equated with *treating* everyday things as enduring entities.

In Kant there are hints that will point to the same direction. Accordingly he offers a 'pragmatic' understanding of certainty, qualifying it in terms of an unalterable commitment. Hence, also for Kant 'God' can be understood as a concept we live by. Unlike Wittgenstein and Rhees, Kant is still fond of 'architectural clarity', while he doesn't appreciate the mess of overlapping and intertwined language games. In Kant's analysis, the concept of God serves as a mediator for the concepts of justice and happiness, while the latter are both built upon the con-

---

53 Cf. Rhees (1997, 58): "What is wrong is the idea of something like a ground for religious belief, outside the belief itself. Something which perhaps the teacher has seen but which we cannot see, although we can understand, or at any rate adopt and follow, the view of God which he brings to us."
54 The first one to emphasize a Wittgensteinian notion of basicality over and against Reformed Epistemology was late Dewi Phillips. Cf. Phillips (1988, 3–127).
55 Rhees asks us to compare the language of religion with the language of love; cf. Rhees (1997, 39–40).
56 Cf. Rhees (1997, 49, 56).

cept of freedom. Insofar as I unavoidably have to consider myself as being free (and, therefore, morally responsible), I must arrive at the concept of God as a concept to live by. Furthermore, according to Kant, it is the concept of God that gives meaning to subordinate concepts we unavoidably live by.[57] The certainty we have is tied to the seriousness of our commitment[58], which is in alignment with the seriousness of our lives.[59]

6 Religious Experience as Interpretation

It is quite interesting to see that Alvin Plantinga tried a lot to get around the admittedly sticky business of taking religious experience into consideration—as a means of justifying religious belief. His discussion of William P. Alston is very

---

[57] Cf. Kant (*Kritik der praktischen Vernunft*, A 223–237, esp. A 226–227: "Hier ist nun wohl zu merken, daß diese moralische Notwendigkeit *subjektiv*, d.i. Bedürfnis, und nicht *objektiv*, d.i. selbst Pflicht sei; denn es kann gar keine Pflicht geben, die Existenz eines Dinges anzunehmen (weil dieses bloß den theoretischen Gebrauch der Vernunft angeht). Auch wird hierunter nicht verstanden, daß die Annehmung des Daseins Gottes, *als eines Grundes aller Verbindlichkeit überhaupt*, notwendig sei (denn dieser beruht, wie hinreichend bewiesen worden, lediglich auf der Autonomie der Vernunft selbst). Zur Pflicht gehört hier nur die Bearbeitung zur Hervorbringung und Beförderung des höchsten Guts in der Welt, dessen Möglichkeit also postuliert werden kann, die aber unsere Vernunft nicht anders denkbar findet, als unter Voraussetzung einer höchsten Intelligenz, deren Dasein anzunehmen also mit dem Bewußtsein unserer Pflicht verbunden ist, obzwar diese Annehmung selbst für die theoretische Vernunft gehört, in Ansehung deren allein sie, als Erklärungsgrund betrachtet, *Hypothese*, in Beziehung aber auf die Verständlichkeit eines uns doch durchs moralische Gesetz aufgegebenen Objekts (des höchsten Guts), mithin eines Bedürfnisses in praktischer Absicht, *Glaube*, und zwar reiner *Vernunftglaube*, heißen kann, weil bloß reine Vernunft [...] die Quelle ist, daraus er entspringt."

[58] Cf. Kant (*Kritik der Urteilskraft*, B 462–463): "*Glaube* [...] ist die moralische Denkungsart der Vernunft im Fürwahrhalten desjenigen, was für die theoretische Erkenntnis unzugänglich ist. Es ist also der beharrliche Grundsatz des Gemüts, das, was zur Möglichkeit des höchsten moralischen Endzwecks als Bedingung vorauszusetzen notwendig ist, wegen der Verbindlichkeit zu demselben als wahr anzunehmen [...]. Der Glaube (schlechthin so genannt) ist ein Vertrauen zu der Erreichung einer Absicht, deren Beförderung Pflicht, die Möglichkeit der Ausführung derselben aber für uns nicht *einzusehen* ist [...]."

[59] Cf. Kant (*Kritik der Urteilskraft*, B 459): "Dagegen ist der von uns zu bewirkende höchste Endzweck, das, wodurch wir allein würdig werden können selbst Endzweck einer Schöpfung zu sein, eine Idee, die für uns in praktischer Beziehung objektive Realität hat, und Sache; aber darum, weil wir diesem Begriffe in theoretischer Absicht dieser Realität nicht verschaffen können, bloße Glaubenssache der reinen Vernunft, mit ihm aber zugleich Gott und Unsterblichkeit, als die Bedingungen, unter denen allein wir nach der Beschaffenheit unserer (der menschlichen) Vernunft uns die Möglichkeit jenes Effekts des gesetzmäßigen Gebrauchs unserer Freiheit denken können."

aware of the structural problems attached to almost any concept of religious experience. To realize the merits of Plantinga's method we might as well listen carefully to Charlie Martin's caveat. For Martin, 'religious experience' has a psychological aspect, i.e. the mental event of experiencing, and a theological aspect, i.e. referring to God. The crucial problem now is to explain how it might be possible to deduce θ-sentences (expressing theistic propositions) from ψ-sentences (sentences reporting some of our inner events):

> Unfortunately this deduction is useless. The addition of the existential claim 'God exists' to the psychological claim of having religious experiences must be shown to be warrantable. It cannot be shown to be warrantable to any deductive argument, because psychological statements of the form:
> (1) I feel as if an unseen person were interested in (willed) my welfare.
> (2) I feel a relation quite unlike any I have ever felt before.
> (3) I have feelings of guilt and shame at my sinfulness.
> (4) I feel as if I were committed to bending all of my efforts to living a certain way, etc., etc.
> can make the claim only that I have these complex feelings and sensations. Nothing else follows deductively. No matter what the existential statement might be that is added to the psychological statement, it is always logically possible for future psychological statements to call this existential claim in doubt. (Martin 1963², 78–79).

A possible way around this dilemma would be to show that—as for other forms of experience—God must be causally responsible for the mental event as physical objects are causally responsible for those mental events that point to physical things (like feeling a hardwood floor underneath my feet) or respond to the effects of physical things (like feeling aching pain in my knee because of my encounter with the desk in front of me). But, of course, to build an argument of this sort in favor of the trustworthiness of religious experience is risky. Plantinga is able to avoid Martin's problems as well as further charges, which come as costs of resolving these problems, by changing the whole layout. He insists that there is no inferential connection between psychological sentences and theistic sentences. Rather, there are psychological/mental events, which will trigger the *sensus divinitatis* to produce theistic sentences.[60] This is an ingenious step; nevertheless, the solution comes at very high costs. In abandoning the inference-situation, Plantinga also closes the door on the interpretation-aspect of religious experience. There is no need to get into the details of the trustworthiness of a *sensus divinitatis* again (or to wonder whether this admirable capacity really exists). Instead, I simply want to ask whether Plantinga's picture is correct with re-

---

60 Cf. WCB, 326–331.

spect to the phenomenon of religious experience. So, what exactly happens when I look at the brilliant, crystal clear night sky that gives me a taste of infinity while I utter the words: "O God, you are the creator of beauty and unsurpassable in your own beauty"? As a matter of fact, I just observe and watch the night sky. I do not have a direct encounter with God. Although watching the night sky is responsible for my praising the Lord, it is not a direct cause for my utterance, since it is not a necessary antecedent of my prayer. Counterfactually, I could have uttered the sentence spontaneously or while being confronted with something entirely different. So, the night sky is neither the object nor the cause of my religious utterance. But what's my praise about? In Wittgensteinian terms, my prayer would be comparable to an interpretation of a situation in order to make sense of this very situation. Of course, interpretation in this case does not mean scientific interpretation. Rather, it has to do with relating a situation to a concept we live by.

Rush Rhees has pointed out that there is an ongoing risk of misconceiving the concept of religious experience:

> I know there are those who say that a belief in God may rest on 'the evidence of religious experience'. I think I have some idea of what leads them to speak that way, but I do not want to enter that now. I will say only that I think they are confused in what they make of it. It is not evidence for belief at all. They sometimes talk as though they observed God in these occasions. And this invites the question, 'How do you know it was God?', Frank Buchman answers, 'Well how do you know red's red?'; and I suppose someone might also say 'Well, how do you know it was your brother you were talking with just now?' But that will not do. I have means of identifying a man, and if anyone doubts my first assumption I can check. I know it is red because I know red when I see it; i.e. because I know what 'red' means, i.e. because I have learned the word by ostensive definition and the rest of the usual method. Nothing of that sort can apply to an 'experience of God'. And the question 'How do you know it was God?' would not mean anything like 'How do you know it was this man as opposed to that or some other?" [...] If it was God, then it was the creator of all there is, it was that in which all things live and move and have their being. The point of the question was that you cannot have experience of that. [...] Winston Churchill may be Prime Minister and also a company director, but I might come to know him without knowing this. But I could not know God without knowing that he was the Creator and Father of all things. That would be like saying that I might come to know Churchill without knowing that he had a face, hands, body, voice or any of the attributes of a human being. (Rhees 1997, 47).

The point of this remark is that we cannot encounter divine attributes directly; but it doesn't make sense to say that we arrive at them indirectly. Whatever we experience in this world is not the least bit equivalent to divine properties. Plantinga offers a way to get around this problem in saying that whatever we encounter in this world doesn't have to be equivalent because its role is just the role of a stimulus. However, this version cuts off the interpretation-aspect of so-called religious experience. If we start re-reading divine attributes as concepts we live by we can apply them to certain situations so that they serve as forms of interpretation. In doing so we will get beyond the problem of equivalence as well as the problematic aspects of the stimulus-concept.

So, what is religious experience, if it is neither a case of observing God nor a set of stimuli meant to trigger the *sensus divinitatis?* Let us try to imagine an instance of religious experience, which is within the 'variety of religious experience', but more or less in the middle of the spectrum. If I have, for example, a religious experience, let's say, while driving all night long and watching the burning of a mountain top in central Montana, this would be clearly the case when religious experience reveals itself to be an interpretation of a situation. The burning trees on the mountain top with nobody around to care, because there is no human being in danger given the vast and empty spaces covered only by forests and wildlife, might remind me of my existential finitude: the fact that I am just a marginal spot in a majestic universe. To feel completely unimportant but, at the same time, to realize that I am the only witness of this natural spectacle, which takes place in a wilderness unaffected by human beings, can create a specific situation of awareness (comparable with what Charles S. Peirce once described as 'musement'), which makes it fit to turn to the concept of God as an interpretation of the situation, if I already have this concept of God to live by. Possibly, my astonishment results in sentences like: "God, you are even greater than this, please strengthen me in my nothingness". Or I may quote those psalms that praise God's mercy, which has exalted human existence from sheer nothingness to the glory of self-awareness and awareness of the divine. What I express verbally will document the depth of the impact the concept I live by really has on my life. Taking this case at face value, we can conclude that the essence of religious experience is to see something as something else: to see a specific situation in the light of the divine. To get to this we already need to have a concept of the divine we live by. In fact, the religious experience is an interpretation of an extraordinary situation (whereas, in principle, it doesn't always have to be out of the ordinary). Mutually, the situation and the concept we live by can serve as stimuli, although there is no mechanism that generates some sort of religious output from some sort of sensory input with a 100 per cent certainty. It is the concept we live by that inspires the situation. And it is the situation that, speaking figuratively, 'invites' and 'awaits' the concept. Whether the concept we apply in interpreting the situation in the light of the divine makes sense or appears to be rational is part of a—to allude to Alston[61]—*hermeneutical practice*. This very practice does not dictate that I interpret the above-mentioned situation in the light of the divine; but this practice permits me to do so without losing my reputation as a rational being. One measure of rationality is the depth of the impact the concept, which I am applying, has on my life. Another benchmark might be how the situation I am interpreting in light of the divine gets interwoven with my life, especially with all my other life experiences (and, so to say, the rest of the concepts I do live by).

Well, the benign reader may wonder what will count in favor of my picture of religious experience. This time I am inclined to advise him to take a look at the religious and non-religious people around him. Why is it that some say: "God, thank you for your mercy" when they escaped a dangerous accident, while others say: "This was darn luck, wasn't it"? Is it because the latter party's *sensus divinitatis* is malfunctioning, while the former party's SD is doing fine and is working properly? I can hardly believe that. Actually, what I do think is that both parties offer different interpretations of a situation, see those situations in a different light—involving procedures that are equally valid, based on the guiding concepts they live by. Nevertheless, we are able to ask what the consequences of each concept are and in which ways the concepts have an impact on human lives. If, by chance, both parties shared a common concept to live by, we would be able to evaluate the differences of the above-mentioned concepts and to start a rational discussion of the necessities and challenges of concepts in order to make sense. In saying this, I am not approving non-cognitivism for religion. But I want to remind the benign reader that our cognitive capacities would be useless or remain abstract potentials, if they weren't guided by the concepts we live by. Furthermore, this isn't plain anti-realism either. Because from the notion of concepts we live by we cannot and must not descend to

---

[61] I think that certain aspects of what Alston has called a doxastic practice can be taken into account by analogy; cf. Alston (1991, 146–183). But, of course, there remain disanalogies. For a hermeneutical practice one has to focus even more on the instantiation of a practice accomplished by an individual. Although I know that this concept is subject to Plantinga's substantial critique of Alston (cf. WCB, 117–134), I see a more plausible concept of religious experience being closer to Alston than to Plantinga. Why is that? I think it is for the simple reason that in religious experiences there is a certain liberty of experiencing. I may be compelled, may feel dumbstruck and astonished by the divine as I feel overwhelmed and stirred up by a work of art. But the experiences of the divine as the experience of beauty cannot be put into a framework that—as the stimulus/SD conception does—looks like the necessary connection of cause and effect. In Rhees' terms, the rationality of a hermeneutical practice with respect to religious experiences should be compared to the problem how we would respond to the question *whether there is a right way to play Mozart*. Cf. Rhees (1997, 59).

the idea that we might deal with abstract entities, which are an offspring of our minds only. Instead, we have to take into account again that 'being real' is not an unequivocal expression and, moreover, that 'being real' is in itself a concept we live by and which is applied differently in various forms of life: Just imagine what 'being real' means for physical objects as opposed to laws of nature or instances of beauty or goodness. The same goes for the 'reality' of the divine.

Literature

Abaelard, Peter (1997[3]): Theologia summi boni: Tractatus de unitate et trinitate divina, I, Hamburg.
Alper, Matthew (2006): The 'God' Part of the Brain: A Scientific Interpretation of Human Spirituality and God, Naperville.
Alston, William P. (1991): Perceiving God: The Epistemology of Religious Experience, Ithaca, London.
Askew, Richard (1988): "On Fideism and Alvin Plantinga", in: International Journal for Philosophy of Religion 23, 3–16.
Bordt, Michael (2006): Platons Theologie, Freiburg i.B., München.
Broom, Donald M. (2003): The Evolution of Morality and Religion, Cambridge.
Dalferth, Ingolf U. (1998): Kombinatorische Theologie: Probleme theologischer Rationalität. Freiburg i.B.
Dawes, Gregory W. (2009): Theism and Explanation, London.
Evans, C. Stephan (1998): Faith Beyond Reason: A Kierkegaardian Account, Edinburgh.
Geach, Peter T. (1969): "On Worshipping the Right God," in: God and the Soul, London.
Goodman, Nelson (1978): Ways of Worldmaking, Hassocks.
Levine, Michael P. (2000): "Contemporary Christian Analytic Philosophy of Religion: Biblical Fundamentalism, Terrible Solutions to a Horrible Problem, And Hearing God", in: International Journal for Philosophy of Religion 48, 89–119.
Löffler, Winfried (2003): "Externalistsche Erkenntnistheorie oder theologische Anthropologie? Anmerkungen zur Reformed Epistemology", in: Ludwig Nagl (Ed.): Religion nach der Religionskritik, Wien, Berlin 2003, 123–147.
Lonergan, Bernard (1992): Insight: A Study of Human Understanding, ed. Frederick E. Crowe and Robert M. Doran, Toronto–Buffalo–London 1992 (RP 2005).
Martin, Charlie B. (1961[3]): "A Religious Way of Knowing," in: Antony Flew/Alasdair McIntyre (Eds.): New Essays in Philosophical Theology, London 1961 (RP 1963), 76–95.
Mascord, Keith (2006): Alvin Plantinga and Christian Apologetics, Eugene.
Merricks, Trenton (1995): "Warrant Entails Truth" in: Philosophy and Phenomenological Research 45, 841–855.
Newberg, Andrew/Waldman, Mark Robert (2006): Why We Believe What We Believe: Uncovering Our Biological Need for Meaning, Spirituality, and Truth, New York, London, 167–245.
Nielsen, Kai/Phillips, Dewi Z. (2005): Wittgensteinian Fideism? London.
Parsons, Keith (1990): God and the Burden of Proof: Plantinga, Swinburne, and the Analytic Defense of Theism, Buffalo.

Parsons, Keith (2007): "Some Contemporary Theistic Arguments", in: Michael Martin (Ed.): The Cambridge Companion to Atheism, Cambridge 2007, 102–117.
Penelhum, Terrence (1983): God and Skepticism: A Study in Skepticism and Fideism, Dordrecht.
Phillips, Dewi (1988): Faith after Foundationalism. London, New York.
Phillips, Dewi Z. (2001): Religion and the Hermeneutics of Contemplation, Cambridge.
Plantinga, Alvin (1993a): Warrant: The Current Debate, New York.
Plantinga, Alvin (1993b): Warrant and Proper Function, New York.
Plantinga, Alvin (2000): Warranted Christian Belief, New York.
Plantinga, Alvin (2011): Where the Conflict Really Lies. Science, Religion, and Naturalism, Oxford.
Rehnman, Sebastian (2012): "A Reformed Natural Theology?", in: European Journal for Philosophy of Religion 4, 151–175.
Rhees, Rush (1997): On Religion and Philosophy, Dewi Z. Phillips (Ed.), Cambridge.
Roberts, Robert C./Wood, W. Jay (2007): Intellectual Virtues: An Essay in Regulative Epistemology, Oxford.
Schärtl, Thomas (2008): "Erfahrung, Exerzitium, Autorität und Einsicht: Überlegungen zur rationalen Verantwortung für religiöse Überzeugungen", in: Franz-Josef Bormann/Bernd Irlenborn (Eds.): Religiöse Überzeugungen und öffentliche Vernunft, Freiburg i.B., Basel, Wien 2008 (= Quaestiones disputatae 228), 132–173.
Steup, Matthias (1995): "Proper and Improper Use of Cognitive Faculties: A Counterexample to Plantinga's Proper Functioning Theory", in: Philosophy and Phenomenological Research 45, 409–413.
Swinburne, Richard (2001): "Plantinga on Warrant", in: Religious Studies 37, 203–214.
Wenz, Gunther (2012): "Hegels Geistphilosophie als Ort theologischer Erkenntnis," in: Christoph Böttigheimer/Florian Bruckmann: Glaubensverantwortung im Horizont der Zeichen der Zeit, Freiburg i.B. 2012, 304–328.
Wilson, David S. (2002): Darwin's Cathedral: Evolution, Religion, and the Nature of Society, Chicago.
Wittgenstein, Ludwig (1990^4): "Vermischte Bemerkungen", in: Werkausgabe, Bd. 8., Frankfurt a.M.
Zagzebski, Linda (1998^2): Virtues of the Mind: An Inquiry into the Nature of Virtue and the Ethical Foundations of Knowledge, Cambridge, 326–329.
Zagzebski, Linda T. (1993): Rational Faith: Catholic Responses to Reformed Epistemology, Notre Dame.
Zeis, John (1998): "Plantinga's Theory of Warrant: Religious Beliefs and Higher Level Epistemic Judgements", in: American Catholic Philosophical Quarterly 72, 23–38.

Anita Renusch
Thank God it's the right religion!— Plantinga on religious diversity

1 Introduction

In his *Warranted Christian Belief* (WCB) Plantinga presents the so-called Aquinas/Calvin (A/C) Model in order to show that if Christian belief is true then there is no sound objection to its epistemological righteousness; in other words, Christian belief is most probably justified, rational and warranted according to Plantinga. Plantinga also presents an extension of the model—the extended A/C Model—which he employs for devising an interesting response to the challenge many religious people feel when pondering the facts of religious diversity. The extended A/C Model is intended as an inner-Christian account and hence presupposes what Plantinga claims to be Christian doctrines: God had wanted human beings to know him and thus created all of them with something like a *sensus divinitatis*, a cognitive faculty that functions properly according to God's design plan and in an appropriate environment produces true Christian beliefs in a basic way, just as memory or perceptual beliefs are produced by their corresponding cognitive processes. Unfortunately though, humans fell into sin and therefore this particular belief-producing faculty was severely damaged; hence it is not possible to know God as it was before sin entered the world. However, the A/C Model continues, God provided the means to salvation, through his son, which are revealed in the Bible, and he restored the *sensus divinitatis* by something like the Internal Instigation of the Holy Spirit—he did so for Christians but for reasons we do not fully understand the *sensus divinitatis* was not restored (or at least not to the extent as it was in Christians) in Non-Christians.[1] What is interesting with respect to the problem of religious diversity is the answer the extended A/C Model provides to that problem for the Christian:

> [The Christian] therefore thinks she is in a better epistemic position [...] than those who do not share her convictions; for she believes she has the witness of the divinely guided church, or the internal testimony of the Holy Spirit, or perhaps still another source for this knowledge. She may be *mistaken*, in so thinking [...] but she needn't be culpable in holding this belief. [...] the believer nonculpably believes that she has a source of knowl-

---

[1] Plantinga thereby suggests a model that could have also been different in his view (WCB, 170). So, for our purpose, we do not have to discuss its details.

edge or true belief denied those who disagree with her. This protects her from epistemic egoism, as well as from the defeater that might accompany awareness of it. (WCB, 454)

In summary, believing that due to the work of the *sensus divinitatis* and the Holy Spirit she got it right and the adherents of other religions got it wrong, sticking to her beliefs in the face of religious diversity is rational for the Christian believer. Christians—Plantinga lets us know—nonculpably believe that they are in a "better epistemic position" than those holding beliefs incompatible with Christian belief.

Nonculpably, I hope, in misunderstanding such a great philosopher as Professor Plantinga is, I am going to argue in this text that believing oneself to be in a better epistemic position is not as easy as Plantinga thinks it is. More precisely, I won't contest the claim that Christians in fact are epistemically privileged but the claim that believing so is rational in religious disagreement. After a short introduction sketching the problem of religious diversity I, therefore, consider the question of how to assess one's dissenter's epistemic competence in a disagreement. Subsequently, I argue that Plantinga does not take into account these considerations to a sufficient degree in his defense of Christian belief and that he thus disregards part of the trouble the problem of religious diversity causes for religious believers.

Plantinga's discussion of the problem of religious diversity can be seen as a reaction to objections raised by Hick and others against religious exclusivism, the view that "the tenets or some of the tenets of one religion [...] are in fact true [...and] that any propositions, including other religious beliefs, that are incompatible with those tenets are false" (WCB, 440).[2] Apart from moral and probabilistic aspects Plantinga mostly concentrates on the epistemological challenge of religious diversity and thus on the question: Can a person rationally stick to her religious beliefs when faced with religious disagreement?

Of course, this question might not only be posed with respect to religious beliefs but other beliefs as well. However, though much of what I have to say regarding that kind of belief and disagreement is compatible with answers to similar questions on non-religious beliefs, I nonetheless focus on religious beliefs in this treatment simply because Plantinga does. Plantinga finds his adversary most clearly expressed in the writings of Gutting, saying:

---

[2] There are other ways to specify "religious exclusivism" though none is as useful for epistemological purposes than that given by Plantinga. Note that the conception of "religious exclusivism" usually includes soteriological elements as well—a fact Plantinga gives astonishingly little attention.

[B]ecause believers have many epistemic peers who do not share their belief in God (and even more who do not share their belief that ‚God exists' is properly basic), they have no right to maintain their belief without a justification. If they do so, they are guilty of epistemological egoism. (Gutting 1982, 90)

Hence, according to Gutting the problem he points to is roughly this: Take a religious believer, who is aware that there are people holding beliefs that are incompatible to her own religious beliefs—among them many adherents of other religions. The believer acknowledges that those people are as intelligent as she is, that they are equally reflective and honest, perhaps also equally pious, and that they are aware of the phenomenon of religious diversity as she herself is. Furthermore, they seem to think that their beliefs are coherent and that they gain support by various arguments and from religious experience in a similar way to how she holds her beliefs to be coherent and to be supported by evidence and thus being rational. However, there seems to be no argument that every side agrees to be sound, no generally recognized source of authority and no other neutral way to come to a conclusion about which of the rival attitudes are true. What is the right reaction for the believer? How should the awareness of the disagreement affect her beliefs given the fact that just one of two incompatible claims could be true?

2 Disagreeing

Let us take a closer look at disagreements. For the sake of simplicity, I focus on situations in which one person believes that p and another person believes that non-p. Needless to say, many of the conflicts people have are not as easy as that but involve more than two people or more than one controversial proposition. In addition, there are conflicts about beliefs that are different but do not contradict each other. My excuse for reducing complexity by concentrating on this pure case is that I hope to gain some results which are worthy of being carried over to the more complex situations in the future.

Whenever I and another agent disagree on p there are basically three options:
a) I can or even should stick to my belief. I can (or should) do so if I believe that I have better evidence for my belief than my opponent has for his belief, if I take myself to be more familiar with the controversial issue and if, all things considered, I regard myself as more competent with respect to the relevant question whether p is true or false.

b) I should abandon my belief and adopt its denial.³ I should do this if I believe that my evidence for my belief is worse than my opponent's for his belief, if I take myself to be less familiar with the controversial issue, and if, all things considered, I regard myself as less competent with respect to the relevant question whether p is true or false.
c) I should withhold my belief. I should do this if I believe that we both have equally good evidence for our beliefs, if I take us to be equally familiar with the controversial issue and if, all things considered, I regard us to be equally competent with respect to the relevant question whether my belief is true or false.

The third option calls for a "conciliatory attitude" or "conciliationism".⁴ Although there is fairly broad agreement about the required consequences in situations like a) and b) there is not nearly such a consensus when it comes to the third. Gutting's use of the expression "epistemic peer" indicates that he seems to have in mind situations of this third kind—cases of peer disagreement so to say. However, what motivates the conciliatory view? Why should we be required to suspend belief in a peer disagreement?

There is a strong intuition that becoming aware of peer disagreement affects and should affect our beliefs. Sidgwick already put it this way:

> For if I find any of my judgments, intuitive or inferential, in direct conflict with a judgment of some other mind, there must be error somewhere: and if I have no more reason to suspect error in the other mind than in my own reflective comparison between the two judgments necessarily reduces me temporarily to a state of neutrality. (Sidgwick 1893, 342)

That sounds plausible for many situations like the following example:⁵ Two friends, let us call them Jack and Rose, dine at a restaurant. They have done so regularly for many years now. When it is time to pay, they always proceed in the same way: They add a 20% tip and then split the bill. Jack and Rose each calculate in their heads once the waiter brings the check. In the past they agreed on the result most of the time. Disagreement rarely occurred and

---

3 Again this implies simplification. Instead of keeping my belief I could also be required to keep it with diminished confidence or instead of abandoning my belief completely I could give it up partly.
4 I owe these terms to David Christensen, who introduced them into the philosophical debate on "peer disagreement"; cf., for instance, his Christensen (2009).
5 The example is one that is quite often referred to in the literature. As far as I am aware Christensen was the first one to use it in his "Epistemology of Disagreement: the Good News" (cf. Christensen 2007). I recall it here slightly different and abridged.

if it did, it was Jack as often as it was Rose who was right in the end. Today none of them had reason to think that he or she is more tired than the other one (or more tipsy or affected in another way). So they both take each other to be equally good at mental math when they are doing their latest calculations. However, upon being confident that it is $43, Jack hears Rose say that it is $45. It would be awkward for Jack to insist on his figure and that, of course, holds for Rose the other way around. The conciliatory response sounds like the mandatory strategy in this case. However, does this hold for any situation of peer disagreement?

Three different replies might be defended. *The first one says: Yes*, whenever a person finds one of her opinions in contradiction with that of an epistemic peer she should suspend her belief as long as there is no consensus on the critical issue. However, a solution to Jack's and Rose's disagreement is easily available, which is certainly not the case in quite a few long-standing controversies, such as people have, on religious, political, philosophical, or moral topics. If, according to conciliationism, a person can or should no longer believe what she believed prior to becoming aware of peer disagreement, conciliationism threatens to foster widespread skepticism in all controversial areas. This is a rather unattractive price to pay and the question is whether these costs can be avoided.

The second reply says: No, maintaining their beliefs is permitted or even obligatory for people having acknowledged that they disagree with an epistemic peer. Alston, for instance, argues that a person can reasonably stick to her belief in a disagreement in some situations, although at least for Alston it is for reasons other than those pertaining to the epistemic justification of her belief.[6] Apart from the question of the normative value of such practical reasons, an advocate of this account would have to explain why it finds application in some situations (as Alston wants it to apply for beliefs in religious disagreements) but not in others (as it certainly does not apply in the restaurant case).

Plantinga adds a third reply saying: Yes, but even in controversial fields like religion people have fewer epistemic peers than objectors like Gutting think they have. Therefore, maintaining beliefs in the face of peer disagreement is rational in many conflicts over religious beliefs. More precisely, Plantinga's argument is this: He first concedes that acknowledged peer disagreement can diminish one's epistemic confidence or that it should lead to belief suspension respectively.[7] However, he then argues that Christians need not regard people claiming contradictory claims to be true as their epistemic peers and that most Christians do not in fact do so. Thus, Plantinga concludes, Christians need not withhold

---

6 Cf. Alston (1993, chap. 7).
7 Cf. WCB, 453.

their beliefs when faced with disagreement. Even if it is generally rational to suspend belief in the face of peer disagreement, it does not lead to skepticism on Christian belief because Christians need not or should not regard their religious opponents as their epistemic peers. To put it in a different way: The problem of religious diversity does not affect the rationality of Christian beliefs.

My target is the second premise in Plantinga's argument. What do Christians believe about the epistemic stance of non-Christians and what is rational for them to believe? Recent debates focus on criteria like the following for determining epistemic peerhood:

> Let us say that two individuals are epistemic peers with respect to some question if and only if they satisfy the following two conditions:
> (i) they are equals with respect to their familiarity with the evidence and arguments which bear on that question, and
> (ii) they are equals with respect to general epistemic virtues such as intelligence, thoughtfulness, and freedom from bias. (Kelly 2005, 174)

There are a number of problems linked to this account and to the notion "epistemic peer" in general. So let me clarify how I will employ it and give further explanations on the two elements Kelly points to. It is important to note that there are two different ways of understanding, which should be kept apart from each other. First, one can talk of a person *being* another person's epistemic peer and, second, one can say that one person (or more than one) *regards* another person as her epistemic peer.[8] Ignoring these different readings clearly causes confusion. What happens, for instance, if two people are epistemic peers but do not recognize that this is so? What happens if just one of them does? How do we deal with situations in which both take each other to be epistemic peers but in fact they are not peers?

We will seldom have certainty about two people actually and undoubtedly being peers. Anyway, with respect to the question of how to react in a disagreement, the second understanding is the more interesting one. Most people will usually take into account more than one alternative in a disagreement when thinking about their dissenters:[9] Apart from the option that they have to deal with an epistemic peer, they will also consider the option that the dissenter is in a better epistemic position or the option that he is epistemically inferior. In at least two of the three options—superiority and epistemic peerhood—it is un-

---

[8] Cf. for this distinction Enoch (2011, 970 ff.).
[9] As usual, exceptions confirm the rule. An absolute expert, for instance, would not contemplate the question of whether some layperson is in a better epistemic position to know one of the propositions in the field of expertise.

clear according to the current philosophical stand, whether sticking to one's belief is rational or not.[10] So let us look at how we assess the epistemic credentials of a dissenter in more detail. In the course of this, Kelly's distinction between the evidential side of equality and the cognitive side will guide us.

3 Assessing the epistemic credentials of a dissenter

Evidential equality requires taking the other person as equally informed and familiar with respect to the evidence and arguments that bear on a controversial question, as Kelly's definition says—a state which is ideally achieved by a full disclosure of all relevant evidence that bears on that controversial question. This might be easy in situations like the restaurant case but turns out to be quite difficult for more complex questions, for which it is sometimes extremely troublesome to communicate all evidence completely. Some evidence is difficult to put into words, some loses its force when transmitted from one person to another, and some may be valid evidence for me but not for you. Therefore, in a disagreement on a certain proposition p, the participants will often also argue on what counts as evidence for p and what does not, since what we believe is usually related to what we believe is good evidence.[11] If someone believes p to be true, evidence for p will also look more favorable to her than to someone believing p to be false. Two people claiming incompatible beliefs to be true thus probably refer to different pieces of evidence since not every proposition that one person regards as supporting her view is seen as good evidence by another person with a different view. People's assessment of evidence is often not independent of what they believe to be true.

So usually dissenters will not have the same evidence, at least not exactly. However, this fact should not lead us to conclude that what has been discussed under the heading of peer disagreement is of little or no epistemic relevance. Although dissenters quite seldom (or perhaps never) *have* exactly the same body of evidence, it is possible for them to *tell* each other what they think supports the proposition they disagree on. Thus it is possible to account for and to take note of another person's evidence to a certain degree. Accounting for the evidence of

---

10 For the question of whether it is rational once epistemic superiors are involved cf. Frances (2010). For the question of whether it is rational to stick to one's belief when having a peer disagreement see, among others, the following collection of texts: Feldman/Warfield (2010).
11 For more on this cf. Timothy Williamson (2010, 212).

another person can take on different scopes if we allow for there being different kinds of evidence. A first step consists in reporting what, in line with King, I will call "dialectical evidence".[12] According to King, a person has dialectical evidence for a proposition p if she is "aware of an argument for [p] whose premises beg no questions against someone who currently does not believe [p]" (King 2011, 6).[13] Dialectical evidence can be disclosed, it is intersubjectively accessible, and it seems possible that two people *have* the same dialectical evidence (which, of course, immediately leads to the question whether rational disagreement is possible in this case).

Sometimes, however, explaining disagreements involves another kind of evidence, one that is just partly intersubjectively comprehensible, its main elements being intuitions, insights, and experiences.[14] It is obvious that the exchange of this kind of evidence is more difficult than the exchange of dialectical evidence. Still, *reporting* experiences or intuitions is possible to a certain extent even though this does not result in others *having* the same such evidence. Rather we would say in at least some cases that the other party has equally good evidence. The descriptions of a Muslim mystic and a Christian mystic, for example, deal with different experiences and support different religious beliefs. However, even if the Muslim mystic thus does not share the Christian's experience he can acknowledge that the Christian experienced something that can be compared with his own experience.

Finally, some might want to add a third step in taking note of each other's evidence and that is done by disclosing background beliefs. Disclosure with regard to this kind of evidence (if we are willing to call it that) is not required to a great extent in disagreements such as the restaurant case. However, many beliefs gain their support from other beliefs a person holds, which themselves are in need of support from other beliefs, and so on. A person's stance on the question whether abortion should be permitted, for example, is likely to depend on other beliefs she has, beliefs about the value of human life and the question of when it

---

12 Cf. King (2011, 254), to whose text I owe the following distinction between different broad conceptions of evidence, starting with dialectical evidence. I will not argue here that the other two on which I further comment in what follows—experience and background knowledge—could be legitimately referred to using "evidence", too. Instead, I will simply assume for the purpose of this text that the evidentialist conception of evidence (that excludes them) is too strict. For a critical discussion of the latter see, for instance, Van Inwagen (1996, 137–53).
13 Cf. also Kelly (2011, 171).
14 Note that some philosophers would not call these items "evidence" at all and that for each of the three terms it is not quite clear what they refer to. However, I trust that the reader has some kind of intuitive access allowing him or her to see that there is a difference between this kind of evidence and dialectical evidence.

starts, beliefs about the needs and rights of a pregnant woman, beliefs about what a mother can and cannot bear and so on.

However, listing these different sorts of evidence casts a shadow on our previously given notion of evidential equality: If our concept of evidence incorporates experiences, intuitions as well as insights, and even background beliefs, two persons having the same evidence seems virtually impossible. Who, at any rate, knows someone entertaining exactly the same set of background beliefs? And how can someone find that out for sure?—That should be difficult. This difficulty does not mean, however, that in some cases there is not such a thing as a very high degree of evidential correspondence. And whereas genuine peer disagreement (that is, disagreement in which both parties have *exactly* the same evidence) might be an ideal, disagreements in which people come close to that ideal without matching it are not without any epistemic significance. We could also express that by saying evidential equality and hence epistemic peerhood is not a matter of all-or-nothing but comes in degrees, its epistemic impact rising to the extent the conditions of peerhood are fulfilled. The more a person thinks that she has evidence in common with her dissenter, the more troubled she will and should be by the current disagreement she has with that person. The closer one person takes another one to be, the spicier the disagreement.

Thus, the use of the concept of "evidential equality" can be vindicated even though it turns out to be difficult to find paradigm cases in which all of its conditions are fulfilled in an ideal way. Assuming evidential equality occurs on different levels on a spectrum between having much in common and differing on almost every belief. The closer the two agents get in sharing dialectical evidence, background beliefs, and having equally good experiences and intuitions, the higher the epistemic significance of their actual belief conflict.

Evidential equality, however, might be of little interest with regard to religious beliefs if Plantinga's claim is true that it is not the evidence that is crucial with respect to the question whether religious beliefs are rational or whether they have warrant for a person. If religious people indeed do not hold their religious beliefs on the basis of evidence, estimation of the overall cognitive competence of a dissenter is paramount to assessing whether he has the same or equally good evidence. The same is true when the participants of the disagreement do not have any hints suggesting evidential asymmetry. Seeking to explain the disagreement in both situations people will be interested in the following questions: Is there a reason to think that one's dissenter is as equally likely to arrive at a true belief as one thinks oneself to be? Could he be a better assessor of the evidence or a worse one? Is he perhaps more intelligent or less or does he have better reasoning skills that are relevant to the controversial question? Or is there another difference with respect to the items Kelly's definition of cognitive equality summarized as "epistemic virtues"?

The most straightforward way to find out whether my dissenter is one of my cognitive equals with respect to a certain issue or whether he is in a better or worse epistemic position would be to compare our *track records* with respect to the type of beliefs we are disagreeing about—a similar track record indicating that the other person is my peer. Presupposing a common or equally good body of evidence, finding out that my dissenter was right in the past just as often as I was gives me reason to assume that he is equally likely to have a true belief on the current matter in question than it is likely that I do (and correspondingly that it is also equally likely that he has a false belief, as it is likely that I have) which is why peer disagreement is epistemically significant for social agents. Here is an example of how assessment of one's dissenter's epistemic credentials could proceed by using track records:

Take Jack and Rose again dining in a restaurant, splitting the check at the end of their get-together, and, today, arriving at different results. Before asking the waitress for a calculator, Jack makes one of the following observations:[15]

i. 'The last ten nights we ate together, both of us figured out the correct result in each case (or both of us figured it out nine times and one time both of us got the wrong result, or both of us had five correct and five false, or both of us never had a correct result). All things being equal (I have no reason to think that I am or Rose is more tired or tipsy today than the other, or suffers from another kind of impairment the other one does not, or that the arithmetic task is more difficult today than the tasks were in the past) Rose's chances for calculating the right figure today are equally as high as mine.' That is to say Jack takes Rose as his cognitive equal.

ii. 'The last ten nights we ate together, Rose figured out the correct result in each case whereas I was wrong every time (or Rose figured out the correct result nine times and I just one time, or Rose was right eight times and I was wrong eight times, and so on). All things being equal, Rose is more likely to figure out the right result today than I am.' That is to say that Jack takes Rose as being epistemically superior with respect to the matter of calculating their shares.

iii. 'The last ten nights we ate together, I figured out the correct result in each case whereas Rose was wrong every time (or I figured out the correct result

---

15 I would say that much of the following happens rather implicitly. Setting it down in a detailed way like this, however, gives us some insights by making explicit some of the thoughts that are in the background of the agent's mind.

nine times and Rose just one time, or I was right eight times and Rose was wrong eight times, and so on). All things being equal, Rose is less likely to figure out the right result today than I am.' That is to say that Jack takes Rose as being epistemically inferior with respect to the matter of calculating their shares.

It is important to note that track records are available to the agents in this case and thus can be used for the assessment of one's dissenter.[16] Jack and Rose can be sure at least afterwards who was right in each of their foregone disagreements. I believe that this is true for many disagreements about non-inferential beliefs but not, for instance, for philosophical, religious or moral beliefs (unfortunately, there is no calculator settling questions in these areas), which makes the evaluation of a dissenter's cognitive credentials more complicated in these cases. Let me introduce another couple in order to explain the problem. Emma disagrees with Tom about proposition p, which concerns, let us say, a moral issue. If Emma wants to know whether Tom is equally (or less or more) likely to give the right answer to a question as she herself is, she might say: "Look, I believe that p and Tom believes that non-p. However, Tom also disagreed on the propositions q, r and s in the past. In all those cases I was right and Tom was wrong. Tom also disagrees now. Therefore he will be wrong this time too and I will be right on whether p or not." This procedure can be question-begging. In some circumstances, however, it also can be legitimate. Whether it is question-begging or not is a matter of degree and a question of whether all the disagreements Emma bases her estimation of Tom's epistemic competence on are independent of each other.

Imagine that Tom and Emma disagree not only on p but on almost every belief Emma has in any area you could think of. Among Emma's beliefs, however, there will be some she will have good evidence for and some she holds with a high degree of confidence; some that most reasonable people hold to be true and some that she knows she is an expert on. If she finds herself to be in such a vast disagreement with Tom and if she has no reason to think that she is mentally impaired, she will and should think that she is in a better epistemic position with respect to p than Tom is. The more disagreement Emma comes across the more likely it is that she takes Tom to be "deranged".[17] "How can

---

16 Furthermore, it is easy to define the relevant type of belief, which it is not in many other situations.
17 Christensen (2011, 13) makes the same point and White (2009, 247 ff.) develops a similar idea, too.

he reject all those things I hold to be true?" she might wonder and judge, "he must be strange".

If there is minor disagreement however, or disagreement in just one realm, or if the additional disagreements their mutual disclosure reveals are not independent of each other, then it is less likely that Emma will think so, particularly if the beliefs they disagreed on in the past are such that she could not know who was right. Finally, if Emma finds out that there is broad agreement between her and Tom apart from p and some related claims, she will be inclined to think that Tom is equally epistemically virtuous and thus equally likely to have a true belief regarding p. "Why does such an intelligent person as Tom, with whom I share so many of my beliefs, disagree on p?" she might wonder. In this case the disagreement probably affects her belief that p and it would be question-begging if she tried to show her epistemic superiority by pointing to cases of disagreement about propositions q, r, and s, which are related to p. Emma has reason in this situation to think of Tom as her epistemic peer because she has a couple of beliefs about Tom among them many suggesting that Tom is her peer in a way that is independent of their current disagreement. In the first case when she and Tom disagreed in every area, she lacks that common basis providing reason to think that Tom is her peer in the same way that she lacks that basis when disagreeing with a stranger she knows little about. The more reason a person has to think that a dissenter is her epistemic peer the greater the impact of the disagreement.

4 Being in a better epistemic position

Let Emma now be a Christian and Tom a non-Christian, having beliefs that are incompatible with Emma's Christian convictions. Now, according to Plantinga, Emma believes the difference between her and Tom to be this: She has a special source of true beliefs for her Christian beliefs whereas Tom does not have one for his non-Christian beliefs. Recall what Plantinga claims about the Christian's stance with respect to religious disagreement:

> She [the Christian] therefore thinks she is in a better epistemic position with respect to this proposition than those who do not share her convictions; for she believes she has the witness of the divinely guided church, or the internal testimony of the Holy Spirit, or perhaps still another source for this knowledge. [...] As a result, of course, the serious believer will not take it that we are all, believers and unbelievers alike, epistemic peers on the topic of Christian belief. [...] If something like the extended Aquinas/Calvin (A/C) model [...] is in fact correct, then there is a significant difference between the epistemic situation of those who accept Christian belief and those who do not. (WCB, 454 f.)

Having a belief source that reliably produces true beliefs requires proper function according to Plantinga, which means "the absence of dysfunction or pathology. [...] It requires, first, proper function with respect to the formation of the sensory experience on which perceptual belief is based. And it consists, second, in the formation of the right kind of doxastic experience—that is, the sort of doxastic experience required by proper function" (WCB 110, 112). According to the extended A/C Model Christians display this kind of proper function with respect to their *sensus divinitatis* supported by the Internal Instigation of the Holy Spirit whereas non-Christians remain in an epistemically unsatisfactory state.

Note that proper function is at the same time the essential part of what Plantinga claims "warrant" to be—that property or quantity, enough of which makes the difference between knowledge and mere true belief. Having warrant in its core means having a belief that is the result of properly functioning cognitive faculties or processes according to Plantinga. He further enriches this concept by adding that belief formation happens in an appropriate cognitive environment, "according to a design plan that is successfully aimed at the production of true belief" (WCB, XI). If cognitive faculties or processes function properly, they are a reliable source for true beliefs. The use of "successfully aimed at" indicates that a person having warrant in this sense and her beliefs being false nonetheless is not impossible.[18] However, it also says that having warrant and believing something false is very unlikely.

Plantinga argues that if it is true that God arranged Christians to know him by the production of true beliefs via the *sensus divinitatis* and by the Internal Instigation of the Holy Spirit, then Christian belief is probably warranted for Christians. If it is not, Christian belief probably lacks warrant for Christians. However, as Plantinga admits, "warrant seems to have a *contextual* character; the degree of warrant necessary for knowledge seems to depend, to some extent, on circumstances and context" (WCB, 161, emphasis original). As Plantinga does not dwell on this remark, let us do so here.

The first thing to note is that it is difficult to say whether a belief has been produced by properly functioning faculties or processes and whether it was formed in an appropriate environment according to a design plan. There is no empirical evidence for the existence of a *sensus divinitatis* (and for its proper function).[19] This point alone does not speak against the truth of the model; most of the functioning of our cognitive faculties is far from being fully explored

---

18 After all, the beliefs' acquisition could happen under exceptional circumstances such as for those of the title character in the film "The Truman Show".
19 It is even difficult to imagine what such evidence would look like; cf. Fales (2003, 361).

by scientists. People usually take their faculties to function properly without being able to prove that this is so. Furthermore, in order to think about the proper functioning of our belief-forming processes we have to rely on those processes and their proper functioning, which makes our investigation even more complicated. However, it is a fact that some sources work properly and some do not. That is, some faculties or processes reliably produce true beliefs whereas others do not. Is there a way to distinguish between them apart from having meta-knowledge about their proper functioning? How can agents figure out whether to rely on a belief source or not?

There is an element in Plantinga's epistemology that could play the role of an indicator for the proper functioning of cognitive faculties, one that is at the agent's disposal. In *Warranted Christian Belief* Plantinga specifies this element as "doxastic experience" (WCB, 111) which he determines as a certain *seeming*, that is, the belief in question seems obviously true to the agent like perceptual or memory beliefs often simply seem to be true to the agent. Plantinga believes that this kind of doxastic experience is also present in the formation of Christian beliefs. According to the extended A/C Model, to the Christian believer "the great things of the gospel seem clearly true, obvious, compelling" (WCB, 264). It appears to the believer: "Yes, that's right, that's the truth on the matter; this is indeed the word of the Lord" (WCB, 250). The pivotal question now is this: Can or even should the Christian stick to her belief in the face of disagreement and thereby think that she is in a better epistemic position because what she believes seems utterly obvious to her, that is, because she has this certain kind of doxastic experience?

In his writings Plantinga makes frequent use of examples like the following one for the purpose of illustration:

> (Hiker) "I am a suspect in a crime committed yesterday afternoon; I have means, motive, opportunity. I am known to have committed this kind of crime before, and a credible eyewitness claims to have seen me at the crime scene. Nevertheless, I clearly remember spending yesterday afternoon on a solitary hike miles from the scene of the crime."
> (Plantinga 2001, 220)

To give the hiker's dissenter a name, think of a prosecutor. We could possibly assume that the hiker has a disagreement with the prosecutor in this case; the prosecutor believes that hiker was not on a solitary hike miles away on that afternoon, whereas our hiker does believe that he was. Plantinga wants this case to be analogous to the situation of the religious believer. However, there is an important difference between the two. There is no one in the epistemic environment of the hiker, whom the hiker takes as knowing as well as he does what happened on that crucial afternoon. The hiker need not doubt his epistemically privileged position (at least under normal circumstances) because he can quite easily refer to his positive track record with respect to his memory beliefs (arguably he is the most reliable person when it comes to his own memory beliefs). Christians cannot refer to something like this for their Christian beliefs. Many and perhaps most Christians today are surrounded by witnesses of other faiths, who claim or could claim like Christians themselves according to the A/C Model do that they have some source of knowledge other people lack. At least there are lots of people contesting the claim that Christians are in a better epistemic position.

In order to specify this idea let us call the hiker Jack and the Christian Emma again. Jack had never been in a situation like this before—being accused of committing a crime he is not actually responsible for. He is not aware of having suffered from malfunction of his memory in the past (at least not to a great extent). Further, he has evidence for many of his other memory beliefs, he crosschecked them with other agents, and all his other mental capacities seem to be fine. The situation would be different if his memory beliefs had been constantly questioned in the past and if he knows that he suffered from mental blackouts. However, the latter not being the case, his insistence on his innocence is rational for him even in the face of disagreement.

The picture looks very different on the other side for the Christian Emma or at least for many of the Emmas we could think of. As epistemic circumstances of Christians vary, think of an Emma first, who was raised in a Christian community, read what the priest told her to read, has not encountered believers of other faiths so far, and perhaps also thinks that "the great things of the gospel seem clearly true, obvious, compelling" (WCB, 264). When she finally becomes aware that another person disagrees on one or some of her religious beliefs she might regard this event as an exception, the way the hiker does not regard the prosecutor's claim as a serious challenge to his own belief that his memory functions properly. This down-home Emma may thus rationally believe that she is in a better epistemic situation than her opponent. However, Plantinga wants his Model not only to apply to this kind of religious believer but also to capture the "sophisticated, aware, educated, turn-of-the-millennium people who have read their Freud and Nietzsche, their Hume and Mackie" and who are "fully aware of other faiths, have had their existence and their claims called to [their] attention [...] and [...] have noted that the adherents of other religions sometimes appear to display great intelligence, moral excellence, and spiritual insight and have [...] reflected on the problem of pluralism..." (WCB, 200, 440). So let us test the hiker analogy with respect to an educated Emma living in a pluralistic context, too. This Emma was raised learning that her religious beliefs are constantly being challenged. Although she also belongs to a Christian community confidence in her Christian beliefs varies. She believes there is some evidence in favor of her beliefs but she also knows evidence against it. She believes that God wants her to know him but she is puzzled by the fact that many people obviously do not know him. As for the adherents of other faiths, she counts some of them to be her closest friends, who share almost all the beliefs she has—moral, scientific, everyday, and even some religious beliefs. Yet, Emma and one of her friends still differ on a certain religious belief p (and perhaps some other beliefs r, s, and t, too). This belief has the "feel of being right" (WCB, 451) for Emma. However, such feelings can be misleading, which is often indicated by the disagreement of others.

Emma could still doubt in that situation that her friend's belief is accompanied by a doxastic phenomenology similar to what her belief that p is. However, having listened to what he said and having no reason to doubt his testimony, why should she do so? So let us assume that Emma acknowledges that she and her friend have the same sort of internally available phenomenology for their different beliefs, a condition whose existence Plantinga is willing to concede.[20] Bewildered by the constant disagreement, Emma tries to assess her dissenter's cognitive credentials in this case. As we learned, she cannot go for a comparison of track records in this case as their religious beliefs are not like the numbers in the restaurant case. She perhaps thinks that her friend is less qualified to answer the question whether p because he is less intelligent than she is or because he is known to let himself be guided by prejudice, in which case she would have a reason to think that she is in a better position as he is. However, perhaps she believes, instead, that he is as intelligent as she is, that he is equally honest and wary of bias as she is and so on. If she further agrees with him in a vast variety of other questions, she will have a reason to think that he is one of her cognitive equals which makes it difficult for her to tell why her belief should be right and her friend's belief should be wrong.

Plantinga's hiker analogy, thus, is misleading at least for some instances. It is not as clear as it is in the case of the hiker Jack, that Christians like Emma could rationally stick to their beliefs in the same way that Jack does. That his memory beliefs are challenged is an exception for Jack, whereas for Emma, inquiry into her Christian belief is a rule. Thus, it is far less problematic for the hiker to rely on his memory faculty as it is for Emma to rely on the *sensus divinitatis*. Contrary to what Jack thinks about his memory beliefs, it is much less easy for Emma to think that her Christian beliefs result from properly functioning faculties.

---

[20] Cf. Plantinga (2000, 181).

Think of another hiker analogy, one in which Jack enjoyed the company of his friend Rose in the mountains. As a friend, Rose does not intervene in Jack's disagreement with the prosecutor. However, when Jack and Rose are on their own, Rose reminds Jack that—contrary to their usual habit—this time they had departed after having walked together for some miles, Jack saying that he wanted to get back to town. So depending on whether this was true, there would have been enough time for him to commit the crime. Jack himself does not remember having done so. However, given Rose's confidential statement in addition to the prosecutor's evidence, and in the absence of a reason for not trusting Rose, it feels more and more appropriate for Jack to question his belief too, even if he holds it in a basic way.[21] This is so because in the past Rose's memory beliefs proved to be true as often as Jack's own memory beliefs did. Very much as in the restaurant case, Jack reasons using his and Rose's known track records, this time with respect not to arithmetic but to their memory beliefs. If Rose showed herself to be an unreliable source of memory beliefs in the past, Jack will not put much weight on her view on the hiking-crime case. If Jack showed himself, however, to be unreliable with respect to memory beliefs when compared to Rose or if he comes to think that Rose's memory is equally reliable, Rose's statement probably undermines Jack's confidence in his own belief.

The Christian Emma cannot compare track records with respect to her Christian beliefs as Jack does with respect to his memory beliefs or with arithmetic in the restaurant. She might think that she was right in other cases of disagreements she had with her friend about religious beliefs. However, many of hiking Jack's memory beliefs have been confirmed by sources other than his own memory and his figures in the restaurant have been checked via calculator. Emma in contrast has her belief that she has been blessed by the Internal Instigation of the Holy Spirit and the work of the *sensus divinitatis*—a belief that itself relies on the proper function of the process it stems from. That seems very little to oppose the assumption indicated by her current disagreement that her "Yes, that's right" experience could deceive her. Yet, let us assume that it is enough for the purpose of argument to see what follows.

---

21 The time elapsed since the event they are disagreeing about seems to be an important factor in this case, too, as the gap between beliefs produced by an unreliable and a reliable person becomes greater the further in the past the issue of disagreement is.

5 Varying confidence

It is an undeniable fact that many religious believers lack the doxastic "yes, that's right"-experience altogether,[22] a detail Plantinga acknowledges in a footnote:

> In typical cases, therefore, as opposed to paradigmatic cases, degree of belief will be less than maximal. Furthermore, degree of belief, on the part of the person who has faith, typically varies from time to time, from circumstance to circumstance. (WCB, 264, Fn. 43)[23]

At first view, this sounds puzzling given Plantinga's assumption of the *sensus divinitatis* as a proper functioning cognitive faculty. As we have learned proper function results in having the right kind of doxastic experience. So if Christians indeed display proper function of the *sensus divinitatis* it is hard to see how their degree of belief could be less than maximal. Lack of epistemic confidence can be explained, however, by means of what Plantinga says about the work of the Holy Spirit in his extended A/C Model: Due to sin the *sensus divinitatis* had been corrupted, Plantinga explains. Apart from its other consequences, sin hinders us from knowing God in a way in which it had been possible to know him before sin entered the world.[24] In order to limit the damage, God, however, makes up the cognitive loss by sending his Holy Spirit:

> By virtue of the work of the Holy Spirit in the hearts of those to whom faith is given, the ravages of sin (including the cognitive damage) are repaired, *gradually or suddenly, to a greater or lesser extent*. (WCB, 243f., my emphasis).

With respect to the question of why some or even many Christians do not have the right kind of doxastic experience, the last quoted words are important because they seem to indicate that the work of the Holy Spirit often results in beliefs having less than the maximal degree of confidence—an assumption that causes some difficulties for Plantinga's account.

Firstly, it is not clear whether these beliefs thus gained through the Internal Instigation of the Holy Spirit have enough warrant. Plantinga describes the work

---

[22] That is why Chignell (2002) objects that Plantinga offers an "epistemology for saints".
[23] Interestingly, Plantinga had previously argued in another context not only that Christian beliefs have warrant for Christians, if true, but that those beliefs have warrant for "most Christians" ibid., 201. So the question is not quite clear as to how many believers Plantinga's account is supposed to cover.
[24] For Plantinga's detailed account of how sin works, cf. WCB, 205, 115ff.

of the Holy Spirit as "a cognitive process that produces in us belief in the main lines of the Christian story" (WCB, 206). For beliefs resulting from properly functioning processes, Plantinga defines the right kind of doxastic experience as the impression "Yes, that's right". Furthermore, according to Plantinga, the strength of belief determines the degree of its warrant (and thus its eligibility for counting as knowledge).[25] Do believers whose *sensus divinitatis* has only been partially repaired or to a lesser extent have the right kind of doxastic experience and hence a high degree of warrant for their beliefs? It seems that they do not and that thus Plantinga cannot have both: an explanation for the lack of epistemic confidence familiar to many believers, in terms of the Holy Spirit producing beliefs with less than the maximal degree of confidence and the claim that Christian beliefs are warranted for (many or most) Christians.

The second difficulty directly bears on the question of how to react when faced with religious disagreement. Let us return to the question we started with and pay attention to the fact that in the typical case Christian belief is not joined by the "Yes, that's right"-experience. Are believers in those typical cases rational if they stick to their beliefs in a disagreement in the same way that perhaps those Christians are, whose beliefs go along with the feeling of being right? What reason could the typical Christian have to believe that she is in a better epistemic position in a disagreement if her beliefs do not enjoy the high degree of confidence which warranted beliefs usually have according to Plantinga? If the Christian does not think that she has got a "knock-down, drag-out argument, a demonstration or conclusive proof" (WCB, 440)[26] of her beliefs, she will try to get an idea of the other agent's cognitive abilities. Lacking the appropriate degree of belief she will (and should) probably not think that she is in a better epistemic position because her belief enjoys warrant whereas the other one does not. As for general epistemic virtues like intelligence, thoughtfulness, and so on, she knows that those factors are not limited by the borders of a certain religion. What is more, the typical Christian might know adherents of other religions disagreeing on her religious beliefs, for whom she has reason to think that they are her epistemic peers. They might be her friends, with whom she agrees in almost every area (morality, politics, science), except that some of their religious beliefs differ. That person has enough dispute-independent evidence for thinking that her dissenters are equally likely to arrive at a true belief as she is and demoting them based on their current disagreement (or by reference to related disagreements) would be question-begging.

---

25 Cf. WCB, 258.
26 Which most Christians do not think, according to Plantinga.

For Christians of the latter type the skeptical challenge of the conciliatory position persists. If they are in a position to think that it is equally likely that the other side made a mistake or failed in some sense as it is likely that they themselves did, then it is hard to see why they should think that their belief is true and that the incompatible one is false. Believing oneself to be in a better epistemic position is not possible for them. One can argue, however, whether this pertains to many Christians or not. Perhaps there are not so many Christians whose closest friends are staunch atheists or who belong to a different religion seen as equally epistemically virtuous by their fellow Christians. However, as we stated earlier in this text, equality comes in degrees and so does the disagreement's relevance. And thus more than a few people are likely to be affected.

6 Conclusion

So contrary to Plantinga's assumption that the awareness of religious disagreement need not undermine confidence in Christian beliefs, it still does for many religious believers. Recall Plantinga's "Yes, but"- answer to the problem of religious diversity which was already described earlier in this text: Plantinga first concedes that acknowledged peer disagreement should diminish one's epistemic confidence or that it can or even should lead to belief suspension respectively. However, he then argues that Christians need not regard people holding contradictory claims to be true as their epistemic peers and that they in fact do not do so. Thus, Plantinga concludes, Christians need not withhold their beliefs faced with disagreement. Even if it is generally rational to suspend belief in the face of peer disagreement, it does not lead to skepticism of Christian belief because Christians need not or even should not regard their religious opponents as their epistemic peers.

My argument consists of a criticism of the second premise. Contrary to Plantinga, I hold that many Christians have reason for regarding (some of) their religious dissenters as their epistemic peers and that they thus have a religious peer disagreement. Do we have to conclude that Christians and other religious believers should adopt the conciliatory response suspending their beliefs or trying to believe with less firmness? Remember that we started by listing three possible answers to the problem of religious diversity:

The first one opts for *conciliationism*, that is, for suspension of belief in the face of peer disagreement. With respect to this option we learned that religious skepticism looms large.

Plantinga's option, which is inapplicable for many believers as I argued in this text, was to say: *Yes, but* even in controversial fields like religion, people have fewer epistemic peers than an objector like Gutting thinks they have. Therefore, maintaining beliefs in the face of peer disagreement is rational in many conflicts on religious beliefs.

However, even if Plantinga's defense is only available for some but not for many believers, there is an account that promises to avoid the dreaded consequences of *conciliationism* even for those believers whose confidence varies, which is something like Alston's employment of practical considerations—an account that in my view deserves further exploration.[27]

Literature

Alston, William P. (1993): Perceiving God: The Epistemology of Religious Experience, 1. Paperback Print, Ithaca, New York, chap. 7.
Chignell, Andrew (2002): "Epistemology for Saints: Alvin Plantinga's magnum opus", in: Books and Culture—A Christian Review.
Christensen, David (2007): "Epistemology of Disagreement: the Good News", in: Philosophical Review, 116, no. 2.
Christensen, David (2009): "Introduction: The Epistemology of Disagreement", in: Episteme 6, no. 03.
Christensen, David (2011): "Disagreement, Question-Begging and Epistemic Self-Criticism", in: Philosophers' Imprint 6.
Enoch, David (2011): "Not Just a Truthometer: Taking Oneself Seriously (but not Too Seriously) in Cases of Peer Disagreement", in: Mind 119, no. 476.
Fales, Evan (2003): Review of: "Alvin Plantinga 'Warranted Christian Belief'", in: Noûs 37.
Feldman, Richard/Warfield, Ted A. (2010): Disagreement, New York.
Frances, Bryan (2010): "The Reflective Epistemic Renegade", in: Philosophy and Phenomenological Research 81, no. 2.
Gutting, Gary (1982): Religious Belief and Religious Skepticism, Notre Dame.
Kelly, Thomas (2005): "The Epistemic Significance of Disagreement", in: John Hawthorne/Tamar Gendler: Oxford Studies in Epistemology, vol. 1, Oxford, 167–196.
King, Nathan (2011): "Disagreement: What's the Problem? or A Good Peer is Hard to Find", in: Philosophy and Phenomenological Research 85, no. 2, 249–272.
Plantinga, Alvin (2000): "Pluralism: A Defense of Religious Exclusivism", in: Philip L. Quinn/Kevin Meeker (Eds.): The Philosophical Challenge of Religious Diversity, Oxford, 172–192.
Plantinga, Alvin (2000): Warranted Christian Belief, New York.
Plantinga, Alvin (2001): "Rationality and Public Evidence", in: Religious Studies 37, 220.

---

[27] I am most deeply indebted to Katherine Munn and Oliver Wiertz for many valuable comments on the argument. Many thanks also to Maggie Bell, Dieter Schönecker, Thomas Schmidt, as well as the participants of a workshop on the papers contained in this anthology, and the members of a research group founded by the John Templeton Foundation, who all red and discussed earlier versions of this paper.

Sidgwick, Henry (1893): The Methods of Ethics, London.
Van Inwagen, Peter (1996): "It Is Wrong, Everywhere, Always, and for Anyone, to Believe Anything upon Insufficient Evidence", in: Jeff Jordan and Daniel Howard-Snyder (Eds.): Faith, Freedom, and Rationality: Philosophy of Religion Today, Lanham Md., 137–153.
White, Roger (2009): "On Treating Oneself and Others as Thermometers", in: Episteme 6, no. 3.
Williamson, Timothy (2010): The Philosophy of Philosophy, The Blackwell/Brown lectures in philosophy 2, Malden, MA.

Georg Plasger
Does Calvin teach a sensus divinitatis? Reflections on Alvin Plantinga's Interpretation of Calvin

In the following reflections I will not attempt to analyze or review the entire religious-philosophical work of Plantinga. His considerations are powerful and challenging—and are therefore interesting as a topic for serious discussion, especially for theological scholarship. My question is far more modest. In Plantinga's major work *Warranted Christian Belief* (WCB)[1] it becomes clear that he develops his concept in a continual dialogue with the Geneva reformer, John Calvin.

First of all, this is something to be welcomed. For John Calvin in particular has the problematic reputation for being overly severe in his life and excessively strict in his teaching (especially with regard to the "double predestination" theory). While in theology (for the most part), where Calvinistic theology was widely influential, and to some extent still is (fueled by the 2009 anniversary of Calvin's birth), in contemporary philosophy there has been no really significant discussion and interpretation of Calvin apart from Plantinga (and other Reformed Epistemologists), as far as I know. It is striking and interesting to see how Plantinga finds ideas in Calvin's work that also serve him as a foundation for his approach. However, the question to be asked is whether the way in which Plantinga absorbs Calvin can be accepted insofar as it is supposed to be based on the texts of Calvin—and to examine this question is precisely the purpose of my paper.

1 Alvin Plantinga reads John Calvin

This first part is solely concerned with clarifying this initial point—or in other words: how Plantinga interprets and responds to John Calvin. I am limiting myself in my presentation and analysis to WCB, in order to ensure a reasonably secure overview. Plantinga mainly refers to texts from Calvin's major work *"Institutio Christianae religionis"* (in its final form from 1559), and in some points also to Calvin's works of biblical commentary; for our specific purposes here a focus on the first chapter of Paul's Letter to the Romans is important.

---

[1] New York 2000.

The basic thought that Plantinga finds in John Calvin's work (and in that of Thomas of Aquinas) is that every human being possesses "a kind of natural knowledge of God" (WCB, 170). According to Calvin, as Plantinga understands him, faith originates from this innate human knowledge of God, which displays itself in various forms: "Calvin's basic claim is that there is a sort of instinct, a natural human tendency, a disposition, a nisus to form beliefs about God under a variety of conditions and in a variety of situations" (WCB, 171). And it is this basic thought which must be more precisely discussed and understood. First of all we must address the question of what this "natural knowledge of God" is, a notion which, in Calvin's work, is simply an explication of a statement made by the apostle Paul in the first chapter of Romans. This "natural knowledge of God" is what Calvin calls "a sensus divinitatis or sense of divinity, which in a wide variety of circumstances produces in us beliefs about God" (WCB, 172)—and this sensus divinitatis is "a kind of faculty or a cognitive mechanism" (WCB, 172). This "natural knowledge of God" is innate—at least this is how Plantinga understands Calvin. Plantinga, however, has problems with the term "innate" in that he can only understand Calvin to suggest that "innate" means a "capacity", because, as Plantinga sees it, the knowledge of God cannot be attributed to each and every newborn child, even if this is sometimes manifested in young children. However, he is not so certain about whether he understands Calvin correctly here —but his own model, in any case, views the sensus divinitatis as a fundamental "capacity" that is to be understood as a "disposition, or set of dispositions" (WCB, 173).[2] How exactly does this "natural knowledge of God" work? "You see the blazing glory of heavens from a mountainside at 13,000 feet; you think about those unimaginable distances; you find yourself filled with awe and wonder, and you form the belief that God must be great to have created this magnificent heavenly host" (WCB, 173). Thus it can be seen here that Plantinga proposes a twofold approach: The ability to know God is innate, but what one does with this knowledge ("form") is a second stage. In other words: Human beings already have a knowledge of God before they are confronted with arguments that speak in favour of (or against) the belief in God: "The heavens declare the glory of God and the skies proclaim the work of his hands: but not by way of serving as premises for an argument" (WCB, 175). That humans have such a natural sense of God is fundamental. This "sensus divinitatis is a belief-producing faculty (or power, or mechanism) that under right conditions produces belief that is not evidentially based on other beliefs. On this model, our cognitive faculties have been de-

---

[2] As we shall show further on, Plantinga has noticed a possible divergence in this regard between Calvin's approach and his own. However, he does not elaborate on this.

signed and created by God ... The purpose of the sensus divinitatis is to enable us to have true beliefs about God" (WCB, 179). According to Plantinga, God has created this basal knowledge of God within humanity, and it is something fundamental with which He endowed each and every human being at creation. This innate knowledge of God is to be distinguished from the precise knowledge of God that the Holy Spirit imparts: "This work of the Holy Spirit, therefore, is a very special kind of cognitive instrument or agency; it is a belief-producing process, all right, but one that is very much out of the ordinary" (WCB, 180). So while the natural knowledge of God is an innate ability of all humanity, the knowledge that the Holy Spirit imparts is not given to all, but only to a selection of people (it is "out of the ordinary"). Both of these ways of having knowledge of God cannot be identified with one another; however, there is an explicit connection between them—and this connection is to be described in the context of universal human sin. For the "natural knowledge of God" could also have led to the right belief in God if sin had not intervened: The sensus divinitatis "would no doubt have been part of our epistemic establishment even if humanity had not fallen into sin" (WCB, 180). If humanity had not sinned, according to Plantinga, the sensus divinitatis, in its purpose of giving a reliable knowledge of God, would still be at work. This, however, is no longer the case: "Finally, according to the A/C model this natural knowledge of God has been compromised, weakened, reduced, smothered, overlaid, or impeded by sin and its consequences" (WCB, 184). What this means is that the sensus divinitatis is disturbed in its actual purpose and can lead to a false form of belief in God[3]—in any case the de facto existing "sensus divinitatis", which is limited in its purpose, does not lead to the specific Christian God. So because of sin, the sensus divinitatis is limited and hindered in its actual purpose of producing knowledge of God—and therefore, according to Plantinga, it is necessary to look at the work of the Holy Spirit, who gives faith: "The principal answer is that faith is at work—the main work, according to Calvin—of the Holy Spirit; it is produced in us by the Holy Spirit" (WCB, 249). This coming of the Holy Spirit thus repairs the disorder, which entered because of human sin, and allows us the ability to recognize God: "First, there is the repair of the sensus divinitatis, so that once again we can see God and be put in mind of him in the sorts of situations in which that belief-producing process is designed to work" (WCB, 281). Nevertheless—according to Plantinga—the Holy Spirit delivers more than the knowledge of God through creation (namely, what the sensus divinitatis could have known about God in the condition of sinlessness); in fact, it delivers a more specific knowledge of

---

3 Cf. WCB, 215.

God, including the meaning of the incarnate God in Jesus Christ and the meaning of his crucifixion and his resurrection.[4]

Plantinga therefore proposes a threefold model of the knowledge of God. The "sensus divinitatis" is principally there so that we can recognize God as the creator, who created heaven and earth, and whose beauty is reflected in the world. Now apart from fixating human beings on loving themselves, sin has limited their cognitive ability, or more precisely: "the sensus divinitatis has been damaged and deformed" (WCB, 205), so that we no longer recognize God in the same way as we recognize the world and other people, so that this rebellion in human beings grows to such a point that they do not want to recognize God at all. The third stage is the repair of the sensus divinitatis (and, furthermore, its extension toward the more precise knowledge of God)[5] and therefore the renewed implementation of this innate ability: The human being enlightened by the Holy Spirit recognizes God in creation.

Plantinga understands Calvin in such a way that the "sensus divinitatis" would produce belief in the condition of sinlessness. Nevertheless, as Plantinga sees it, given that humans are indeed sinners, the sensus divinitatis is damaged but not entirely destroyed: "it remains partially functional in most of us. We therefore typically have some grasp of God's presence and properties and demands, but this knowledge is covered over, impeded, suppressed" (WCB, 210). Plantinga thus suggests that most people do have some sort of sense or awareness of God, which is to be seen as the remainder of the sensus divinitatis—the human being cannot recognize God correctly any more since his or her original ability to do so has been deformed.

Now it is also important to mention that Plantinga sees a strong connection between Thomas Aquinas and John Calvin, which is why Plantinga speaks of the A/C model, the Aquinas-Calvin-model. For Aquinas, Plantinga suggests, it is a characteristic claim that: "To know in a general and confused way that God exists is implanted in us by nature" (WCB, 170)—and he believes that this statement also holds for Calvin's sensus divinitatis. It is possible that Plantinga wants to emphasize here that he places his model on a broader ecumenical base than simply that of the so-called Reformed Epistemology, and wishes to indicate that his model is interesting for all Christians, regardless of their particular religious denomination.

---

4 Cf. WCB, 281.
5 Cf. WCB, 280 ff.

2 Calvin's concept of the knowledge of God

John Calvin, being a reformer of the second generation, is especially interested in deepening the foundations of "reformed" knowledge. His main work, *Institutio Christianae Religionis* (Inst.),[6] written in several stages until its completion in 1559, is best translated as an "instruction in Christian worship" because "religio" is not identical with the word "religion" and is not regarded by Calvin as a meta-term for instituted religions in general. Although Calvin refers to many passages of Luther's theological work and positively accepts much of it, the *Institutio* is still one of the first expressions of evangelical dogmatics because of the way it takes up and interprets the theology of the early church and that of the medieval world. In the *Institutio*, one strongly senses the influence of his own commentaries on the Bible, a work of interpretation which Calvin engaged in throughout his life.

Calvin opens the *Institutio* with the well-known claim: "Nearly all the wisdom we possess, that is to say, true and sound wisdom, consists of two parts: the knowledge of God and of ourselves".[7] This clearly indicates that Calvin gives an extremely high priority to the knowledge of God—the *Institutio* begins with it and it is considered the sum of all human wisdom. This knowledge of God, however, is not to be understood without the connection to the knowledge of oneself; rather, both of these represent a continuous process, which the Christian will never complete. In contrast to Luther, who teaches a schematic order of law (where the human being recognizes his sin from the impossibility of following God's will) and the Gospel as the acquittal of humanity, Calvin rejects a defined order. He proposes that the knowledge of God and the knowledge of oneself are always linked to one another in the life of Christians: in the light of God's compassion one realizes one's distance from God and the realization of one's sin allows the love of God, which one does not have to earn, to shine all the brighter.

Before asking how human beings come to this knowledge of God, one must ask about its content: What do the knowledge of God, and the knowledge of oneself, consist of? This question is so fundamental because here the answer—at least according to Calvin—decides whether the knowledge of God and the knowledge of oneself do actually take place. For Calvin the knowledge of God means that God shows himself as he really is: He is triune as Father, Son and Holy Spi-

---

[6] Cf. Plasger/Calvin (2009).
[7] "Tota fere sapientiae nostrae summa, quae vera demum ac solida sapientia censeri debeat, duabus partibus constat, Dei cognitione et nostri" (Inst. I,1,1). All English translations are coming from: McNeill (1960, here p. 35).

rit. He is the creator of the world, which he created in the beginning and preserves and governs up to the present. He is the redeemer in Jesus Christ, which is at the heart of Calvinistic theology. This is the reason why Calvin gives an affirmative answer to the following question: "The foundation and beginning of confidence in God is then, the knowledge of him in Christ?"[8] It is thus clear that Calvin does not attempt to give a tangible definition of God because, for him, to know God in Christ is like hearing a story and coming to an understanding of it. A story about a human being who has enslaved himself under sin, whose nature is consequently corrupted and who no longer has the free will to draw close to God. God himself draws close to this human and saves him by becoming human himself in Christ, purchasing life for humanity by dying on the cross and rising again. And this already implies a certain self-recognition. What does the human being realize in view of the love that God demonstrates for him? "Thus, from the feeling of our own ignorance, vanity, poverty, infirmity, and—what is more—depravity and corruption, we recognize ourselves" (Inst. I,1,1, 36)[9]—and all this leads human beings to search after the knowledge of the riches of God. The human being does not find in himself the life that God has in mind for him—he finds the sin of humankind, which, according to Calvin, is not to be fathomed with moral categories. This sin is only fathomed when one moves towards, or when one attains, the knowledge of God. On the one hand, sin prompts the human being to look for fulfilment, which he cannot find in himself. On the other hand, in the light of God's overwhelming grace, power and love, the human being realizes his wretchedness all the more. The redeemer shows the human being his need for redemption and this need impels the human to seek it ("But that primal worthiness cannot come to mind without the sorry spectacle of our foulness and dishonor presenting itself by way of contrast, since in the person of the first man we have fallen from our original condition." Inst. II,1,1, 242).[10]

Consequently, Calvin speaks in his Geneva Catechism of 1542 of the knowledge of God as not being a merely cognitive act but an act that concerns the whole human, for this knowledge must be demonstrated in the active practice of honouring God:

---

[8] "Fiduciae ergo in Deo collocandae fundamentum ac principium est, eum in Christo novisse." (CO 6, 12); the English translation comes from: Waterman (1815, 11).

[9] "Ita ex ignorantiae, vanitatis, inopiae, infirmitatis, pravitatis denique et corruptionis propriae sensu recognoscimus" (CO 2, 31).

[10] "quin mox ex altera parte se offerat triste foeditatis et ignominiae nostrae spectaculum, ex quo in primi hominis persona ab origine nostra excidimus." (CO 2, 175)

> What is the true and correct knowledge of God? When he is so known, that the honour, which is his due, is rendered to him. What is the true method of rendering him true honour? It is to put our whole trust in him; to serve him by obedience to his will, all our life; to call upon him in all our necessities; seeking in him salvation, and every good thing that can be desired; and finally, to acknowledge, both in the heart and with the mouth, that he is the sole author of all blessings (Waterman, 1815, 9).[11]

So it can be concluded then that the knowledge of God only transpires in Christians because only they recognize God, who shows himself in Jesus Christ.

When we look more closely, we notice that Calvin, in the *Institutio*, also speaks of a "twofold knowledge of God" (Inst. I,2,1, 40)[12]—specifically, the knowledge of God as creator and as redeemer. Furthermore, it is also worth noting that the first two books of the *Institutio* correspond precisely to this twofold knowledge: "The knowledge of God the Creator" (Inst. I, 35)[13] is the title of the first book and "The knowledge of God the Redeemer in Christ, First Disclosed to the Fathers Under the Law, and Then to Us in the Gospel" (Inst. II, 241)[14] is the title of the second book. If we simply consider the following sentences of the *Institutio* 1:2:

> First, in the fashioning of the universe and in the general teaching of Scripture the Lord shows himself to be the Creator. Then in the face of Christ he shows himself to be the Redeemer (Inst. I,2,1, 40),[15]

then it might appear as though Calvin assumes a twofold knowledge of God, which can be understood as two stages that are built onto one another: Firstly, each and every human being can recognize God in nature, and then the knowledge of God in Jesus Christ would be an additional second stage in the knowledge of God, which would not necessarily be possessed by everyone.

How then does the knowledge of God as the creator arise, according to Calvin? As a matter of fact, Calvin fundamentally believes—and this sets him apart

---

11 "Porro, quaenam vera est ac recta Dei cognitio? Ubi ita cognoscitur, ut suus illi ac debitus exhibeatur honor. Quaenam vero eius rite honorandi est ratio? Si in eo sita sit tota nostra fiducia: si illum tota vita colere, voluntati eius obsequendo, studeamus: si eum, quoties aliqua nos urget necessitas, invocemus, salutem in eo quaerentes, et quidquid expeti potest bonorum: si postremo, tum corde, tum ore, illum bonorum omnium solum autorem agnoscamus." (CO 6, 10)
12 "hinc duplex emergit eius cognition" (CO 2, 34).
13 "De cognitione Dei creatoris" Inst I (CO 2, 31).
14 "De Cognitione Dei Redemptoris in Christo, quae Patribus sub Lege primum, deinde et Nobis in Evangelio patefacta est." (CO 2, 175)
15 "Quia ergo Dominus primum simpliciter creator tam in mundi opificio, quam in generali scripturae doctrina, deinde in Christi facie redemptor apparet" (CO 2, 34).

from most of our contemporaries—that: "The knowledge of God shines forth in the fashioning of the universe and the continuing government of it" (Inst. I, 5, 51).[16] Is this knowledge of God, which radiates in this world for humanity to see, thus the natural knowledge of God, which at least potentially leads all human beings toward God if, for instance, they behold the beauty in nature? Calvin clearly indicates at the end of the paragraph of *Institutio* 1:5 that humankind does *not* have this ability to recognize God as the creator by simply observing nature. As Calvin concludes:

> Moreover, by the erroneous estimate we form, we either so obscure or pervert his daily works, as at once to rob them of their glory and the author of them of his just praise (Inst I,5, 15).[17]

Although, at this point, we see that Calvin has specified humankind's inability to recognize God in nature, he has not yet completed his train of thought. For even if the human being is no longer able on his own to recognize God as the creator, the knowledge of God as the creator is still basically possible. However, for this it is necessary to have the Bible: "Scripture is needed as guide and teacher for anyone who would come to God the creator" (Inst. I, 6, 69).[18] In order to recognize that God is the creator of this world, it is necessary to have the Bible, which explains and illustrates this. This thus suggests, according to the next line of thought, that instead of talking of a direct recognition of God in nature in Calvin, one should rather talk of identifying him through the given hints in nature: it is because the Bible speaks of these fingerprints of God that the human being can then discover them. On his own, according to Calvin, the human being cannot relate what he perceives in nature back to God. Perhaps he can connect what he perceives with a thought about God, but not with God himself. Why exactly is the Bible an authority here? The Bible is indeed a trustworthy and important book, which should make a due impression on the rational human being. However, for the human being who recognizes God as the creator according to the testimony of the Bible, it is crucial, according to Calvin, that there is no authority beyond the Bible but the testimony of the Holy Spirit: "Scripture must be con-

---

16 "Dei notitiam in mundi fabrica et continua eius gubernatione lucere" Inst I,5 (CO 2, 41).
17 "Quotidiana porro eius facta ita aut obscuramus aut invertimus prave aestimando, ut et suam illis gloriam, et autori debitam laudem praeripiamus." Inst I,5, 15 (CO 2, 52).
18 "Ut ad Deum creatorem quis perveniat, opus esse scriptura duce et magistra." (CO 2, 53)

firmed by the witness of the Spirit. Thus may its authority be established as certain" (Inst. I,7, 74).[19]

Thus the human being does not recognize God as the creator because of his perception of creation, but because the Holy Scriptures, through the authority of the Holy Spirit, show the human being that God is the creator—yet it is uncertain to whom the Holy Spirit gives this knowledge; Calvin is in any case certain that only a select number of people receive this.[20] Further on in the *Institutio* it becomes clear that for Calvin the recognition of God as Creator involves more than merely seeing the hints to the fact that this world has been created. In fact, the continual government of the world (*concursus* or *gubernatio dei*, theologically termed), the concept of the Trinity and the creation of humankind in God's image, are all parts of recognizing God's act of creation. In the second stage of recognizing God, where it concerns a specific knowledge of Christ, it is not even considered that the human could recognize this "by nature"—Calvin assumes that this dimension of recognizing God needs to be "revealed" to humankind. Nonetheless, according to Calvin, it also needs to be revealed to the human being that God is the creator, and this happens through the authorization of the Holy Scriptures. So it cannot be said that there is a first, generally accessible stage of recognizing creation onto which one could then add a second stage of redemption. Or to put it another way: the knowledge of God as the creator as well as the knowledge of him as the redeemer are both an act of faith.

3 Calvin and the sensus divinitatis or the semen religionis

It may have been noticed that up until now Calvin has not said anything at all about the "sensus divinitatis". In the first place, this is because, as a linguistic fact, Calvin does not use this as a *terminus technicus*—as Plantinga at least seems to do in deploying this term throughout his work. The term appears only a few times in Calvin's work, one example being in his commentary on the prophet Jeremiah: "Interea nulla est in illis religio, et nullus sensus divinitatis."(CO 37, 622)—"Meanwhile there is nothing in their religion, and no sense of the divine." Here people who mock God (according to Calvin, in his interpretation of Jeremiah 5:12) are being described, and Calvin writes that these are people

---

19 "Quo testimonio scripturam oporteat sanciri, nempe spiritus: ut certa constet eius autoritas" (CO 2, 56).
20 Here one may refer back to the doctrine of predestination.

who do not honour God—and that they do not even have a sense of the existence of a god. In his interpretation of Isaiah 61:8 Calvin states that despite the innate and incorruptible "sensus divinitatis", God is not honoured. In the section that Plantinga refers to quite closely (*Institutio* 1:3–5), the term "semen religionis", which Plantinga himself does not use, can sometimes be found—and also in his commentary on Romans 1:18–19, which Plantinga also refers to.[21] However, the term used here is not decisive; the issue at hand is this: whether there is a knowledge of God innate in all of humanity. So how does Calvin argue in the section of *Institutio* 1:3–4, in which he actually assumes that such an innate knowledge of God exists?—Calvin's line of argumentation in the *Institutio* is reminiscent of Paul, in the first chapter of Romans. To encapsulate the central concern of Paul's letter to the Romans: Paul describes the Gospel here as the power of God that came to sinners—which all human beings are. Sinners, according to Paul, are therefore not only those who consciously break God's commandments although they knew them—and here it would be possible to name the Jews as they were the chosen people to whom God's commandments were entrusted. Sinners are also those who did not know his commandments, which can be found in the Old Testament—thus this also includes the Gentiles; the non-Jews.

> For the wrath of God is revealed from heaven against all ungodliness and wickedness of those who by their wickedness suppress the truth. For what can be known about God is plain to them, because God has shown it to them. Ever since the creation of the world his eternal power and divine nature, invisible though they are, have been understood and seen through the things he has made. So they are without excuse; for though they knew God, they did not honour him as God or give thanks to him, but they became futile in their thinking, and their senseless minds were darkened. (Romans 1:18–21)[22]

The theological discussion about the fundamental question of whether human beings have a natural knowledge of God, and what this could mean, fills volumes and cannot be included here—it is, however, to be noticed that in view of this rather narrow textual basis, the danger of overrating this passage cannot be excluded. What does Calvin do with this statement? The basic message is made clear right at the beginning:

> There is within the human mind, and indeed by natural instinct, an awareness of divinity. This we take to be beyond controversy. To prevent anyone from taking refuge in the pretense of ignorance, God himself has implanted in all men a certain understanding of his divine

---

21 Cf. WCB, 171.
22 Translation of the New Revised Standard Revision.

majesty. Ever renewing its memory, he repeatedly sheds fresh drops. Since, therefore, men one and all perceive that there is a God and that he is their Maker, they are condemned by their own testimony because they have failed to honor him and to consecrate their lives to his will. (Inst. I,3,1, 43 f.)[23]

All human beings, according to Calvin, have a kind of sensitivity, a sensorium, an awareness of God—and here Paul's influence on Calvin becomes clear—but with Paul (and also with Calvin), this awareness has the sole consequence of leaving human beings without excuse before God.

Calvin, however, does not just refer back to Paul, whose aforementioned verses are his only observations on this topic, as we have already mentioned. Calvin mainly refers back to Cicero[24] (incidentally, in his comments regarding the letter to the Romans), who had also claimed that there is no one who does not share a fundamental sense that a god exists. The fact that people have other gods is an indication for Calvin that—even for those who deny the existence of God—knowledge about God (aliqua Dei notitia), although sometimes blocked, exists, because their consciences can also be pricked with feelings of conviction. According to Calvin, human beings do not lose this knowledge; it is innate. What happens then with this innate knowledge of God? In practice, this disposition does not just lead people to honour God; on the contrary, this innate notion often leads people to confuse fictitious ideas with God: "Thus all who set up their own false rites to God worship and adore their own ravings" (Inst. I,4,3, 49).[25] That, according to Calvin, is the given reality: that despite their innate idea of God, people do not use it to honour him. Nevertheless—as Calvin never tires of emphasizing—God shows himself in creation in manifold ways: "The knowledge of God shines forth in the fashioning of the universe and the continuing government of it" (Inst. I,5, 51).[26] Thus for Calvin it is essential that despite this activity of God, which is seen in creation, human beings display no knowledge of God. Actually, the human being should be able to recognize all the many hints that point to God, which he is confronted with in creation, and recognize them as signs from God—and Calvin is talking here about both

---

23 "Quemdam inesse humanae menti, et quidem naturali instinctu, divinitatis sensum, extra controversiam ponimus; si quidem, ne quis ad ignorantiae praetextum confugeret, quamdam sui numinis intelligentiam universis Deus ipse indidit, cuius memoriam assidue renovans, novas subinde guttas instillat: ut quum ad unum omnes intelligant Deum esse, et suum esse opificem, suo ipsorum testimonio damnentur quod non et illum coluerint, et eius voluntati vitam suam consecrarint." Inst. I,3,1 (CO 2,36).
24 Cf. Inst. I,3,1, 44.
25 "Sua ergo deliria colunt et adorant quicunque cultus Deo commentitios erigunt" (CO 2, 40).
26 "Dei notitiam in mundi fabrica et continua eius gubernatione lucere." Inst I,5 (CO, 41).

the existence of the world and God's continual preservation of it. "Knowledge of this sort, then, ought not only to arouse us to the worship of God but also to awaken and encourage us to the hope of the future life." (Inst. I,5,10, 62).[27] The result is, nevertheless, that in spite of all these hints, the human being does not recognize God, and therefore does not honour him. No human being does. Consequently, all the hints that point to God's existence, which he gives to human beings so that they will recognize him, are to no avail; human beings lack the eyes to see the hints that God gives them.[28] Additionally, Calvin suggests that Paul, in Romans 1:19, did not mean that God could be known, but that he in fact is not known by human beings, so that they are without excuse. Calvin also suggests that the inability to recognize God is not a failure of creation but the fault of human beings on account of their innate sense of inaction. The background to Calvin's discussion here is the concept of original sin, taught since Augustine. Because of Adam's sin the human being finds himself a sinner; indeed, sin has been passed on from Adam to all humankind. Augustine taught the passing on of sin through the *concupiscentia* in the act of intercourse, but for Calvin this idea is too limited, so he more generally speaks of Adam as the prototype of all humanity, and that what was lost in him was also lost in all human beings to come—the righteousness, the free will, and so on. The conclusion in any case is this: In Adam, the human being is to be recognized as someone who has turned away from God's righteousness. Therefore, the human being is to be seen as a sinner. Regarding the question of where this sin originates, Calvin cannot and does not want to give an answer, just as the Bible does not—and Calvin denies the possibility that God created it as a part of the imperfect nature of humankind. This sin now also applies to the free will of humankind. According to Augustine and Calvin, Adam had the opportunity to live in accordance with God— he had the free will to shape his life according to God's will. But free will also includes the knowledge of God. Adam had the opportunity to know God. But because human beings became sinners through Adam, they no longer have this ability to turn to God. The knowledge of God in Calvin's work is always described as the act of honouring God and is therefore not to be reduced to merely the knowledge that God exists—to know God is thus to have faith in him. The sinner does not have the opportunity to honour God because he is caught up in his sin and is not able to free himself from it—or in other words: without God himself turning toward the human being and freeing him, the human being cannot be-

---

[27] "Deinde eiusmodi notitia non modo ad Dei cultum excitare nos debet, sed ad spem quoque futurae vitae expergefacere, et erigere." (CO, 48)
[28] Cf. Inst. I,5, 14.

lieve, recognize or honour God. Calvin can also describe this with the metaphor of imago dei. "Accordingly, the integrity with which Adam was endowed is expressed by this word [sc. image of God G.P.], when he had full possession of right understanding, when he had his affections kept within the bounds of reason, all his senses tempered in right order, and he truly referred his excellence to exceptional gifts bestowed upon him by his Maker" (Inst. I, 15, 3, 188).[29] But Adam after the Fall is not the same image of God as before: "There is no doubt that Adam, when he fell from his state, was by this defection alienated from God" (Inst. I, 15, 4, 189).[30] And even when Calvin is unable to deny that there is any image of God in human beings after the Fall, he does not see any positive possibility of working with this:

> Therefore, even though we grant that God's image was not totally annihilated and destroyed in him, yet it was so corrupted that whatever remains is frightful deformity.
> (Inst., I, 15, 4, 189)[31]

And because there is nothing in the human being which can be seen as basic belief, Calvin teaches that Christ has to reform us into God's image—through the Holy Spirit. How exactly is it possible now that the Holy Spirit can turn toward human beings? What is crucial for Calvin is the story of Jesus Christ. Jesus Christ died on the cross and rose again. Calvin here employs the Pauline argumentation of the Adam-Christ-typology in Romans 5. In Adam, human beings are to be identified as sinners, because by him original sin came into the world. But in Jesus Christ the human being has overcome the sin and is to be seen as righteous. To grasp Calvin's essential line of thought here it is necessary to understand the concept of substitution: because in his death, Jesus Christ suffered the distance from God representatively for all human beings and gives life to them by forgiving their sins. What then does the Holy Spirit do? The Holy Spirit gives the human being the faith that this was also done for him; that his sin is also forgiven and thus he is no longer a sinner; he is now righteous. With regard to himself, the human being still continuously sees "Adam", because he sees his own imperfection. Yet looking to Christ the human being sees his new righteousness. The Holy Spirit now teaches the human being that God is gracious towards

---

29 "Proinde hac voce notatur integritas qua praeditus fuit Adam quum recta intelligentia polleret, affectus haberet compositos ad rationem, sensus omnes recto ordine temperatos, vereque eximiis dotibus opificis sui excellentiam referret." (CO, 138)
30 "Quin Adam, ubi excidit e gradu suo, hac defectione a Deo alienatus sit minime dubium est." (CO, 138).
31 "Quare etsi demus, non prorsus exinanitam ac deletam in eo fuisse Dei imaginem, sic tamen corrupta fuit, ut quidquid superest, horrenda sit deformitas." (CO, 138)

him and that he can only receive this grace as a gift, and thus this has happened freely and gratuitously. So the Holy Spirit gives knowledge of God—and the knowledge of oneself. If human beings believe that their sin has been forgiven, then knowledge of God and of themselves is imparted to them. The aforementioned "semen religionis", however, no longer plays a role regarding this knowledge of God. For this awareness of a god, which exists in every human being, is—according to Calvin—limited to the fact that human beings can realize that they are sinners.

4 Does the semen religionis remain the basis for every belief in God?

One of Plantinga's theses is that the semen religionis or the sensus divinitatis is the foundation out of which faith is formed because it is the "disposition ... to form beliefs" (WCB, 171). So he suggests that if human beings were not sinners, then the sensus divinitatis would enable them to recognize God. Plantinga correctly sees that, according to Calvin, the human being originally, as he was intended by God, was able to conclude from the beauty of this world that a creator must exist (Calvin, referring to Romans 1:19);[32] in the *Institutio* Calvin calls this the "primal and simple knowledge to which the very order of nature would have led us if Adam had remained upright" (Inst. I,2,1, 40).[33] Plantinga has also correctly seen that, according to Calvin, the actual purpose of the natural knowledge of God, which is essentially to recognize him, has been perverted by sin: the human being is no longer able to recognize God. Plantinga, despite sharing the same basic perspective, is more moderate than Calvin—and is aware of this.[34] For instance, Calvin's main conclusion is that the human spirit now has a "perpetuam ... idolorum fabricam" (CO 80)—"a perpetual factory of idols" (Inst. I,11,8, 108), because instead of honouring the one true God humans now turn away and invent for themselves another god or even multiple gods.[35] Maybe Plantinga's restraint is based on his effort not to limit his model solely to the Christian religion; Calvin, on the other hand, is far more polemical here. Nevertheless, Plantinga still fundamentally shares the Calvinist line of ar-

---

32 This is also quoted by WCB, 171.
33 "sed tantum de prima illa et simplici loquor, ad quam nos deduceret genuinus naturae ordo si integer stetisset Adam." Inst I,2,1 (CO 2, 34).
34 Cf. WCB, 177.
35 Cf. Inst. I,4, 3.

gument here.[36] However, Plantinga then takes it a step further. He says that this innate ability to recognize God is basically able to form the correct faith in God. Plantinga always talks here in *potentialis:* under very specific conditions this innate, natural knowledge of God is able to lead to faith; this disposition of the human being is essentially always there, even if it is not implemented—but it is possible that this inherent trait can be utilized. This argumentation that the natural knowledge of God can lead to faith does not correspond to Calvin's argument. For Calvin only refers to this innate knowledge in purely negative terms—it is one that leads to wrong beliefs. This innate, natural knowledge of God, although Adam could have implemented it to come to know God, is now not even a possibility—it is an entire *irrealis*. When Plantinga says that the "sensus divinitatis" is essentially able to produce faith, he disregards the absoluteness of the *irrealis* in Calvin's work.

Now one could object that Plantinga does not adopt this idea of Calvin because Calvin understands Adam in a pre-Enlightenment fashion as an actual historical figure and therefore reasons in too historical a way; but he does not say this. The crucial point is this: Calvin uses neither the concept of the semen religionis nor the natural knowledge of God in the further course of the *Institutio*, because the faith imparted by the Holy Spirit is something completely new. However, Plantinga also argues that there is no simple continuity that leads from the natural knowledge of God toward the correct belief, but he sees both of these possibilities as far more complementary than Calvin does. Plantinga understands the sensus divinitatis as continually relevant, whereas Calvin does not consider it to have any significance whatsoever with regard to faith.

In the theology of the 20th century there were theological concepts which postulated a so-called point of contact, because, according to this theology, without this point of contact the human being would not be able to recognize God.[37] And here I see exactly the same intention in Plantinga's work: The Holy Spirit, who gives faith, needs a point of contact with creation, possibly because otherwise the universality of humankind would not be sufficiently acknowledged. Calvin's approach is not so apologetic. He only refers to the natural knowledge of God because the human cannot excuse himself, instead—so that whether he is part of a church or not—idols come forth out of his heart. Calvin's approach is therefore primarily critical of religion—and therefore the knowledge of God and of oneself is an ongoing task.

---

36 Cf. Jeffreys (1997, 428–430).
37 Cf. for example the theology of Paul Althaus (1969), who starts with an "Original Revelation".

5 Is faith linked to the semen religionis?

Alongside the aforementioned thesis, there is another thesis of Plantinga which needs to treated critically. Plantinga had claimed that, according to Calvin, faith and the correct worship of God remain based on the semen religionis—this can be seen, for instance, by looking at the semen religionis as a persisting human disposition that is still available to us. But this is exactly what must be denied. Since the purpose of the semen religionis does not actually function—because human beings are sinners, God adopts an entirely different approach: Instead of by the way of nature, God himself now comes to human beings by his Holy Spirit and gives knowledge of Himself in that way. This coming, however, is not linked to any sensus divinitatis which may exist in human nature. In the Calvinistic argumentation, the human being's sense in regards to the existence of a deity no longer actually appears. That God shows himself in nature is only seen by those who have faith in him—and thus this is not a second stage. In Plantinga's work, it appears as if the innate, natural knowledge of God is either disrupted (sin) or intact (faith)—and the latter only functions through the Holy Spirit. The problem here is that the sensus divinitatis remains the continuum, which is in the process of being repaired—and faith is therefore the medium for recovering the sensus divinitatis—and of course for even more than that. From a purely formal point of view, it is possible to read the following statement: "So Scripture, gathering up the otherwise confused knowledge of God in our minds, having dispersed our dullness, clearly shows us the true God" (Inst. I, 6, 1, 70) [38] as being mainly concerned with this *confused knowledge*—and this is exactly what Plantinga does when he interprets this quote to mean that the Bible "clarifies what we learn by way of the sensus divinitatis" (WCB, 281). But this is exactly what Calvin does not want to say. The confused knowledge is not the basis or the point of contact; on the contrary, the key message is to be found in the work of Scripture. Whether the knowledge is confused, or even non-existent, is irrelevant here—because with the confused knowledge comes darkness. This means, contrary to Plantinga, that it is not faith which is connected to the sensus divinitatis, but rather the reverse; it means that the aim of the sensus divinitatis actually comes into the picture only when faith is already present: "Besides, if all men are born and live to the end that they may know God" (Inst. I,3,3, 46) [39]. From this we can see that for Calvin the objective was that all would come

---

[38] "ita, scriptura confusam alioqui Dei notitiam in mentibus nostris colligens, discussa caligine liquido nobis verum Deum ostendit." (CO 2, 53)
[39] "Porro si ea conditione nati sunt omnes ac vivunt ut Deum cognoscant" (CO 2, 38).

to faith. The semen religionis, possessed by every human being, therefore points to God's intention, and is linked to faith, which is its actual purpose that it sadly does not achieve.

6 Is the coming of the Holy Spirit a repair of the sensus divinitatis?

The connection between the faith given by the Holy Spirit and the sensus divinitatis—in regards to the aforementioned objection—is still to be examined critically. Plantinga claims that the coming of the Holy Spirit, who imparts faith, signifies that the "sensus divinitatis is partly healed and restored to proper function by faith and the commitment work of the Holy Spirit in one's heart" (WCB, 186). Here too the continuity of the sensus divinitatis can be seen—it is healed (at least partly) and restored. Therefore, according to Plantinga, the creational dimension is the constant, on which the Holy Spirit and faith are based. The problem is that the destruction of the knowledge of God is seen here as merely partial rather than total—whereas Calvin suggests that the Holy Spirit imparts faith as something completely new, without the prerequisite of the human being having any notion of God. This particular notion, which every human was endowed with at creation, is not simultaneously employed by Calvin to accomplish a "retreading"—according to Calvin everything is new. This is why it is significant that Plantinga does not leave any room for the Calvinistic rejection of the free will. In addition, for Calvin, the knowledge of God as the creator is not a continuation or an enhancement of the sensus divinitatis; rather, it is an entirely new knowledge of the triune God, which is why the recognition of God as the creator especially includes the rejection of the free will.

7 Would humankind, without sin, believe in a natural way?

One of Plantinga's theses is that the sensus divinitatis is to be seen as a human disposition to believe in God—so that when belief occurs, he reaches his destiny.[40] Through his sin, however, the human being is prevented from using his for-

---

40 Cf. WCB, 173.

mer natural knowledge of God.⁴¹ This raises the question: Could the human being, if he had not become a sinner, have come to faith based solely on his innate ability to be aware of God? Although Plantinga emphasizes that all human beings are sinners, and because of this do not use their innate ability, he suggests that, nevertheless, without sin they would still, even now, be able to recognize God naturally. Calvin does not argue in this way. Following Paul, he assumes that the factual result is that no human being is even able to conclude, through his own natural awareness, that God is the creator. At one point, it seems very clear that Plantinga separates himself from Calvin—and does so more distinctly than he might be aware of. When talking about the inborn "sensus divinitatis", Plantinga emphasizes that he cannot imagine that Calvin believes that one already has this knowledge even in one's mother's womb; rather, he presumes that Calvin's belief is that one does not possess this knowledge until it has developed in a specific phase in life (maybe already even in very young children).⁴² The original sin, to the concept of which Calvin subscribes, is already within the human being in his mother's womb. If now the purpose of the sensus divinitatis is to leave human beings without excuse, according to Calvin, and the youngest of children already find themselves alienated from God, then Plantinga's idea, which suggests that the sensus divinitatis requires a certain age, entirely misses Calvin's point.

That the sensus divinitatis could possibly function is not even conceivable, according to Calvin's line of thought, because human beings are in fact sinners and are in need of a revelation from God to be able to recognize him in the first place. Augustine said of Adam that he did not have to sin, but that all other people, who are in Adam (so all other people after him), are unable not to sin. And exactly this idea is also seen in Calvin's work: The actual condition of human beings is that they are sinners—and the semen religionis, at best, shows them that they find themselves alienated from God. So Calvin does not make a claim that would support Plantinga's thesis—he actually denies the latter, because sin is not potentially, but rather universally, real.

---

41 Cf. WCB, 184.
42 Cf. WCB, 173.

8 Do Thomas Aquinas and Calvin argue on similar lines here?

Plantinga calls his model the A/C-model and he does so, I suppose, because he thinks they Aquinas and Calvin are brothers in spirit.[43] This is not the place to present a detailed analysis of Aquinas's writings—and Plantinga too only refers marginally to Aquinas. However, what can we say in brief about Acquinas's work regarding the knowledge of God? In the so-called proofs of God's existence it is made clear that Aquinas entertains a twofold scheme: the human being is able to behold his surroundings and identify in them the unmoved Mover. He, whose existence everyone can infer, is called God by Christians and is identified as the triune God. According to Aquinas, the latter knowledge is based on grace, which is not imparted to all people. It is, however, possible for all humans to come to the conclusion that God exists, for this ability is innate. The reason why it is possible to come to a realization of the creator is because human beings are created in God's image: nature and grace do not contradict, rather they complement one another: "gratia non tollit naturam sed perficiet" (Aquinas, Summa Theologiae I, 1, 8)—Grace does not destroy but perfects nature". This dichotomy is the result of Aquinas's philosophical basis, which has its foundations in Aristotle. According to this basis, the reality of this world must be the starting point for the supernatural, and thus must already be connected with the supernatural, to be able to function as the starting point.

Calvin does not share or start from this Aristotelian duality, so that his own model is not twofold in this sense at all, but rather involves an antagonism between the semen religionis and faith. So when Plantinga speaks of the A/C-model it might be possible to speak of the A-model—but, again, to do so would require a close reading of Aquinas's writings.

9 In conclusion

It was not my aim to assess the basic sustainability of Plantinga's approach. My question was more limited: Does the representation of Calvin in Plantinga's work truly reflect Calvinistic theology? My result is critical in this regard; I believe that I have shown that significant misunderstandings of Calvin have crept into Plantinga's work.

---

[43] Cf. WCB, 170.

Basically Plantinga tries to find an approach to natural theology in Calvin's work. He is neither the first, nor the only one, to do so. Back in the 16th and 17th centuries there were repeated attempts to develop a *theologia naturalis*, even by the reformed theologians.[44] More specifically, in the 20th century, we find Emil Brunner attempting to find a kind of natural theology in Calvin's writings.[45] According to Brunner, Calvin assumes two revelations; one that is found in the Holy Scriptures and the other one which, as the revelation of God in nature, complements the first revelation in an important way, but does not compete with it—rather, this general revelation is the prerequisite for the special, historic one.[46] Like Plantinga, Brunner also sees a continuity in humanity by virtue of our being created in God's image.[47] German scholars at least have almost unanimously objected to Emil Brunner's interpretation and emphasized that, from their point of view, there can be no question of a complementary relationship between the natural knowledge of God and one that is imparted by the Holy Spirit.[48] But why then does Brunner want to presuppose the persisting significance of this general revelation? In Brunner one can quite clearly sense an apologetic-missionary interest—and Deane-Peter Baker also sees this in Plantinga.[49] These results of Plantinga's interpretation of Calvin, which basically move in the same direction as Emil Brunner, should therefore be regarded critically, in my opinion.

For one thing, these results reflect a highly problematic exegesis of Calvin. From a theological point of view, it should be added that the distinctiveness of the Christian faith is thereby always put at risk of being understood (only) in terms of continuity, and therefore within the confines of a natural knowledge of God.

Literature

Althaus, Paul (1969): Die Christliche Wahrheit. Lehrbuch der Dogmatik, 8th edition, Gütersloh.
Baker, Deane-Peter (2005): "Plantinga's Reformed Epistemology: What's the Question?", in: International Journal for Philosophy of Religion, 77–103.

---

44 Cf. for example to Gijsbert Voetsius the study of Beck (2007).
45 Cf. Brunner (1934) and Brunner (1941). Jeffreys (1997, 423) notes that Plantinga has not taken any notice of this debate.
46 Cf. Emil Brunner (1941, 63).
47 Cf. WCB, 205.
48 Cf. for example Barth (1935); Niesel (1938, 39–49); Busch (2009); Werner (1999, 29–47); Plasger (2009, 19–26).
49 Cf. Baker (2005).

Barth, Peter (1935): Das Problem der natürlichen Theologie bei Calvin, München.
Beck, Andreas J. (2007): Gisbertus Voetius (1589–1676). Sein Theologieverständnis und seine Gotteslehre, Göttingen.
Brunner, Emil (1934): Natur und Gnade, Tübingen
Brunner, Emil (1941): Offenbarung und Vernunft, Zürich.
Busch, Eberhard (2009): "God and Humanity", in: Herman J. Selderhuis (Ed.): The Calvin Handbook, Grand Rapids 2009, 224–235.
Calvin, John (1863–1900): Calvini Opera Omnia i.e. Ioannes Calvini Opera Quae Supersunt Omnia. Vol I-LIX. Ediderunt G. Baum, E. Cunitz & E. Reuss. Vol I-LIX, in: Corpus Reformatorum, Vol. XXIX-LXXXVII. Brunsvigae/Berolini, C.A. Schwetschke et filium, 1863–1900.
Jeffreys, Derek S. (1997): "How Reformed is Reformed Epistemology? Alvin Plantinga and Calvin's 'Sensus Divinitatis'", in: Religious Studies 33, no. 4, 428–430.
McNeill, John T. (1960): Calvin: Institutes of the Christian Religion, Philadelphia, Westminster.
Niesel, Wilhelm (1938): Die Theologie Calvins, München.
Plantinga, Alvin (2000): Warranted Christian Belief, New York.
Plasger, Georg (2009): Johannes Calvins Theologie—Eine Einführung, Göttingen.
Plasger, Georg/Calvin, Johannes (2009): "Institutio Christianae religionis", in: Christian Danz (Ed.): Kanon der Theologie. 45 Schlüsseltexte im Portrait, Darmstadt 2009, 224–231.
Waterman, Elijah (1815): The Catechism of the Church of Geneva, Hartford.
Werner, Ilka (1999): Calvin und Schleiermacher im Gespräch mit der Weltweisheit, Neukirchen-Vluyn.

Christian Illies
Is Suffering the Rock of Atheism?

1 Evil as a potential defeater

For many, the reality of evil in the world argues against the proposition that God is its creator. "Suffering is the rock of atheism," Georg Büchner famously remarks.[1] There have, of course, been many instances where people have lost their faith in the face of some great atrocity.[2] Satan takes this tack when he asks God for permission to tempt the believer Job by making him suffer (Job 1:9ff.). God, however, knows that this will not undermine Job's faith and theism. And indeed, even after losing all his children and property (and left with nothing but a nagging wife) Job remains a firm believer. This is for good reasons, Alvin Plantinga argues in *Warranted Christian Belief* (WCB): the true believer's faith finds sufficient warrant to withstand all suffering.

The possibility of faith remaining robust in the face of suffering might be argued for psychologically—but the argument in WCB is an epistemological one. Plantinga's central claim is that evil does not provide decisive evidence against theism. To use Plantinga's (slightly surprising)[3] terminology, suffering is no "atheological argument", i.e. not an argument "against the existence [...] of an all-powerful, all-knowing, and wholly good person who has created the world and loves the creatures he has created." (WCB, 459). For Plantinga, this amounts to saying that evil is not *de facto* a defeater of theism. By "de facto" he means something "we are alleged to know" that shows straightforwardly that "Christian belief must be false (or at any rate improbable)" (WCB, ix).

Plantinga does not deny the fact of suffering and evil in the world but questions their evidential force. More precisely, he denies their evidential force *for the theist* with a properly working *sensus divinitatis*. He admits that evil can cloud the theist's experience of God and that it might even make her *sensus divinitatis*

---

[1] *Dantons Tod*, Act 3.
[2] Though, many more people lose faith when living in luxury and indulgence. Satan seems to have learned this lesson, and that is why in the Gospel of Matthew, he tempts Jesus by promising him all the wealth and power of this world if he changes his alliance.
[3] It seems more plausible to talk about an "anti-theological" argument if it is directed against the basis of all theology. Furthermore, it is not clear whether the "atheological argument" is supposed to be decisive (in the sense of a proof of God's non-existence) or whether it is merely an objection to God's existence (in the same sense that there might be some evidence for, and some against, the truth of a proposition).

become dysfunctional. All of this is possible, he says, but evil does not supply us with an argument. It is at most a "spiritual and pastoral" (WCB, 483) problem for the believer.

Plantinga's very impressive and original approach (in chapter 14) would, if successful, be of great importance for any rational defence of theism. But is Plantinga right? In order to investigate the strength of his reasoning, I will first give an account of his principal arguments as far as I understand them (II.1) and then place his analysis within the traditional debate of theodicy (II.2). An evaluation of his arguments follows (III). His central point seems forceful, namely that theism can be held rationally even in the face of evil and suffering. Here I agree with Plantinga (III.1) but belive he overestimates the reach of his argument. Plantinga claims that even the undecided "person on the fence" will realise that he has "little if any reason to prefer atheism to theism" (WCB, 481). The Book of Job tells us a different story; Job's friends are *not* preferring theism when they see Job suffer. And these friends, too, have good reasons for their view. It all depends on the weight one gives to the reality of suffering—if one takes the experience of suffering as a basic truth (like Schopenhauer does) then one can find strong warrant for an atheist world-view, or so I will argue (III.2).

2 Outline of Plantinga's arguments

2.1 Does evil make atheism more plausible?

Plantinga's thesis, that evil and suffering do not provide an atheological argument, unfolds in several steps. (a) Firstly, he questions whether the reality of evil in this world provides *any* evidence at all. (b) Secondly, he argues that even if evil provided *some* evidence against the existence of God, this would not matter too much so long as there be sufficient evidence for him.[4] (c) He then turns in more detail to two arguments according to which evil and suffering make theism less plausible, namely the arguments by Paul Draper and William Bower. If they are right, then theism, though still logically possible, becomes a rather unlikely assumption. The theist's warrant would be undermined. (d) After having rejected Draper and Bower, Plantinga adds some reflection on evil as a "spiritual and pastoral" problem for the believer.

---

[4] Surprisingly, Plantinga presents the two arguments in reverse order. But it seems more plausible to start with the question of whether evil provides any evidence at all.

Re (a): Plantinga's possible-worlds-argument

Does evil provide an "atheological argument"? Plantinga doubts this and supports his claim with a possible-worlds-argument: even if our world is characterized by evil and suffering, it could be that there are many worlds in which more goodness and less evil can be found.

> [P]erhaps God has created countless worlds, in fact, all the worlds (all the universes) in which there is a substantial overall balance of good over evil. In some of these worlds there is no suffering and evil; in some a good deal; as it happens, we find ourselves in one of the worlds where there is a good deal. But the probability of theism, given the whole ensemble of worlds, isn't particularly low. (WCB, 463)

This argument is similar to that which Leibniz gives in the first part of his *Theodicy* (Section 19): there are probably many planets with inhabitants who are possibly much happier than we are. The entire universe might be filled with joy so that our suffering in our world amounts to a "nearly-nothing" compared to the whole sum of universal happiness.[5]

As Plantinga remarks, this argument is an inversion of the objection to the intelligent-design argument. It has been argued by Daniel Dennett and others[6] that even if the world *looks* fine-tuned especially for us (because its fundamental parameters are just right for life to be possible) this does not show much. We may just happen to live in one of the few worlds which is favourable to life—but there are possibly billions of worlds that are not sufficiently fine-tuned. And obviously, in these other worlds there is no-one who could reflect on the universe and why it makes life possible. These billion worlds do not indicate an intelligent creator. Given this possibility, the fine-tuning of our universe seems much less of a wonder (less design-like) than it appears to those who think that there is only one world.

If Dennett's argument is sound and sufficient to refute the intelligent-design-argument, then a similar argument can also be used, Plantinga claims, to refute that evil is any evidence against God's existence. If we have many possible worlds, then we do not have to provide reasons as to why God designed our world with suffering and evil. It might be merely bad luck that we happen to live in a world with such a sad record. (There might be billions of worlds with substantially less suffering, where no-one has raised her voice against theism.)

---

5 Cf. Leibniz (1996, 239) (my translation); cf. Farrer (1952, p. 135). I am grateful to Dieter Schönecker to have pointed out this passage to me.
6 Cf. Dennett (1996, 63).

Thus, Plantinga concludes, God is off the hook. Nothing follows from the strong presence of evil in *our* world.

(It is perhaps noteworthy that Charles Darwin argues in a similar fashion that his theory of evolution meliorates the problem of theodicy, because God would only have created the general laws of evolution. He would no longer be held responsible for having directly made all those species which make their prey suffer.)[7]

Re (b): Plantinga's total-evidence-argument

Let us assume that there are terrible events in this world and that we cannot square this experience with our idea of an omnipotent, omniscient, and perfectly good God. Plantinga argues that, even if we accept this as *some* counter-evidence to theism, not much follows. There are many propositions which people rationally accept even in the face of *some* counter-evidence. Plantinga gives the example of poker-playing. It might be highly unlikely "on the rest of what I know or believe" to have drawn an "inside straight" (WCB, 464), but I will not doubt if these are the cards in my hands. The visual evidence is strong enough to provide warrant for my belief against all counter-evidence (it is unlikely etc.). Accordingly, evil's counter-evidence *against* God's existence can be rationally put to one side if there is sufficiently strong supportive evidence *for* it.

Plantinga argues that to make theism implausible, evil would have to make "the existence of God ... improbable with respect to our *total evidence*, all the rest of what we know or believe" (WCB, 462). But that is more than evil can demonstrate, even if it provides some evidence against theism. For evil to be decisive *all* evidence for and against God would have to be taken into account:

> the atheologian would have to look into all the evidence *for* the existence of God—the traditional ontological, cosmological, and teleological arguments, as well as many others; he would be obliged to weigh the relative merits of all of these arguments, and weigh them against the evidential argument from evil in order to reach the indicated conclusion.
> (WCB, 462f.)

---

[7] Cf. Darwin (1988, 174f.). Darwin's argument does not provide a full theodicy, but makes the problem of evil a little less problematic.

Re (c): Plantinga's rejection of probabilistic arguments

There are many philosophers who have argued that the reality of evil and suffering, together with all other background knowledge that we have, makes the truth of theism improbable, even if evil is *logically consistent* with the existence of God. Plantinga turns to two of these arguments in some detail, namely those by Rowe and Draper.

William Rowe's version of the argument runs, in brief, as follows:[8] we can identify particular evils (occasions of human suffering) (Rowe calls them E1 or E2) that are so terrible that we cannot see how a God could possibly rectify them in any future state or, indeed, make sense of them. The evidence of this world does not support any such conjecture. The impossibility of finding any such justification for E1 or E2 is the basis for Rowe's claim that theism is ultimately less likely than atheism: if we cannot think of any good reasons why a God might create a world such as ours, this speaks powerfully against theism being a rational assumption. Thus the existence of a creator God is implausible.

Plantinga rejects Rowe's argument by emphasizing the limitations of human understanding. Even if God has very good reasons for having created our world complete with all its suffering and evil, why should we expect to be able to understand these? Our mental capacities are limited and the "epistemic distance between us and God" might simply be too big (WCB, 467):

> suppose we try to figure out what that reason might be: is it likely that we would come up with the right answer? Is it even likely that we would wind up with plausible candidates for God's reason? (WCB, 466)

Rowe responds to this type of reaction by developing his argument further (or by possibly presenting a new argument—so Plantinga reads him (WCB, 467). He starts from the assumption that the probability of God existing or not existing is 0.5 either way. Yet the existence of God becomes ultimately less probable if we add the proposition that there is no "known good such that the latter justifies the former in permitting E1 and E2" (WCB, 467). But even if this proposition makes God's existence less likely, Plantinga objects, we can also find other propositions which make it, by the same reasoning, more likely. An example he gives is: "No evil we know of is such that no perfect being would permit it" (WCB, 468).

Paul Draper's argument is similar to Rowe's. He also states that the theist assumption is not very plausible given evil in this world:

---

8 Cf. Rowe (1979)

> A statement reporting the observations and testimony upon which our knowledge about pain and pleasure [for short "O"; C.I.] is based bears a certain significant negative evidential relation to theism. (Draper 1989, 331)

Draper's point is that an alternative metaphysical hypothesis seems much more plausible as an explanation of evil and suffering, namely the "hypothesis of indifference" ("HI", for short). It claims that if a supernatural being exist at all, then it is indifferent to our sufferings. It would follow that "neither the nature nor the condition of sentient beings on earth is the result of benevolent or malevolent actions performed by non-human persons."[9] According to Draper, HI explains this world better and, because it is incompatible with the good creator God thesis, it provides an evidentiary problem for the theism:

> the problem is evidential. And because of this, we have a *prima facie* good epistemic reason to reject theism—that is, a reason that is sufficient for rejecting theism unless overridden by other reasons for not rejecting theism. (Draper 1989, 331)

With other words, the thoughtful believer has good reasons for giving up his belief, unless he finds strong reasons for theism which outweigh the evidential challenge proposed by evil and suffering. If sound, then Draper's argument would indeed be a defeater of theism (Plantinga's terminology).

The crucial notion, on which Draper's argument is built, is the "antecedent probability" of theism or H1 being the basis for a world as ours. This "probability" is an epistemic notion; it refers to the "probability of O on something like the rest of what I know." (WCB, 480). The exact definition of 'epistemic probability' reads as follows: "Relative to K, p is epistemically more probable than q, where K is an epistemic situation and p and q are proposition. In case any full rational person in K would have a higher degree or belief in p than in q."[10] What exactly characterizes K? It seems that K is the result of all relevant reasons I have. Hence, if I have no strong reason for theism in the first place, then the greater plausibility of O on HI provides me with a defeater for theism.

Plantinga's response to Draper is very much in line with his total-evidence argument: the theist with a functional *sensus divinitatis* is in an epistemic situation where she has good reasons (warrant) for her theism. Even if we followed Draper's point that O is more likely on HI, and thus a *prima facie* reason to accept HI, this, Plantinga argues, would not mean much: any such *prima facie* reason would vanish in face of the strong arguments for theism, because the believ-

---

[9] The Problem, p. 13. Quoted from WCB, 470.
[10] The Problem, p. 27, footnote 2.

er has stronger evidence for than against God. Draper's evidential challenge is not strong enough to make theism implausible.

Plantinga adds that probably "most of the propositions I believe" are evidentially challenged in some way or another (WCB 476), but that this does not make these beliefs irrational or unlikely. In the end, it is all a question of the overall warrant that I have *for* a particular belief—more precisely, whether I have a "significant degree" of warrant for it (WCB, 478). If this is the case then I can rationally continue to believe in God, and nothing changes: "If I had sufficient warrant for knowledge before you made your point about it being evidentially challenged, it still has sufficient warrant." (WCB, 479)

Plantinga finishes his discussion of evidential arguments by making some interesting remarks. He argues that Draper's argument would not even work in the case of someone who has *wrong* warrant for her theism, so long as she is rationally justified in taking it to be sufficient warrant.

> Under those conditions, my theistic belief does not, in fact, have warrant; nevertheless, my learning that it is subject to an evidential challenge does not compromise its rationality and does not give me a defeater for it. (WCB, 480)

Plantinga further remarks that there are merely two situations in which Draper's argument would provide a defeater, namely (1) where someone believed in theism but thought that her "reasons for it are absolutely minimal" (WCB, 480) and (2) where someone believed in God because she regarded God as the best explanation for exactly the facts that are crucial to the evidential challenge (when she learns that they are *better* explained by HI, then her theism has strong warrant no longer). These are the situations in which the evidential challenge is a defeater, Plantinga argues, but they are not the situation of "most theists". (WCB, 481)

Re (d): "Non-argumentative defeaters"

Even if evil and suffering are not the basis for an evidential challenge they might still raise a problem for the believer. Although it does not make theism less likely, it might be a "serious obstacle" (WCB, 482) to it. Plantinga states that in this case evil would not be a defeater but rather a "spiritual or pastoral problem" for the theist (WCB, 483). However, he admits that the problem of evil could be so enormous, the atrocities so terrible, that the believer might ask whether it is not

> apparent, just evident that a being living up to God's reputation couldn't permit things like that? Don't I have a defeater here, even if there is no good antitheistic argument from evil? (WCB, 484)

This is, according to Plantinga, the strongest version of the "atheological case from evil" (WCB, 484).

He carefully speaks about an atheological "case" rather than argument, because this version of the objection is a practical way of putting someone in the situation where he just *sees* that no God could possibly have allowed this evil to happen:

> The claim is essentially that one who is properly sensitive and fully aware of the sheer horror of the evil displayed in our somber and unhappy world will simply see that no being of the sort God is alleged to be could possibly permit it. This is a sort of inverse *sensus divinitatis:* perhaps there is no good antitheistic argument from evil; but no argument is needed. (WCB, 484)

What Plantinga has in mind is a kind of non-argumentative defeater, a kind of reference to the self-evidence of a certain fact.

Is evil a defeater or not? Plantinga seems to say *no* and *yes* at the same time, but his position becomes clear in the light of a certain distinction he makes: evil is no defeater for someone who has full knowledge of God, that is someone with

> *fully rational* noetic structures—noetic structure with no cognitive dysfunction, one in which all cognitive faculties and processes are functioning properly. (WCB, 488)

A fully functional noetic structure includes, of course, the *sensus divinitatis*. Things are different for the person who lacks this knowledge and has but weak faith; Plantinga does not deny that for someone with "*that* cognitive malfunction" (WCB, 486) evil can lead to atheism.

> Indeed, it is the person who gives up belief in God under these circumstances who displays cognitive dysfunction; for such a person, the *sensus divinitatis* must be at least partly disordered. (WCB, 492)

But this does not show that evil as such is a defeater *tout court*—it has no decisive atheological evidence for the rational person.

Things are more complicated, Plantinga admits, because, after the Fall, human beings on the whole lack fully rational noetic structures. One might therefore object that for us *as we actually are* (fallen creatures), evil does provide a defeater after all. But Plantinga sees hope:

> the damage to the *sensus divinitatis* is in principle and increasingly repaired in the process of faith ... and regeneration. The person of faith may be once more such that, at least on some occasions, the presence of God is completely evident to her. (WCB, 487)

That explains why evil is more a 'spiritual problem': if evil and suffering trouble someone to the point of becoming a defeater for her, this is not an *epistemic* challenge but, rather, demands a restoration of her faith. She must try to turn (back) to God: the Christian God will help her make sense of her suffering.

Plantinga concedes the somewhat peculiar features of this situation: he has shown that evil and suffering are not defeaters for someone who holds theism to be true. Only if the believer has not sufficient warrant in the first place, might evil and suffering become proper defeaters of a weak belief in God. So it all depends on whether theism finds warrant to begin with. The believer will think so for good reasons, naturally enough, *for her* theism is true (and evil is no defeater). And according to Plantinga, if she has good epistemic reason to stick with her belief, then there are no external reasons (defeaters) that could demonstrate to her that her beliefs are wrong:

> She will see her belief as the product of cognitive faculties functioning properly, functioning in the way God intended them to (and aimed at producing true beliefs). (WCB, 492)

2.2 The place of Plantinga's arguments in the debate on evil

In the history of philosophy and theology, the overwhelming presence of evil and suffering has troubled many, if not most, theists. Very different answers have been given to the central question as to whether and how such a world as ours could have been created by a good God. The answers given range from elaborate defences of God (e.g. Leibniz) to strong objections to theism (e.g. Mackie who argues that belief in God is "positively irrational") (Mackie 1955). We might order the different positions as follows:
1. *Strong defence:*
    1.1. attempts to explain God's purpose behind evil and suffering (for example: evil is the price we pay for human freedom, which is a superior good).
    1.2. Attempts to minimize evil in world (it only *appears* to be bad for us etc.)
2. *Weak defence:*
    2.1. theoretical version: claim that God has a plan but that it (must) remain(s) mysterious to us (mystery-argument)
    2.2. practical version: we must not try to understand God's reasons but act, do good, focus on God etc.
3. *Evidential arguments:* evil and suffering make God's existence unlikely, implausible etc.

4. *Strong arguments against God:* evil and the good creator God are not compatible; belief is irrational.

In WCB, Plantinga is neither proposing a strong defence of God's existence in the face of the reality of evil, nor is he concerned with the strong argument against God (that the experience of evil and suffering make any belief in God "positively irrational"). A major part of his argument is based upon our epistemological restrictions (and is thus a kind of negative theology): human reason has limits and we must allow for there being a plan or good purpose that "passeth all understanding" (Ephesians 3:19 on the "peace of God"). God can have good (godly) reasons for creating (and sustaining) a world wherein lies evil, even if these reasons are not intelligible to us.

Plantinga's alliance to the mystery-argument explains why he is interested neither in (1) nor in (4).

On the one hand, the mystery-argument takes away from the theist the burden of having to provide a strong defence, i.e. a proper explanation for a world which contains so much evil as in position (1.1). A weak defence is enough, because a proper explanation will always be beyond us. And that is why we do not have to worry if we fail to find such an explanation. As Plantinga says:

> I will not be making any attempt to 'justify the ways of God to man' or to give an answer to the question why God permits evil generally or why he permits some specially heinous forms of evil. (WCB, 459 f.)

The mystery-argument explains on the other hand, why (4) fails: we cannot positively show the incompatibility of God and evil in our world because God might well have reasons we cannot grasp due to our epistemological limitations. They remain mysterious for us—but from our ignorance it does not follow that evil is "flatly incompatible" (WCB, 462) with God's existence. For example, God's standard of good and bad might be different from ours, or the mechanism and connection of good and evil in this world might be too subtle for us. There is no logical inconsistency in such a possibility. (This had already been conceded by Hume in his *Dialogues* on natural religion where he argues: "I will allow that pain or misery in man is *compatible* with infinite power and goodness in the Deity, even in your sense of these attributes"; D 103).

Plantinga's epistemological model of knowledge seeks the possibility of supportive evidence, which is warrant, not proof, of God's existence. That is why he is concerned with the robustness of the warrant theism finds—his focus is therefore the weak atheological argument (2). Even if an almighty and good God is not incompatible with evil, belief in his existence might still be unwarranted. The discussion of this objection is the central aim of this chapter. Plantinga turns to those who argue that "the facts of evil offer *powerful evidence against* the existence of God" (WCB, 462).

> More precisely, his question reads:
> [C]an I be mature, both intellectually and spiritually, be aware of the enormous and impressive amounts and depths of suffering and evil in our world, be aware also of the best atheological arguments starting from the facts of evil, and still be such that Christian belief is rational and warranted for me? (WCB, 460)

Unsurprisingly, his answer is affirmative: "yes indeed", evil is not evidence of any kind against my belief or its warrant.

3 Is evil a defeater? What Plantinga achieves

Plantinga's rich and subtle analysis of the evidential force of evil and suffering against theism is intended to show that they are not defeaters for the believer. He starts by arguing that evil is no counter-evidence in the first place, and continues by saying that even if it amounted to some counter-evidence, it would be negligible. He then rejects two attempts to show that the counter-evidence is strong (and sufficient to make belief implausible). But is this not too quick? After all, evil and suffering cause many to lose their belief in God. It is this phenomenon that Plantinga wants to explain in the conclusion of his chapter: evil and suffering can have this negative effect on a person's belief—but only on someone who does not believe properly in the first place (whose *sensus divinitatis* does not function properly). The true believer remains unshaken, while the weak person falls away.

3.1 The possible-worlds-argument

Let us begin by looking at Plantinga's possible-worlds-argument. Does it show that not much can be concluded from evil and suffering in the first place? I do not think so. The atheological objection is that a good God could not possibly have created a world such as ours—and this accusation is not mellowed by the possibility of there being many worlds that are better than ours. The atheist will ask: why should God not restrict himself to creating *only* those better worlds in which evil is marginal? That these better worlds might also exist (and co-exist with the world we know) does not seem any explanation or justification for *our* world with all its atrocities.

If a trustworthy boy tells us that his father beats him cruelly and shows us his bruises, this amounts to strong evidence against this father being a good, caring father. I cannot see why this evidence should be weakened if the father has other children whom he treats much better. The better treatment of others does *not* take him off the hook. He still has to account for the cruelty against the little boy and we will rightly call him cruel if he shows these qualities so clearly even in one case. (The fact that he is caring to the other children might even add the objection that he is *unfair*.) Similarly, even if there are many possible worlds with different balances of good and evil, God has to explain why he created our world with all its atrocities and why he did not restrict himself to creating only worlds with an overall positive balance.

There *may be* an explanation: it might be that there are many worlds with different balances because God could not restrict himself to creating only the better ones or best one. Perhaps worlds can only be created as a package containing some with a better, some with a worse, balance of good and evil. (This comes close to Darwin's argument mentioned above: perhaps the best way to create worlds is to use some evolutionary mechanism which requires a lot of variation.)[11] Plantinga should certainly say much more about possible worlds if he wants us to be convinced by his argument.

Alternatively, Plantinga could follow Leibniz' path, but this would amount to going in a very different direction. Leibniz outlines a *strong defence* of God. One of his central arguments is that the happiness of all sentient beings is a standard (not the only one) by which the goodness of the world is to be judged. But then all these countless planets with happier inhabitants would make a difference; they could push the overall balance of happiness towards the positive and thus make it plausible why God created the universe according to this standard. But to show this is not Plantinga's goal—he (merely) argues that evil provides no substantial evidence against God. *Prima facie*, it seems a more modest enterprise, but it turns out to be more demanding with regard to *particular* evils.

---

11 Alternatively, the explanation for our world is that all other possible worlds are worse than ours (and ours is still better than no world). Thus a rational God could not have created any world with an overall better balance. This is, of course, Leibniz's argument. Without some such supportive explanation Plantinga's possible-worlds-argument does not work: as it stands, it fails to show that the evil in our world does not provide evidence against a good God. But with a Leibnizian extension of his argument, Plantinga faces the old problem of theodicy on a higher level. Rather than (merely) explaining why our world is only possible (and is, overall, good) with the evil in it, he would have to argue why the package is only possible (and, overall, good) with some worlds of a negative good/evil balance.

We might even add a further objection to Plantinga's possible-worlds-argument.[12] It is, of course, possible that there are many worlds with a *worse* balance than ours; worlds of mere suffering and no happiness or joy at all. If this cannot be excluded, why should we see the possibility of better worlds as an argument at all? It seems that Plantinga's reflection on possible worlds, and on the balance of evil and good within these worlds, does not reveal much.

3.2 What sort of evidence is evil?

Is evil's counter-evidence negligible because of the overall evidence that we have *for* God's existence? That is the central point of Plantinga's *total evidence argument*—and it is the central argument of chapter 14. In its most general form, Plantinga's argument is certainly powerful. It can be rational to hold a belief in the face of *some* counter-evidence, as long as the supportive evidence is sufficiently strong and the counter-evidence is not decisive. Plantinga gives many examples to illustrate this point. These examples fall, roughly, into two groups. (1) I have such strong evidence for my belief that I can ignore the apparent counter-evidence. This is the situation of the poker player who sees the cards in his hand and simply knows that he drew an "inside straight", even if it is highly unlikely that he might do so. (2) I have a messier situation in which I have some pro- and counter-evidence and must weigh them against each other. As Plantinga states, this process "is vastly messier and more problematic than a terse and elegant demonstration of a contradiction" in one of the two assumptions (WCB, 463). Henry James' *Turn of the Screw* is a good example of (2): Does the young governess actually see ghosts which control the orphaned children *or* is she simply paranoid? There is evidence for both understandings and the reader has to balance the evidence and make up his mind. For Plantinga, reflecting on the plausibility of theism is similarly 'messy', at least for ordinary people. It seems to be different, though, for the strong believer, for whom theism is fully warranted. His situation is an example of (1), where the counter-evidence is no challenge.

Plantinga's argument follows a model he uses at other points in WCB. He asks whether some epistemic requirement is necessary for theism to be rational. Then he gives examples of every-day life situations in which we are rationally entitled to hold a belief even if this requirement is not fulfilled. He concludes that this requirement must not *necessarily* be fulfilled for theism to be rational.

---

12 This has been suggested by Dieter Schönecker.

It follows that theism can be held rationally even in face of the counter-evidence that evil and suffering might provide.

In general, Plantinga's argument is convincing. But it depends on the particular case, that is, on what sort of belief we hold and what sort of evidence or counter-evidence can be offered. If, for example, I have *strong* counter-evidence against some belief, then it is probably no longer rational to hold this belief. Therefore, if the evidential challenge of theism by evil were very strong, then we could no longer ignore it, even if we had strong pro-evidence. The crucial issue is, therefore, the strength of the evidences involved. Is the counter-evidence just one among many evidences, or is it decisive? Plantinga holds that it is not decisive, at least for the believer.

That is why he looks at the arguments of Rowe and Draper in so much detail; he wants to show that evil does not make atheism more likely. And his objections are that stochastic calculations seem to be based on questionable assumptions about what is more or less likely. Plantinga rightly asks how we could possibly "judge, with respect to any kinds of evils, the likelihood that an omniscient, omnipotent, and wholly good being would permit them" (WCB, 469). Reflections on quantitative likelihood are, indeed, inadequate in these speculative matters; judging between theism and atheism is not like a chemical analysis, where we can hope for a clear and distinct result.

But what about the person who regards the counter-evidence of evil as *qualitatively* strong—so strong that it outweighs any pro-evidence? We might tell the story of the poker-game the other way round. Perhaps my negative belief (that evil speaks against any good God) is something I take as given. Then God's non-existence is like the full 'straight' in my hands, independently of what my background knowledge tells me about God's existence. That seems to be Ivan's situation as described by Dostoyevsky in *The Brothers Karamazov*. He cannot avoid being overwhelmed by the horror of evil; and it all speaks so powerfully against the existence of a good God. Consider a real-word example. Arthur Schopenhauer experienced the world as fundamentally lost and as a place of endless suffering. For him, it was obvious that an indifferent or even wicked force must have brought it about. This atheistic impression was powerful enough to sweep away all possible evidence to the contrary. According to Plantinga's understanding of 'basic beliefs', for Schopenhauer an indifferent world-creating force, with evil as its expression, is such a belief.

Admittedly, Plantinga discusses cases like this and rejects them. He observes that someone might regard evil and its incompatibility with God as a self-evident truth. But cases like this, he argues, do not provide any evidence against theism. They merely show that some people are epistemically limited—otherwise their *sensus divinitatis* would make them realise that there is an all-powerful God who has a plan for this world (even if we do not understand it fully). If someone sees evil as decisive counter-evidence, as a defeater for theism, then his *sensus divinitatis* is simply dysfunctional. All of this follows directly from the extended Aquinas/Calvin model: if the *sensus divinitatis* functions properly in a person S, "then the belief that there is such a person as God will automatically have warrant for S." (WCB, 486)

There is no inconsistency in Plantinga's position. It follows stringently from the epistemic model that he develops in WCB, and there are situations where we would argue just like Plantinga. If the colour-blind person thinks that he has strong counter-evidence against my belief that the tomato is red, then I will argue that he is epistemically limited. If the colour-sense is functioning properly in S, then the belief that the tomato is red will automatically have warrant for S. His self-evident experience of a brown tomato is no *de facto* defeater of my belief in it being red.

Plantinga's argument is valid, but not without flaw: it introduces a subjective element—the strength someone gives to certain evidence—at a crucial point in the argument. For the believer with his *sensus divinitatis*, evil is not a serious problem. Thus the process of balancing the relative weight given to counter-evidence depends on who he is; and a true believer will never give too much weight to any counter-evidence. If there is a threat in doing so, he can always take refuge in the *sensus divinitatis* and the possibility of it being dysfunctional. Thus the argument might have an awkward consequence; it seems to turn into a strategy of self-immunisation. But, before looking at this possible objection in III.5, let us turn to the mystery-argument.

3.3 The (mysterious) mystery-argument

Plantinga relies at several points on the mystery-argument. We cannot automatically exclude the possibility that God has reasons beyond our understanding. There is, however, a problem with this argument: it is at odds with what Plantinga says elsewhere. The reasoning of WCB starts with the assumption that it "seems likely" (and even is "the natural thing to think") that God, "who desires that we know and love him, and who is such that it is our end and good to know and love him" would also "of course intend that we be able to be aware of his presence and to know something about him" (WCB, 188). If we follow Plantinga's strong intuition about what God should do,[13] then it will seem rather odd that

---

[13] Plantinga simply *affirms* this claim without rational argument; but the assumption is certain-

the same God who is driven by an urge to reveal himself should hide himself so completely to many people.

Such an ambiguous revelation is not *impossible*. We might even argue, in a fashion similar to Plantinga's argument, that our mental capacities are too limited to understand God's (second-order) reason to hide his (first-order) reasons for having created a world with evil and suffering. We might reformulate Plantinga's argument and say:

> suppose we try to figure out what that [second-order—CI] reason might be: is it likely that we would come up with the right answer? Is it even likely that we should find plausible candidates for God's [second-order] reason? (cf. WCB, 466)

However, even a half-hidden God is *possible*. But if, it is just rather odd that the God of revelation should limit himself on this second order level. If so much depends on our holding the right beliefs (a least according to some Christian denominations), why did God make it so difficult for people to understand him?

This does not defeat Plantinga's A/C-model nor provide strong objection to the mystery-argument. It is rather a reservation. If Plantinga could answer it, the mystery-argument would be more convincing. And indeed, I think there are (second-order) reasons we could think of as to why God should conceal his first-order reasons for allowing evil and suffering to be part of our world: If we must think of evil as something which needs to be eradicated (at least to be fought with all our power), then it might be just wise of God to hide his (first-order) reasons. Only if evil remains inexplicable will it have the full force of something that we try to eliminate as much as possible. A full understanding of God's master-plan will always be in danger of taking away some of our resistance to evil. If God wanted it to be part of his world, and revealed his reasons for doing so, then evil might not seem to be too bad after all. Knowing the deeper meaning of evil, we are likely to tolerate it too easily. But if God does not want us ever to fall into this error, he would be very wise to hide his first-order reasons thoroughly. The mystery of evil, its inexplicable presence, might be what best impels the theist to fight it.[14]

---

ly plausible. See, for example, Richard Swinburne: "It is natural to suppose that God created us in such a way that we would come to the true belief that He exists" (Swinburne 2001, 205).
14 For a more detailed argumentation on these lines cf. Illies (2000).

3.4 The limited reach of Plantinga's argument— a trouble about the addressee

As early as 1983, in his inaugural lecture as the John O'Brien Professor of Philosophy at the University of Notre Dame, Plantinga was distinguishing different ways of doing philosophy of religion. In this 'Advice to Christian Philosophers' he proposes:

> What I want to urge is that the Christian philosophical community ought not think of itself as engaged in this common effort to determine the probability or philosophical plausibility of belief in God. The Christian philosopher quite properly *starts from* the existence of God, and presupposes it in philosophical work, whether or not he can show it to be probable or plausible with respect to premises accepted by all philosophers, or most philosophers at the great contemporary centers of philosophy.[15]

The aim of chapter 14, however, seems to be different: at least at times Plantinga argues as if to a wider audience. Plantinga wonders, for example, whether the arguments of Rowe and Draper can convince someone who is "reasonable and well-informed" (WCB 462). And he concludes after having rejected Rowe's and Draper's evidential challenge: "They fail to provide a defeater for theistic belief and, indeed, give the person on the fence little if any reason to prefer atheism to theism" (WCB, 481). The "person on the fence" is probably the "intellectually sophisticated adult in our culture" whom Plantinga also mentions as his addressee (WCB, 358, referring to Philip Quinn), i.e. someone who is not already a committed believer.

Can he be convinced? I do not think so. Plantinga gives the person on the fence no strong reason to jump to the right side. Let us assume that the unbiased observer wants to know whether theism is plausible in a world of suffering and evil. For him, Plantinga's argument must seem like explaining the obscure by the more obscure: the mystery-argument is the first obscurity because it explains something by stating that he cannot understand the explanation:

> Given that he is omniscient and given our very substantial epistemic limitations, it isn't at all surprising that his reasons for some of what he does or permits completely escape us.
> (WCB, 467)

'Why are you so sure that this is the way it is?', the person on the fence will ask the theist. 'Well, because I have a special sense that allows me to grasp it', the theist answers. '*He that hath* ears to hear, *let him hear.* But your ears do not func-

---

15 http://www.leaderu.com/truth/1truth10.html

tion and you will therefore not fully understand how things truly are.' Here the person on the fence is deeply puzzled. Is he too blind to see that God has reasons that no one understands?

Even if there is no inconsistency within the theist's position, the total evidence will not help the person on the fence discern who is right, the atheist or the theist. The theist as much as the atheist seem to have (contrary) basic beliefs. For the theist the belief in God's existence is self-evident and incorrigible; and for people like Schopenhauer the belief that all is, in the end, meaningless suffering is similarly basic. Both sides can claim to have warrant for their beliefs; and if conviction and subjective certainty are fundamental in this regard, then there is no obvious way to decide which side is more likely to be right. Both might refer to a special sense that we have or need: the theist talks about the *sensus divinitatis* and the atheist could imagine another sense, a strong sensibility toward all suffering in our world. (Furthermore, the atheist might argue, with Adorno, that anyone who defends God from the problem of evil is *dangerously* blind to unjust states of affairs in the world. Any theodicy, he might argue, belittles the unjust suffering of people by giving it some alleged meaning; theism is in conspiracy with the evil forces of capitalism, Adorno adds.)

In short, the two opposed positions look very similar to the person on the fence. If he lacks either special sense (be it of the divine or that of Adorno) he is in no position to determine as to whether the total evidence speaks for atheism or theism. If he has one of the two senses, then he will find good reasons to believe in one of these options. Of course, things would be different if the arguments of natural theology and the counter-arguments of naturalism were included in the overall process of balancing the evidence. But then Plantinga would have to become "engaged in this common effort to determine the probability or philosophical plausibility of belief in God", something he does not wish to venture into—that is a different project, not the one Plantinga is pursuing in WCB.

But perhaps the person on the fence is not really the addressee after all. When Plantinga articulates his goal he writes:

> Can I be mature, both intellectually and spiritually, be aware of the enormous and impressive amounts and depths of suffering and evil in our world, be aware also of the best atheological arguments starting from the facts of evil, and still be such that Christian belief is rational and warranted for me? (WCB, 358)

Here he refers to the 'spiritually mature' person—and that is probably a theist whose *sensus divinitatis* is functioning well. After all, someone whose faith is shaken by experience of evil has a "spiritual problem", as Plantinga states. It seems that Plantinga is not really thinking about someone who is sitting on the fence; the addressee has already landed to the side of theism.

3.5 Self-immunisation or a robust argument?

If we pushed this point further we might come to a more serious problem. Does Plantinga portray theism in a way that moves it beyond any possible critique? Obviously, Plantinga presents a consistent and strong epistemic model. But it might be too robust with regard to the theist and too weak with regard to atheists or people on the fence.

To the theist Plantinga's reasoning might seem a strategy of self-immunization. If we accept the A/C model, then the rejection of evil and suffering as a defeater follows immediately. A defeater seems impossible by definition for the theist if he believes that theism is right. "The atheologian can properly claim that evil constitutes a defeater for Christian belief, therefore, only if he already assumes that Christian belief is false" (WCB, 480). This result is correct in an unsurprising way. A hypothesis can only "properly" be defeated if it is false. If something is true, then it cannot be false. Thus if theism is true, it cannot be wrong. But the result applies also in a more interesting sense to the internal situation of the believer. According to Plantinga's epistemic model, the believer cannot *imagine* anything that would make him *rationally* doubt his theism (if he believes that his theism is right; but as a believer he does so by definition). The moment he starts to doubt, he already "displays cognitive dysfunction; for such a person, the *sensus divinitatis* must be at least partly disordered." (WCB, 492)—at least that is the way in which he must see himself. But this argument seems nearly universally applicable; *whatever* case someone might present against theism, the mystery-argument in combination with the *sensus divinitatis* will be enough to reject it.

This objection is not *entirely* fair. What else could Plantinga have done? He establishes an epistemic model, looks for possible defeaters, and rejects them. That seems, overall, an appropriate defense. And one might add that defeaters remain *imaginable* according to the A/C model, namely atheological arguments that show the inconsistency of theism. Plantinga refers to the accusation of Mackie and others (that evil and theism are *logically incompatible*) and argues that this would be "a terse and elegant demonstration" (WCB, 301) of theism being wrong. If such a defeater could be found, then even the theist with a well functioning *sensus divinitatis* would have to acknowledge that his belief is wrong (and that his *sensus divinitatis* is merely a sense of self-delusion). But the accusation of inconsistency seems the only objection which might trouble a rational theist (while irrational theism, like Kierkegaard's, would not be troubled by this objection). Otherwise the A/C model is water-tight and immune to all possible critique.

According to Popper, a good scientific theory is potentially falsifiable; and the more testable the better. A good theory, he argues, must have conjectures that are '*risky*' or '*bold*'. That does not seem to be the case for the A/C model; theism seems immune from falsification. Only in quite a different, non-epistemic, sense does one need to be *bold* to be a theist.

But can Popper's concern be directed against Plantinga's reasoning? After all, theism is not a *scientific* theory—and for *metaphysical* theories the demand of testability might not hold.[16] Metaphysics might contain analytical truths or other robust elements that withstand all possible criticism. Still, it seems strange that a metaphysical theory could be (almost) immune to possible critique, but merely *in the eyes of someone who accepts the theory*. Such an addressee-dependence is not impossible—we cannot blame the only one with seeing eyes in a crowd of blind people for seeing the sun when the others don't—but it limits the use of the theory. The blind person on the fence will not begin to see when he reads WCB. And those for whom evil and suffering are the rock of atheism will not find an argument which proves to them that their rejection of an omnipotent, absolutely good God is built on sand. The true atheist remains unshaken. *In the eyes of the atheist*, atheism remains as firmly grounded as before.

Literature

Darwin, Charles (1988, First Edition 1859): "The Origin of Species by Means of Natural Selection, or the Preservation of Favoured Races in the Struggle for Life" in: The Works of Charles Darwin, Vol. 15, London 1988.
Dennett, Daniel (1996): Darwin's Dangerous Idea, Harmondsworth.
Draper, Paul (1989): "Pain and Pleasure: An Evidential Problem for Theists", in: Noûs 23, 331–350.
Farrer, Austin (1952): Theodicy, New Haven: Yale UP.
Illies, Christian (2000): "Theodizee der Theodizeelosigkeit", in: Philosophisches Jahrbuch 107/2, 410–428.
Leibniz, Gottfried Wilhelm (1996): Die Theodizee I, Frankfurt/Main.
Mackie, John Leslie (1955): "Evil and Omnipotence", in: Mind, *Vol.* 64, no. 254, 200–212.
Plantinga, Alvin (2000): Warranted Christian Belief, New York.

---

16 For Popper, metaphysical theories (which cannot be tested) are immature scientific theories; where science *begins*.

Rowe, William (1979): "The Problem of Evil and Some Varieties of Atheism", in: American Philosophical Quarterly 16, 335–41.
Swinburne, Richard (2001): "Plantinga on Warrant", in: Religious Studies 37, 203–214.

Gregor Nickel
Dwindling Probability.
Mathematical and Philosophical Notes in Margin

> Die Menschen leugnen mit ebensowenig Gefühl das göttliche Dasein, als die meisten es annehmen. Sogar in unsere wahren Systeme sammeln wir immer nur Wörter, Spielmarken und Medaillen ein, wie Geizige Münzkabinetter; (...) Auch hab' ich die Absicht, mit meiner Dichtung einige lesende oder gelesene Magister in Furcht zu setzen, da wahrlich diese Leute jetzo (...) das Dasein Gottes so kaltblütig und kaltherzig erwägen, als ob vom Dasein des Kraken und Einhorns die Rede wäre.
>
> *Jean Paul*[1]

> A coherent philosopher would be a strange and unlovely creature.
>
> *Alvin Plantinga*[2]

In fact, it may be only in mathematics where we can find a *strictly* coherent bulk of beliefs without having the impression that we encounter something strange or unlovely.[3] Mathematics might be able to enfold or construct these clearcut and coherent—but nontrivial and non absurd—structures by an ascetic abstinence from content and by the humility not to claim any absoluteness. Though in a certain sense universally valid, mathematical knowledge (if it might be called knowledge) is always dependent on assumptions, on a priorly fixed framework.[4] Therefore, any attempt to *imitate* the precision of mathematical definitions and the rigor of mathematical proof in philosophy reaches its limitations quite early.

---

1 Cf. Richter (1826, 154). "Men, as a class, deny God's existence with about the same small amount of true consideration, conviction, and feeling as that with which most individual men admit it. Even in our regularly established systems of belief we form collections of mere words, gamecounters, medallions—just as coin-collectors accumulate cabinetsful of coins; (...) I would also fain awaken, with this piece of fiction, some alarm in the hearts of certain masters and teachers (reading as well as read); for, in truth, these men (...) discuss God's existence as cold-bloodedly and chill-heartedly as though it were a question of the existence of the kraken or the unicorn." Jean Paul (eng. 1897, 259).
2 Cf. WCD, 146.—I shall use the following abbreviations: WCB = *Warranted Christian Belief*; WCD = *Warrant: The Current Debate*; WPF = *Warrant and Proper Function*.
3 Of course, this easy feeling might be limited to understood—thus for almost all observers quite small—parts of mathematics and it might solely hold with respect to coherence. Moreover, (parts of) mathematics only in a narrow sense exhibit this strict form of coherence. The important role of contradictions and counterexamples, e.g., for the history of mathematics is explicitly well-known since the pioneering works of Imre Lakatos.
4 The *locus classicus* for this thesis is, of course, Platon's *Politeia* 510c.

Similar limitations hold for a direct *use* of mathematical formalism in philosophical debates. Here, the appearance of a (mathematical) probability concept and the usage of the probability calculus within the philosophy of religion might serve as an example to observe and discuss the relation between these two human enterprises—mathematics and philosophy—in general.

Indeed, the concept of probability plays a considerable role in Alvin Plantinga's apologetic project. First of all, it is a built in feature of his central concept of *warrant* since warrant implies proper function and proper function implies a design plan successfully aimed at truth (at least within a suitable cognitive environment) which in turn means that "there is a high statistical probability that a belief produced under those conditions will be true" (WPF, 46). Moreover, there are two important arguments in *Warranted Christian Belief* where probability calculations enter the stage. First, we find a probabilistic argument against the rationality of (any form of) naturalism and against its truth.[5] And second, there is the argument of the *dwindling probabilities* claiming to show that a "historical case" could not be successful. While the first argument makes a productive use of the probability calculus the second argues that this very calculus is almost useless for any historical argumentation in the philosophy of religion.

Thus, there seems to be enough reason to discuss Plantinga's concept of probability and its role in WCB. The present paper is divided into two major parts. In the first section we will discuss the general concept and fix some notations. The second section is devoted to the argument from dwindling probabilities and the debate around that argument. A discussion of Plantinga's positive use of the probability calculus showing the failure of naturalism must be left to later times or to more competent hands.

1 Absolute Probabilities?—Some Remarks on the Notion and Notation of Probability

In WPF, Plantinga rightly emphasizes the difficulties connected with the probability concept. Before entering the (somewhat technical) details of the following section it seems appropriate to state some selected comments on Plantinga's concept of probability in general and, in particular, about the "absolute probabilities" (e.g., WCB, 272), he refers to. Moreover, we will fix some notations needed for the arguments in the formalized version. Thereby I will hopefully avoid to

---

[5] In WCB, 227 we find a revised and updated form of the argument with respect to the version in WPF.

enlarge the "paradox, mystery, confusion, darkness, despair" (WPF, 139) bristeling in this area.

Of course, the notion "probability" is neither mathematicians' nor philosophers' property. However, if we find equations, calculations, or estimates dealing with probabilities represented by a real number between 0 and 1 in the philosophical literature, we might expect that these are at least in some way related to the mathematical concepts. Moreover, a philosophical discussion of "epistemic probabilities" (WPF, 137)[6] should not almost completely ignore (the history of) mathematical probability theory which is quite successfully dealing with the phenomenon of chance, data-sampling, statistics, large time behavior, prognoses, *et cetera*. In the following we will thus strongly rely on the well established mathematical probability (and measure) theory.

1.1 Probability—a problematic notion

Ian Hacking is rightly quoted by Plantinga emphasizing the two major characteristics of probability:

> the probability that emerged so suddenly [in the decade around 1660] is Janus-faced. On the one side it is statistical, concerning itself with stochastic laws of chance processes. On the other side it is epistemological, dedicated to assessing reasonable degrees of belief in propositions quite devoid of statistical background.[7]

Probability can thus refer to events supposed to be *often and identically repeatable* on the one hand or to *individual* propositions or hypotheses about events on the other; moreover, it can be interpreted either to represent a more or less *objective* property of an object (in the broadest sense) under consideration or a *sub-*

---

6 Remark that (philosophically) discussing and referring to a mathematical theory is quite different from simply using it or imitating its style of argumentation.

7 Cf. Hacking (1975, 12). When Plantinga rightly remarks that this Janus-face can be found already in Aristotle the reader might be pleased to find an analytic philosopher referring to history when looking for a systematically relevant content. And in fact, all too often classical authors describe and discuss philosophical concepts with higher accuracy and deeper insight just pinpointing the really important features while contemporary debates muddle on technical details without clarifying (let alone solving) the question. Plantinga's intensive reference to and reverence for selected classical authors shall thus be explicitly acknowledged. With respect to the current example Plantinga's critique, however, should not blame Ian Hacking since Hacking's considerations are devoted to the mathematical conceptualization of probability (cf. WPF, 159). And this, in fact, is starting only in the middle of the 17th century.

jective degree of belief on the side of an observer. To make the picture even more complicated, these two pairs can be combined in various ways, e.g., classical statistics deals with objective probabilities connected to single events only on the basis of numerous repetitions,[8] while the Bayesian epistemology in general refers to a subjective degree of belief referring to a single proposition,[9] and Plantinga's (epistemic) probability, finally, is claimed to be an objective property of a single proposition. And in fact, traces of this double-face can still be found within the (verbal conceptualization of) actual mathematical probability theory and statistics; and, of course, apparently in the quarrels between frequentist and Bayesian statisticians.[10] We will now state some notes in margin to Plantinga's discussion on probability in general with reference to WPF.

First, Bayesianism is severely criticized by Plantinga; he claims its "central problem" to be the fact that Bayesian probabilities are always relative to the individual observer.[11] In fact, Bayesian epistemology typically refers to individual propositions (or hypotheses) and considers probability to be the subjective degree of belief of an observer. However, at least the mathematical Bayesian is not so hopelessly subjective as Plantinga depicts it. Firstly, there is a vast amount of different arguments, e.g., a Dutch book approach showing a connection between certain rationality assumptions for the observer and (objective) rules for the probability calculus he will use.[12] In fact, Plantinga is well aware of these arguments,[13] but he claims that they cannot show that Bayesianism accounts for an overall rationality.[14] That's true enough. However, a 'working Bayesian' will necessarily refer to a fixed (and accepted) framework. *If* you agree to bet (according to certain rules) and *if* you like to win, you *should* bet according to the Bayesian rationality. In general, mathematicians are wise enough not to univer-

---

[8] A justification for this procedure can be seen in the 'law of a large number' of n-fold repetitions of an 'identical' experiment. A typical textbook formulation is, e.g. : "For large n the probability that the frequency of the event differs by more than ε from the probability p of the event is very small" (my translation) (Krengel 1988, 59). The double appearance of probability—on the 'object level' and on the 'meta level'—indicates the difficulties to connect the axiomatic probability concept with the empirical notion of frequency.

[9] Bayesian statistics, however, deals with subjective beliefs about repeated events.

[10] It should be mentioned that there is no disagreement about the calculations itself, Bayesian as well as classical statisticians are calculating within the same mathematics. Disagreement concerns only the correct modeling of the situation or interpretation of the results.

[11] Cf. WPF, 143.

[12] Cf., e.g., Earman (1992) for an overview.

[13] Cf. WCD, 114.

[14] It should be noted that there are promising attempts to integrate also non contingent propositions into a Bayesian framework in a nontrivial way, cf. Corfield (2003).

salize their formalism—or at least one should hope so. Thus secondly, the 'subjective' part in Bayesian statistics consists in the open presentation of the modeling assumptions (which, by the way, a frequentist would also have to give) *and* the assumed prior probabilities (this seems to be a crucial difference between a classical and a Bayesian approach) depending on his experience with the object and context under consideration. Then, however, the (Bayesian) probability calculus objectively gives posteriori probabilities depending on the data. Everybody supposing the same (or a nearby) prior will obtain the same (or a nearby) posterior. Bayesian probabilities therefore have a fairly objective flavor.

Second, in a section of WPF on a "logical theory of probability"[15] Plantinga mentions "serious" problems "with infinite magnitudes".[16] These problems appear in the context of mathematical measure theory serving as the basal framework for the mathematical probability calculus. Here Plantinga attempts to play the serpent in Cantor's paradise. But he does not succeed to seduce the impeccable mathematical mind. One paradox Plantinga mentions is the following:

> Consider a real line segment closed at both ends. It is composed of uncountably many points—each of which, paradoxically, has no length. How do all those unextended points add up to something with length? (WPF, 146)

This problem is wellknown from the history of mathematics (see Zenon of Elea or Sextus Empiricus to mention only two classical authors) and Plantinga will certainly know that. In fact, it took centuries to develop and understand the concepts of measure theory. The variety of different mathematical concepts related to the continuum—set theoretical, topological, measure theoretical being the most prominent—shows that Leibniz' famous second labyrinth is indeed a complex object.[17] But today—standing on the shoulders of giants—it only takes some

---

15 Cf. WPF, 146. Here, unfortunately one of the best references clarifying the connection between (formal) logic and (classical as well as Bayesian) probability theory could not be used, cf. Jaynes (2003).

16 It should be mentioned that the proper goal of Plantinga's critique is showing that it is not sensible to assume a universal existence of "logical probabilities" and that their connection to epistemic probabilities is problematic. Again, this is true enough. In my view, however, the real problem with "logical probabilities" is that these are assumed to be absolutely independent from any modeling context (cf. the following discussion and footnote 37). Thus our critique does not aim at Plantinga's thesis but at his arguments.

17 I will just give one example for these differences—formulated in the reference frame of standard modern mathematics. Consider the subset of the rational numbers $\mathbb{Q}$ contained in the set of real numbers $\mathbb{R}$ (identifiable with the "continuum"). *Set theoretically* $\mathbb{Q}$ is 'small' since it is only countably infinite, while $\mathbb{R}$ is uncountable, *topologically* it is 'large' since $\mathbb{Q}$ is dense in $\mathbb{R}$ (there are rational numbers in each arbitrarily small neighborhood of every real number), and *measure*

training (and experience with concrete examples, calculations, and argumentations) to find it also intuitively clear.[18] In fact, measuring subsets of the continuum is not as easy as counting points; that's one reason why students of mathematical probability theory must be bothered with density functions and integration theory. But, for sure, they survive it. On the level of mathematical measure theory there is thus no serious problem. Summing up, to me it seems much more fruitful to describe and to analyze *how* modern mathematics *manage to* refer to and handle the continuum than to declare *that* mathematicians *cannot* or even *should not* deal with it.

Third and most important, there are various passages, where we find the notion of an "absolute" or "intrinsic" probability.[19] As a matter of fact, there is no such thing. At least we will not find it within calculations of any mathematical probability theory. Probabilities (in an abstract or in a more concrete statistical approach) will always depend on modeling assumptions which reflect the author's perspective on or the preconceptions of the considered situation. Therefore we will always deal with conditioned probabilities $P_M(A)$ of some event A (being an element of a suitable collection) under the modeling assumptions M. Since this is generally understood, for reasons of notational elegance, the conditions M are normally omitted. Plantinga seems, but only seems to acknowledge that: "a proposition is probable only with respect to some other proposition" (WCB, 272). A footnote on the same page states, however: "The *absolute* or *logical* probability of a proposition would then be its probability with respect to necessary truth." This "*absolute* probability" might be an accepted concept within debates of academic philosophers, but it does not appear in any mathematical con-

---

theoretically it is 'very small' since its (Borel) measure is zero. Even worse, there are uncountable, thus set theoretically 'large' subsets of ℝ with zero measure. It is, however, hardly mysterious that different conceptual perspectives yield different aspects of the 'object' under consideration—if we might be allowed to use that kind of Platonistic terminology for the time being. And in fact, not to the least part it was the intelligent critique of Zenon, Sextus, Berkeley, *e tutti quanti* provoking the differentiated concept formation by various mathematicians.

18 Contrary to the quote in footnote 21 WPF, 146 (for a standard analyst) it seems to be quite intuitive that not *every* subset of ℝ is measurable and, on the other hand, within the framework of non-standard analysis there exists a measure of the requested type. In general, what is considered to be "intuitively satisfactory" (WPF, 146) heavily depends on the historical situation and the individual training. At least in the context of the quoted passage against mathematical measure theory the missing "satisfaction" boils down to a mere subjective animosity.

19 Cf., e.g., WPF, 145 for the reference to Swinburne's intrinsic probability which is judged to be a more suitable concept than *a priori* probabilities.

text.[20] It is thus a purely metaphysical concept which might be legitimate as long as one does not try to calculate anything. The paradox of the *two envelopes* could neatly illustrate the necessary involvement of the modeling context.[21]

Example 1.1 *Two players, A and B, are playing the following game. Each one gets a sealed envelope with money and they are informed that one envelope contains twice as much money as the other. But they do not know which contains the larger sum and which the smaller. After both players had secretly looked into their envelope they are asked whether they want to change the envelopes. Now A might argue as follows: "Since I found n € in my envelope B's envelope could contain 2n € (with probability p) or n/2 € (with probability 1 − p). If I suppose each alternative to be equally probable (p = 0.5)—and seemingly there is no sensible reason against that probability value—the expectation value for changing the envelope will be*

$$E(change) = \frac{1}{2}(2n) + \frac{1}{2}\left(\frac{n}{2}\right) = \left(n + \frac{n}{4}\right).$$

This is certainly more than the amount of n € which I will get if I am not changing the envelope. Thus changing is clearly the better option." However, B will make the same reasoning. Thus for both players changing is the better option. This seems to be a paradoxical result.

A solution of this paradox focuses on the unmentioned preconceptions of the players and the circumstances of the game which are, however, crucial for a reasonable estimate of the probability p. Let, e.g., A and B be the philosophy professors Albert and Bertram and let the head of department organize the game. Now, if Albert finds 50 € he might ask himself whether his department invested 150 € or only 75 € and the answer will determine his decision. If he finds 50.000 € he could be almost sure to have got the larger amount and he will certainly decide against the change. In general, the greater the amount of money he finds the smaller will be his estimate of p. The general message from this exam-

---

20 One reason for the difference might be that mathematicians relate all special concepts to priorly given well defined collections (sets in general); an event A will be defined as a (special sort of, namely a "measurable") subset of a given set Ω, the "state space" of the object under consideration. The definition of Ω and the collection of "measurable" subsets Σ (closed under complementation and countable unions) already tells something about the preconceptions; cf. also the following subsection. This specified framework is alltoo often missing in the epistemological literature (with some commendable exceptions, e.g., Earman (1992), cf. the following section).
21 A slightly different version of this paradox is discussed in a series of papers, cf. Katz/Olin (2007), Katz/Olin (2010), Sutton (2010).

ple is that concrete determination of probability values p (between 0 and 1) will always depend on the assumed model of the investigated situation.[22] Especially when dealing with a Bayesian formalism one should emphasize the importance of the prior estimate for the probabilities. Every Bayesian statistical calculation starts with putting the prior openly on the table. In fact, this is one of the major differences to classical (frequentist) statistics. However, anybody using statistical methods (classical or Bayesian) should be aware of the fact that the modeling assumptions are crucial for the calculation and thus for the results. Therefore, every numerically calculated probability—as long as this calculation takes place within mathematics—is relative.

Finally, here is Plantinga's own attempt for a definition of a conditional *epistemic probability* P(A|B) of a proposition A under the assumption that another proposition B holds true:

> P(A|B) = [x, y] iff [x, y] is the smallest interval which contains all of the intervals which represent the degree to which a rational human being S (for whom the conditions necessary for warrant hold) could believe A if she believed B, had no undercutting defeater for A, had no other source of warrant either for A or for $\neg$ A, was aware that she believed B, and considered the evidential bearing of B on A. (WPF, 168).

Besides its clumsiness[23] this definition is in several ways problematic and Plantinga himself summarizes some of the possible critiques in WPF (168). But one important point he did not mention: The warrant concept itself contains a crucial reference to probabilities. By definition, a belief is only warranted if the cognitive apparatus of the subject holding that belief is working properly, and this implies a high "statistical or objective probability" (WPF, 18) for the belief to be true. We thus inherit all problems of the statistical approach to probability which Plantinga rightly expounded.[24] Moreover, the involved concept of warrant is defined using the concept of probability and, in turn, the mysterious concept of (epistemic) probability is defined using the similarly mysterious concept of warrant. It seems as if our thinking jogs in labyrinthine lanes without becoming healthier.

---

22 Consider as an exercise the following modification of the game. Instead of the amounts n € and $2n$ € we take as a rule n € and $10n$ € or even n € and $1,000n$ €. If you then found 100 € woudn't you be almost sure that the other envelope contained 0.10 € and not 100,000 €?
23 One simplification may be the following. Since there are only finitely many members of the species S is taken from, the somewhat complicated notion "smallest interval which contains all of the intervals..." can be simplified to $[x_{min}, y_{max}]$ where $x_{min} \in [0, 1]$ is the smallest and $x_{max} \in [0, 1]$ is the largest degree to which a rational human being S could believe A etc...
24 Cf. WPF, 151.

Despite the fact, that Plantinga's "epistemic probability does not conform to the calculus of probabilities" (WPF, 173), we find in WCB probabilistic calculations. And here Plantinga uses the standard formulas from the calculus of probability (sometimes with a reference to Reverend Bayes). He thus does not make use of his own—laboriously enough conquered—concept of epistemic probability. It is thus an open question how we should understand the probability values Plantinga calculates and underpins his argumentation with. Be that as it may, in the following section we will analyze one prominent probabilistic argumentation, the argument from the "dwindling probabilities".[25] Before that it will be necessary to fix some notations.

1.2 Notation

An important reason for irritations between mathematician's and philosopher's probability concepts seems to be the use of quite different reference frames. While standard mathematical probability theory assigns a probability to an 'event' represented by a subset $A \subseteq \Omega$ of a suitable set of 'elementary events' Ω within debates of (mostly analytic) epistemology probabilities are assigned to propositions (or theories) in the context of some logical framework. This could be represented by a fixed collection of propositions $\mathcal{A}$. The content and structure of $\mathcal{A}$ will vary from context to context, but at minimum it is assumed that $\mathcal{A}$ is closed under finite truth-functional combinations, i.e., conjunction (denoted by $\land$), disjunction (denoted by $\lor$), and negation (denoted by $\neg$). For any proposition $A \in \mathcal{A}$ we will denote by $\vDash A$ that A is true in all models or all 'possible worlds' considered in our context (we can thus treat A as a tautological element of $\mathcal{A}$).[26] We will now give parallel sketches of the basic notions and notations of a probability calculus within the framework of logic or set theory, respectively.

Assumption 1.2 (Logical Probability Function) *We assume a fixed collection $\mathcal{A}$ of propositions closed under finite logical operations ($\lor$, $\neg$) and a map*

---

[25] The question for the epistemic status of the probability values might be less troublesome in this discussion since here Plantinga's result is skeptical thus it implies the abandoning of probabilistic calculations anyway. However, the question is much more important with respect to his probabilistic argument against naturalism.

[26] Again it should be noted that $\vDash$ depends on our context: "[T]he content and structure of the models or possible worlds will depend upon the context" (Earman 1992, 36). For a concise presentation of this framework of epistemology cf. Earman (1992, 35).

P: $\mathcal{A} \to \mathbb{R}$ from $\mathcal{A}$ into the real numbers $\mathbb{R}$ such that

$P(A) \geq 0 \quad\quad \text{for all } A \in \mathcal{A},$ (1)
$P(A) = 1 \quad\quad \text{if } \vDash A,$ (2)
$P(A \lor B) = P(A)+P(B) \quad \text{if } \vDash \neg (A \land B)$ (3)

i.e., if A and B *are mutually incompatible elements of* $\mathcal{A}$.
The map P: $\mathcal{A} \to \mathbb{R}$ *is called a* **probability function.**

Proposition 1.3 For any probability function P: $\mathcal{A} \to \mathbb{R}$ the following rules can be shown easily.

$P(A) \leq 1 \quad\quad\quad\quad\quad\quad\quad\quad\quad \text{for all } A \in \mathcal{A},$ (4)
$P(\neg A) = 1 - P(A) \quad\quad\quad\quad\quad\quad \text{for all } A \in \mathcal{A},$ (5)
$P(A) = P(B) \quad\quad\quad\quad\quad\quad\quad \text{for all } A, B \in \mathcal{A} \text{ with } \vDash (A \leftrightarrow B),$ (6)
$P(A) = P(A \land B) + P(A \land \neg B) \text{ for all } A, B \in \mathcal{A},$ (7)
$P(A \lor B) = P(A)+P(B)-P(A \land B) \text{ for all } A, B \in \mathcal{A},$ (8)
$P(A) \leq P(B) \quad\quad\quad\quad\quad\quad\quad \text{for all } A, B \in \mathcal{A}, \text{ with } \vDash (A \to B).$ (9)

Based on this notions one can define *conditional probability*.[27]

Definition 1.4 (Conditional probability) *For any given probability function* P: $\mathcal{A} \to \mathbb{R}$ *and fixed* $B \in \mathcal{A}$ *with* $P(B) \neq 0$ *we define the* **conditional probability** $P(A|B)$ *of* A *with respect to* B *by*

$$P(A|B) := \frac{P(A \land B)}{P(B)}.$$ (10)

A simple and straight forward consequence of these definitions is now the famous theorem of Thomas Bayes (1701–1761).

Theorem 1.5 (Bayes Formula) For any given probability function P: $\mathcal{A} \to \mathbb{R}$ and $A, B \in \mathcal{A}$ with $P(B) \neq 0$ we obtain

$$P(A|B) = \frac{P(B|A)P(A)}{P(B)}.$$ (11)

---

[27] An alternative approach could take conditional probabilities $P(\cdot,\cdot)$ as the primitive concept (denoting the probability of the first entry conditioned by the second) and define on that basis unconditioned probability $P(\cdot) := P(\cdot, N)$ where $N \in \mathcal{A}$ could be chosen to be any fixed tautology contained in $\mathcal{A}$, cf. Earman (1992, 59). Notice that we do not obtain "absolute" probabilities by this definition. The framework—symbolized by the set of propositions $\mathcal{A}$ and the supposed probability measure $P(\cdot,\cdot)$—still relativizes the result.

For many applications it is necessary to study infinite collections of propositions. The probability function is then assumed to be 'compatible' with infinite logical operations.

Assumption 1.6 (Continuity condition (C)) *We call a probability function P: $\mathcal{A} \to \mathbb{R}$* **continuous** *if for all sequences of propositions $A_1, A_2 \ldots$ fulfilling*
(i) $\models (A_{i+1} \to A_i)$ for all i=1,2,3... and
(ii) $\{ A_1, A_2 \ldots \}$ is inconsistent (i.e., the A_i are not all true in any possible world)

we obtain

$$\lim_{i \to \infty} P(A_i) = 0.$$

This condition (C) is one reason for a phenomenon bothering Plantinga; we quote this from Earman:[28]

> Continuity or countable additivity does not come without intuitive cost. Consider a denumerably infinite list $H_1, H_2 \ldots$ of pairwise incompatible and mutually exhaustive hypotheses. One might think that it should at least be possible to treat these hypotheses in an evenhanded manner by assigning them all the same probability. But this we cannot do consistently with (C), since (C) implies that $\sum_{i=1}^{\infty} P(H_i) = 1$. Continuity thus forces us to play favourites   (Earman 1992, 37).

The dealing with countable infinite operations is generally a built in feature of the framework of mathematical probability theory following the axiomatics of Andrei Nikolajewitsch Kolmogorow (1903–1987). The reference frame is now a collection of events represented by subsets of a given *set*.

---

[28] This quote continues by: "(Sticking to finite additivity would allow for a draconian even-handedness in the form $P(H_i)=0$ for all *i*.)" It is thus not really helpful to weaken the requirement to *finite* additivity since then for a denumerably infinite set of hypotheses there is only one possible assignment of equally distributed probabilities, namely zero probability for every hypotheses.

We see here once more the dependence of every sensible probability calculus on the assumed framework or model. In WCD, 141 and slightly modified in WPF, 147 Plantinga discusses ornithological examples of the following general form. We consider countably infinite, mutually incompatible propositions $\{A_0, A_1, A_2, \ldots\}$. If these are supposed to contain "the same degree of content" (however this may be determined) we infer by the "principle of intrinsic probability" (PIP) that they must be equally probable. But it is not possible to assign equal probabilities to each A_i without violating (countable) additivity. In contrast to Plantinga's conclusion we just see that preconceptions about the propositions $\{A_0, A_1, A_2, \ldots\}$ must be taken into account; there simply is no equidistribution on infinite sample spaces. In this perspective (PIP) seems to be quite dubious.

Definition 1.7 (Measurable space) *Let $\Omega \neq \emptyset$ be any nonempty set and let Σ be a collection of subsets of Ω such that*

$$\Omega \in \Sigma, \tag{12}$$
$$A \in \Sigma \quad \text{implies} \quad A^c := \Omega \setminus A := \{x \in \Omega : x \notin A\} \in \Sigma, \tag{13}$$
$$A_1, A_2 \ldots \in \Sigma \text{ implies } \cap_{i=1}^{\infty} A_i \in \Sigma. \tag{14}$$

Thus Σ is closed under complementation and countable intersection.[29] *The pair (Ω, Σ) is called a **measurable space**. An element $A \in \Sigma$, thus a subset $A \subseteq \Omega$ is called an **event**.*

Assumption 8 (Probability space, Probability measure) *Let (Ω, Σ) be a measurable space. We consider a function $P: \Sigma \to \mathbb{R}$ such that*

$$P(A) \geq 0 \text{ for all } A \in \Sigma, \tag{15}$$
$$P(\Omega) = 1, \tag{16}$$
$$P(\cup_{i=1}^{\infty} A_i) = \sum_{i=1}^{\infty} P(A_i) \tag{17}$$

*for all countable collections $A_1, A_2 \ldots \in \Sigma$ which are pairwise disjoint. We thus assume: P is positive, the probability of the 'sure event' Ω is 1, and P is countably additive. The triple (Ω, Σ, P) is called a **probability space**, P is called a **probability measure**.*

Similar to Proposition 1.3, any probability measure fulfills several elementary properties.

Proposition 1.9 *For any probability function $P: \Sigma \to \mathbb{R}$ the following can be shown easily.*

$$P(A) \leq 1 \text{ for all } A \in \Sigma, \tag{18}$$
$$P(A^c) = 1 - P(A) \text{ for all } A \in \Sigma, \tag{19}$$
$$P(A \cup B) = P(A) + P(A) - P(A \cap B) \text{ for all } A, B \in \Sigma. \tag{20}$$

Conditional probabilities can now be defined analogous to the above Definition 1.4 and Bayes' theorem follows just by the same easy calculation.

The following table will present a summary of the parallel concepts of the two formalisms.

---

29 This implies that $\emptyset \in \Sigma$ and Σ is also closed under countable unions.

Probability within epistemology (logic)	Mathematical probability concept
Probability is assigned to propositions	Probability is assigned to subsets
$\mathcal{A}$ is closed under $\wedge, \vee, \neg$	Σ is closed under $\cup, \cap, (\cdot)^c$
(finite or countable)	(countable)
$P(A \vee B) = P(A) + P(B) - P(A \wedge B)$	$P(A \cup B) = P(A) + P(B) - P(A \cap B)$
$P(A) = 1$ if $\vdash A$	$P(\Omega) = 1$
$A \to B$ implies $P(A) \leq P(B)$	$A \subset B$ implies $P(A) \leq P(B)$
$A \leftrightarrow B$ implies $P(A) = P(B)$	$A = B$ implies $P(A) = P(B)$

It should be noted that there are ways to translate from the one language to the other.[30] For our context it is important to note that either framework has built in prior assumptions about the object under consideration. Once more: within no probability calculus we will find 'absolute probabilities'.

2 Dwindling Probabilities

A somewhat entangled debate about the correct calculation of iterated conditional probabilities started with Plantinga's argumentation for the necessity of the "extravagant means" by which—due to Plantinga—Christian belief obtains warrant.[31] The initial question is thus, "*given* that recalibration [of affections, aims, intentions by special divine aid, G.N.], couldn't you *then* see and appreciate the historical case for the truth of the main lines of Christianity without any special work of the Holy Spirit?" (WCB, 271). Plantinga's answer is: "that case isn't strong enough to produce warranted belief (...) at most, it could produce the warranted belief, that the main lines of Christian teaching aren't particularly improbable" (WCB, 271). He now reconstructs a stepwise argumentation—the "historical case"[32] which is assigned to Richard Swinburne. Let us fix (with Plantinga) the following abbreviations:[33]

---

[30] Cf., e.g. Earman (1992, 37): "One can move (...) to the mathematical conception by taking Ω to be the set of models of the language of $\mathcal{A}$, Σ to be the field generated by sets of models of the form mod(A) for a sentence $A \in \mathcal{A}$, and P to be a measure satisfying $P(A) = P(\text{mod}(A))$." The opposite translation is somewhat more difficult since the sigma field Σ allows infinite intersections while the collection of propositions $\mathcal{A}$ does not allow infinite disjunctions in general.

[31] Cf. WCB, 268: "Chapter III, Section 8. The Extended Aquinas/Calvin Model, Subsection VI. Why necessary?"

[32] There is already some disagreement on the very concept of a "historical case"; suffice it here to quote Swinburne calling his goal a "ramified natural theology" which is "a natural extension of bare natural theology to produce arguments from generally agreed historical data for the detailed claims of a particular religion" Swinburne (2004b, 533).

- *K* is "some body of background knowledge (...) what we all or nearly all know or take for granted or firmly believe (...)",
- *G* is the conjunction of the "central Christian claims",
- *T* is the "existence of God",[34]

---

[33] Cf. WCB, 272.

[34] It seems to be appropriate to state, at least shortly, my perplexity about Plantinga's intrepidness when addressing huge metaphysical (not to mention theological or religious) concepts. Compare the initial passage in WCB (WCB, vii): "This book is about the intellectual or rational acceptability of Christian belief. (...) Classical Christian belief includes, in the first place, that there is such a person as God. (...) God is thus all-knowing, and all-powerful; he is also perfectly good and wholly loving. Still further, he has created the universe and constantly upholds and providentially guides it."

"Such a person" defined here by some (highly problematic!) predicates and functions can enter the scene, however, in a completely different manner (for the following quotes cf. Dalferth, 1992, 1): "Nichts ist einfacher als Gott. Gerade deshalb ist nichts schwieriger, als Gott zu denken." Right from the beginning of his considerations Ingolf U. Dalferth accentuates a fundamental tension *connecting* the highest ontological demand with equally high epistemological difficulties. Right from the start he repudiates any analogical thinking trying to control its concept of God: "Auch anderes macht uns Denkschwierigkeiten, die uns vor kaum lösbare Probleme stellen: die Welt etwa, oder wir selbst. Aber die Schwierigkeiten sind anderer Art. (...) Wir können (...) die Welt nicht denken, ohne daß unser Denken an seine Grenzen stößt, weil die Welt immer noch komplexer ist als der komplexeste Gedanke von ihr, den wir zu denken vermögen: Unsere Weltgewißheit wird dadurch aber nicht ernsthaft in Frage gestellt. (...) Bei Gott ist das anders. (...) Gott [können] wir überhaupt nicht als Gott denken, ohne seine ganz und gar dysfunktionale Differenz zu all unserem Wünschen, Wollen, Brauchen und Erklären ernst zu nehmen und ihn damit unmißverständlich von uns selbst und von der Welt zu unterscheiden."

Dalferth's problem is not arguing for the existence of an already wellknown 'God' or for the acceptability of his own creed but how to *think* God at all instead of building his own idle idol. The question how to start thinking and speeking (about, of, from ...) God seems unavoidable and fortunately everlasting and it must always be regarded with respect to the addressee of the thinking and the thinking itself at the same time. Sadly enough Platinga seems to perceive (or take serious) little of the long Christian tradition of sceptical or mystical or negative theology. What Freud criticized from the 'outside' can quite similarly be criticized from the 'inside'; following Dalferth the recent boom of efforts in the philosophy of religion results from a search for reinsurance in confusing and disquieting times (cf. WCB, 422), it seems that "(...) unserer verunsicherte Vernunft in ihren diversen Sinnkrisen die funktionale Stabilisierung durch Religion wiederentdeckt (...) Denken wir Gott aber nur als wohlfeile und von uns dringend benötigte Sinnressource, dann haben wir überhaupt noch nicht begonnen ihn zu denken, weil wir damit noch ganz in den Vorstellungszusammenhängen unseres Wunschdenkens (...) befangen sind: In Gottesbildern maskiert denken wir dann nur unsere eigenen Probleme (...)"

Again, mathematics is in a completely different and much easier position with respect to its object(s): Just clearly state your axioms, postulates, and definitions and begin with your calculation. That even (a substantial reflection on) mathematics can virtuously be integrated in a form

- A is the proposition that "God would make some kind of revelation (...) to humankind",
- B is the proposition that "Jesus teachings were such that they could be sensibly interpreted and extrapolated to G",
- C is the proposition that "Jesus rose from the dead",
- D is the proposition that "[in] raising Jesus from the dead, God endorsed his teachings",
- E is the proposition that the "extension and extrapolation of Jesus' teachings to G is true".

The goal of the historical argument is to show that G is 'probable' on the basis of K, thus $P(G|K)$ is reasonably high (Plantinga's goal is showing that this argumentation fails). The strategy to show this starts by claiming that

1. T is probable on the basis of K, thus $P(T|K)$ is high,
2. A is probable on the basis of $T \wedge K$ (K and T), thus $P(A|T \wedge K)$ is high,
3. B is probable on the basis of $A \wedge T \wedge K$, thus $P(B|A \wedge T \wedge K)$ is high,
4. C is probable on the basis of $B \wedge A \wedge T \wedge K$, thus $P(C|B \wedge A \wedge T \wedge K)$ is high,
5. D is probable on the basis of $C \wedge B \wedge A \wedge T \wedge K$, thus ...
6. E is probable on the basis of $D \wedge C \wedge B \wedge A \wedge T \wedge K$.

If the argument works and since E is claimed to imply G "you might conclude that G is in fact probable with respect to what we know" (WCB, 273). Now, however, Plantinga's dwindling begins. An elementary consideration from the calculus of probabilities yields for any three propositions X, Y_1, Y_2 (see equation (7) and recall that we denote by $\neg Z$ the negation of any proposition Z)

$$\begin{aligned} P(X|Y_1) &= P(X \wedge Y_2|Y_1) + P(X \wedge \neg Y_2|Y_1) \\ &= P(X|Y_1 \wedge Y_2)\, P(Y_2|Y_1) + P(X|Y_1 \wedge \neg Y_2)\, P(\neg Y_2|Y_1) \\ &\geq P(X|Y_1 \wedge Y_2)\, P(Y_2|Y_1). \end{aligned} \quad (21)$$

This obvious claim can be found in WCB, p. 273 and in footnote No. 62 on the same page. Here we used the following equation (again obtained by elementary calculations, cf. Definition 1.4)[35]

$$P(Y_1 \wedge Y_2|X) = P(Y_2|Y_1 \wedge X)\, P(Y_1|X). \quad (22)$$

---

of mystical theology can be seen in the works of Nikolaus Cusanus (1401–1464), cf. Nickel/Nickel-Schwäbisch (2005, 67–92), Nickel (2005, 9–28, 23), Nickel (2011, 193–212).

35 As it is stated in WCB, 279.

Using these two relations (21) and (22) Plantinga[36] now obtains by elementary calculations the following estimate[37]

$$P(E|K) \geq P(E|K \wedge T \wedge A \wedge B \wedge C \wedge D) \, P(T \wedge A \wedge B \wedge C \wedge D|K)$$
$$= P(E|K \wedge T \wedge A \wedge B \wedge C \wedge D) \cdot$$
$$P(D|K \wedge T \wedge A \wedge B \wedge C) \, P(T \wedge A \wedge B \wedge C|K)$$
$$= P(E|K \wedge T \wedge A \wedge B \wedge C \wedge D) \, P(D|K \wedge T \wedge A \wedge B \wedge C) \cdot$$
$$P(C|K \wedge T \wedge A \wedge B) \, P(T \wedge A \wedge B|K)$$
$$= P(E|K \wedge T \wedge A \wedge B \wedge C \wedge D) \, P(D|K \wedge T \wedge A \wedge B \wedge C) \cdot$$
$$P(C|K \wedge T \wedge A \wedge B) \, P(B|K \wedge T \wedge A) \, P(T \wedge A|K)$$
$$= P(E|K \wedge T \wedge A \wedge B \wedge C \wedge D) \, P(D|K \wedge T \wedge A \wedge B \wedge C) \cdot$$
$$P(C|K \wedge T \wedge A \wedge B) \, P(B|K \wedge T \wedge A) \, P(A|K \wedge T) \, P(T|K).$$

Though he rightly calls it "ludicrous to assign real numbers to these probabilities" (WCB, 279), Plantinga amuses himself and possibly his readers by doing so. Since no proposition is known for certain, thus every factor obtains at most a value strictly less than 1, the product will shrink with every new factor (assigning, e.g., 0.9 to every factor we would obtain $P(E|K) \geq 0.9^6 \approx 0.53$). Even by "generous" assignments near 0.9 he obtains by multiplication the almost useless estimate[38]

$$P(E|K) \geq 0.35.$$

In fact, following this argument we can only infer that the probability $P(E|K)$ is not very small,[39] and thus: "our background knowledge, historical and otherwise

---

[36] We omit some further details in Plantinga's reconstruction, e.g., that E is replaced by a series of 5 different propositions.
[37] Cf. WCB, 278.
[38] Cf. WCB, 279.
[39] One may ask what kind of information or argument or insight an estimate of the claimed kind $P(E|K) \geq 0.35$ represents at all. Who will be impressed or agitated or moved by such a calculation? And what kind of consequences could follow? A closer look into the history of this type of argument could help answering these questions. The first one combining theological problems with calculations of mathematical probability theory certainly was Blaise Pascal (1623–1662) in his famous fragment *Infini–rien*. The credit of priority must be given to Pascal for the simple reason that in this short piece of text central concepts of probability and decision theory are developed in the first place (cf. the careful reconstruction of Ian Hacking 1994). Sadly enough among the authors of the dwindling controversy it is only Plantinga who adds a short note mentioning Pascal. However, Pascal's decision theoretic framework could clarify the epistemic status of the obtained probability; moreover, Pascal presents a clear and true-to-life context for the argumentation: his fictitious dialogue partner being a member of the Jeunesse dorée

(excluding what we know by way of faith or revelation), isn't anywhere nearly sufficient to support serious belief in G (WCB, 280). Plantinga calls his considerations "principle of dwindling probabilities" and summarizes it as follows:

> [T]he fact that in giving such historical argument, we can't simply annex the intermediate propositions to K (as I'm afraid many who employ this sort of argument actually do) but must instead *multiply* the relevant probabilities. (WCB, 280)

The above sketched considerations led to a series of critical papers (see Colwell 2003, Swinburne 2004b, McGrew 2004, McGrew 2006 and a reply of Plantinga 2006). We will now try to summarize the debate and add some further comments.

The critique focuses mainly on one general and two technical points. In general it is argued that *every* historical argumentation would become problematic if Plantinga was right. But since "in these areas we can reach conclusions which are very probable" (Swinburne 2004b, 540) Plantinga must be wrong. We will come back to this point later.

The technical points are the following. First, the authors emphasize that Plantinga obtained only a—small since poorly estimated—*lower* bound for the probability $P(G|K)$ under consideration. But then he argued as if nobody could ever obtain any better one. In fact, for deriving the estimate (21) the second term $P(X|Y_1 \wedge \neg Y_2) P(\neg Y_2|Y_1)$ containing the negation $\neg Y_2$ of the evidence was ignored. Therefore, taking the negation into account a more careful consideration could improve the estimate.[40] Swinburne,[41] e.g., after an incorrect quote of Plan-

---

knows the gambling situation Pascal is referring to quite well. The whole argument is explicitly written for this kind of educated agnostic and it does not stop after the formal proof but continues the dialogue sketching and offering possible consequences for a change in lifestyle. In my opinion a careful reading of Pascal's fragment—which, however, is also a source for quite problematic interpretations—would be much more fruitful than working through the intricate debate on 'dwindling probabilities'.

40 In a hardly noticed paper Jason Colwell substitutes the abstract negations by two different lines of concrete propositions, one going back to the "Old Testament prophecies" and the other considering the "apostles who spread the message of Christianity" and "died for that message" (Colwell 2003, 153). The "historical argument" now consists in three separate lines of argument which are claimed to be "independent". Colwell states that the "principle of dwindling probabilities" now *supports* the "historical argument", since "although each (...) probability that the ith chain fails is large, the (...) probability that *at least one* of the chains succeeds may be large" (Colwell 2003, 152). Denoting the conjunction of the respective propositions of each of the three lines by Y_1, Y_2, or Y_3, respectively, he obtains the following network of arguments:

$$
\begin{array}{c}
 \nearrow\ Y_1\ \searrow \\
K\ \to\ Y_2\ \to\ G. \\
 \searrow\ Y_3\ \nearrow
\end{array}
$$

tinga,[42] emphasizes that a careful argumentation must also take the lesser probability $P(X|Y_1 \land \neg Y_2)$ $P(\neg Y_2|Y_1)$ into account:

> [I]f the probabilities along the other routes from K to G are significant, they could make a significant difference to the overall probability. Maybe, for example, in raising Jesus from the dead, God was not endorsing his teaching—so not-D; but God was endorsing the teaching of the church which Jesus founded, although what it taught was not a sensible extrapolation from Jesus's teachings (and so not-B). Maybe this is not very probable, but to get the overall value of $P(G|K)$ we need to add in the value of the probability of G along the route $K \to T \to A \to$ not-$B \to C \to$ not-$D \to E \to G$. (Swinburne 2004b, 539)

Timothy McGrew[43] took the trouble to write down all 16 different paths from K over A, $\neg A$, B, $\neg B$ C, $\neg C$, D, $\neg D$ to E and complains: "what he [Plantinga, GN] does not make clear is why the remaining paths can be ignored" (McGrew 2004, 11). Moreover, he argues that Plantinga's reconstruction of the historical argument "seems to reverse the natural order of inference. Surely many reasonable people who have held T have assigned a very low probability to C, but it is hard to imagine a reasonable person who held C without believing T."[44]

He supposes (in accordance with Plantinga) that $P_i := P(G \land Y_i|K)$ ($i=1, 2, 3$) is small thus the probability of the complement $P(\neg(G \land Y_i)|K)$ is considerably high. Now this in turn—following Colwell—implies that
$$P(\neg(G \land Y_1) \land \neg(G \land Y_2) \land \neg(G \land Y_3)|K) = (1 - P_1)(1 - P_2)(1 - P_3) \qquad (23)$$
may be small and, consequently,
$$P((G \land Y_1) \lor (G \land Y_2) \lor (G \land Y_3)|K) = 1 - (1 - P_1)(1 - P_2)(1 - P_3)$$
may be high. Plugging in the "generously" calculated value of Plantinga for every P_i, i.e., assuming $P_1 = P_2 = P_3 = 0.35$ he obtains $P(G|K) \geq 0.725$.—Hallelujah!
The whole mathematical deduction, in particular equation (23), however, depends on the assumption that
$$(G \land Y_1), (G \land Y_2), (G \land Y_3) \text{ are stochastically independent (with respect to K).} \quad (24)$$
This, however, is *not* equivalent to (nor implied by) the independence (with respect to K) of Y_1, Y_2, Y_3. Summing up, Colwell presents neither a material argument for the independence of his three separate arguments, nor does he show how this assumption could be related to the independence (24) he needs for the calculation.—Alas!

41 Cf. Swinburne (2004b).

42 In his summary of Plantinga's argumentation he imputes (by misquotation) the generally false equation
$$P(E|K) = P(E|K \land T \land A \land B \land C \land D) \, P(D|K \land T \land A \land B \land C) \ldots P(T|K)$$
to Plantinga. Only some lines later, he adds "Now, strictly speaking—as Plantinga acknowledges, but takes no further—$P(E|K)$ is the sum of the probabilities of the different routes to it" (Swinburne 2004b, 539).

43 Cf. McGrew (2004).

44 It seems not *so* difficult to find a classical author who did not have problems to imagine such a reasonable person holding C but denying T. In the first "Blumenstück", Richter (1826, 155), of

In reply to this first aspect of the critique Plantinga[45] considered also the missing paths and argues that the respective probabilities are either 0 or inscrutable. Moreover, he apologizes for ignoring them in WCB, since "*Swinburne*, as I understood him, ignored them" (Plantinga 2006, 11). Concerning the order of inference, he refers once more to Swinburne: "*[M]y* reason for putting T below C in the lattice is that I am evaluating *Swinburne*'s argument, and that's how he does it" (Plantinga 2006, 13). As a result his position remains unchanged.

The second point concerns the more or less skilled usage of many different pieces of evidence and is less easy to understand.[46] Swinburne claims that is was important

> [...] to note that the 'dwindling' arises from the fact that in Plantinga's discussion he supposes that all the evidence is put on the table at the beginning. [...] But the force of evidence may often be better appreciated if we do not put all our evidence on the table at the beginning; and instead as we add each conjunct to the hypothesis, we also add a new piece of evidence. (Swinburne 2004b, 541)

He claims to have clarified his own approach in the recent publication (Swinburne 2003). McGrew emphasizes this point as well:

> This multi-stage approach to the argument is what Swinburne himself originally had in mind, as a careful reading of his works makes plain. (McGrew 2004, 19)

Here Plantinga seems to accept the critique and that a new perspective could be opened:

> This is certainly a different way of proceeding, and a significantly different way. Of course, adding new propositions to complex bodies of evidence can have unforeseen results; it's

---

his great novel "Siebenkäs" Johann Paul Friedrich Richter (1763–1825) writes: "Für andere, die nicht so weit sind wie ein lesender Magistrand, merk' ich noch an, daß mit dem Glauben an den Atheismus sich ohne Widerspruch der Glaube an Unsterblichkeit verknüpfen lasse; denn dieselbe Notwendigkeit, die in diesem Leben meinen lichten Tautropfen von Ich in einen Blumenkelch und unter eine Sonne warf, kann es ja im zweiten wiederholen;—ja noch leichter kann sie mich zum zweiten Male verkörpern als zum ersten Male."

An atheistic creed can be combined with the assumption of immortality (though with dramatically changed character), since the same necessity which embodies a person the first time could do it also a second. Consequently, for Jean Paul it is not difficult to assume that the monumental "Proclamation that there was no God" is held by the reanimated Christ.

45 Cf. Plantinga (2006).
46 The whole complex of Bayesian epistemology in a technical sense, however, is hardly touched in the debate under consideration (for an introduction cf., e.g., Bovens/Hartmann 2003).

important to see that the earlier conclusions can also be *less* likely on the later evidence. [...] Nevertheless, this proposal for the structure of historical arguments is certainly promising and certainly deserves detailed exploration. (Plantinga 2006, 17)

However, he could not find any such (diachronic) argumentation in Swinburne's writings:[47]

> I can only report that after several careful readings of those pages, I still can't see that they make plain McGrew's interpretation; and some of what Swinburne says here clearly suggests the synchronic interpretation. (Plantinga 2006, 17)

In fact, the Appendix to (Swinburne 2003) does not reveal any new approach exceeding a simple application of Bayes' formula (at least to my reading). Moreover, we learn step by step indeed, but it is not easy to see why, in the end, we shouldn't take stock and lay all claims and all arguments or evidences on the table at once. Of course, for the *rhetoric* of an attorney addressing the court the timely order of the arguments is of utmost importance. But this should not be the case for the *logic* of a philosophical argumentation. In fact, a Bayesian statistician may update his posteriori probability distribution every time new data are collected. For many situations, however, one can show that the result of an encompassing step calculation will be the same: It is an easy to prove, however important, feature of Bayesian statistics[48] that for n *independent* data an n-fold stepwise updating of the probability results in exactly the same value as one application of Bayes' theorem for the whole bundle of data.

Let us—for a moment—forget about all these confusing calculations and try to understand the philosophical difference between Plantinga and Swinburne with respect to the above issue. At first glance it seems to be the old struggle between the arguments of natural theology—highly confident in human rationality and experience—and the pessimism of reformed theologians—emphasizing the hopeless (epistemic) situation of mankind. However, perhaps the two positions are closer related than they believe to be—at least pragmatically. At the end of his paper Swinburne wonders why people so often do not grasp his all too clear arguments. His pessimistic answer is, that people in general are stupid and lazy ("sunk in sin" Plantinga could add or translate), though his formulation is a little bit more polite:

---

47 Strange engough we find here an example that analytic philosophers apparently do not manage to make their arguments clear and explicite.
48 Cf., e.g. Koch (2007, 16).

> Part of the answer must be that humans are only partly rational. [...] We have a built-in inclination to reject arguments which might lead us to [...] a change in our life style.
> (Swinburne 2004b, 542)

And on the other hand, Plantinga tries to convince his opponent(s) not by denying the value of a strictly rationalistic argumentation and changing to another style of language but by adopting the formalism and using the very same probability calculus.

Taking stock: Is there any moral we can draw from the above sketched debate about dwindling probabilities? Perhaps the following. First, concerning the technical side of the dispute Plantinga's critique remains more or less valid. It can be similarly related, however, to all historical argumentations. Strange enough there still exists history within the sphere of academics. Moreover, in general we don't find any probabilistic calculations in historical works. So possibly historians are not mainly interested in (probabilistically) proving the validity of historical facts. Whether a (Bayesian) approach could quantify, e. g., the coherence of *independent* information and thus enable a quantification of the validity of material arguments seems to be an open question which should be discussed, however, in concrete contexts where the assumed *priori* probabilities are sufficiently plausible. Anyway, the more serious part of Plantinga's critique lies in the short remark that it was "ludicrous to assign real numbers to these probabilities" (WCB, 279).[49] In fact, we hardly find convincing considerations about the sense of these probabilities in the whole debate. So second, the use of the mathematical formalism which is quite excessive on Swinburne's side does not seem to help deciding or at least clarifying the philosophical discussion. Even worse, the poor reader struggles with formulas and calculations instead of considering concepts or phenomena. Sadly enough, we neither changed our conviction with respect to any theologically relevant issue nor did we gain any better understanding of the phenomena and (Biblical) reports the debate claimed to be concerned with.

And even Plantinga could be lovelier and less strange if he sometimes ceased struggling for a cogent argumentation (which does not work anyway) and strengthened the efforts to draw a rich, endearing and therefore convincing picture of the Christian creed.

---

[49] With respect to this sentence we could interpret the whole section in WCB as being pure irony. However, the following quite serious debate speaks a different language.

3 Epilogue

The Babel fish is small yellow and leech-like, and probably the oddest thing in the Universe [...] if you stick a Babel fish in your ear you can instantly understand anything said to you in any form of language. Now it is such a bizarrely improbable coincidence that anything so mindbogglingly useful could have evolved purely by chance that some thinkers have chosen to see it as a final and clinching proof of the nonexistence of God. The argument goes something like this: "I refuse to prove that I exist," says God, "for proof denies faith, and without faith I am nothing." "But," says Man, "the Babel fish is a dead giveaway isn't it? It could not have evolved by chance. It proves that you exist, and so therefore, by your own arguments, you don't. QED." "Oh dear," says God, "I hadn't thought of that," and promptly disappears in a puff of logic. "Oh, that was easy," says Man, and for an encore goes on to prove that black is white and gets himself killed on the next zebra crossing.
Douglas Adams

Literature

Bovens, Luc/Hartmann, Stephan (2003): Bayesian Epistemology, Oxford.
Colwell, Jason (2003): "The Historical Argument for the Christian Faith: A Response to Alvin Plantinga", in: International Journal for Philosophy of Religion 53, 2003, 147–161.
Corfield, David (2003): Towards a Philosophy of Real Mathematics, Cambridge.
Dalferth, Ingolf U. (1992): Gott. Philosophisch-theologische Denkversuche, Tübingen.
Earman, John (1992): Bayes or Bust? A Critical Examination of Bayesian Confirmation Theory, London.
Earman, John (2000): Hume's Abject Failure. The Argument against Miracles, Oxford.
Hacking, Ian (1975): The Emergence of Probability, Cambridge.
Hacking, Ian (1994): "The Logic of Pascal's Wager", in: Jordan (Ed.): Gambling on God, Lanham 1994.
Howard-Snyder, Daniel (2004): "Was Jesus Mad, Bad, or God? ... or Merely Mistaken", in: Faith and Philosophy 21.
Jaynes, Edwin Thompson (2003): Probability Theory: The Logic of Science, Cambridge.
Katz, Bernard D./Olin, Doris (2007): "A Tale of Two Envelopes", in: Mind 116, 903–926.
Katz, Bernard D./Olin, Doris (2010): "Conditionals, Probabilities, and Utilities: More on Two Envelopes", in: Mind 119, 171–183.
Koch, Karl-Rudolf (2007): Introduction to Bayesian Statistics, Berlin.
Krengel, Ulrich (1988): Einführung in die Wahrscheinlichkeitstheorie, Braunschweig.
McGrew, Timothy (2004): "Has Plantinga Refuted the Historical Argument?", in: Philosophia Christi 6, 7–26.

McGrew, Timothy/McGrew, Lydia (2006): "On the Historical Argument. A Rejoinder to Plantinga", in: Philosophia Christi 8, 23–38.
Nickel, Gregor (2005): "Nikolaus von Kues: Zur Möglichkeit von theologischer Mathematik und mathematischer Theologie.", in: I. Bocken/H. Schwaetzer (Eds.): Spiegel und Porträt. Zur Bedeutung zweier zentraler Bilder im Denken des Nicolaus Cusanus. Maastricht 2005, 9–28.
Nickel, Gregor (2011): "Mutmaßendes Sehen oder wahrscheinliche Wahrnehmung?—Kues contra Oxford", in: E. Heinrich/D. Schönecker (Eds.): Wirklichkeit und Wahrnehmung des Heiligen, Schönen, Guten, Paderborn 2011, 193–212.
Nickel, Gregor/Nickel-Schwäbisch, Andrea (2005): "Visio Dei ante omnia quae differunt. Niklas aus Lüneburg beobachtet Nikolaus von Kues", in: K. Reinhardt/H. Schwaetzer (Eds.): Cusanus-Rezeption in der Philosophie des 20. Jahrhunderts, Regensburg 2005, 67–92.
Plantinga, Alvin (1993): Warrant and Proper Function, Oxford.
Plantinga, Alvin (2000): Warrant: The Current Debate, Oxford.
Plantinga, Alvin (2000): Warranted Christian Belief, Oxford.
Plantinga, Alvin (2006): "Historical Arguments and Dwindling Probabilities", in: Philosophia Christi 8, 7–22.
Richter, Jean Paul Friedrich (1826): "Blumen- Frucht- Und Dornenstücke; Oder, Ehestandt, Tod und Hochzeit des Armenadvokaten F. St. Siebenkäs Im Reichsmarktflecken Kuhschnappel", in: Sämtliche Werke Dritte Lieferung, Zweiter Band, Berlin.
Richter, Jean Paul Friedrich (1897): Flower, Fruit, and Thorn Pieces; or the Wedded Life, Death, and Marriage of Firmian Stanislaus Siebenkäs, Parish Advocate in the Burgh of Kuhschnappel, transl. by Alexander Ewing, London 1897.
Sutton, Peter A. (2010): "The Epoch of Incredulity: A Response to Katz and Olin's 'A Tale of Two Envelopes'", in: Mind 119, 2010, 160–169.
Swinburne, Richard (1979): The Existence of God. Oxford.
Swinburne, Richard (2003): The Resurrection of God Incarnate. Oxford.
Swinburne, Richard (2004): The Existence of God. Second Edition, Oxford.
Swinburne, Richard (2004b): "Natural Theology, its 'Dwindling Probabilities' and 'Lack of Rapport'", in: Faith and Philosophy 21, 2004, 533–546.

Alvin Plantinga
Replies to my commentators

I deeply admire and appreciate this series of essays on my work, the more so since they emanate from Germany with its magnificent philosophical tradition.

Ad Schönecker

I'm certainly grateful to Dieter Schönecker for his careful and detailed effort to answer the question "What is *Warranted Christian Belief* all about?" And I'm also perfectly willing to concede that, as Kant suggests in a different connection, Schönecker may have a better answer to that question than I do. Nevertheless, I'll give it a try.

First Schönecker is certainly correct in saying that the main point of WCB is not just the thought that if Christian belief is true, then very likely it does have warrant (call this claim 'TW'.) But then what is it? The first thing to see is that WCB is a sequel to earlier works, in particular *God and Other Minds* and "Reason and Belief in God". It's a sequel in the following way. In G&OM, I "set out to investigate the rational justification of belief in the existence of God . . . ." However, I didn't spend any time thinking about the meaning of "rational justification," taking for granted, in a sort of unreflective way, the usual understanding of that notion current at that time. On this understanding, justification in general is *deontological*, a matter of conforming to duty; and rational justification is a matter of conforming to duties with respect to the formation and maintenance of belief. Although there were few detailed investigations into the nature of rational justification, this deontological conception was often expressed, e.g., by Roderick Chisholm, Brand Blanshard, Michael Scriven, and others. An earlier and particularly heartfelt expression of this view is found in W. K. Clifford, according to whom

> if a belief has been accepted on insufficient evidence, the pleasure is a stolen one. Not only does it deceive ourselves by giving us a sense of power which we do not really possess, but it is sinful . . . . To sum up, it is wrong always, everywhere, and for anyone to believe anything upon insufficient evidence.
> (William James remarks on the "robustious pathos" of Clifford's *cri de couer.*)

In G&OM I simply assumed this deontological notion of 'rational justification' and argued that belief in God and belief in other minds were in the same boat with respect to it. In RBG, I looked a bit more deeply into this idea of rational justification, asking whether there are such (intellectual) duties, and if so, whether a believer in God who doesn't believe on the basis of (propositional) evidence was in violation of them. I argued (among other things) that there do seem to be intellectual duties, but that the believer who takes belief in God as basic is not just as such in violation of them. Hence such belief is or can be *properly* basic, i.e., basic with respect to deontological justification.

In WCB, I looked further into the notions of rational justification, rationality and allied notions, concluding that there were three basic notions here: (1) justification taken deontologically, or at least in ethical terms, (2) rationality in a sense involving the proper function of *ratio*, i.e., rational faculties, and (3) warrant, that property or quality a sufficient amount of which distinguishes knowledge from mere true belief. I asked which of these, if any are enjoyed by theistic belief, but went on to ask the same question about explicitly Christian belief. So I broadened the investigation undertaken in G&OM and R&BG in two ways: by considering Christian belief as opposed to mere theistic belief, and by considering rationality and warrant as well as justification.

I took it to be fairly obvious that Christian belief is or can be deontologically justified, even if taken in the basic way: one need be flouting no intellectual duties in thus embracing it. I also thought it fairly obvious that (basic) Christian belief is or can be *internally* rational; i.e., there need be no lack of proper function in the operation of cognitive faculties 'downstream' from experience. Here I take experience to include 'seemings'—for example, the seeming-to-be-true of various propositions.

What about *external* rationality—what about experience and those seemings? Here too, of course, there can be malfunction. Upon being appeared to in a familiar fashion, it seems to me that I see a tree. Of course things could go wrong; that way of being appeared to could fail to produce the appropriate seeming-to-be-true, either producing no seeming at all, or producing an inappropriate seeming. Marx, I think, would concede that religious belief seems to many to be true; but he claims that this seeming-to-be-true of religious belief arises from some kind of malfunction of cognitive powers. This malfunction, furthermore, is due to some kind of pathology or malfunction in society itself; social malfunction induces individual malfunction. I said it's pretty obvious that Christian belief is or can be deontologically justified and internally rational; but it's not just obvious that Marx's claim here—that this seeming is due to pathology —is mistaken (although I certainly think it *is* mistaken).

People like Freud, on the other hand, argue that religious belief is a product of *wish-fulfillment*. Here the suggestion is not that religious belief is a product of cognitive faculties that are malfunctioning; belief on the basis of wish-fulfillment is not necessarily a sign of cognitive malfunction. Wish fulfillment has its uses, and our cognitive architecture or design plan seems to have a place for it. Perhaps I think I am more clever, or socially more adept, or less funny looking than I actually am; this sort of mild illusion isn't so much a sign of cognitive malfunction as a mechanism that enables me to function better (for example, by avoiding depression). So the problem with religious belief, according to Freud, is not cognitive malfunction, but rather that the cognitive processes involved in the formation and maintenance of religion belief are not aimed at the production of *true* belief; they are instead aimed at the production of belief with some other quality, such as the ability to carry on in this cold cruel world. And again, it isn't just obvious that Freud and his cohorts are wrong (though again, of course, I think they are).

This brings us to *warrant*. I argued that a belief has warrant if it is produced by cognitive powers that are functioning properly in a congenial epistemic environment according to a design plan that is successfully aimed at truth. And once more, it isn't just obvious that religious beliefs meet this condition. It is clear, however (even if not obvious) that (probably) Christian belief meets this condition if and only if it is true (and this is where TW fits in); for if it is true, then probably the faculties that produce Christian belief—the internal witness of the Holy spirit, for example—are indeed aimed at truth and functioning properly in a congenial epistemic environment. I then went on to deal with several kinds of potential defeaters.

As Schönecker points out, several people take TW (the thought that both Christian and theistic belief are probably warranted if they are true) to be the main thesis of WCB, and then express disappointment that I didn't go on to argue that Christian belief is in fact true. But TW is a small part of a much larger project. First, I was aiming to make a contribution to specifically Christian philosophy by presenting a model of the way in which Christian belief has or can have warrant. But second, I was also trying to make a contribution to a conversation about philosophy of religion among people of all sorts—believers and unbelievers alike. In *that* context, I wanted to argue that there aren't any decent *de jure* objections to Christian belief—that is, there aren't any decent *de jure* arguments that are not based on *de facto* arguments. I was arguing that the atheologian can't sensibly object to the *rationality* of Christian belief without first objecting to its *truth*. This is a significant claim, for two reasons. First, many, perhaps most atheological objectors, both to theistic and to more specifically Christian belief, argue that Christian belief is irrational, without arguing that it is false. Schönecker seems to doubt that there are all that many objectors of this kind. But I should think there are: I'm thinking of the whole atheological evidentialist tradition according to which Christian belief, whether true or false, is at any rate irrational, just because there is insufficient evidence for it. Here W. K. Clifford would be an early and enthusiastic representative of this view (that "tone of robustious pathos"); others would be Brand Blanshard, Michael Scriven, and an exceedingly strong oral tradition. And second, as far as I know, there aren't any decent arguments for the falsehood of Christian belief.

Why didn't I go on to argue for the *truth* of Christian belief? Well, in the context of a discussion involving both believers and unbelievers, such an argument should have premises accepted by the majority of the parties to the discussion, i.e, by unbelievers as well as believers. And the fact is I don't know of any sufficiently strong arguments of that sort for the truth of Christian belief. Of course I do believe the Christian faith; indeed, I'd say, *know* that it is true (contrary to Schönecker, p. 20). But this knowledge is a matter of faith. And as far as I can see, there are no purely philosophical arguments sufficiently strong to undergird serious Christian belief. As Schönecker points out, however, I do propose a powerful (so I say, anyway) philosophical argument against the main current alternative to theistic belief, namely naturalism.

It's worth noting, I think, that those who lament the fact that I produced no such arguments do not for the most part themselves produce such arguments. The exception would be Richard Swinburne, who does indeed put forth such arguments. But Swinburne takes it that the belief that p is really just the belief that p is more likely than not with respect to the relevant evidence; and surely no one would think that I *know* p if the best I can say for it is that it is more probable than not with respect to the relevant evidence.

So this is how I see the structure of WCB. On reflection, it certainly does look fairly complicated; it is no wonder, perhaps, that many have misunderstood that structure. Schönecker has certainly done us a service in so carefully and fully canvassing this question.

Ad Tapp

I should like to begin by thanking Christian Tapp for his interesting discussion of infinity and the possibility of reference to an infinite being. Much of what Tapp says seems to me both insightful and clearly true. At a couple of places, however, I find myself less than wholly convinced.

I took issue with Gordon Kaufman's suggestion that God is really a mental construct, not an actual person, and I suggested that it was absurd to suppose that a mental construct had created the world; Tapp gently chides me for being a bit uncharitable:

> A real property such as 'being creator' is predicated of a mental construct—that is indeed absurd. Wouldn't it be a much more charitable interpretation of a Kantian standpoint to locate the predicated property 'being creator' also at the anti-realist reinterpretation level, i.e., to take it too as some sort of mental construction (a mental construction that applies to certain other mental construction as their property in a very special sense)? If one does so, the absurdity is by far not that obvious. (p. 44).

I accept the criticism that I was insufficiently charitable towards Kaufman. But I'm not sure how to construe Tapp's suggestion as to how to be more charitable: I don't really understand his suggestion.

The idea seems to be this. Kaufman suggests that when we say, e.g., 'God has created the heavens and the earth,' we ordinarily use the name 'God,' not as the name of an omnipotent, omniscient wholly good person, but rather as a name of a mental construct, something we have ourselves have brought into being. Taken at face values, he seems to be thinking that we are then predicating the property *having created the heavens and the earth* of a mental construct (whatever that is). Tapp thinks of this as Kaufman's proposing an anti-realist interpretation of the word 'God': instead of referring to the being endorsed by theism, we are really referring to a certain mental or imaginative construct. This would be anti-realist in the way the nominalist is anti-realistic about universals: the nominalist proposes that when we allegedly talk about universals, we are really referring to linguistic items, names, nomina.

So far this makes good sense. But what is it to "locate the predicated property 'being a creator' also at the anti-realist level, i.e., to take it too as some sort of mental construction (a mental construction that applies to certain other mental constructions as their property in a very special sense)"? To be anti-realist about universals, as I've suggested, is to take it that there really aren't any universals; what there are instead is names, nomina. To be anti-realist about horses, by parity, would be to suggest that there really aren't any such things as horses; what there really are, are things of some other sort—maybe horse-images. To be anti-realist about the property *being a creator* would be, I guess, to think that there is no such thing as that property; what there is, is something different. But what? What would this something different be? What sort of thing would it be? Would it be some other property?

Here's a suggestion—I don't know whether it is close to what Tapp has in mind. Perhaps he thinks the charitable way to construe Kaufman here is to take him to be suggesting that when we say "God created the world" we are not predicating the property *creator of the world* of a mental construct, but are instead predicating of that construct the property of *being such that if it were not a mental construct but a concrete being, then that being would have created the world*.

Does this make sense? I'm not sure. What I am sure of is that this is certainly not how Christians or other theists think of what they are doing when, as they assert that God has created the world, created us human beings in his image, and so on. Nor is there any reason to believe that, contrary to what they think, this is what they are really doing.

Tapp identifies another point at which he thinks I'm uncharitable to Kaufman. Kaufman suggests that we should reinterpret the grand claims of the Christian faith; for example, when we say, e.g., "God is real", we should take this as meaning "There are forces in the world that contribute to human flourishing". I took some umbrage at this, suggesting that it is at best misleading double talk, enabling someone who is in fact an atheist or agnostic to appear to agree with Christians, perhaps those Christians sitting in the pews of his congregation.

Tapp suggests that there is a more constructive way of understanding Kaufman: we should take him as suggesting a mapping from the sentences that express traditional Christian belief, to some other sentences having two properties: (1) these sentences express propositions entailed by traditional Christian belief, and (2) those propositions can also be accepted by contemporary secularists. Doing this, says Tapp, "may be helpful for mystagogical and apologetic purposes" (p. 50); it "represents something akin to a preliminary stage of Christian faith for modern, rational and open-minded people" (p. 50). He says that "By Kaufman's work, we may learn that an interpretation of Christian faith exists that . . . makes sense, is morally appealing and in accordance with reason . . . and strikes some necessary chords to enable a secular minded person to discover his 'religion musicality' (Max Weber)." (p. 50)

Now I certainly appreciate Tapp's apologetic concerns. But I'd like to make two points. First, the sentences Kaufman proposes as the values of that mapping are not in fact an *interpretation* of Christian belief. Not just any sentences entailed by a given sentence are an interpretation of that sentence. You say "Einstein was the greatest scientist of the twentieth century"; I propose to interpret you as saying "Einstein probably took a science course in school". You would certainly have the right to say I haven't interpreted what you said—not even badly. What I attribute to you is not an interpretation of what you said—not even a bad interpretation.

And second, even if Kaufman's proposed substitutes *are* interpretations, what is the point of making them? I have a hard time seeing them as of much apologetic value. I tell my secular colleagues: here's an interpretation of Christian belief: when we say, for example, "God is real", you can interpret that as "The universe displays some forces that conduce to human flourishing". I'd expect them to reply something like "Well, if *that's* all you mean, I'd say you've been expressing yourself rather badly. I thought you were talking about God, a being who is eternal, all powerful, all-knowing and perfectly good, and claiming that such a being really exists. Of course I agree that there are some forces that conduce to human flourishing, but if that's all you mean, why don't you just say it?"

I really can't see how this reinterpretation is at all likely to lead my colleagues closer to Christian belief.

Ad Löffler

I really have little—little of importance, anyway—to say in response to Winfried Löffler's very interesting paper. I agree that my account of what he calls world-view beliefs (such as that there are other persons, that here has been a past, that time doesn't reverse its direction, and the like) is underdeveloped, and that a great deal more needs to be said about such beliefs. I agree that his 7-fold classification of beliefs is useful, perhaps more useful than my division of beliefs into basic and non-basic beliefs. And I agree that world-view beliefs are very interesting, and require something like special epistemological treatment.

Still, I'd like to make a couple of comments. Löffler suggests that I take these world-view beliefs to be neither basic nor inferential: "In *Warranted Christian Belief* we find a confirmation that these world-view beliefs are neither properly basic nor inferential" (p. 70); he goes on to add a bit later, "the importance of world-view beliefs remains rather underexplored and their positive epistemological characterization remains open: if they are neither basic nor inferential, what are they?" (p. 72). I don't have the space, here, to explore this question in sufficient detail and depth, but I'd like to make a suggestion or two.

In the first place, I was thinking of the basic/non-basic distinction as exhaustive: every belief (on the part of a given person, at a given time) is one or the other but not both (and I'm prepared to take 'inferential' as a synonym for 'non-basic'). A belief is basic if it is not accepted on the evidential basis of other beliefs; otherwise it is non-basic. If so, however, I can't follow Löffler in the thought that world-view beliefs are neither basic nor inferential. So how can we think of them?

Consider my belief that there are other persons. I start my cognitive life, presumably, by accepting beliefs that entail this belief—perhaps as a young child I believe such things as *Momma likes me, Daddy is angry with me, my little brother tattles on me,* and the like. According to to Löffler, "Spelled out in another terminology, we may say that a world-view has a guiding function and provides the necessary context and background in the light of which we understand our world" (p. 77). But a small child may not have these world-view beliefs, at least not explicitly. As a small child, I may have remembered riding my tricycle earlier in the day, but I probably had never formed the belief that there has been a past.

Would it be right to say that when I believed *this morning I rode my trike*, I believed the proposition *there has been a past* and other world-view propositions in a sort of *implicit* or perhaps *dispositional* sense? According to Löffler "'Believing', of course, is taken here in the tacit, dispositional sense: you need not actually think of these contents, but on being asked about them, you would assent to them. I think that any plausible analysis of belief systems relies on this sense of believing" (p. 79, footnote 23). But *is* there any such sense of 'believing'? It's true, certainly, that I presently believe many propositions that I'm not presently thinking about or entertaining. I certainly believed, a moment ago, that China has a large population, even though at that moment I was not thinking of or entertaining that proposition. Someone who believes China has a large population doesn't go around always explicitly and consciously thinking the thought *China has a large population*. Perhaps there are puzzles about such beliefs—beliefs that one isn't consciously entertaining—but surely there are such beliefs.

On the other hand, a proposition's being such that *if I were asked about it, I would assent to it* is not sufficient, I think, for my believing it. There are, first, the usual problems with such counterfactual accounts (in response to the question "Do I look good in this dress?" I would probably make an affirmative reply, whatever my actual belief on that head). Setting these pitfalls aside, I think we can still see that being such that *if asked, I would assent to the proposition p* is insufficient for my believing *p*. For it might be that my hearing and considering the question "What do you think about p? Is it true?" induces in me for the first time a grasp of a concept the grasping of which is a necessary condition of believing *p*. Perhaps I have never thought about the fact that some numbers have prime factors, and don't have the concept of a prime factor of a number. By a series of clever questions you get me to respond affirmatively to the question "If the prime factors of a number are the prime numbers that exactly divide it, are 2 and 3 the prime factors of 6 and 12?" Before you asked that question it was true of me that if asked, I would respond affirmatively; it wasn't true, so I think, that before you asked that question I believed that proposition. I'd be inclined to think you don't believe any proposition you have never explicitly considered.

But then what about such early beliefs as *Momma likes me*? The first times I believe this, perhaps I don't really believe such propositions as *there are persons*, or *there are other other persons*, or *there is such an affection as liking*. Löffler points out, however, that these world-view propositions seem to play an important role with respect to beliefs such as *Momma likes me*. To quote him again,

"Spelled out in another terminology, we may say that a world-view has a guiding function and provides the necessary context and background in light of which we understand our world" (p. 77). If I don't initially *believe* these propositions, however, how are they related to those early beliefs? That's a very good question, one to which at the moment I don't know the answer.

My idea is that these world-view beliefs are in fact basic. Nevertheless, one begins cognitive life without them. The question is whether one (typically) infers them from other more specific beliefs. Of course they may differ here—perhaps some such beliefs are basic and some are not. But consider the belief that there's been a past. First, I doubt very much that most or many people form this belief by *inferring* it from more specific beliefs. I doubt, for example, that anyone would reason like this: "I had breakfast a couple of hours ago; if so, there must have been a past; therefore there has been a past". On the other hand, this belief is presumably not one anyone holds *before* forming such more specific beliefs as *Yesterday was a nice day* or *Daddy was here a minute ago*. Perhaps it's rather that one forms this belief as soon as the question arises—which may be only in a philosophy class. This belief is one that isn't inferred from more specific temporal beliefs (or indeed any other beliefs); one the other hand, we wouldn't form this belief unless we had had more specific temporally beliefs. So this more general belief is in a way dependent upon more specific beliefs, but not by way of being inferred from them.

Ad Wiertz

For the most part Oliver Wiertz understands me very well. I certainly appreciate his elaborate and cogent defense of my project against the charge of circularity. And I'm gratified to note that he recognizes that my AC model plays two quite different roles: "In WCB Alvin Plantinga pursues two main goals: First, he wishes to contribute to Christian apologetics by showing that if the Christian faith is true, it is most likely in good epistemic order. Second, he wants to provide an epistemology of theistic belief from a Christian perspective, and in so doing make a contribution to Christian philosophy." (p. 85) Just so.

I take it there are three main themes in Wiertz's interesting paper. First, there is the theme indicated by the title: the question whether my AC model is an example of ideologically tainted philosophy. Second, there is the thought that my response to the "son of Great Pumpkin" objection to my model is inadequate. And third, there is the thought that, in WCB and perhaps else where, I am not sufficiently sensitive to the difficulties of holding Christian belief in a pluralistic western society: "Less mistaken, it seems to me, is the impression that Plantinga at times appears to underestimate the concrete epistemic situation of many intellectual theists in contemporary, pluralist, liberal Western societies and consequently the epistemic starting point for an apologetic for theism" (p. 111). I'll take these up in turn.

Is my AC model ideologically tainted? This depends, of course, on what ideological taint consists in, and here I had a bit of difficulty. What is ideological taint?

> For my purposes I define the basic idea of the pejorative use of "ideology" as a divergence between the real underlying purpose of something and an ideology's intellectual justification for it. Characteristically, ideologies in this sense are not concerned with weighing the reasons for and against the truth of a belief i.e. not concerned with the search for truth, but rather about providing legitimacy for already fixed beliefs by providing them with an "intellectual alibi" [...]. As a result, ideologies are not open to critical inquiry but try to avoid it at all costs [...]. Ideology thus bars our access to reality. Correspondingly, Hans Kelsen has defined "ideology" (in the pejorative sense) as "... a representation of the object which is non-objective, influenced by subjective value judgments, concealing, transfiguring or disfiguring the object of knowledge ..." (Wiertz, p. 84)

There are several ideas here. Ideologies are not concerned with weighing the reasons for and against the truth of a belief, i.e., not concerned with the search for truth, but rather about providing legitimacy for already fixed beliefs by providing them with an "intellectual alibi". Well, I must confess that in WCB and elsewhere I don't engage in a search for the truth about *theism* or *Christian belief*, although I do search for the truth about other things. I believe theism, as well as Christian belief, is in fact true. But I'm not sure why this should be thought improper. Consider a philosopher who firmly believes, e.g., that there are other minds (or a past, or an external world, or that induction is trustworthy), and then sets out to show how such belief could have warrant. This philosopher doesn't first produce arguments for the existence of other minds; she takes it for granted that there are, and is interested in investigating how we could know such a thing. Would it by way of an argument from analogy? Or by way of Thomas Reid's natural signs? Or what? Perhaps this could be construed as something like "providing legitimacy for already fixed beliefs" (I don't know about that 'intellectual alibi' part); but what is wrong with that? This philosopher seems to me to be proceeding in a perfectly proper, untainted fashion.

A central part of the notion of ideology, it seems, is that it involves some kind of deception (that "divergence between the real underlying purpose of something and an ideology's intellectual justification for it"). There is a kind of dishonesty here, a pretending to do one thing when actually you are doing something quite different. Marxists sometimes seem to be making such accusations: liberal political theory, for example, poses as an investigation of certain philosophical or political questions, but is in fact an effort to do something wholly different: prop up an unjust and outmoded capitalist system. The ideologue, in this sense, doesn't really believe what he or she says, or at any rate doesn't care whether it is true: her aim, what she cares about, is quite different, lies in a different direction.

Well, if this is what ideology involves, I plead not guilty. I do indeed care about the truth of what I say, and I do indeed believe what I say. As far as I can see, there is no misdirection or deception or dishonesty involved in my AC model. I used it to suggest a way to think about, from a Christian perspective, how Christian belief has warrant; I also use it to show that *de jure* objections to Christian belief presuppose *de facto* objections, in that if Christian belief is true, then very likely it has warrant. I am perfectly willing to swear, in an American or German court of law, that this is what I believe.

Second, Wiertz believes that I don't have a decent response to the Son-of-Great-Pumpkin objection to my model. Now the Great Pumpkin objection is essentially this: if, as I say, religious belief can be properly accepted in the basic way, the same goes for any other belief, including bizarre beliefs like Linus' belief that the Great Pumpkin returns every Halloween. This objection is clearly a nonstarter. Son-of Great Pumpkin (SGP), however, is a bit more formidable. I argued that theistic and Christian belief has a certain important property: they are very likely warranted if they are true. This means that any *de jure* objection to such belief will have to be grounded in a *de facto* objection; to argue that Christian or theist belief lacks warrant, one would first have to argue that such belief isn't true. Now according to (SGP), the same goes for any other belief, no matter how absurd: for example, Great pumpkinism. Wiertz believes that I don't have a convincing rejoinder, because, he thinks, the argument I gave for the conclusion that theistic belief has this warranted-if-true property can indeed be replicated for any other belief.

This seems to me mistaken. I argued as follows. Suppose theism is true: there is such a person as God: an all-powerful, all-knowing and perfectly good person, who has created the world and created human kind in his own image. If so, very likely God would want us human beings to know about his presence; he would therefore have created us with a cognitive process whereby we do come to know about his presence and properties. But then our belief in God would meet the conditions necessary and sufficient for warrant. Now Wiertz argues that the same story could be told by the Great Pumpkinist: if Great Pumpkinism is true, there will be a *sensus cucurbitatis* which is the source of belief in the Great Pumpkin; but such belief will then be warranted, so that if Great Pumpkinism is true, then very likely it is warranted as well.

But why think it likely that if Great Pumpkinism is true, there will be a *sensus cucurbitatis*? Why think the Great Pumpkin has created us? Why think this pumpkin would care about whether human beings know anything about it? Indeed, why think this Great Pumpkin has any personal properties at all? Why think it is conscious, capable of knowledge, and the like? All the story says is that there is this very large and scary-looking pumpkin that returns to Linus' pumpkin patch every Halloween. The argument for their being a *sensus cucurbitatis* if Great Pumpkinism is true, has very little going for it.

Now of course Great Pumpkinism can be elaborated. We can add that the Great pumpkin is indeed a person, and has created the world and us in his image, and is all knowing; we can add that he loves the people he has created and intends that they know about his presence and properties, and has therefore created us with that *sensus cucurbitatis*. (And perhaps Wiertz is thinking of Greaet Pumpkinism as thus as elaborated.) If we do this, however, then 'the Great Pumpkin' seems to be no more than another name for God—with the addition, perhaps, that God has an unusual and hitherto undetected interest in pumpkins.

It isn't true, therefore, that just any bizarre belief has the property of being warranted if true. But certainly Christian belief isn't the only belief with that property. Perhaps Judaism and Islam also have that property. Perhaps any near relative of theism has the property. Well, perhaps so: but how exactly is that a problem? My aim was to argue that Christian and theistic belief is warranted if true. Why is it a problem for me if Judaism and Islam also have that property? Perhaps they too are such that if true, they are very likely warranted.

Wiertz goes on to suggest that

> perhaps the one decisive weakness of the A/C model and Plantinga's apologetic strategy centering on this model [...] becomes clear: Plantinga has no good (dialectical) reason [...] to accept the truth of central theistic beliefs. Correspondingly, Plantinga's remarks on the *sensus divinitatis* and the proper basicality of central theistic beliefs in his A/C model take the form of a conditional: *if* theistic beliefs are true, *then* they are most likely the products of a properly functioning *sensus divinitatis* and therefore have warrant. But the A/C model leaves open the following issues: the question of the truth of theism, the reasons for the truth of theistic belief, and the reasons for believing in the existence of a properly functioning *sensus divinitatis*. (p. 95f.)

Here I'm not convinced. A dialectical reason for theistic belief, says Wiertz, is a reason which is accepted by all parties as a reason (footnote 39)—all who take part in the discussion, I take it. But why must I propose such reasons for my project to succeed? As Wiertz says, there are two parts to my project: (a) contribute to Christian philosophy by proposing a good way to think about the epistemology of religious (Christian theistic) belief, and (b) show that there aren't any decent *de jure* objections that do not presuppose *de facto* objections. Clearly the success of (a) doesn't require having dialectical reasons for the truth of theistic or Christian belief; but neither does (b). What's required for the success of (b), perhaps, is having dialectical reasons for the proposition that if the A/C model is possibly true, if things could be the way the A/C model suggests, then *de jure* objections to Christian belief presuppose *de facto* objection. But I *did* propose what I took to be dialectical reasons for that.

Finally, a word about underestimating "the concrete epistemic situation of many intellectual theists in contemporary, pluralist, liberal Western societies" (p. 111). Perhaps I should just plead guilty here. But I don't think the facts of pluralism really offer a defeater for Christian belief—anymore than the fact of philosophical pluralism offers a defeater for each philosophical view. On the other hand, I *do* recognize that there is psychological difficulty in maintaining a position or way of thinking that is rejected by your colleagues and others around you. One can feel beleaguered, out of step, a bit weird. When I began my career at Wayne State University, my colleagues were gifted philosophers whom I admired, respected, and liked. They were also atheists or agnostics, and I did feel beleaguered, and out of step, and a bit weird. But what are we to make of that from a philosophical point of view? For a partial answer, see my reply to Anita Renusch, below.

Ad Schärtl

Many thanks to Thomas Schärtl for his intriguing comments on WCB. There is a good bit of what Schärtl says that I can't claim to understand, perhaps for the same reason that there are substantial swaths of Wittgenstein, Rush Rhees, and D. Z. Phillips that I can't claim to understand. There is also a good bit of Schärtl's comments I do understand and with which I wholly agree. But there are also some areas where I think I understand him, and disagree.

There is one area in particular, I think, where Schärtl and I do not see eye to eye. He apparently believes that philosophy must be in some sense neutral, or must have a neutral starting point, or something like that. Perhaps the idea is that a properly philosophical treatment of a problem or topic must employ, as premises or means of interpretation, only propositions that are accepted by all or most of those who address that problem; or perhaps he thinks that only the deliverances of reason can be used here. *Theology*, no doubt, can appeal to theological presuppositions or beliefs, but philosophy must be neutral: "And isn't the whole idea of a human nature equipped with a cognitive capacity that secures the 'production' of reliably basic beliefs a rather *theological* answer to a *philosophical* problem? (p. 115 f.) Elsewhere he says:

> In this paragraph Alvin Plantinga very clearly reveals that his concept of a *sensus divinitatis* is plain Barthianism in disguise. Let's name it: what in fact makes the Christian believer superior to a non-Christian believer is *revelation*. As long as she can count on revelation as an additional source to gain knowledge, she has the right not to be ashamed of feeling superior. I have to admit that this is an attractive position *theologically*; nevertheless, *philosophically* it is disastrous because the appeal to revelation does no good in the philosophers' rulebooks. (p. 128)

Here I must demure. There are many different philosophical projects, and philosophical projects of many different kinds. Take naturalism to be the view that there is no such person as God or anything like God. One philosophical project would be that of trying to convince others that naturalism is in fact the truth of the matter: here arguments from premises that are widely accepted, or perhaps arguments from the deliverances of reason would be appropriate. And another perfectly proper philosophical project, one that is in fact widely practiced, is that of trying to give a naturalistic understanding of, say, human action, or the development of the kind of cognitive capacities human beings actually have, including the ability to successfully pursue advanced mathematics, science, and philosophy. Here one takes naturalism for granted and then tries to give an account of various phenomena. This is a perfectly sensible philosophical project, and he who pursues this project is not under a prior obligation to convince other philosophers that naturalism is in fact true.

But the same goes for Christian philosophers. One project, that associated with natural theology, would be an attempt to persuade others of the truth of theism, or Christianity. Today's foremost exponent of this project would be Richard Swinburne, with his sophisticated and powerful arguments for the truth of theism, and for at least certain portions of Christian belief. But another and equally proper project is that of starting from Christian belief, working at the question philosophers ask and answer, the topics and problems they pursue and address, from the perspective of Christian belief.

Christian philosophers have a perfect right to start with the views they hold as Christians; these are quite as suitable as starting points for philosophical inquiry as the naturalistic perspective from which most contemporary philosophers do in fact start. Christian philosophers who pursue this project are under no obligation first to prove that Christianity or theism follow from or are probable with respect to premises widely accepted in the contemporary secular philosophical academy before trying to work out its implications for epistemology and ontology, for ethics and logic, for aesthetics and philosophy of mathematics.

In this spirit I set out to develop an epistemological account of specifically Christian belief. Here the aim was to start from the truth of the great things of the gospel, as Jonathan Edwards called them, and come up with a satisfying account of its epistemology. My account involved (borrowing from John Calvin) both a *sensus divinitatis* and an internal witness of the Holy Spirit.

Now Schärtl points out that

> No atheist is going to buy that referring to the possibility-wise unrefutable claim that there might exist a *sensus divinitatis* (strengthened by IIHS) will be enough to establish the religious believer's entitlement to be considered rational; to the atheist the whole strategy might look like a sophisticated way of religious people to duck and to henceforth ignore the 'gunfire' of an enlightenment and post-enlightenment critique of religion (p. 120).

I suspect this is true: it is also irrelevant. The aim, here, is not to persuade the atheist that Christian belief is rational or warranted; the aim instead is to propose a sensible way for the Christian, philosopher or not, to think about the epistemology of theistic and/or Christian belief. The success of this project does not depend upon convincing or gaining the approval of the atheist.

But this is not the only project involving the Sensus Divinitatis and the IIHS. I also aim to show that there are no decent *de jure* objections to Christian belief that do not presuppose the falsehood of Christian belief: *de jure* objections presuppose *de facto* objections. As I put it in the Preface to WCB,

> This book can be thought of in at least two quite different ways. On the one hand, it is an exercise in apologetics and philosophy of religion, an attempt to demonstrate the failure of a range of objections to Christian belief. *De jure* objections, so the argument goes, are either obviously implausible, like those based on the claim that Christian belief is not or cannot be justified, or else they presuppose that Christian belief is not true, as with those based on the claim that Christian belief lacks external rational or lacks warrant. Hence there aren't any decent *de jure* objections that do not depend on *de facto* objections. (p. XIII)

In this second project it would not be appropriate to start from Christian belief; this is a project or argument addressed to all philosophers (and any one else who is interested) not just Christians. And here what I offer to the non-Christian or nontheist philosopher is the proposition that if Christian belief is true, then (very likely) it has warrant, and has it in something like the way the model suggests. Given that there is no independent route to determining the warrant of Christian or theistic belief, it follows that there aren't any decent *de jure* objections that do not presuppose the falsehood of such belief.

Of course there is much more to be addressed in Schärtl's stimulating comments; Schärtl starts far more hares than I can chase. The rest will have to wait for another time.

Ad Renusch

Anita Renusch's thoughtful paper has much to be said for—for example her thorough and insightful account of epistemic peerhood and the difficulties of determining it. I am not sure, however, that (or where) she and I disagree. She begins her section 6, "conclusion", by saying, "So contrary to Plantinga's assumption that the awareness of religious disagreement need not undermine confidence in Christian beliefs, it still does for many religious believers." (p. 166) But I don't see the contrariety here. I did indeed say that awareness of religious disagreement need not undermine confidence in Christian belief; but I also said, "For at least some Christian believers, an awareness of the enormous variety of human religious responses does seem to reduce the level of confidence in their own Christian belief" (WCB, 456).

Still, I think we do have significant disagreement. She reports me as arguing "that Christians need not regard people holding contradictory claims to be true as their epistemic peers and that they in fact do not do so" (p. 166) and goes on to say that her target is this proposition. This target proposition, the one Renusch takes issue with, has two parts: (a) Christians *need not* regard people holding contradictory claims (i.e., claims inconsistent with Christian belief) to be true as their epistemic peers, and (b) Christians in fact do not hold such people to be their epistemic peers. With respect to (b), I don't have a lot to say. Peerhood, of course, varies from topic to topic; I take my departmental colleagues to be my peers with respect to philosophy, but not with respect to rock-climbing (or my own personal history), about which I know more than they do. So the question is whether Christians do or don't take it that people who reject Christian belief are their epistemic peers with respect to Christian belief. I don't think I said much about that one way or the other; I suppose the right answer is that some Christians do and others don't. Perhaps most don't, because taking it that someone with views contradictory to yours is your epistemic peer with respect to the topic of those views would tend to make it hard to continue to hold those views.

I'm more interested in the other question, i.e., the question whether Christians *need* to regard as their peers people who hold views inconsistent with Christian belief. I think Renusch believes the answer is 'yes': "Contrary to Plantinga, I hold that many Christians have reason for regarding (some of) their religious dissenters as their epistemic peers and that they thus have a religious peer disagreement." (p. 166) So do Christians need to regard non-Christians as their epistemic peers with respect to Christian belief? The first question is: need for *what?* Here the possibilities would seem to be (1) for justification, (2) for rationality, and (3) for warrant.

What about justification? Suppose a Christian thinks people with religious views contrary to hers are not her epistemic peers with respect to such views: can she be within her epistemic rights in so thinking? Can she be justified? In my first philosophy position, at Wayne State University in Detroit, I had as colleagues a number of other young philosophers, all of them extremely competent and some with better philosophical training than I had. I respected them greatly, and thought of them in general, at least, as my philosophical peers or maybe my philosophical betters. I also liked them immensely, and as it turned out we had great camaraderie and made common cause on many philosophical ventures. But, as it also turned out, they were all agnostics or atheists. Did I have reason to regard them as my philosophical peers with respect to the question of theism?

Given my esteem for these colleagues, I of course took their views seriously; how could I fail to? But the more I thought about God, the more it seemed to me that there really was such a person. In church I sometimes felt very close to God, as also in prayer, in reading the Bible, and in some other circumstances, for example in the mountains. I was inclined to doubt that the same was true of my colleagues; they didn't go to church, and, as far as I knew, they didn't pray or read the Bible. So I doubted that they had the same kind of religious experience as I had. This led me to doubt that they were my epistemic peers with respect to belief in God. As far as I can see, I wasn't going contrary to any epistemic duties in so thinking.

Furthermore, it really wasn't within my power to cease believing. Indeed, it is seldom within one's power to adopt or reject a given belief. So presumably I was within my rights in holding the belief in question; but wouldn't I then be entirely sensible, and entirely within my rights in concluding that someone who held beliefs incompatible with that one wasn't really my epistemic par with respect to that belief? I am therefore inclined to think that a person who believes in God need not, on pain of being unjustified, believe that those who don't accept such beliefs are her epistemic peers.

What about rationality? Does my doubting that my colleagues were my epistemic peers with respect to theism go contrary to my evidence, or to some deliverance of reason? Again, I can't see how. I take it there was nothing contrary to reason in my belief in God; after all, as I said, in at least some circumstances it seemed to me that I was experiencing God's presence. But then if I doubted that the same was true for my unbelieving colleagues, it wouldn't be going contrary to my evidence to doubt that they were my epistemic peers on this particular topic.

How about warrant? Would my belief that my colleagues were not my epistemic peers on this topic have warrant, that property which distinguishes or quality enough of which distinguishes knowledge from mere true belief? I think of warrant (roughly) as follows; a belief has warrant for me if it is produced by cognitive faculties functioning properly in a congenial epistemic environment, according to a design plan successfully aimed at truth. As I argue in WCB, (probably) my belief in God has warrant just if it is true. So if theism is true, my belief in God has warrant. But then if that belief has warrant, and I go on to infer that my unbelieving colleagues are not my epistemic peers, that belief too, I should think, would have warrant. After all it is inferred from beliefs that have warrant. On the other hand, if my belief in God *lacks* warrant, then presumably the same would go for my belief that my unbelieving colleagues are not my epistemic peers with respect to theism.

Return to the other branch of Renusch's thesis: that many Christians have reason to think that their unbelieving friends or colleagues are their epistemic peers. I'm inclined to doubt that this is true. But it is also true that the wide prevalence or currency of unbelief in our secular society, in particular among the intellectual elite of our secular society, makes it more difficult for Christians to maintain a robust faith. We human beings are social animals, heavily influenced by our peers, and that, whether or not those peers are our epistemic peers. Those Christians who are not surrounded by unbelievers are in this respect blessed; and unbelief itself is a trial for Christians.

I therefore remain unconvinced that Christians need not take their unbelieving colleagues to be their epistemic peers with respect to belief in God or more specifically with respect to Christian belief. I do agree, though, that our currently secular intellectual environment poses special problems for Christians and may make it more difficult to maintain robust Christian belief.

Ad Plasger

As Georg Plasger suggests in his impressive paper, I do indeed develop my ideas on the epistemology of theistic and Christian belief in constant dialogue with John Calvin. I take it my Aquinas/Calvin model is at least fairly close to what Calvin had in mind with respect to the epistemology of Christian and theistic belief. Of course Calvin wasn't first of all an epistemologist, and, as far as that goes, was also not first of all a systematic theologian. As many have pointed out, his main interests were for the most part practical, not theoretical.

By the same token, my central interest in Calvin was (and is) not to try to figure out precisely what his views were on this topic, and then propose or adopt those views. Indeed, since Calvin isn't primarily a systematic theologian, it is sometimes not at all easy to figure out just what his views were. Furthermore, as I said, Calvin wasn't an epistemologist. In the effort to develop an adequate epistemology of Christian and/or theistic belief, therefore, one can't simply present Calvin's views as such an epistemology. My aim was to develop such an epistemology, and Calvin played into this effort as a source of some general ideas—ideas that I proposed to develop in my own way, whatever Calvin had in mind. As I said somewhere, it's my model, not Calvin's.

Still, I think Plasger sometimes mistakenly attributes to me certain understandings of Calvin. For example, he says (p. 170) "According to Calvin, as Plantinga understands him, faith originates from this innate human knowledge of God, which displays itself in various forms..." That's not what I was thinking: as I understand Calvin, faith, as he defines it anyway, doesn't originate in this innate natural knowledge of God; it is instead a product of the "internal witness of the Holy Spirit". As Calvin puts his definition, faith is "a sure and certain knowledge of the Divine benevolence toward us, which being founded upon the truth of the gratuitous promise in Christ is both revealed to our minds and sealed in our hearts by the Holy Spirit." I take it Calvin doesn't see the *sensus divinitatis* as the origin of this "sure and certain knowledge". As I understand him, Calvin sees the *sensus divinitatis* as wounded, corrupted, overlaid by sin. Furthermore, faith has to do with "the gratuitous promise in Christ"; the *sensus divinitatis*, on the other hand, doesn't produce belief in or knowledge of Christ and his works.

Also, according to Plasger, "One of Plantinga's theses is that the semen religionis or the sensus divinitatis is the foundation out of which faith is formed because it is the 'disposition ... to form beliefs'" (p. 182). Here there is misunderstanding. I wasn't thinking that the *sensus divinitatis* or the *semen religionis* is the foundation out of which faith is formed. In my model, I do take the *sensus divinitatis* to be a disposition to form certain beliefs—certain beliefs about God. But that doesn't mean that it is the foundation of faith. Perhaps the confusion here is due to the fact that 'belief' and faith' are sometimes taken as synonyms. But I wasn't so taking them: I was following Calvin in taking faith to be "a sure and certain knowledge of God's benevolence to us...", while I was taking belief much more broadly. For example, my endorsement of the propositions that China is a large country and that water freezes at 32 degrees Fahrenheit are examples of belief, but not, of course, of faith.

In this same connection, Plasger thinks I propose, in my model, that "this innate ability to recognize God is basically able to form the correct faith in

God" (p. 183). This isn't part of my model. I take faith, on its cognitive side, to be a grasp or apprehension of or belief in the great things of the gospel—for example, the salvific work of Christ; this belief, and the accompanying affections, is the result of the Internal Instigation of the Holy Spirit. The *sensus divinitatis*, on the other hand, does not produce belief in the great things of the gospel. Had it not been for sin, the *sensus divinitatis* would no doubt have functioned differently; but it would not have produced belief in the great things of the gospel—just because, had it not been for sin, God's grand scheme of salvation for us sinners would not have been necessary.

Plasger also says (p. 184) "Plantinga had claimed that, according to Calvin faith and the correct worship of God remain based on the semen religionis." But I didn't state that, and certainly didn't intend that. I'd say instead that according to Calvin, because of human sin, God instituted his grand scheme of salvation for sinners. He then went beyond the provisions of the *sensus divinitatis* and, as Plasger nicely puts it, "God himself now comes to humans by his Holy Spirit and gives knowledge of Himself in that way" (p. 184).

In sections 2 and 3 of his paper, Plasger, as I understand him, appears to me to be arguing that according to Calvin there really is no knowledge or apprehension of God. Rather, any kind of knowledge of God, according to Calvin, is a result of faith. Here I must defer to his expertise; I am not a Calvin scholar and Plasger is. I should point out, though, that the experts differ here; some experts do think that according to Calvin, there is a natural knowledge of God, even if it is impeded and distorted by sin. Here is a dilemma that confronts us non-experts: the experts don't agree! So then what is a poor non-expert to do?

Nevertheless, I should have thought that the passage Plasger quotes on p. 178f. strongly implies that Calvin thought human beings, all human beings, or perhaps all normal human beings, perceive that there is a God and that he is their maker: "Since, therefore, men one and all perceive that there is a God that he is their Maker, they are condemned by their own testimony because they have failed to honor him and to consecrate their lives to his will" (Institutes I, 3, 1). It therefore puzzles me when Plasger says, "thus for Calvin it is essential that despite this activity of God, which is seen in creation, humans display no knowledge of God" (p. 179). He also says: "For this awareness of a god, which exists in every human being, is—according to Calvin—limited to the fact that humans can realize that they are sinners" (p. 182). But if all I know about God is that I am a sinner, can I properly be said to "perceive that there is a God"? I don't see how. Perhaps, indeed, the fact that I am a sinner *entails* that there is such a person as God, for perhaps the notion of sin presupposes a divine Lawgiver. And perhaps someone might think that if I know a proposition p, and p entails some other proposition q, then I must know that proposition q. But of course this would be an error; the fact that I know p and that p entails q does not entail that I know q, or even that I believe q, or even that I could understand q if it were proposed to me. For example, I know the (Peano) axioms for arithmetic; I certainly don't know or believe all of the theorems, and in fact some of those theorems are such that I couldn't even grasp them.

In conclusion I'd like to stress the main point: I wasn't proposing an interpretation of Calvin (and haven't read nearly all of Calvin), and I'm certainly prepared to defer to Plasger's expertise in these matters. My A/C model is indeed inspired by Calvin; once more, however, it's my model, not Calvin's.

Ad Illies

There is much to admire in Christian Illies' paper. For example, he points out (p. 206) that "there are (second-order) reasons we could think as to why God should conceal his first-order reasons for allowing evil and suffering to be part of our world", and then he proposes some plausible such second-order reasons. There is also much that calls for comment in what he says; I shall be able to reply to only a bit of his rich and thoughtful paper.

First, there is what Illies calls "Plantinga's possible-worlds-argument" (p. 193). I was thinking as follows: if we believe there are or could be other universes, on the order of the other universes in the many-worlds response to fine-tuning arguments, perhaps we could suppose that God creates all those universes or worlds where there is a balance of good over evil. In many of these worlds there will be quite a lot of evil, although in none of them will there be more evil than good. If we did think along these lines, we could hardly suppose that the existence of evil in our world or even of a great deal of it, is serious evidence against theism.

By way of comment, Illies suggests that "the atheist will ask: why should God not restrict himself to creating *only* those worlds where evil is marginal?" (p. 201) The answer, I should think, is that the existence of a world which is on balance good—a world in which there is more good than evil—contributes to the total value in the universe (or multiverse). But then he goes on to say just a bit later: "Similarly, even if there are many possible worlds with different balances of good and evil, God has to explain why he created our world with all its atrocities and why he did not restrict himself to creating only worlds with an overall positive balance." (p. 202) Well, of course God doesn't really have to explain himself to us on this or any other topic. I was supposing, however, that *this* world—the world in which we find ourselves—is a world with an overall positive balance. I'd certainly agree that if our world has a negative balance, if there is more evil than good in it, then it would be really hard to see why God would have created it.

I'd like to go on a bit more about why I think our world is a very good world.[1] Suppose initially we think about the matter as follows. God intends to create a world. He considers all the uncountably many possible worlds, each with its own degree of excellence or value. How shall we think of the value or goodness of a possible world? Well, what sorts of things are good or valuable or excellent, on the one hand, or bad or unhappy or deplorable on the other? What are good-making qualities among worlds—what sort of features will make one world better than another? Here one thinks, for example, of the amount of creaturely happiness; a world with a great deal of creaturely happiness (i.e., a world such that if it were actual, there would be a great deal of creaturely happiness) is so far forth a better world than one in which there is little such happiness. Other characteristics on which the goodness of a world depends would be the amount of beauty, justice, creaturely goodness, performance of duty, and the like. The existence of creatures who conform to the divine law to love God above all and their neighbor as themselves (which presumably holds not just for humans but for other rational creatures—angels, other rational species in our universe, if there are any others) would also be an important determinant of a world's goodness or excellence. And of course there are also badmaking characteristics of a world: containing suffering, pain, creaturely rejection of God, hatred, sin and the like. Fundamentally, a world W is a better world than a world W* just if God would prefer the actuality of W to the actuality of W*.

However, there is another quite different sort of good-making characteristic of our world—one that isn't present in all worlds—that towers enormously above all the rest of the contingent states of affairs included in our world: the unthinkably great good of divine Incarnation and Atonement. Jesus Christ, the second person of the divine trinity, incomparably good, holy, and sinless, was willing to empty himself, to take on our flesh and become incarnate, and to suffer and die so that we human beings can have life and be reconciled to the Father. In order to accomplish this, he was willing to undergo suffering of a depth and intensity we cannot so much as imagine, including even the shattering climax of being abandoned by God the Father himself: "My God, My God, why have you forsaken me?" God the Father, the first being of the whole universe, perfectly good and holy, all-powerful and all-knowing, was willing to permit his Son to

---

[1] The next page or so summarizes what I explain in more detail in "Supralapsarianism, or 'O Felix Culpa'" (in Peter van Inwagen, ed., *Christian Faith and the Problem of Evil* (Grand Rapids, 2004), pp. 48ff.

undergo this suffering, and to undergo enormous suffering himself, in order to make it possible for us human beings to be reconciled to him. And this in face of the fact that we have turned our back upon God, have rejected him, are sunk in sin, indeed, are inclined, as the Heidelberg Catechism puts it, "to resent God and our neighbor". Could there be a display of love to rival this? More to the present purpose, could there be a good-making feature of a world to rival this?

I don't think there could be. So I conclude that many of the very best possible worlds include Incarnation and Atonement. But then those worlds also include sin, and its resultant misery and suffering—and not just a tiny bit of sin, as of a peccadillo on the part of an otherwise admirably disposed angel. If there is to be a proper proportionality between sin and its remedy, there will have to be a very considerable amount of sin. Hence I am inclined to think the answer to the question "Why does God create a world in which there is a great deal of sin and suffering and evil?" is "Some of the very best possible worlds contain a great deal of sin and suffering."

In the brief space I still have left, I'd like to reply to one further problem Illies finds (3.4): it's not clear to him who I was addressing. Some of what I say seems directed to Christians and involves, among other things, suggestions as to how Christians should think about sin and evil. Other parts of what I say suggest that I am addressing a wider audience, including some who may be on the fence. Who am I actually addressing?

The answer, as I said in the Preface, is that I was undertaking two quite different projects. One was to contribute to "Christian philosophy" by suggesting how Christians can sensibly think about justification and warrant, and the warrant enjoyed by theistic and Christian belief. The other was to respond to a certain sort of objection to Christian and theistic belief. The first project is really addressed to Christians, although others might find it interesting to see how Christians do or can think about these epistemological problems (just as Christians might be interested in seeing how naturalists think about the epistemological questions that arise for them). This project, naturally enough, involves as presupposition the whole Christian way of thinking about the world, and is not designed to convince those who don't accept Christian belief.

The second project is addressed to people more generally, whether Christian or not. And here the aim is to show that a certain kind of objection to the rationality of Christian belief doesn't hold: the sort of objection that attacks the rationality of Christian belief without addressing the question whether Christian belief is true—i.e., in the terminology of the book, *de jure* objections that don't presuppose *de facto* objections. An example would be the so-called *evidentialist* objection: the thought that Christian or theistic belief is irrational because there isn't sufficient (propositional) evidence for it. The claim is that this is so whether or not Christian belief is true: either way, it's irrational, because either way there is insufficient evidence for it. (As I pointed out in my reply to Schönecker this is a very common objection, perhaps the most common objection.) Here I am addressing people generally, and I expect or at least hope that the fence sitter with respect to the viability of such objections will jump off on my side. Indeed, I hope at least some of those who offer that sort of objection will reconsider.

Ad Nickel

I turn finally to Gregor Nickel's mathematical ruminations on probability, as treated in particular in mathematics, but also in philosophy. I found his contribution of great interest, but also in spots a bit puzzling. I'll mention a couple of such spots.

First, 'intrinsic' or 'absolute' probability. Nickel intends to have no truck with such probabilities, but attributes to me the thought that such probabilities do indeed exist. This is certainly beyond reproach, since in WCB, p. 272, fn. 58, I say, "The *absolute* or *logical* probability of a proposition would then be its probability with respect to a necessary truth". Here I was thinking, perhaps incautiously, that for any proposition A, there is such a thing as the probability of A on any necessary truth, or, equivalently, on the conjunction of all the necessary truths. Here I'm thinking of all propositions, not some particular class of propositions. Nickel apparently doesn't agree, citing the fact that any ascription of probability must be relativised to a particular model or context. But why does he think so? Here he cites the paradox of the two envelopes (p. 219), and points out that some perhaps initially not implausible ascriptions of probability (assigning a probability of .5 to each of

(1) the other envelope contains twice what mine does

and

(2) the other envelope contains half what mine does)

leads to trouble. This is certainly correct; but accepting absolute or logical probabilities does not require one to ascribe those particular offending probabilities to (1) and (2).

He is also right in pointing out that a realistic assignment of probabilities here will depend on many other considerations: how much my envelope contains, who is handing out these envelopes, how much money they have or are likely to have, and the like. Now suppose we abstract away from all considerations, and insist on asking after the probability of these propositions on nothing but necessary truths. Here we find ourselves completely at a loss. How can we make so much as a stab at these probabilities? We can't sensibly appeal to a principle of indifference here, arguing that since our evidence doesn't distinguish between (1) and (2), we should assign them the same probabilities; the problem is, of course, that there are any number of other propositions p such that our evidence doesn't distinguish between (1) and p. For example there is

(1) the other envelope contains four times what my envelope contains;

following that principle of indifference here as well would lead to obvious trouble. So what would be the absolute probabilities of these propositions? Do we have even the faintest idea? This problem is even more obvious if we think about propositions such as *Paul is riding his bicycle just now* or *there are three flying donkeys:* what is the probability of these propositions on necessary truths? So perhaps the best way to understand Nickel's aversion to absolute or intrinsic probabilities as the entirely correct claim that even if there are such probabilities, in many contexts they will be of no earthly use.

Second, a comment on epistemic probabilities. Aristotle distinguished two kinds of probability, one having to do with frequencies, and the other with the correct, or proper, or rational degree of belief in a proposition, given a particular epistemic situation. Following current custom, I called the second kind of probability 'epistemic' probability, giving a definition of it that Nickel quotes on p. 220. Nickel doesn't approve of this definition. He claims it is clumsy, which is true; but his other animadversions are a bit off the mark. He points out that this definition involves the notion of warrant, which in turn itself involves the notion of probability—statistical or objective probability. He then suggests that, "We thus inherit all problems of the statistical approach to probability which Plantinga rightly expounded" (p. 220). But here there is misunderstanding. I didn't expound any problems with objective or statistical probability as such; rather, I argued that *epistemic* probability can't be *explained* in terms of statistical probability. There may be problems with the notion of statistical probability, but it is certainly a notion we need and regularly use. My thought was only that epistemic probability can't be reduced to or explained just in terms of statistical probability (and here I am following Aristotle, Hacking, and very many others).

Nickel goes on: "Moreover, the involved concept of warrant is defined using the concept of probability and, in turn, the mysterious concept of (epistemic) probability is defined using the similarly mysterious concept of warrant. It seems as if our thinking jogs in labyrinthine lanes without becoming healthier" (p. 220). In addition to mystery, Nickel seems to suspect circularity here: but again, this is a misunderstanding. *Epistemic* probability is explained in terms of warrant, and warrant is defined or explained in terms of *statistical* probability plus other notions. No circle here. Nor is there (undue) mystery: a belief has warrant for me if it is produced by cognitive faculties functioning properly according to a design plan successfully aimed at truth, where the last clause, *being successfully aimed at truth*, is explained in terms of statistical probability. All of this is pretty straightforward. Epistemic probability is defined or explained in terms of warrant together with the notions of rationality, defeater, and degrees of belief—again, all pretty straightforward. Of course mystery is in the eye of the beholder; and admittedly these notions don't have the lapidary character of such mathematical notions as, e.g., *prime factor* or *derivative*. Of course these notions depend on the concept of *number*, where it isn't all that easy to say what *that* is.

Finally, I'd like to thank Nickel for his treatment of the problem of dwindling probabilities. Here I won't trouble the reader by recapitulating that problem and the subsequent discussion; instead, I'll just quote Nickel:

> We learn step by step indeed, but it is not easy to see why, in the end, we shouldn't take stock and lay all claims and all arguments or evidences on the table at once. Of course, for the *rhetoric* of an attorney addressing the court the timely order of the arguments is of utmost importance. But this should not be the case for the *logic* of a philosophical argumentation.

Just so.

Once again, I'd like to thank all eight contributors for their careful and insightful comments. I have learned much from them.

Index of persons

Abaelard, Peter 127
Adam 180–183, 186
Adams, Douglas 234
Adorno, Theodor W. 208
Alston, William P. 1, 6, 9, 25, 88, 108, 116, 140, 144, 151
Anderson, James N. 11
Aquinas, Thomas 11, 57, 117, 124, 147, 158, 170, 172, 187, 254
Aristotle 25, 57, 77, 111, 187, 261
Augustine 180, 186

Bavinck, Herman 10
Bayes, Thomas 221f., 224, 232
Bolzano, Bernard 61f.
Büchner, Georg 191
Buddha 37

Calvin, John 2, 11f., 117, 124, 147, 158, 169–189, 251, 254–257
Carroll, Michael P. 29
Christensen, David 150, 157
Clark, Kelly 12
Copan, Paul 13, 20
Craig, William L. 11, 18
Cupit, Don 29
Cusanus, Nicolaus 134, 227

Dalferth, Ingolf 135, 226
Damschen, Gregor 3
Daniels, Charles 29
Darwin, Charles 194, 202
Dennett, Daniel 1, 21, 26, 37, 123, 193
Descartes, René 71, 92
Dostoyevsky, Fjodor M. 204
Draper, Paul 192, 195–197, 204, 207

Earman, John 216, 219, 221–223, 225
Ellis, Albert 29
Ephesians 200

Fales, Evan 1, 159
Farrer, Austin 193
Fichte, Johann G. 2

Flew, Anthony 79
Forrest, Peter 12
Frege, Gottlob 58
Freud, Sigmund 15, 27–30, 109, 121, 123–125, 161, 226, 238f.
Frye, Northrop 29

Gale, Richard 9
Geivett, R. Douglas 18, 36
Greco, John 12, 36
Groothius, Douglas 11
Gutting, Gary 148–151, 167

Hacking, Ian 215, 228, 261
Haldane, John 115
Hegel, Georg F. W. 2, 92, 135
Helm, Paul 12
Herder, Johann G. 2
Hibbs, Thomas S. 12
Hick, John 5, 42, 44f., 50–55, 62–64, 148
Hösle, Vittorio 6
Hume, David 29, 71, 161, 200

Illies, Christian 191, 206, 257, 259
Isaye, Gaston 78

James, Henry 203, 237
Jean Paul 213, 231
Jesson, Greg 1, 18, 36
Job 191f.

Kant, Immanuel 1, 3, 5, 44–46, 51, 55, 116, 120, 130–136, 139f., 237
Kaufman, Gordon 5, 44–50, 53, 55–57, 62, 64, 134, 240–242
Kelly, Thomas 152–154, 156
Kierkegaard, Søren 210
King, Nathan 154
Kolmogorow, Andrei N. 223
Körner, Stephan 67, 76
Kretzmann, Norman 8
Kripke, Saul 58
Kuhn, Robert L. 17

Index of persons

Lehrer, Keith 19
Leibniz, Gottfried W. 193, 199, 202, 217
Levine, Michael 115
Locke, John 71
Löffler, Winfried 13, 65, 67, 87, 111, 116, 243f.
Lonergan, Bernard 119

Mackie, John 8, 27, 87, 161, 199, 209
Martin, Charlie 141
Martin, Michael 27, 93, 141
Marx, Karl 15, 27–30, 84, 121, 123–125, 238
Mavrodes, George I. 1
Moore, G. E. 65, 67
Moreland, James P. 11, 18
Moser, Paul K. 12, 87

Nagasawa, Yujin 62
Newberg, Andrew 120
Newman, J. H. 70f., 111
Nickel, Gregor 11, 18, 213, 227, 260–262
Nietzsche, Friedrich 1, 28, 123–125, 161

O'Hear, Anthony 27

Pascal, Blaise 228f.
Paul (the Apostle) 79, 169f., 178–180, 183, 186, 231, 261
Peirce, Charles S. 143
Phillips, Dewi Z. 13, 120, 136, 139, 249
Plantinga, Alvin 1–37, 41–66, 68–73, 77f., 80f., 83–111, 115–118, 120–128, 130, 133–136, 140–142, 144, 147f., 151f., 155, 158–162, 164–167, 169–172, 177f., 182–188, 191–210, 213–218, 220f., 223, 225–233, 237, 245, 248, 250, 252, 255–257, 261
Plasger, Georg 1f., 169, 173, 188, 254–257
Plato 126–128, 213
Popper, Karl 210

Quinn, Philip 207

Reid, Thomas 10, 69, 71, 246
Rentsch, Thomas 24
Rhees, Rush 135, 137–139, 142, 144, 249
Richter, Johann P. F. 213, 230f.
Rorty, Richard 26
Rousseau, Jean-Jacques 29
Rowe, William 195, 204, 207
Russell, Bertrand 58

Schelling, Friedrich W. J. 2
Schönecker, Dieter 1, 3, 11, 69, 81, 90, 111, 167, 193, 203, 237, 239f., 260
Schopenhauer, Arthur 192, 204, 208
Senor, Thomas D. 12
Sextus Empiricus 217
Socrates 128
Strawson, Peter F. 67
Swinburne, Richard 5, 11, 18, 24, 29, 36, 43, 96, 101, 111, 117f., 124, 206, 218, 225, 229–233, 240, 250

Tapp, Christian 2, 18, 22, 41, 61, 111, 240–242
Trigg, Roger 12
Thomas Aquinas 170, 172, 187

van Inwagen, Peter 115, 154, 258

Wachter, Daniel von 12
Wiertz, Oliver 83, 167, 245–248
Williamson, Timothy 153
Wilson, Warren 29, 125
Wittgenstein, Ludwig 67, 119, 135f., 138f., 249
Wolterstorff, Nicholas 2, 5
Wykstra, Stephen J. 13, 29

Zagzebski, Linda 12f., 31, 33, 36, 120, 127
Zenon of Elea 217

Subject Index

absence of limits   62 f.
absolute probability   214 f., 218
A/C model   12, 16, 19–23, 30–32, 34, 42 f., 85 f., 88–92, 94–101, 104, 147, 159–161, 164, 171 f., 209 f., 248 f., 257
Adam   180–183, 186
Advice to Christian Philosophers   5, 207
agnostic attitude   27–29, 36, 42
alethological proof of God's existence   121
anti-realism   44, 46 f., 130, 116, 145
anti-realists in the philosophy of science   47
apologetics   20, 41, 85, 90, 96, 99, 111, 117 f., 245, 251
apophatic   55, 57
argument
– atheological a.   191–193, 200 f., 208 f.
– historical a.   227, 229 f., 232
– intelligent-design a.   193
– mystery-a.   199 f., 205–207, 209
– parity-a.   4 f., 9, 12, 22, 35, 69
– possible-worlds-a.   193, 201–203, 257
– retortion a.   78
– theistic a.   5
– total evidence a.   203
atheist-theologian   48

Babel fish   234
Barthianism   126, 128, 135, 250
basic convictions   68, 102–104, 115, 119, 147, 158
basic intuition   45, 47, 119 f., 150, 154 f., 205
basicality; *see* proper basicality
Bayes Formula   222
Bayesian epistemology   216 f., 231, 232
Bayesian statistics   216 f., 232
belief   2 f., 5–10, 12 f., 15, 20 f., 26 f., 29–33, 35 f., 38, 42–44, 49, 52 f., 59, 65–81, 83–86, 88, 90–110, 115, 117, 122 f., 125, 128 f., 138, 147–167, 170 f., 182 f., 197, 199, 204, 206, 208, 213, 216, 239, 243–250, 253–255
– Christian b. as knowledge   42
– incorrigible b.   6–8, 32, 71, 208

– in God   1, 4–10, 12, 16, 24, 30–34, 50, 69, 78, 94, 117–119, 122 f., 135, 142, 149, 170 f., 174, 177, 182 f., 185, 187 f., 197–201, 207 f., 237 f., 247, 253 f., 256
– moral b.   8, 75, 79, 148, 151, 157, 161 f., 174, 233
– perceptual b.   5–7, 9, 30, 69 f., 110, 147, 159 f.
– properly basic; *see* proper basicality
– religious b.   13, 28, 52, 56, 77, 78–81, 83, 85, 88, 97, 100, 117 f., 129, 138, 140, 148 f., 151, 154 f., 161–163, 165, 167, 238 f.
– theistic b.   2, 5, 9–13, 15 f., 19, 24, 28 f., 31–33, 35, 37, 48, 50, 54, 59, 68, 76, 78, 80, 83, 85 f., 88–98, 100–105, 107–111, 118, 122–125, 197, 207, 238–240, 245, 247–249, 251, 254 f., 259
– true b.   1, 3–6, 8 f., 11–18, 20–25, 27–31, 34–38, 41–43, 47, 50, 55 f., 58, 60, 77, 80, 85 f., 88–92, 95–98, 101, 103–105, 107, 109, 115, 117, 122 f., 128 f., 138, 147–151, 153, 155–161, 163–166, 171, 173, 175, 182, 184, 191, 199, 201, 205 f., 209 f., 213 f., 216 f., 220 f., 223, 227 f., 237–240, 244–254, 259–261
– warranted true b.   37, 115
believing that   9, 35, 44, 91, 123, 148
Bible   8, 79, 87, 115, 128, 135, 137, 147, 173, 176–178, 180, 184, 188, 253
Big Bang   47

causal theory of meaning   58 f.
certainty   70, 101, 104 f., 107–109, 115 f., 129 f., 134–140, 143, 152, 208
– kinds of c.   13, 71, 154, 204, 239, 261
– nature of c.   87, 116, 180, 237
– of faith   5, 36, 109, 115, 130, 135, 137, 177, 191, 198, 229, 240, 255 f.
Christian philosophy   20, 85, 92, 239, 245, 248, 259
circularity   80, 87–93, 111, 117, 245, 262
cognitive capacities   101 f., 115, 120 f., 123, 125, 127, 133, 135–137, 161, 195, 206, 250

cognitive faculties   6, 15, 25–27, 34, 42 f., 56, 68, 86, 92, 133, 139, 159 f., 162, 171, 198 f., 238 f., 254, 262
concept of God   4 f., 19, 21, 24, 42, 44–48, 56, 58, 65, 68, 77, 86, 116, 119, 126 f., 129–131, 133 f., 138, 140, 143, 170–188, 191 f., 194 f., 198–202, 206 f., 226, 234, 237, 255 f., 258
concept to live by   136–138, 140, 143 f.
conceptual agnosticism (CA)   44–46, 50 f., 55–57, 62–64
conceptual frameworks   67
conciliationism   150 f., 166 f.
conditional probability   222
contemplation   120, 127, 132
cosmic forces   44, 49 f.
critique of religion   120, 124, 251

de facto objection   14–16, 36, 42 f., 85, 95, 98 f., 105, 247, 249, 251, 259
defeaters   8, 23 f., 42, 80, 85 f., 93, 100 f., 106 f., 109 f., 197, 199, 201, 209, 239
defeater-defeaters, internal (intrinsic)   85
definite description   52, 56–58
de jure attitude   28–30, 42 f.
de jure objection   14–16, 20, 25–27, 29, 36, 42, 44, 85 f., 95, 98, 105, 239, 247, 249, 251, 259
deontologism   32
design plan   15, 22, 27, 30, 34, 42 f., 86, 98, 101, 122, 147, 159, 214, 239, 254, 262
dialectical evidence   154 f.
differencia specifica   57
disagreement   102, 116, 138, 148–158, 160–163, 165–167, 252–254
divine attributes   42, 52, 59, 65, 74, 76, 78, 97, 129, 142 f., 200, 255, 260
divine infinity   42, 46 f., 54, 56, 59–64, 116, 135, 142, 240
divine properties   41, 47 f., 51–55, 57, 60–64, 74, 97, 130, 132–135, 138, 143, 172, 224, 242, 247 f.
doxastic experience   8, 26, 103 f., 108, 159 f., 164 f.
doxastic phenomenology   162
dwindling probability; *see* probability

epistemic confidence   11, 73, 75, 150 f., 157, 161, 163–167, 174, 252
epistemic distance between us and God   195
epistemic possibility; *see* possibility, epistemic
epistemic imperialism   6
epistemic peer   149–153, 155 f., 158, 165–167, 252–254
epistemological antirealism   116
epistemology   2, 10, 12, 20 f., 25, 42, 44, 65, 73, 80 f., 83, 85, 89 f., 92 f., 96, 110 f., 115–117, 121 f., 136, 150, 160, 164, 221, 225, 245, 248, 251, 254 f.
– of religion   10, 20, 42, 58, 61, 67, 83, 88, 103, 136, 183, 207, 214, 226, 239, 251
– reformed e.   1 f., 7, 11 f., 69, 83, 96 f., 99, 121, 125, 139, 172, 169, 173, 188, 232
– religious e.   2, 8 f., 11–13, 28 f., 76–81, 83, 85, 88, 93, 96 f., 99–101, 104, 107, 109, 115–122, 147–149, 151 f., 154 f., 157 f., 160–167, 169, 172, 226, 238 f., 247, 249, 251–253
essential properties   61
events, psychological/mental   110, 141, 194, 215 f., 221, 223
evidence   4–11, 15, 24, 28 f., 37, 43, 53, 86, 96 f., 99, 103–107, 109 f., 118, 124 f., 132, 134, 137, 142, 149 f., 152–157, 159, 161–163, 165, 191–198, 200–205, 208, 229, 231 f., 237 f., 240, 253 f., 257, 260–262
– propositional e.   5, 9, 37, 88, 100, 104, 107, 130, 238, 260
evidential equality   153, 155
evidentialism   4 f., 8, 10 f., 11, 28, 32, 37, 77–79, 85 f., 95, 99, 104, 118–120, 138 f., 147 f., 154, 161, 166, 182, 196 f., 199, 203 f., 207, 239, 259
evolutionary theory   23, 37, 92, 125
experience
– mystical e.   9, 132, 226 f.
– of God   4 f., 19, 21, 24, 42, 44–48, 56, 62 f., 65, 68, 77, 86, 115 f., 118 f., 121, 125–134, 138–140, 143, 170–188, 191 f., 194 f., 198–202, 206 f., 226, 234, 237, 255 f., 258
– religious e.   2, 8 f., 11–13, 28 f., 52–54, 56, 62–68, 76–81, 83, 85, 88, 93, 96 f.,

99–101, 104, 107, 109, 120, 141–144, 147–149, 151f., 154f., 157f., 160–167, 169, 172, 226, 238f., 247, 249, 251–253
experience   2, 8f., 11, 15, 26, 45–47, 51, 53, 58, 62, 74, 76–81, 101, 103, 108–110, 120, 130, 132f., 137, 139, 141–144, 149, 154f., 159, 163–165, 192, 194, 200, 205, 208, 217f., 232, 238, 253
experimental contact   51f.
explanatory and prognostic success   55
extended Aquinas/Calvin model   19, 42, 205, 225
externalism   121
– theistic e.   2, 5, 9–13, 15f., 19, 24, 28f., 31–33, 35, 37, 68, 76, 78, 80, 83, 85f., 88–98, 100–105, 107–111, 115f., 118–120, 122–125, 134, 141, 197, 207, 238–240, 245, 247–249, 251, 254f., 259

faith   43, 49f., 85–87, 90, 94, 96–98, 100–105, 109, 116, 119, 122, 124f., 129, 135–137, 161f., 164, 170f., 180–188, 191, 198f., 208, 234, 240, 242, 245, 254–256, 258
– nature of f.   55–57, 87, 116, 180, 237
– religious f.   2, 8f., 11–13, 28f., 48, 50, 52–54, 56, 60, 62, 64–68, 76–81, 83, 85, 88, 93, 96f., 99–101, 104, 107, 109, 120, 124f., 137, 147–149, 151f., 154f., 157f., 160–167, 169, 172, 226, 238f., 247, 249, 251–253
Fall   8, 19, 37, 41, 43, 49f., 70, 79, 171, 174, 198, 201, 203, 206
– after the F.   2, 181, 198
finite object   57
first-order approximation   50
flying spaghetti monsters   37
formal property, *see* properties   48, 51f.
foundationalism   6f., 10, 28, 32, 71–73
– classical f.   6f., 10, 21, 23, 32, 71f., 71–73., 78, 215–217, 220, 226, 230
– modern f.   7, 71, 108, 217f., 242
free will   174, 180, 185
frequentism   216–220
Freud-and-Marx Complaint   27–30, 124f.
functions properly   42, 86, 97, 147, 161, 205

genus proximum   57
German Idealism   2, 134
God
– all-knowing G.   56, 59–64
– all-powerful G.   56, 59–63, 204
– available G.   46
– creator   56
– experience of G.   52f., 61–64, 116, 142, 191
– as symbol   48
– hiddenness of G.   18f., 206
– infinity of G.   41–64
– perfect being conception   42
– personality of G.   59
– reference to G.   5, 21f., 41–64
– unexperienceable G.   55
– unknowability of G.   55
– unlimited G.   63f.
– wholly good G.   56
God and Other Minds   1f., 4, 65, 237
Goodman-world   122
great pumpkin objection (son and grandson of great pumpkin objection)   7, 23, 27, 80, 85, 93–106, 247f.

Hegelian dialectics   135
hermeneutical practice   144
hinge propositions   67
hiddenness; *see* God, hiddenness of
historical argument   227, 229f., 232
Holy Scriptures; *see* Bible
Holy Spirit   19, 80, 87, 104, 108, 115, 128, 135, 147f., 158f., 163–165, 171f., 174, 176f., 181–185, 188, 225, 239, 251, 255f.
– instigation of the H.S.   19, 128, 147, 159, 163f., 256

identity-criteria   130, 133
ideology   83–85, 92, 106, 111, 246f.
illusion (religion)   28f., 124, 239
immunization strategy   99
inconsistency, self-referential   97, 200, 205, 208f.
inferentialism   119
infinite, transcendent and ultimate being (ITUB)   41, 43f., 52, 55–64, 200, 217, 223, 225, 240

infinity 42, 46f., 54, 59–64, 116, 135, 142, 240
instantiation 127, 144
interpretation 2f., 11–13, 24f., 28, 31f., 34–36, 43–51, 62–64, 66, 78f., 93, 98, 101, 122, 141–144, 169, 173, 177f., 188, 216, 229, 232, 241f., 249, 257

justification 7, 10, 15, 24–27, 31f., 35–37, 43, 65, 69, 73, 77, 81, 83f., 88, 92f., 96, 108, 110, 123, 129, 137f., 149, 151, 237f., 246, 253, 259

knowledge 5, 7f., 12f., 15, 18f., 21, 24, 31, 35, 37f., 42f., 45, 59–63, 79, 84, 86, 89–92, 97, 99–101, 105, 115f., 119–121, 123, 126–136, 138, 147f., 154, 158–161, 165, 170–180, 182–188, 195–198, 200, 204, 213, 226, 228, 238, 240, 246, 248, 250, 254–256
– of entailments 130
– of God 4f., 19, 21, 24, 42, 44–48, 54f., 58, 62f., 65, 68, 77, 86, 115f., 121, 127, 132–134, 170–188, 191f., 194f., 198–202, 206f., 226, 234, 237, 255f., 258
– religious k. 2, 8f., 11–13, 28f., 48, 50, 52–54, 56, 60, 62, 64–68, 76–81, 83, 85, 88, 93, 96f., 99–101, 104, 107, 109, 120f., 147–149, 151f., 154f., 157f., 160–167, 169, 172, 226, 238f., 247, 249, 251–253
– serious k. 16, 19, 24–26, 72, 84, 116, 130–134, 158, 161, 169, 197, 205, 209, 217f., 226, 229, 233, 240, 257
– serious k. objection 134
– source of k. 9, 69, 103, 107, 147, 149, 158, 161, 163, 220, 247, 255

Leibniz Principle 76
Letztbegründung 6
life-experience 137, 140

materialism 29
mathematical objects 55
mathematics 8, 213f., 216–218, 220, 226, 250f., 260
maximal degree of qualities 59–63
MaximalGod Thesis 62

maximality 60f.
measure theory 217f.
mental construction 45–47, 64, 241
metaquestion 14f.
moral beliefs; *see* beliefs

naturalism 1, 23f., 34, 37f., 78, 92, 96, 115, 121, 137, 208, 214, 221, 240, 250
natural theology 5, 58, 99, 110f., 115, 119–121, 123, 125, 129, 188, 208, 225, 232, 250
negative theology 5, 21, 42, 52, 55, 63, 134, 200, 226
noetic structures 72f., 75f., 81, 198
non-inferentiality, non-inferential knowledge 118, 120
non-reductionist view of religion 120
nuomena 45

OmniGod Thesis 62
omnipotence 56, 59, 62, 63, 126, 134, 194, 204, 210, 241
omniscience 56, 58, 59, 61, 63, 194, 204, 207, 241

parity argument; *see* argument
perception of God 62
perfect being 61f.
person on the fence 192, 207f., 210
phenomenal realm 45
Plantingianism 1f.
pluralism 23, 109, 126, 249
possibility, epistemic 6, 16, 19, 21–23, 41, 52, 54, 56, 62, 64, 79, 89f., 92, 94f., 100, 102, 104, 118, 120, 122, 132, 180f., 183, 191, 193, 200f., 203, 205, 240, 251
predicates 42, 47f., 53, 55–59, 226
– categorical p. 57
– nonformal p. 51–53, 56
predication 41, 43, 45–48, 55–57
– categorial p. 45, 57
– logical p. 57
– real p. 56
prejudice 124f., 162
principle of credulity 9, 11, 101
principle of dwindling probabilities 223; *see also* probability

principle of intrinsic probability   223
principle of non-contradiction   77
principle of rationality   105 f.
principle of testimonial evidence   105
probability   11, 16–18, 30, 92, 97, 109 f., 115, 193, 195 f., 207 f., 214–225, 228–230, 232 f., 260–262
– calculus p.   214, 216 f., 221, 223, 225, 227, 233
– dwindling p.   213 f., 215 f., 225–233, 262
– measure p.   74, 144, 215, 217 f., 222, 224 f.
– space   25, 32, 93, 143, 219, 223 f., 243, 259
problem of equivalence   143
proper basicality   2–10, 12, 15, 22, 25–27, 31–36, 43, 68–73, 78, 80, 86, 88–98, 100–102, 105, 115, 118, 127, 134 f., 149, 159 f., 162, 165, 191, 198 f., 201, 205, 207, 209, 220, 238 f., 243, 247–249, 254, 256, 262
– as internal rationality   33
– as justification   31, 238
– as warrant   33, 35
– conditions of p.b.   7, 109, 155
– criteria for p.b.   7, 105
– of theistic beliefs   83, 89, 93, 100, 109, 111
properties   41, 43, 46, 47 f., 51–58, 60–64, 74, 97, 130, 132–135, 138, 143, 172, 224, 242, 247 f.
– divine p.   52
– essential p.   51
– formal p.   51 f.,
– great-making p.   60–63, 86 f., 159, 191, 215 f., 238, 241, 247 f., 254
– of which we have a grasp   51–54, 63
– of which we have no grasp   52, 54, 63
– positive p.   51–54
– theory of p.   54
– types of p.   51
propositions   1, 4, 6–10, 17, 21–23, 30, 32, 60, 69, 71–73, 87, 91, 103, 115, 117–120 120, 122, 125, 129, 148 f., 152–154, 157 f., 191, 194–197, 215 f., 218, 220–225, 227–229, 231, 238, 242, 244 f., 249, 251 f., 255 f., 260 f.
– basic p.   6, 32, 115, 120, 129, 135

– hinge p.   67
– religious p.   120
– theistic p.   118–120, 127, 141
public evidence   43
purloined letter example   106–110

rationality   5, 7, 10, 31, 42–44, 50, 65, 80, 92 f., 96, 105 f., 117 f., 121 f., 125–127, 135, 137, 144, 197, 214, 216, 232, 238, 253, 262
– external r.   15, 25 f., 33, 37 f., 70 f., 77 f., 100, 199, 238, 246, 251
– functional r.   137, 172, 196, 198, 221
– internal r.   15, 25 f., 36 f., 90, 100, 106, 108 f., 158 f., 163 f., 209, 239, 251, 255 f.
– meta-r.   121–124, 126
– procedural r.   137
– of Christian belief   117, 152, 239, 259
– of theism   125
realism, theological   22, 32, 43 f., 56, 61, 64, 68, 80, 90, 102, 169, 173, 178, 183, 188, 191, 226, 228, 241, 249 f.
real referent   46–48
reason   3 f., 6–8, 10, 12, 15 f., 18 f., 23, 26 f., 29, 35, 37, 41 f., 44, 46 f., 50, 54, 57, 62, 67, 69, 74, 80, 84, 87 f., 95–98, 100–103, 105–108, 110, 117, 121 f., 124–126, 128 f., 135, 138 f., 144, 147, 150 f., 155–158, 162 f., 165 f., 174, 181, 183, 187, 191–193, 195–197, 199 f., 205–208, 214, 218 f., 221, 223, 228, 231, 239, 242, 245 f., 248–250, 252–254, 257
– pure r.   3, 45, 127, 129, 133
Reason and Belief in God   1 f., 5, 65, 69, 85, 93, 237
reductionist explanations of religion   120
reinterpretation of Christian faith   46, 48 f., 64
religious diversity   116, 147–149, 152, 166
religious musicality   50, 242
religious pluralism   23, 109, 126, 249
religious plurality   67, 117, 122
religious worldview   24, 96 f., 117, 127
retortion arguments   78
revelation   128 f., 135, 183, 186, 188, 206, 227, 229, 250
rooted in experience   119

Satan 66, 191
self-evidence 7, 198
semen religionis 177f., 182–187, 255f.
sensus divinitatis 2, 5, 12f., 19, 22, 30f., 42f., 80, 86–92, 95–98, 101f., 104f., 107f., 115, 117f., 120, 123–129, 133, 135, 141–144, 147f., 159, 162–165, 169–172, 177f., 182–186, 191, 196, 198, 201, 204f., 208f., 248, 250f., 255f.
sin 5, 19, 42, 86, 88, 102, 104, 108, 115, 147, 164, 171–174, 180–182, 184–186, 232, 255f., 258f.
situation of awareness 143
son and grandson of great pumpkin objection; *see* great pumpkin objection
speech acts 64
spiritually mature person 201, 208
straight knowledge dogma 133
strategy of self-immunisation 205
strength of belief 165
structuralists 47
suffering 191–193, 195–197, 199–201, 203f., 206–210, 257–259
supernaturalism 92, 137
supreme cause 65f., 77, 99, 132, 134, 142, 144, 148, 152, 164, 201, 253
supreme wisdom 134, 173
supreme Being 131f.
system of reference 136

tertium non datur 57
theism 13, 19, 23f., 29, 37f., 49, 59, 79, 85, 88–91, 93–102, 105–107, 109, 111, 119, 124f., 191–197, 199–201, 203–205, 207–210, 241, 246f., 250, 253f., 257; *see also* belief, theistic
theology 42, 44, 49, 55, 58–60, 62, 72, 78, 111, 115, 120, 122f., 130, 169, 173f., 183, 187, 191, 199, 227, 249
– classical th. 55
– implicit th. 67f.
theoretical entities 55
theory of positive and negative properties 53
The Real 25, 51–54, 62–64, 84, 217, 246
– authentic manifestations of T.R. 54

– empty concept of T.R. 54
The Ultimate 52
track record 156f., 161–163
transcendence 56, 116, 119
trinity 19, 59, 177, 258
truth 11, 15, 21f., 24f., 27f., 30, 34, 36, 38, 42f., 47, 68, 77, 80, 84–105, 108, 111, 119, 121–128, 159f., 178, 191f., 195, 204, 207, 210, 213f., 218, 221, 225, 239, 246–251, 254f., 260–262
– Christian belief, truth of 1–7, 11–38, 41–44, 48–50, 54f., 59, 64f., 70, 78, 80, 83, 85f., 90, 96, 102, 108, 110, 147f., 152, 158–166, 169, 191, 201, 208f., 213f., 225f., 237–240, 242f., 245–254, 259f.
– of theism 11, 15, 34, 37, 85, 88–92, 94f., 97, 99f., 102, 104f., 125, 191–193, 195f., 203f., 209, 248, 250, 253
TW (if theistic belief is true, then it probably has warrant) 2, 11–13, 16–22, 24f., 30, 33–37, 237, 239

unexperiencability 47
universals 127, 241
unlimited being 54, 60
unlimitedness 60f., 63

Warrant and Proper Function 1, 13, 30, 59, 65, 73, 85, 213
Warrant. The Current Debate 13, 74, 123, 213, 216, 223
warrant (warranted) 1, 3, 9, 11–13, 15–20, 22, 24f., 27f., 30f., 33–38, 42f., 49f., 62, 65, 73, 77f., 86, 88–110, 115, 117f., 121–129, 155, 159, 164f., 191f., 194, 196f., 199–201, 205, 208, 213f., 220, 225, 237–239, 246–248, 251, 253f., 259, 261f.
source of w. 9, 69, 103, 107, 118, 127f., 147, 149, 158, 161, 163, 220, 247, 255
Weltanschauung; *see* world-view
Where the Conflict Really Lies 1, 23
wish-fulfillment 28, 238
world-view; world-view beliefs 65f., 243–245

www.ingramcontent.com/pod-product-compliance
Lightning Source LLC
Chambersburg PA
CBHW070609170426
43200CB00012B/2628